MODERN SCOTTISH HISTORY
1707 TO THE PRESENT

MODERN SCOTTISH HISTORY
1707 *to the* PRESENT

VOLUME 4: READINGS
1850 TO THE PRESENT

Edited by
Anthony Cooke, Ian Donnachie,
Ann MacSween and Christopher A Whatley

JOHN DONALD

In association with
THE OPEN UNIVERSITY IN SCOTLAND

and
THE UNIVERSITY OF DUNDEE

First published in Great Britain in 1998 by Tuckwell Press Ltd

This edition published in 2007 by
John Donald, an imprint of Birlinn Ltd
West Newington House, 10 Newington Road
Edinburgh EH9 1QS
www.birlinn.co.uk

ISBN 13: 978 1 904607 63 2
ISBN 10: 1 904607 63 2

British Library Cataloguing-in-Publication Data
A catalogue record for this book is available
on request from the British Library

Designed by James Hutcheson

Typeset by Hewer Text UK Ltd, Edinburgh

Printed and bound in Great Britain by Cpod, Trowbridge, Wiltshire

Contents

ACKNOWLEDGEMENTS   vii

PREFACE   ix

Article 25:   I Levitt 'Scottish Sentiment, Administrative
Devolution and Westminster, 1885–1964'   1

Article 26:   RJ Finlay 'National Identity in Crisis: Politicians,
Intellectuals and the "End of Scotland"'   13

Article 27:   J Hunter 'The Politics of Highland Land Reform
1873–1895'   33

Article 28:   EA Cameron 'They Will Listen to no Remonstrance':
Land raids and land raiders in the
Scottish Highlands, 1886–1914   59

Article 29:   R Rodger 'Concentration and Fragmentation:
Capital, Labor and the Structure of Mid-Victorian
Scottish Industry'   82

Article 30:   M Gray 'Scotland in the International Economy
1860–1914'   114

Article 31:   RA Cage 'Infant Mortality Rates and Housing:
Twentieth Century Glasgow'   123

Article 32:   RJ Morris 'Death, Chambers Street and Edinburgh
Corporation'   139

Article 33:   Tom Hart 'Urban Growth and Municipal Government:
Glasgow in a Comparative Context, 1846–1914'   147

Article 34:   F McKichan 'A Burgh's Response to the Problems
of Urban Growth: Stirling, 1780–1880'   153

Article 35: T Gallacher 'Protestant Extremism in Urban Scotland,
1930–1939: Its Growth and Contraction'   171

Article 36: S Reynolds 'Women Compositors in
Edwardian Edinburgh'   196

Article 37: E Gordon 'Women and the Labour Movement
in Scotland, 1850–1914'   207

Article 38: R Anthony 'The Scottish Agricultural Labour Market,
1900–1939: a case of institutional intervention'   220

Article 39: JJ Smyth 'The Independent Labour Party in Glasgow,
1888–1906: the struggle for identity'   242

Article 40: W Gallagher 'The Battle of George Square'   253

Article 41: A Campbell 'From Independent Collier to Militant
Miner: Tradition and change in the trade union
consciousness of the Scottish miners, 1874–1929'   256

Article 42: R Anderson 'In search of the "Lad of Parts":
the Mythical History of Scottish Education'   271

Article 43: A McPherson 'An Angle on the Geist: Persistence
and Change in the Scottish Educational Tradition'   282

Article 44: S Kuper 'Celtic and Rangers, or Rangers and Celtic'   293

Article 45: C Craig 'The Body in the Kit Bag: History and
the Scottish Novel'   305

Article 46: U Kimpel 'Beyond the Caledonian Antisyzygy:
Contemporary Scottish poetry in between cultures'   316

Acknowledgements

Grateful acknowledgement is made to the following sources for permission to reproduce material in this volume:

I Levitt 1993 'Scottish Sentiment, Administrative Devolution and Westminster, 1885–1964', *in* M Lynch (ed) *Scotland, 1850–1979: Society, Politics and the Union*, Historical Association Committee for Scotland and The Historical Association; RJ Finlay 1994 'National Identity in Crisis: Politicians, Intellectuals and the "End of Scotland" ', *History*; J Hunter 1974 'The politics of highland land reform 1873–1895', *Scottish Historical Review*; E Cameron 1997 ' "They will listen to no Remonstrance": Land raids and land raiders in the Scottish Highlands, 1850–1914', *Scottish Economic and Social History* reproduced by permission of the Economic and Social History Society of Scotland; R Rodger 1988 'Concentration and Fragmentation: Capital, Labor and the Structure of Mid-Victorian Scottish Industry', *Journal of Urban History* reproduced by permission of Sage Publications Inc; M Gray 1990 *Scots on the Move: Scots Migrants 1750–1914*, Studies in Scottish Economic and Social History, reproduced by permission of the Economic and Social History Society of Scotland; RA Cage 1994 'Infant Mortality Rates and Housing: Twentieth Century Glasgow', *Scottish Economic and Social History* reproduced by permission of the Economic and Social History Society of Scotland; R Morris 1992 'Death, Chambers Street and Edinburgh Corporation', in *History Teaching Review Year Book 6*; Tom Hart 1982 'Urban Growth and Municipal Government: Glasgow in a Comparative Context, 1846–1914', *in* A Slaven and D Aldcroft *Business, Banking and Urban History* John Donald; F McKichan 1978 'A burgh's response to the problems of urban growth: Stirling, 1780–1880', *Scottish Historical Review*; T Gallacher 1985 'Protestant Extremism in Urban Scotland 1930–1939: Its Growth and Contraction', *Scottish Historical Review*; S Reynolds 1989 *Britannica's Typesetters: Women Compositors in Edwardian Edinburgh*, Edinburgh University Press; E Gordon 1991 *Women and the Labour Movement in Scotland*, Oxford University Press; R Anthony 1993 'The Scottish Agricultural Labour Market, 1900–1939: a case of institutional intervention', *Economic History Review* reproduced by permission of the Economic History Society; JJ Smyth 1990 'The Independent Labour Party in Glasgow, 1888–1906: the struggle for identity', *in* R Morris and JJ Smyth *The Independent Labour Party in Scotland*, Manchester University Press; T Gallagher 1936 *Revolt on the Clyde*, Lawrence and Wishart; A Campbell 1989 'From Independent Collier to Militant Miner: tradition and change in the trade union consciousness of the Scottish miners, 1874–1929', *Scottish Labour History Society*

Journal; R Anderson 1985 'In search of the "Lad of Parts": the Mythical History of Scottish Education', *History Workshop Journal* Oxford University Press; A McPherson 1983 'An Angle on the Geist: Persistence and Change in the Scottish Educational Tradition', *in* W Humes and H Paterson *Scottish Culture and Scottish Education, 1800–1980*, John Donald; S Kuper 1995 *Football Against the Enemy*, Orion Publishing Group; C Craig 1979 'The Body in the Kit Bag: History and the Scottish Novel', *Cencrastus*; U Kimpel 1995 'Beyond the Caledonian Antisyzygy: Contemporary Scottish poetry in between cultures', *in* H-W Ludwig and L Fietz (eds) *Poetry in the British Isles: Non Metropolitan Perspectives*, University of Wales Press.

Preface

This volume and the series of which it is part have as their central purpose the study of the history of Scotland from 1707 until the present. The series seeks to combine the products of more recent research and general findings by some of the most prominent scholars working in the subject with the enthusiasm of those who wish to study it either in a systematic way or simply by reading one or more of these volumes at leisure.

Now is a particularly appropriate time to bring this scholarship and the wider audience together. There is enormous public interest in all periods of Scottish history. This springs from a variety of sources: the new political agenda in Scotland following the re-establishment of parliament in Edinburgh; the 300th anniversary of the Treaty of Union in 2007; the higher profile of Scottish history in school, college and university curricula; the enhanced interest in local and family history; the success of museums and heritage ventures devoted to the more recent past; and the continuous flow of books on so many aspects of Scottish history. However, explicitly academic publications, with a few honourable exceptions, have been little read by any but specialists, so new findings have frequently had little impact on general perceptions of Scotland's more recent past.

There are two main aims encapsulated in these volumes, which are overlapping and complementary. The first is to present an overview of recent scholarly work, drawing on the approaches and findings of political, economic, social, environmental and cultural historians. This should be illuminating, not only for those seeking an up-to-date review of such work, but also for anyone interested in the functioning of Scotland today – the essential historical background of present-day issues and concerns. The second, equally important, aim is to help readers develop their own historical skills, using the volumes as a tool-kit containing a wide range of primary sources and more detailed readings on specific topics. This and the other volumes in the series differ from most conventional academic publications, in that the focus is on *doing* history, rather than just absorbing the facts. The volumes are full of ideas on sources and methods that can be followed up by the interested reader.

Given the vast scope of the subject, we have had to put some limits on the coverage. The timescale is the early eighteenth century to the late twentieth century, a period for which sources not only abound but can also be readily understood and critically assessed. There is no attempt to give a detailed historical narrative of the period from the Union of 1707, which can readily be found elsewhere. Rather we present a blend of topics and themes, selected with a view to providing readers with a reasonably comprehensive introduction to recent work and a context and stimulus for further reading or investigation. Although there is an organisational divide at 1850, many of the themes are explored continuously over the whole period. Hence the first volume begins with the Union of 1707 and Jacobitism, and covers topics including industrialisation, demography, politics, religion, education, class, the environment and culture, as well as looking at the differences between Highland and Lowland society and economy. The second volume, from 1850 to the present, also covers a wide range of topics. Some of these, such as industrialisation, demography, urbanisation, religion, class, education, culture and Highland and Lowland society are continued, while new topics include the state, Scottish identity, leisure and recreation. The third and fourth volumes contain carefully selected readings to accompany the topic/theme volumes and are likely to prove an invaluable resource for any reader wishing to pursue a particular subject in greater depth or perhaps investigate it in a local or regional project. The fifth volume in the series is a collection of primary sources for the history of modern Scotland designed to accompany the other volumes. It makes accessible between the covers of one book many of the documents of national and local importance from the eighteenth century and beyond and provides a unique and detailed insight into the period.

This book forms one part of the University of Dundee/Open University collaborative course, Modern Scottish History: 1707 to the Present. This is an honours level undergraduate course for part-time adult learners studying at a distance, and it is designed to develop the skills, methods and understanding of history and historical analysis with modern Scotland as its focus. However, these volumes are designed to be used, either singly or as a series, by anyone interested in Scottish history. The introduction to recent research findings, together with practical exercises, advice on the critical exploitation of primary sources and suggestions for further reading, should be of wide interest and application. We hope it will encourage users to carry their enthusiasm further by investigating, for example, some aspect of their own community history based on one or more themes covered in the series.

A series of this kind depends on the efforts of many people, and accordingly there are many debts to record. Our enthusiasm was shared by the Scottish Higher Education Funding Council which provided a generous grant to fund the development of the course. Within the University of Dundee, Professor David Swinfen, Vice-Principal, has played a valuable supporting role. The authors produced their contributions to agreed formats and deadlines. While they are responsible for what they have written, they have also been supported by other members of the writing team and our editorial and production specialists. The material was developed collaboratively, reflected too in the cooperation and support we have had from our publisher, Tuckwell Press. Particular thanks to Tracey Walker, the Project Secretary, for her administrative support. Thanks also to Karen Brough and Jen Petrie who transcribed some of the texts for the articles and documents volumes.

USING THIS BOOK

Activities

Volumes 1 and 2 are designed not just as a text to be read through but also as active workbooks. They are therefore punctuated by a series of activities, signalled by a different format. These include short questions, exercises and prompts for the reader articles in Volumes 3 and 4 or documents in Volume 5. Conversely, the readings and documents refer back to topics/themes discussed in detail in Volumes 1 and 2.

Series Editors

Scottish Sentiment, Administrative Devolution and Westminster, 1885–1964

Ian Levitt 1993 *in* Michael Lynch (ed) *Scotland, 1850–1979: Society, Politics and the Union*, London (Historical Association Committee for Scotland and the Historical Association), 35–42.

In 1746, during the last phase of the Jacobite rebellion, the Marquis of Tweeddale was removed from his post as Secretary of State for Scotland.[1] At the time it was partly ascribed to Cabinet intrigue, but it also reflected a deep concern within the Whig Government that a Scottish Secretaryship symbolised and kindled pre-Union sentiment within Scottish opinion. Such a sentiment held back not only the full integration of Scotland within the United Kingdom, but also its development as part of the civilised world of the Enlightenment.

Once the military emergency died down, Scottish administration was transferred to one of the British Secretaries of State (after 1782, the Home Secretary), who in turn delegated much of the detailed work to the Lord Advocate in Edinburgh. By the 1840s, however, with the growth of Benthamite legislation, the need to ensure greater administrative uniformity led to the establishment of Edinburgh boards to monitor and supervise such local services as poor relief, mental welfare and public health. Nevertheless, political control of the boards seemed somewhat vague and parliamentary discussion of Scottish affairs remained perfunctory, if not entirely absent. By the 1880s, there was widespread belief that their detachment from Westminster had made it difficult for distinctive Scottish welfare and other traditions to be protected and promoted.

The response of Gladstone's Liberal Government in 1883 was to promote a Bill to establish a Scottish Local Government board, principally to deal with health and welfare matters. It was not welcomed by the Conservative opposition and fell in the Lords. Their objection was principally twofold. First, they thought the Board would suffer from a failure to access the 'progressive' benefits of Westminster legislation. Second, and for them possibly far worse, an Edinburgh Board, only loosely connected to British administration, might raise demands for greater devolution. In the 1880s, at a time of the widening franchise, what they feared most was a Scotland dominated by the temperance activist, the 'wee free' presbyterian and the Highland land leaguer.

The Liberals, however, knew that some political response was necessary. In 1885, they re-introduced the Bill, but with an important alteration. A Scottish Secretary would be appointed and assume responsibility for a wide range of functions, from health and welfare to law and order. The Scottish Secretary's office, the Scottish Office, would be based in London and have three primary functions. The first was to access parliamentary time more readily for the Edinburgh boards and other Scottish institutions. The second was to liaise with UK and English Departments to ensure that Scottish interests would be heard effectively in the drafting of legislation. The third was to take over certain law and order functions from the Home Office. The Secretary for Scotland, however, was not to be a fully fledged Secretary of State; he was paid a salary equivalent to the Lord Privy Seal, a minister sometimes not in the Cabinet itself. It meant the Scottish Secretary's staff, an under secretary and four clerks, were also paid on a lower scale. It underlined the view that the Scottish Secretaryship was of symbolic as much as administrative importance. The real work of managing Scotland remained as before with the Edinburgh boards. Board members, although appointed and answerable to the Scottish Secretary, in fact, tended to be representative of Scottish interests, the land, the law, local government and by 1900, the medical profession. On the whole, board membership came from outside the British civil service and, being composed of Scotsmen sitting in Edinburgh, was identifiably Scottish.

THE BIRTH OF LABOUR UNIONISM (1919–1925)

In the years before 1914, British government was much more restricted in its activities than today. Central government had only limited power over local authorities and, apart from receiving such welfare benefits as the old age pension, the ordinary public rarely had much contact with what it did. First World War controls and promises of post-war reconstruction greatly altered that. In no area was this so overtly the case as in housing, where the Government had committed itself to fund a substantial post-war new building programme. In Scotland, however, the Labour movement went further and combined a programme of post-war reconstruction with calls for political devolution.

Although Labour had not done well at the 1918 polls, for Lloyd George's Coalition the Labour movement in Scotland did seem to wield enormous power – in the factory and on the street. Moreover, from the various intelligence reports to Cabinet, it seemed a volatile and inflammable movement. So for Scottish administration, historically speaking, what was important about 1919 was that the Cabinet decided not to duplicate its policy for England and create a separate Scottish Ministry of Health, but establish a health board under the Scottish Secretary who would be aided by a new Parliamentary Under Secretary. This was a significant rebuff to the 'Home Rule' movement, but did reflect a reformulation of the British attitude towards administering Scotland. Robert Munro, the Scottish Secretary, made the position clear. What he wanted was a single Scottish department which in its dealings with the Cabinet and Treasury would have 'weight and authority'.[2] Two Scottish ministers would almost certainly have meant separate negotiations with the Treasury and, as the Health Minister's brief included housing, by far and away Scotland's biggest and most polemical problem, Munro feared 'the Scottish Secretary might be worsted'.[3]

What had happened? In the age of mass democracy, with an assertive labour movement and popular demands for social reconstruction, the Government's response had been to underline that the Scottish Secretary and his London office were above certain sectional and (for the Cabinet at least) potentially revolutionary interests – whether it was the miner, the shop steward or the slum dweller. In effect, 1919 saw the birth of 'Labour Unionism' – a political culture that sought to fuse the needs of the radical Scottish voter to the well-oiled wheels of the British administrative system. To Munro, this form of Unionism meant a progressive, but constitutional approach to reform, a shared Empire and the Treasury to fund investment. To Walter Elliot, then a Scottish Office Parliamentary Private Secretary, it meant Scotland would not descend into 'the frightful spectacle of nationalist Middle Europe' with its anarchy, confusion and political chaos.[4] But it meant a changed role for the Scottish boards – less monitoring the quality of local administration, more ensuring Scotland received, as Munro argued, 'her due share of public moneys'.[5] This form of Unionism, then, was less about political rights, participation through devolution of authority, and more about material welfare – satisfying the basic wants of a job, a house and social security.

To achieve this Munro had two strategies. The first meant restructuring the Scottish Office. At that time the Scottish Secretary had only two London-based advisers, the Scottish Office permanent under-secretary and his assistant. Although there were other officials at the Scottish Office, under Civil Service rules they were too junior for a minister to consult. In February 1919, after some correspondence on the range and scope of its work, the Treasury agreed that the Scottish Office should be increased with the addition of two assistant secretaries. Munro had wanted three (to deal with issues such as social welfare, local government and economic development), but it did mean the Scottish Office could be reconstructed on more typical departmental lines with assistant secretaries managing 'divisions'.[6]

Munro, in fact, did not give up and continued to press the Treasury for a third appointment. The Treasury's view was that although the Scottish Office performed certain 'home office' functions it was primarily a parliamentary and liaison office. Many policy issues were 'thrashed out' by the boards and, as such, the Scottish Office was little more than 'a post office' for Edinburgh proposals. Board members were, of course, paid salaries equivalent to the senior officials in London and strictly speaking the relationship between London and Edinburgh was not hierarchical. The Boards would deliberate and make submissions to the Scottish Secretary through his private secretary's office, not through his chief London officials. Munro's view was on an altogether different plane. Although the pace of Government reconstruction legislation was slowing, the onslaught of the depression meant 'a period of social and industrial stress'. The Scottish Office was likely to be faced with questions of high policy concerning 'strikes, land troubles and police matters'. Such questions, with their special Scottish dimension, the crofter and the Clydesider, lay outside the normal range of board functions. He wanted senior advisers in London. In May 1922, the Chancellor of the Exchequer, Sir Robert Horne, a Clydeside MP, agreed and a third assistant secretary, with considerable experience of the Admiralty, was drafted in.

Munro's second strategy was to convert his office into a full Secretaryship of State. If this were to occur then his status in Parliament and the position of his senior officials in Whitehall would be considerably enhanced.[7] It would also effectively put the Scottish Office, not as one of a number of Scottish departments, but as the principal department in administrative control of what the boards did. Munro, a one-time promoter of an Edinburgh Parliament in a federal Britain, now had second thoughts on the advantages of political devolution. Edinburgh, he said, would still be influenced by policy developments south of the border, but would have little influence on policy formulation. As social legislation (and concomitant grants) had come to dominate much of Government time, it was important that the London Office act as 'the guardian' of the Scottish interest in Whitehall.[8]

Lloyd George's Government initially accepted the proposition and in August 1919 introduced a Bill to increase the number of secretaries of state by five, including the Scottish Secretary. At the same time, however, it began a policy of 'retrenchment' and a number of backbench MPs, including some Scottish Liberals, objected.[9] Why, they asked, was the Government proposing to increase ministerial salaries at a time when its reconstruction programme was being cut? The Bill was quickly withdrawn. Although a considerable lobby developed that there was a Scottish interest above a departmental one, the Government refused to re-introduce the measure. In fact, the Treasury had never been 'enamoured' with the idea, Stanley Baldwin, the Financial Secretary, accepting a note from his officials that the Scottish Office was not 'one of the great departments of state'.[10] It meant the boards continued to function as before, with considerable administrative autonomy from the Scottish Office. The difficulties that this caused became evident in 1921 when, despite Treasury assurances to the contrary, Munro was left out of discussion on withdrawing the local authority housing subsidy.

If 1921 had been a difficult year for the Scottish Office, then 1923 was considerably worse. Lord Novar, the new Scottish Secretary, found Bonar Law's Government equally intransigent towards meeting any special Scottish interest. Despite higher unemployment and poorer housing, Novar's pleading for additional grant aid failed. The Government's position was simple. Scotland was part of the UK and as such could not expect England to pay higher levels of taxation, irrespective of any peculiar Scottish needs.

At the same time, Novar was able to restart Cabinet discussion on creating a Secretaryship of State, but the Treasury made it clear they opposed an increase in salary. The Scottish boards were there to implement British policy and in areas such as health, housing and economic development the lead Department was either an all-British department, like the Board of Trade, or an English ministry, like Health. The pressure for change, it argued, was due to historical 'sentiment', not the promotion of Government efficiency.[11] Walter Elliot, the Parliamentary Under Secretary, recognised the issue and told Scottish MPs quite candidly that if Scotland wanted higher grants or other administrative changes it had to be justified 'by arguments of an altogether different order'.[12]

The chance to present a different argument came in 1925, after the Conservatives had won a convincing UK election but narrowly failed on the Clyde. At that time the Scottish housing programme was running into serious difficulty, despite the reintroduction of subsidies under the 1923 and 1924 Housing Acts. This was due largely to the lack of materials and skilled labour. Sir John Gilmour, the Scottish Secretary, tried hard during the early part of 1925 to encourage new methods of construction (such as steel and timber), but with the prospect of industrial action, he reluctantly accepted that a different approach was necessary. Sidestepping Neville Chamberlain, the Minister of Health, Gilmour approached Baldwin, the Prime Minister, and made the Scottish position clear. First, he said that the Conservatives had always believed bad housing was not just a cause of ill health but also of 'social discontent and unrest'.[13] Second, if the Scottish programme failed – were they prepared to give Labour pro-devolution ammunition? The answer was they were not. A

Government agency, a housing association directly under the aegis of the Scottish Secretary, was employed to build houses.

After 1925, each time the issue of housing was considered, Scottish Secretaries were able to draw on the 1925 decision as a precedent that there were in Scotland 'special circumstances' or 'special needs' and that the State would have to provide subsidies far larger than in England. Administratively it also meant the Scottish Secretary's position within Cabinet and the Scottish Office's within Whitehall had been considerably enhanced. In future, the Scottish Secretary would have to be consulted much earlier in policy formulation.

A 'NATIONAL ADMINISTRATION' (1926–1945)

The need to respond positively to the Scottish issue, however, was not confined to housing. Although the pro-devolutionists lost the 1924 'Government of Scotland Bill', the Conservatives realised that their principal concern – Scotland's relatively worsening social and economic position – remained unanswered. Indeed, with some justification, they pointed out that the apparent assimilation of Scottish policy into English had made matters worse. Gilmour's response was to press Baldwin to recognise that he was not just a head of a Department, but a Minister 'who is in charge of a national administration'. This time, in contrast with 1921, the Scottish argument was accepted and in 1926 Gilmour became a Secretary of State, though not with an increased salary. As the *Glasgow Herald* put it, Baldwin had effectively dished 'the visionaries and the extremists'.[14] The Scottish Secretary was no longer 'a subordinate minister' and this was demonstrated almost immediately with Gilmour becoming chairman of the Imperial Conference.[15] The argument after 1926 was thus not about devolution *per se*, but rather about what particular administrative system would enable Scotland to access more effectively the mechanics of British decision-making. What was important, as Sir Archibald Sinclair (Scottish Secretary 1931–2) said, was to have ministers and civil servants 'who knew the Whitehall ropes'.[16]

Gilmour's attempts to improve on Scottish effectiveness, the conversion of boards into departments in 1928, was not particularly successful. In reality, the departments maintained their separate identities and liaison arrangements. But, in order to placate fear of total integration into Whitehall, he did agree that some further reorganisation of departments, with their headquarters in Edinburgh, would be necessary. However, it was left to one of his successors, Sir Godfrey Collins, a Liberal, to push the matter further. Collins accepted, like Munro and Gilmour, that the pace of decision-making and the complexity of government had increased 'the divergence' between Scottish interests and

British policy.[17] But, after Labour's 1931 poll debacle, he also sensed a change in the attitude of the Scottish public. What would replace the 'lost faith' of the ILP – its fervour, its hope and its commitment to devolution? With an economy in structural difficulty and housing little improved, Collins feared that if there was disillusion with the existing political system, an upsurge of Scottish nationalism would result.

To help deflect criticism of a distant, unresponsive Government and 'damp the smouldering spirit of nationalism', Collins agreed in 1934 to move a Scottish Office division from London to Edinburgh (to improve local authority liaison) and then agreed to establish an inquiry into Scottish administration.[18] What he wanted was what Munro had sought in 1919, the Scottish departments under 'the general control' of his Scottish Office permanent under secretary.[19] If this official could oversee departmental co-ordination, reach agreement on the Scottish view and act accordingly, then the Scottish voice would have greater weight. (The senior officials, as well as the Scottish Secretary, would also have to be appropriately paid.) In addition, if the reorganised Scottish Office was located in the new planned St Andrews House in Edinburgh, then administratively, if not politically, the public would sense devolved government in Scotland. Unlike in 1919, the Treasury welcomed an inquiry – it thought the suggested arrangements 'would kill off the idiotic Home Rule movement'.[20]

The Committee on Scottish Administration reported in 1937 and recommended a reorganisation of the Scottish Departments much in the way Collins had suggested. In 1939, four new Edinburgh departments (Health, Home, Education and Agriculture) became the organic Scottish Office, based at St Andrews House. A small parliamentary and liaison office was retained in London, which the permanent under secretary could readily access.

CENTRIPETALISM VERSUS PARALLELISM (1945–1964)

In 1934, Collins successfully persuaded Chamberlain to give the Scottish Office control of a separate Special Areas Commissioner – with unemployment twice England's, Scottish opinion, it was said, 'was rather touchy'.[21] This meant, however, that the Scottish Secretary's brief now formally included economic development. At reorganisation, issues affecting development were concentrated within part of an assistant secretary's brief in the new Home Department. This included the Special Areas Act, the Highlands and Islands, electricity and power supplies, the Scottish Travel Association and the Scottish Development Council. This regrouping of development issues by 'affinity' to each other was meant to indicate the importance attached to regenerating the economy.[22] In 1945, however, under the Coalition Government's post-war reconstruction plans, the Board of Trade took over the responsibility for redistributing industry, essentially to 'steer' industry from the south-east. It was agreed that the Home Department's role was to co-ordinate the activities of such bodies as the Scottish Council of Development and Industry and generally make Scottish interests known. The Department of Health's role was to secure the necessary local planning consent and other services.

The administrative problems that this split responsibility caused did not really surface until early 1947 when, unlike those in England, the Scottish post-war plans began to go astray. The Government estimated 145,000 jobs were required for Clydeside. By 1947 only 80,000 had been planned and even fewer actually secured. However, because of the range of Labour's legislative pro-gramme, Joe Westwood, the Scottish Secretary, was unable to devote much time to the Distribution of Industry Committee and this work was usually left to one of his parliamentary under-secretaries. It meant the Scottish representative held a rank lower than most other ministers.

In May 1947, with increased criticism of the Scottish employment position, Westwood responded by proposing to the Cabinet Office the appointment of a second Scottish Cabinet Minister, an 'identical twin', to tackle a wide range of duties, including economic planning.[23] It received a hostile response. As in 1921, the Cabinet Office thought that the post-war legislative programme would slow and, as a result, the Scottish Office would have more time to improve its effectiveness. A second minister might cause the same constitutional problem that Munro had suggested in 1919 – who would be the real senior minister? But the Cabinet Office also thought that if the Scottish public sensed an administrative failure the demand for greater devolution would be raised. However, Westwood was also being pressed by the Scottish Labour Party to take a different approach and instigate an inquiry into the practicability of further legislative or administrative devolution. In July he withdrew the plan and instead pressed the Government to accept the Labour demands. It received an equally hostile response for three principal reasons. First, the Cabinet Office believed that there was 'no deep rooted demand for devolution'.[24] Second, it re-emphasised that the lead department in the distribution of industry was the Board of Trade. The Scottish Office brief was too wide to handle all the technicalities involved. Third, the Cabinet Office felt that there was not enough native entrepreneurship in Scotland to sustain the kind of development required – car production, aircraft manufacture and the like. That could come only through the Board of Trade using its powers to induce investment from England.

In October 1947 Westwood was sacked and replaced by the more congenial, if somewhat bureaucratic Arthur Woodburn. Woodburn dropped the idea of an additional minister, but instead suggested the establishment, under his authority, of a 'Scottish Production Council to stimulate and co-ordinate the development of industry'.[25] The Council would bring together in one forum the nationalised industries, private industry, the Scottish Office, the Ministry of Supply and other bodies such as the Scottish Council for Development and Industry. He also floated the idea of an inquiry. Both received a similarly hostile response, Woodburn was firmly told that with the dollar crisis almost consuming the Government, if a repetition of 1931 was not to recur, then his loyalty to the Party was essential. All Woodburn secured was an improvement in Commons procedures for Scottish business, a consultative committee on economic development and a commitment to review the organisation of British departments in Scotland. It was not in Scotland's interest to have control over economic planning.

Although a review of Government organisation duly took place, none of the British departments would increase the delegation of authority to their Scottish officials or agree to a modification of Westwood's idea – that a Scottish parliamentary under secretary be appointed to co-ordinate their work. Such an appointment, they said, would not only complicate departmental management but would also raise the constitutional problem of which minister was ultimately answerable for specific decisions. In January 1949 Woodburn, although maintaining further administrative devolution was 'inevitable', reluctantly accepted 'the appointment would not afford a satisfactory solution'.[26] As far as the Labour Government was concerned, the issue was effectively dead.

When the Conservatives returned to power in 1951 they had already decided that the Scottish ministerial team had to be strengthened. Having a somewhat more pluralistic view of Government power than the planned functionalism of Labour, they had no problem about appointing a Minister of State and an additional parliamentary under secretary. All that mattered to them was ensuring that the Scottish Secretary would have more time in London to engage in ministerial power-broking and, with the additional parliamentary secretary, to improve Scottish attendance at committees. On a day-to-day basis the Minister of State, as the resident Edinburgh deputy, could handle Scottish institutions and liaise with British departmental officials.

The Conservatives had also pledged a Royal Commission into Scottish Affairs, but that proved more problematic. On the political side the issue of legislative devolution was ruled out; the Conservatives were the party of the Union. On the economic side, as Labour would not accept an inquiry into the nationalised industries without discussion of the private sector, which the Conservatives would never accept, the mechanics of the Scottish economy had to be ruled out. The Commission therefore had to concentrate on Government organisation and, in effect, review the argument between a 'centripetal' view of Government efficiency and that of 'parallelism'; between functional departments with London as the channel for high-level negotiation and St Andrews House being able to access British departmental officials and reach agreement on as many problems as possible without reference to London.[27] As in 1948, the key issue was how much authority the Scottish ministerial team would have over British officials.

Although Lord Balfour, the Commission's chairman, had been briefed 'not to go any distance', his Commission proved extremely interested in examining the case for devolution.[28] But it tackled the issue in different ways. For roads, which had always been a sensitive issue, it recommended a complete transfer of responsibility from the Ministry of Transport to the Scottish Office, largely on the grounds that, as road development affected Scotland's infrastructure, Scottish ministers would have a better idea of appropriate investment. Although initially hesitant, the Treasury, in the end, fully supported the recommendation as simply another form of functional efficiency. Another of its recommendations was to increase the status of British officials in Scotland. Originally the Commission had wanted each department to be represented by an under-secretary, effectively a departmental deputy, but the Treasury raised objections. Instead they had to settle for a promise that departments would review the delegation of authority to their existing assistant secretaries. The Commission had also wanted the Scottish Office to be consulted by the Board of Trade if firms sought its advice over new factory sites, but again was persuaded by the Treasury that this might be politically as well as administratively difficult. The Welsh might want the same.

On the surface the Commission's report seemed 'barren'.[29] But in reality its tone legitimated the arguments against centripetal economic planning. The Scottish economy had not received the kind of boost war-time planners had assumed. In fact, as the Scottish Office had noticed, since 1947 investment from England in the development areas had steadily declined, only to be matched by increased unemployment. There was some preference in the Treasury for a limited re-organisation of the Scottish departments, based largely on transferring the development division from the Home Department to the small office of the permanent under secretary. But once roads had been transferred to the Home Department in 1956, it meant the Department now had some responsibility for executing economic development within industrial Scotland. Instead, the Treasury asked the Scottish Office to consider a more detailed re-organisation, based on combining the Department of Health's planning functions with the Home Department's road and economic liaison brief. This view accepted that if 'centripetalism' had not promoted economic growth and 'parallelism' posed administrative as well as constitutional problems, then a solution might be to re-organise the Scottish Office and enhance its role over physical planning. The establishment of the Scottish Development Department in 1962 effectively underlined this shift in Scottish Office responsibilities, symbolically as much as administratively. British departments could not operate in Scotland without establishing closer liaison with the Development Department and in that way no change in British policy could be considered unless they had specifically considered Scottish needs.

CONCLUSION

What can be said about the issue of Scottish 'sentiment', devolution and Westminster? The long view of Scottish history would suggest certain deeply held views about the potential for Scottish society to be easily destabilised. Jacobites, temperance activists and Clydeside shop stewards were all passionate believers in causes that a small society could not easily absorb. Political union, this view held, enabled the 'centrifugal forces' to be absorbed.[30] The alternative, a Scottish Parliament, would simply 'revive the unruly factionalism of the stormiest periods of Scottish history'.[31] But the twentieth century required not just political symbols, such as a Scottish Secretary, but material advancement. At a time when Government itself held greater control over social and economic investment, the Scottish Secretary had to be seen to be effective in securing jobs, houses and social security. The real issue was how to achieve it. The political response – administrative devolution – developed as a threefold strategy. First, it sought to restructure Scottish departments so that there could be one mouth-piece for opinion to be heard. Second, it sought to ensure that Scottish administration could articulate needs and satisfactorily implement policy. Third, and perhaps most important of all, it qualitatively sought greater influence within Whitehall. As Tom Johnston once said, if the Scottish Office was to be effective it had to have 'the right to know – and in time'.[32]

NOTES

1 This chapter is based on the author's *The Scottish Office: Depression and Reconstruction, 1919–59* (Scottish History Society, 1992).

2 *Scotsman*, Speech, Scottish Grand Committee, on the Board of Health Bill, 10.4.1919.

3 *Scotsman*, Leader Review on Bill's Progress, 29.3.1919.

4 *Forward*, 'Regionalism versus Nationalism', 12.6.1920.

5 *Glasgow Herald*, 'The Scottish Office: Mr Munro's Review and Retrospect', 17.10.1921.

6 Scottish Office letter to Treasury, on the Re-organisation of Administrative Staff, 20.1.1921; Public Record Office, PRO, T 162/494.

7 *Scotsman*, Speech, 'Status of the Secretary for Scotland', 13.3.1923.

8 *Hansard*, vol 127, Government of Scotland Bill, 16.4.1920.

9 *Scotsman*, Leader Review on Bill's Progress, 21.4.1920.

10 Treasury minute, Secretary of State for Scotland Bill, 24.7.1920, PRO, T 163/3/1.

11 Treasury minute, Re-organisation of Offices (Scotland) Bill, 22.8.1923, PRO, T 163/18/9.

12 *Hansard*, vol 163, Housing (No 2) Bill [Money] Committee, 30.3.1923.

13 *Glasgow Herald*, 'Public Health', 21.7.1925.

14 *Glasgow Herald*, 'The Scottish Secretariat', 24.2.1925.

15 *Scotsman*, 'Scottish Affairs', 25.2.1929.

16 *Hansard*, vol 214, Re-organisation of Offices (Scotland) Bill, 5.3.1928.

17 Treasury minute, on Scottish administration, 23.6.1936. PRO, T 162/476.

18 Letter of Collins to Baldwin, on Scottish administration, 28.11.1935. SRO, HH 1/896.

19 Scottish Office memorandum, on Scottish administration, 13.8.1934. PRO, T 162/998.

20 Treasury minute, on Scottish administration, 24.6.1936. PRO, T 162/476.

21 Comment by Noel Skelton, Scottish Parliamentary Under Secretary, to the Depressed Areas Committee, 18.10.1934. PRO, CAB 27/578, DA(34)2nd.

22 Scottish Home Department, Report of the Advisory Committee on Departmental Organisation, 18.3.1952. PRO, T 222/471.

23 Minute of Joseph Westwood, on Scottish ministerial arrangements, June 1947. PRO, T 222/1048.

24 Official minute for Herbert Morrison, Lord President of the Council, on Scottish Devolution, 13.11.1947. PRO, CAB 124/91.

25 Letter of Woodburn to Herbert Morrison, on Scottish Devolution, 7.11.1947. PRO, CAB 124/911.

26 Scottish Office letter to Treasury, on Scottish administration, 20.1.1949. PRO, T 222/1048.

27 Treasury Notes on Government Organisation – Regional Organisation, June 1946. Scottish Record Office. SRO, HH 1/1231.

28 Treasury minute, on the Balfour Commission, 3.4.1954. PRO, T 222/686.

29 *Scotsman*, 'Scots Devolution', 28.7.1954.

30 *Scotsman*, 'The Election in Scotland', 17.11.1922.

31 *Glasgow Herald*, 'Scottish Home Rule', 7.5.1924.

32 Evidence of Johnston to Balfour Commission, 17.12.1953. SRO, HH 41/690.

National Identity in Crisis: Politicians, Intellectuals and the 'End of Scotland', 1920–1939

Richard J Finlay 1994 *History* 79, 242–59.

I

Although Scotland, along with the rest of the United Kingdom, had emerged victorious from the First World War, it soon became apparent that many of the previously held values and assumptions concerning Scottish national identity and self-perception either were no longer tenable or would have to be adapted to suit the changed political, social, cultural and economic circumstances of the post-1918 era. Pre-war national identity had, to a large extent, been founded on the notion that Scotland was an equal partner with England in the founding and running of the British empire. The imperial connection had lain at the root of economic success, as Glasgow, 'second city of the empire', had amply testified with Clyde-built ships and engineering at every point of the globe. Scottish soldiers, such as General Gordon, missionaries, such as David Livingstone, and colonists, who formed large Scottish communities in the white settler dominion nations, were all engaged in the imperial mission; they had formed a focus of pride for those Scots still at home and helped to divert their attention away from the grim realities of a society which had some of the most appalling social conditions in Western Europe. For those Scots concerned with national identity in the period before the First World War, the empire provided a tailor-made outlet for the exhibition of all those qualities of virility, martial prowess and romanticism which characterized much of later nineteenth-century European nationalism. The impact of the Great War was, however, to throw many of these assumptions into sharp relief and ushered in a period of profound social, cultural, economic and political dislocation. As was common throughout Europe between the wars, politicians and intellectuals grappled with old and new problems in their re-assessment of Scottish national identity.

The problems of national identity and national self-perception were compounded by the fact that the major dislocations experienced by Scottish society in the inter-war era were never satisfactorily resolved, and this added an air of uncertainty which did much to damage national self-confidence. After the war, the economy, which was the linchpin of nineteenth-century Scottish greatness, lay ruined and exposed as over-reliant on the old, heavy, export-related industries. Although this was a general north-western European problem, Scottish industrialists, unlike their European counterparts, were slow to respond to the problem of structural imbalance, which was never rectified during this period: economic recovery was only possible as a result of re-armament in the late 1930s.[1] To the entrenched social problems of bad health and bad housing was added the new one of long-term, mass unemployment. Razor gangs, falling church attendance and the perceived threat of uncontrolled Irish immigration compounded the bourgeoisie's fear that the fabric of Scottish society was disintegrating. Politically, things were no more settled. The long, lingering death of the once mighty Scottish Liberal Party added a note of uncertainty to political life in the early 1920s, delaying the firm establishment of a Tory-Labour divide based on class. Although the late 1920s witnessed a period of relative calm, the impact of the great depression and the political crisis of 1931 skewed normal development and gave the Unionists an unrivalled hegemony as the Labour Party in Scotland was reduced to the point of near-insignificance.[2] The problems which bedevilled Scottish politicians in the inter-war era seemed to be insoluble; and it is against this dismal backdrop of economic, social and political dislocation that debates about culture and national identity were conducted. Not surprisingly, the predominant theme that emerges from these debates is, once again, dislocation.

Historians of Scottish literature have rightly seen this period as an era of cultural 're-awakening' or 'regeneration'. The sentimental Kailyard was ousted by the Scottish literary renaissance and its leading proponents, such as Hugh MacDiarmid, are revered for making the greatest cultural contribution to twentieth-century Scotland.[3] Such an optimistic view of the inter-war period, however, was not shared by contemporaries. Indeed, the need to 're-create' the Scottish language was seen as a sign of weakness; a sort of artificial respiration which did not bode well for the nation's current cultural health. As one commentator acidly put it: 'the so-called renaissance is a myth, believed in by nobody outside a very small circle – if indeed by them. To hark back artificially to older things or to dredge the dictionary for archaic Scottish words, is to achieve nothing new. And this so far is the achievement . . .'[4]

Others claimed that without a national impulse, the Doric would 'become more and more of an anachronism and a debilitating influence to the purpose of those who use it'.[5] For some, it had already died: 'I do not for a moment think that it is possible that after a certain level of education has been reached the vernacular can ever be used again in Scotland for ordinary social intercourse.'[6] Without the benefit of hindsight, contemporaries were more likely to think in negative terms about the future of the Scottish national identity. According to several writers, Scottish culture had become a hollow tartan sham: 'The Scots are incapable of considering their literary geniuses purely as writers and artists. They must be either an excuse for a glass or a text for a sermon.'[7] For them it was a period of great confusion and uncertainty, haunted by the fear that Scotland had ceased to be a living entity. According to one Unionist MP: 'Scotland has passed the stage of nationhood. Her nationhood has been absorbed into a wider area.'[8] For many, all the indicators seemed to point to the fact that the Scottish nation was in a process of terminal decline: 'The first fact about the Scot is that he is a man eclipsed. The Scots are a dying race.'[9] These anxieties crystallized into a series of terse phrases, such as 'the southward drift of industry', 'provincialization', 'the Irish invasion', 'the slum problem', and, most tellingly of all, 'that distressed area: North Britain', all of which dominated the political vocabulary of inter-war Scotland.

II

The state of the Scottish economy lay at the heart of the debate concerning the crisis of national identity, although many of the trends of economic decline would not become apparent until the late 1920s. Initial optimism at the end of the war translated itself in part into persistent demands for home rule, mostly coming from the Labour Party which had inherited this as part of the radical baggage of the Liberal Party. As the 1920s wore on, however, Labour became more and more orientated towards British political priorities, especially as the solution to Scotland's endemic social and economic problems was seen to lie within the context of centralized British control; and, in so doing, the party abandoned its previous enthusiasm for Scottish home rule.[10] The independent nationalist party, the National Party of Scotland, which emerged in 1928, was not taken seriously by its political rivals. Indeed, the party's leftward and separatist stance confirmed many middle-class suspicions that Scottish nationalism was inspired either by socialism or the Catholic Irish.[11] As the cold winds of recession began to blow fiercely with the arrival of the great depression in 1929, however, Scottish economic recovery looked further away than ever and middle-class resentments started to take on an nationalist air, much to the concern of anti-home rule Unionist politicians.

With the benefit of hindsight, contemporaries noted that economic developments in the 1920s began to take on a sinister appearance as Scottish businessmen woke up to the fact that control of the country's economy was slipping away from Scotland. The amalgamation of the railways following the war transferred the management to London and, thereafter, the construction and repair work favoured Derby and Crewe at the expense of Inverness, Kilmarnock and St Rollox.[12] The Scots had also seen four of their main banks fall victim to London takeovers, which, according to the prominent Scottish industrialist, Lord Maclay, meant that:

> Scottish money is liable to be chained more and more to London, making it increasingly difficult for Scottish traders to secure financial assistance. Even now Scottish banks pay higher interest for deposits to customers in London than in Glasgow, and also discount bills cheaper.[13]

Contemporaries were well aware that Scotland's economy was not performing as well as England's. Unemployment remained about 50 per cent higher, with some 400,000 or 26.2 per cent of the insured workforce idle in 1932.[14] New industries were not coming north – largely, it was believed, on account of more expensive local rates, which were the result of higher levels of unemployment and the lack of a sufficient domestic market. Nor did the political reputation of the 'red' Clyde help matters.

Scottish industrialists failed to diversify, pursuing a 'wait-and-see' policy, while the old industries were constantly contracting, and at a faster rate than their counterparts in England. In 1932, twenty new Scots factories were opened and thirty-six closed; in 1933, fourteen were opened and twenty-nine closed; in 1934–5, thirty-eight opened and fifty-eight closed.[15] In the depressed areas of Scotland, the picture was even bleaker. In 1933 only three new factories opened, compared with 467 for the rest of the United Kingdom; in 1934, five opened, compared with 520; in 1935, two opened compared with 514; and in 1936, six opened, compared with 551.[16] Furthermore, Scottish industrial production had been declining since the end of the war and in 1931 was smaller than in 1913, in complete contradistinction to England.[17] Fishing and farming, likewise, were declining both in output and as a source of employment.[18] When comparisons were made with the progress of England – particularly the south of England, for which most of the government's policies seemed tailor-made – discontent began to grow: 'Scotland has her own particular problems and we will never make much progress until masters and men realise that what applies to England does not necessarily apply here'.[19] For many Scottish businessmen it appeared that they were locked into a spiral of economic decline:

Many of the concerns which attract new capital and pay big dividends, are distributive, non-industrial, and, so far as export trade is concerned, non-productive . . . these lucrative enterprises tend to concentrate more and more in the South East of England.[20]

In short, it was claimed that the south had all the advantages and would continue to do well, whereas Scotland was handicapped with no prospect of recovery in sight.

Unlike the early 1920s, when nationalist sentiment was largely led by the left, the growing disgruntlement of the Scottish middle class by the early years of the following decade presented Scottish Unionist politicians with a considerable problem. The idea that something was badly wrong with the Scottish nation had certainly caught the public's imagination. As the leader of a popular newspaper reviewing the past events of 1929 put it:

In certain respects the year which closes today will remain memorable to Scotland as a nation. Certainly no year within memory of any living Scot has witnessed so much heart-searching. Never before has there been so much airing of the question: what is wrong with Scotland?[21]

A whole host of politicians and writers joined in the debate of 'Stands Scotland Where She Did?' The early 1930s saw the publication of a number of books which linked economic decline with national decline; disconcertingly for the Unionist Party, most were written by those from the right of the political spectrum and most advocated some form of self-government as a solution.[22] Social problems were analysed and again the poor Scottish performance in health and housing was highlighted; all of which added fuel to the fire of those preaching national decay. Infant mortality rates did not decline to the same extent as those from England and Wales, while medical opinion universally acknowledged that the average Scot was, physically, in much poorer shape than his English counterpart. Poor housing and slum conditions remained as bad as ever, with overcrowding six times greater in 1935 than south of the border.[23]

The novelist and Unionist MP, John Buchan, made numerous pleas in favour of a strong Scottish national identity, but they were always tinged with a disconcerting lack of optimism: 'We do not want to see Scotland become merely a Northern Province of England. We do not want to become like the Jews a race without a Jerusalem. We must save our national identity while there is still time.'[24] The rather facile statement of John Colville, on the appointment of Sir James Lithgow as head of the Federation of British Industries, that 'if they had more men of his kind [Lithgow] they would not only cease to hear of the drift

from Scotland to the south, they would see a drift of industry to the north again'
was cold comfort.[25] Further platitudes from Sir James himself that 'Scotsmen
only needed to believe in themselves again' did little to stifle the growing
unease.[26]

In the face of such appalling economic and social circumstances, there was
little reason to be confident. Normally acquiescent Unionist allies appeared to
be turning towards a nationalist interpretation of the economic crisis. As the
President of Edinburgh Chamber of Commerce put it in November 1932:
'Business after business was being bought up by English money and factories
one after another closed down . . . If the process of English absorption is not
stopped, Scotland will drop to a position of industrial insignificance.'[27] The
Glasgow Chamber of Commerce was equally gloomy in its assessment of the
Scottish economic situation. Attention focused on the fact that a lack of
control over the economy from within Scotland was handicapping any
effective way out of the continuing malaise of economic distress. Contemporaries believed that they were victims of a system which denied them the
opportunity to put their own house in order and to contribute to their own
economic well-being:

> A Scotland functioning as a real controlling centre of industry, trade,
> agriculture, shipping and finance is a bigger asset to the British Empire, a
> more profitable customer to England, France, Germany and so forth, than a
> Scotland written all over with the words 'branch economy'.[28]

Others succumbed to the growing mood of nationalist discontent and chose to
explain the situation by means of a conspiracy theory. Glasgow had declined,
according to Sir John Samuel, because of

> the changes which have taken place in the spheres of shipping, railways,
> banks, steel, manufacturing, bleaching and calico printing, the drapery and
> soft goods trade, chemical manufacture, and even philanthropy, with the
> extinction or absorption of many Glasgow firms and the falling of others
> under English control. There has been an insidious Campaign of suppression
> of Scottish affairs for a long time.[29]

Unfortunately for the Unionist establishment, such ideas were dangerously
similar to the ones being put about by the nationalists. The Unionist press
walked a precarious tightrope, attempting to air nationalist grievances, but
without succumbing to nationalist solutions. While dismissing any notion of
home rule as unworkable, the *Glasgow Evening Citizen* of 14 October 1931

captured the growing mood of unease, warning against the dangers of nation-alist upsurge, but also drawing attention to the legitimacy of their concerns:

> There is, however, a widespread discontent with economic conditions in Scotland. We see business leaving our country. London is more and more becoming the centre of commerce, finance, law, literature and the arts. More and more ambitious Scotsmen are attracted by the glittering prizes that London can offer. So far as manual workers are concerned, our old industries stagnate and few new ones are rising up; there is unemployment and discouragement. In contrast, the new industrial areas which have London as their centre have never been so prosperous.[30]

Economic rationalization was seen to be a particularly anti-Scottish device. The printing and bleaching works at Thornliebank and the Mossend steelworks were two notorious examples of Scottish factories being closed down in order to safeguard jobs 'elsewhere'.[31] The scant regard paid to Scottish national con-cerns in the process caused widespread resentment. The following comment from *The Scotsman* was typical:

> This transference of the control of Scottish industry is no new thing; but it has received an additional impetus from the present popularity of what is known as rationalisation. It is a movement which is fraught with the most serious consequences to Scotland, and has already caused great loss of work to Scottish people, besides limiting enormously the possibilities of future expansion when trade improves . . . Scottish conditions both industrial and administrative, present their own problems. Continuance of the fundamentally false policy of centralizing everything on London, will, sooner or later, finish Scotland as a nation and reduce her to a mere province of England.[32]

Members of the National Government had no doubt that it was the severity of economic conditions which was fuelling nationalist grievances. Sir Godfrey Collins, the Secretary of State for Scotland, agreed that 'the Depression had caused many to seek a solution to their problems by the setting up of a Parliament in Edinburgh'.[33] Sir Robert Horne likewise noted that nationalism was stirring in 'those communities in Scotland which are most distressed, and I believe that the present movement really had its origin in the state of great depression into which Scottish communities have fallen'.[34]

III

Despite such claims, economic issues were not the only source of grievance. By the late 1920s open day had been declared on any kind of perceived injustice to the Scottish nation. The Local Government Act of 1929 was passed in the face of near-universal opposition from the Convention of Royal Burghs, and widespread resentment was caused by the apparent example of parliamentary indifference to Scottish opinion. According to John Buchan MP, it led 'many people to whom home rule would be an anathema to question in measured terms the wisdom of the whole system'.[35] What caused most anxiety among Unionist politicians was the alienation of moderate and conservative opinion, best represented in this instance by Sir Henry Keith, who claimed that the local government reforms were a violation of the Treaty of Union.[36] A series of embarrassing statistics were produced, one after another, by nationalist and non-nationalist alike to illustrate how Scotland was being treated unfairly. It was shown, for example, that over 97 per cent of salaries paid to government officials were paid to those located in England.[37] The Scottish Office's representative in Scotland was a messenger who was paid £148 a year, while the seventy permanent officials in London received between them £31,051 per annum.[38] The treatment of Scottish libraries and records was another case in point. The National Library of Scotland received only £2,600 in 1931, while its counterpart in Wales received £25,000.[39] Attention was drawn to the fact that the Scottish Record Office was badly underfunded and valuable historical documents 'lay in the basement of Register House in the very sacks which they had been deposited in over a century ago'.[40] The *Scottish Historical Review* ceased publication in 1929, causing considerable concern over the state of the nation's historiography.[41] Furthermore, the teaching of Scottish history in schools was not encouraged, except within the opportunity offered by the Scottish Education Department for 'local history' – a notion which offended many.[42] The formation of the Saltire society in 1936 as an organization designed to promote the nation's cultural heritage was a further indication of the anxiety being expressed about the disappearance of Scottish culture.

To make matters worse for Scottish politicians, an increasing amount of attention was focused on just how little time was devoted to purely Scottish affairs in parliament. Lord Beaverbrook trumpeted this injustice to his readers: 'There have been only two debates on Scottish affairs during the present session of Parliament. One of them was on Derby Day. Parliament is too busy to give adequate attention to Scotland.'[43] David Kirkwood MP moaned to *Daily Record* readers about how Scottish debates were the quickest way to clear the chamber and fill the bars.[44] Even Unionist members began to express unease with the present system:

> I venture to think that Scotland is not receiving sufficient consideration. Scotland has her own special problems which demand special treatment and special legislation . . . I cannot rid my mind of the feeling that Scotland does not receive her due share of parliamentary time.[45]

Of greater concern to many, however, was the habit of applying English Bills to Scotland without reference to the country's peculiar legal system. The Children's Bill and the Town and County Planning Bill were two examples cited in 1931; they needed so many amending clauses in order to conform with Scottish law that they had become largely unintelligible.[46] Another case cited to demonstrate English indifference to Scottish needs was the government subsidies given to the production of wheat and sugar beet. While this benefited English farmers, Scottish farmers were not given subsidies for oats (the most common Scottish crop) and the existing subsidies ruined the Greenock sugar cane refining industry.[47]

Emigration was seen as proof positive that the Scottish nation was in the process of terminal decline. The census of 1931 showed that the Scottish population had fallen by about 40,000, the first recorded decline. The population of England and Wales, on the other hand, had risen in the same period by over two million. Even more alarming for observers of the state of the Scottish nation was the fact that the Scottish birth rate was higher than that in England.[48] Other critics compared the state of Scottish population decline with that of other European nations and concluded that emigration was both the symptom and the cause of national decline.[49] Moreover, in a Europe which was becoming increasingly race conscious, unfettered emigration which allowed the 'life blood of the nation to slip away' was seen as another example of injustice to Scotland: 'Emigration! It is the negation of national policy. It has been – in the insensate form in which we have known it – one of the causes of our impoverishment, one of the sources in the decline in national stamina.'[50] For many, emigration represented a defeatist reaction to the belief that Scotland was naturally and incurably poor, and had no alternative but to send the best of its population abroad. This was seen as particularly dangerous, especially as there was now a declining population and a falling birth rate.

This testament to national decline was compounded by fears that the country was being overrun by 'alien' Irish Catholics who flocked to Scotland to steal jobs from the natives and claim poor relief. This racial scaremongering was largely due to the efforts of the leaders of the Church of Scotland, who hoped to enhance their role as spiritual leaders of the nation by an appeal to Protestant bigotry.[51] In spite of the release of figures from the Scottish Office which showed that such fears were a fabrication, many politicians regularly repeated the wild assertions of the anti-Irish lobby.[52] John Buchan linked Irish immigration and Scottish emigration to produce a woeful picture of national decline:

> Our population is declining, we are losing some of the best of our race stock by the migration and their place is being taken by those, whatever their merits, who are not Scottish. I understand that every fifth child born now in Scotland is an Irish Roman Catholic.[53]

Sir Robert Horne, likewise, recited the exaggerated claims as to the size of the Scoto-Irish, Catholic community in Scotland and warned against the dangers of Scottish nationalism and home rule, claiming that the 'Irish'

> could easily be the determining element in the balance between the Scottish parties and you might find that what you believed to be Scottish home rule, turned out to be a form of very insidious Irish domination in our politics.[54]

The impact of the depression not only produced widespread discontent; it knocked the stuffing out of national self-confidence. The novelist and poet, Edwin Muir, summed up this mood of despondency in 1935:

> a silent clearance is going on in industrial Scotland, a clearance not of human beings, but what they depend upon for life. Everything which could give meaning to their existence in these grotesque industrial towns of Lanarkshire is slipping from them; the surroundings of industrialisation remain, but industry itself is vanishing like a dream. Airdrie and Motherwell are the most improbable places imaginable in which to be left with nothing to do; for only rough work could reconcile anyone to living in them. Yet, a large population lives there in idleness; for there is nowhere to go, and little prospect that Monday will dawn for a long time.[55]

Sir Robert Horne told the House of Commons that the discontent of the distressed areas had led to a 'sense of defeat amongst a considerable proportion of the population, to which the Scottish people were not accustomed. There was a loss of pride.'[56] Other MPs recounted similar tales of woe at the lack of national self-esteem, while one writer summed up the effects upon the younger generation of living in such a climate:

Among the working-classes the old pride of craftmanship is dead; lazy, shiftless, and physically degenerate, they make no effort to find a footing for themselves in a country they believe to be doomed, while at the same time they do not emigrate until compelled to do so.[57]

To many all was not well with the Scottish nation and, according to John Buchan, a sense of nationalist grievance had spread to

young people who are hard headed, ambitious and practical, who are shaping out for themselves careers in medicine and law and business. Very few of that class would agree for a moment to any of the schemes of home rule at present put forward, but they all feel this dissatisfaction. They all believe that much is wrong with Scotland and it is up to Scotsmen to put it right.[58]

Nationalism, it would seem, was in danger of spreading beyond its traditional bounds of cranks and romantics and, perhaps most disconcertingly, for Buchan,

it has infected a very important class who do a good deal of the thinking of the nation. I would have this House remember that it is not any scheme [of home rule] put forward that matters. Those schemes may be crude and foolish enough in all conscience. It is the instinct that matters and unless we face that instinct honestly and fairly, we may drive it underground, and presently it will appear in some irrational and dangerous form.[59]

Having accepted that Scottish national grievances were the result of an 'honourable fear', Buchan concluded that something had to be done to 'satisfy a legitimate national pride and to intensify that consciousness of individuality and idiom, which is what is meant by . . . national spirit'.[60]

IV

Of the main political parties in the early 1930s, the Labour Party had the easiest task in confronting this upsurge of nationalist sentiment. Since the mid-1920s Labour had been committed to economic and social regeneration through the powers of centralized government control, and therefore any measure of home rule was surplus to requirements. Although there were some MPs who maintained a nominal commitment to Scottish self-government, it was not accorded a high priority.[61] Some previous supporters had renounced home rule and

nationalism on account of its bourgeois origins.[62] As the then current bout of
nationalist sentiment was recognized to be of middle-class origin, few Labour
leaders bothered with it and a parliamentary discussion on the subject in 1932
was criticized by George Buchanan and David Kirkwood for wasting time
which would have been put to better use in discussing the effects of the
recession. The former blandly asserted that: 'Far greater than home rule for
Scotland or for England or for Ireland are the great fundamental economic
problems, the problems of a community which is producing untold wealth and
untold poverty'. The latter, meanwhile, claimed: 'Home rule for Scotland is a
mere bagatelle compared with the situation with which the country is faced.'[63]
The Scottish Parliamentary Labour Party was slow to realize that the effects of
the depression were considerably worse in Scotland than in England. In any
case, Labour was still in the process of recovering from the débâcle of 1931
which had massively reduced both the numbers and the intellectual calibre of its
Scottish members.[64]

It was the Unionist Party which had most to fear from the upsurge in nationalist
sentiment. In 1932 the Cathcart Unionist Association seceded because of the
party's attitude towards Scotland. The Duke of Montrose and Andrew Dewar
Gibb had thrown in their lot with the nationalist movement, and other public
figures who might normally be expected to follow the National Government were
doing the same.[65] Even among loyal Tory MPs, discontent was being voiced.
Walter Elliot was unable to contain his frustration at the government's decision
to scrap the Cunard cruiser programme in February 1932:

> The question is not so simple from the point of view of workers on the
> Clyde. Government can scrap cruisers and claim the money for something
> else. But the people of Scotland know that officials are too apt to spend
> saved money on bridges in London, and carrying out other work in England,
> while there is more than enough unemployment in Scotland.[66]

One of the Unionists' most anti-home rule MPs, Robert Boothby, likewise
found it difficult quietly to acquiesce in the government's policies:

> The real interests of Scotland have been sacrificed to those of England.
> Today the Unionists accept the situation but not without protest. Scottish
> Unionists are especially dissatisfied with proposals which worsen the position
> in Scotland compared with England.[67]

Much of the reason for this discontent can be explained by the fact that the
Unionists did not seem to have a coherent Scottish policy; a fact often alluded to

by Tory Scottish MPs. The pre-war opposition to home rule was trotted out in the early 1930s without much forethought, and many of the same arguments employed against Scottish self-government in the Edwardian era were polished up and used again. They were wholly unsuited, however, to the new circumstances of inter-war Scotland.

The Unionist vision of Scottish national identity was based firmly on the role of Scotland in the British empire. It was believed that the Scots had played a notable part in the creation of the greatest empire the world had ever known. The task of administering and running the empire had allowed Scotsmen to prove their talents as an expansive and outward-looking race. Emigration to the colonies was interpreted as a sign of national virility. The martial prowess of the Scottish soldier in conquering and defending the vast domains of the empire was a source of great pride. Glasgow had flourished as second city of the empire because of its imperial connections. All these factors combined to make loyalty to the British imperial ideal the fundamental ideological tenet of Scottish Unionism, and any attempt to weaken or sever the imperial link would be resisted. As Miss Horsburgh MP put it to the House of Commons: 'Are they [the Scottish home rulers] willing to shut out Scotsmen and Scotswomen from taking the biggest positions in the Empire?'[68]

Unfortunately, most of these ideals were no longer relevant to the particular circumstances in which Scots found themselves during the inter-war period. The empire was seen to be drifting apart as the dominion nations attained greater control over their own affairs. Industrial decline had shattered the belief that Scotland was the economic powerhouse of the empire. Emigration to the colonies was seen as a sign of weakness and a demonstration of the lack of social and economic opportunities at home. And, in a society still reeling from the psychological shock of the First World War, military attributes were no longer held in such high esteem. In any case, the naval base at Rosyth had been mothballed in favour of Chatham, in Kent, and several of the most famous Scottish regiments were now stationed in England.[69] The Unionists' pious hope that 'nothing will detract from the fine worth and importance of that wider and nobler imperial patriotism to which Scotsmen have never been indifferent' was becoming increasingly difficult to realize.[70] In fact, Scottish Conservatives were increasingly offering little more than a sentimental appeal to the past.

'We are and we remain an iron race,' was how Robert Boothby reacted to the 'parrot cry' of Scottish home rule: 'It is our phenomenal control over a world-wide Empire that has made the name of Scotland famous, admired and respected in every quarter of the globe.'[71] In his view, Scotland owed everything to the Union and without it she would be nothing:

Prior to 1707, the Scottish people were a pack of miserable savages, living in incredible poverty and squalor, and playing no part in the development of civilisation. Since 1707, they have been partners in the greatest undertaking the world has ever seen. It was the Union that turned the Scottish people into an imperial race.[72]

The iron race was now a bit rusty, however, and the task of ruling themselves was seen by some to be beyond their capabilities, an attitude that revealed major inherent contradictions within the Conservative vision of Scotland. Sir John T. Cargill, Bt., asked readers of *The Scotsman*: 'Could they imagine what a Scottish Parliament would be like? He could and he would not like to dwell upon it.'[73] This knee-jerk loyalty to the concept of 'wider imperial patriotism' meant that Unionist politicians were prone to obsequious outbursts of national self-effacement of the worst kind; all of which did little to boost the nation's self-confidence, which was badly damaged by the savage effects of the depression. Walter Elliot concluded that the Scots had no political tradition and, in any case, like most of his colleagues, sought refuge in the past, claiming that presbyterianism, rather than any quest for a Scottish parliament, represented the soul of the nation:

> We do not know where to worship, and that is the dis-orientation of Scotland to-day. But when our ideal dis-engages itself and stands out once more we shall seek it according to the heritage which our fathers have left us. That is a heritage where the ordinary man exercises his right of vote, of choice, but afterwards does not have the right to recall it again. It is a heritage of nomination and not of democracy . . . These traditions we should study, and their histories are the annals of the parishes, their ministers and their elders. Their annals are the annals of the congregations and their calls, their presbyteries and their general Assemblies, their Moderators and their High Commissioners.[74]

In addition to imperial loyalty and appeals to the past, the other main argument offered by the Unionists against any measure of Scottish self-government was economic:

> Without a doubt Scotland has benefited most from the Union and anything in the way of a severance from England would almost certainly spell disaster. The setting up of a separate Scottish Parliament would certainly result in the removal to England of many Scottish industries and also many merchant traders and others on whom even today Scotland is losing hold.[75]

Prominent industrialists, such as Sir James Lithgow, chimed in with the anti-home rule chorus, claiming that 'it would be most detrimental to the industries with which I am most associated'.[76] If things were bad at the moment, they would become much worse should the Scots opt for home rule, because 'Scotland looks South for her markets'.[77] According to Sir Reginald Macleod of Macleod: 'Let Scotland not by yielding to some fancied enthusiasm expose herself to the material loss which I feel sure would occur if she had her own Parliament.'[78] The harsh message was hammered out that there could not be any loosening of constitutional ties because Scotland needed England to survive and there was simply no alternative. In any case, many industrialists had substantial connections with English firms and had no desire to jeopardize them.[79] Moreover, given the importance of government orders to the traditional heavy industries of the Clyde, few wanted to rock the constitutional boat.[80] Others, such as Sir Robert Horne, based their claim on the fact that Scotland needed English money to pay for the social costs of the depression:

> The Welsh are showing the kind of wisdom that is generally attributed to the Scot, because, knowing that the amount of their unemployment is so much greater than elsewhere, probably they realize that they would find great difficulty in providing unemployment benefit by themselves, and they are wiser to rely on the richer country than to seek separation.[81]

Although this argument did convince many Scots, it was hardly a confident espousal of the principles and benefits of Unionism.

The National Government of the 1930s had the difficult task of recognizing and responding to the legitimacy of Scottish national aspirations and grievances, particularly as it was believed that these were held by many traditional Conservative supporters. This had to be done without giving in to home rule, however, because, it was argued, such measures would not solve the underlying economic problems or meet the immediate needs of the nations. According to John Buchan:

> Real as the needs are, to attempt to meet them by creating an elaborate legislature would be more than those needs require. Such a top heavy structure would not cure Scotland's ills; it would intensify them. It would create artificial differences, hinder cooperation and engender friction.[82]

Walter Elliot reiterated this position, claiming that what Scotland needed was not more government, but good government.[83] The National Government responded by implementing administrative devolution, which had the advantage of bringing the mechanisms of government closer to the people, but without surrendering political control. The decision to move the Scottish Office to Edinburgh in 1932 and the commencement of St Andrew's House were testament to this desire to appease Scottish national identity, although the decision to use an architect from HM Office of Works in London did little to reduce nationalist resentment.[84] Nor did the occasional gaffe by Unionist MPs help matters, especially as the press in Scotland was on the look-out for such choice statements as that offered by Paisley MP, J. P. Maclay, in November, 1932:

> He was as proud as anyone else of Scottish sentiments; and the problem in Scotland was to reconcile Scottish aspirations and sentiments and at the same time maintain the position as an integral part of *England* and the Imperial Parliament.[85]

It was hoped that administrative devolution, as outlined in the Gilmour Report of 1935, would lead to more effective government and that this would in itself help to reduce nationalist resentments.[86] The Scottish Development Council was set up in 1931 with the remit of promoting economic growth, particularly in the new light industries. It did not have the power to effect any great changes, however, and, as critics were quick to point out, it was led by the captains of the old industries who would not want to loosen their grip on the Scottish economy by promoting economic diversification.[87] In many ways the Development Council simply paid lip-service to the task of solving Scottish economic problems, and it offered little in the way of positive remedies. The appointment in 1934 of Sir Arthur Rose as Commissioner for the Special Areas was an attempt to mollify public opinion by showing that the government was genuinely concerned about the distressed areas. His findings, however, were largely greeted with dismay as no immediate or substantial solutions were offered for Scotland's endemic social and economic problems.[88]

Unable to solve those economic problems, concessions were made to Scottish nationhood with a series of gestures. The number of royal visits was increased to encourage loyalty to the British imperial ideal, and it was mooted that the royal residence at Holyrood should be occupied for three months of the year by a representative of the king.[89] Scottish records removed by Edward I in the thirteenth century were returned to Scotland, and improvements were granted to the National Library and the Scottish Record Office. The Glasgow Empire Exhibition of 1938 was an effort to combine the memories of better times with an attempt at economic regeneration. Most of what followed, however, was mere gesture, a fact not lost on the Scottish Secretary of State, Walter Elliot, who in 1937 believed that such ephemeral changes:

will not in themselves dispose of the problems upon whose solution a general improvement in Scottish social and economic conditions depends. It is the consciousness of their existence which is reflected, not in the small and unimportant Nationalist Party, but in the dissatisfaction and unease amongst moderate and reasonable people of every rank – a dissatisfaction expressed in every book written about Scotland now for several years.[90]

Elliot recognized that the source of Scottish grievances and resentments lay in the structural fault of over-dependence on heavy industry in the Scottish economy, and that this had still to be rectified. This was a point constantly referred to by nearly every report on the Scottish economy carried out in the 1930s; to this problem rearmament was only a temporary solution.[91] Consequently, no lasting security against Scottish grievances and the potential for nationalist sentiment would be attained until this was done. The experience of the inter-war years and the intractability of Scotland's social and economic problems all contributed to a feeling of hopelessness, and this meant that Scottish politicians, of all hues, were more than ready to accept the new orthodoxy of centralized government economic planning when it arrived with the out-break of the Second World War.[92]

NOTES

1 See R. H. Campbell, *The Rise and Fall of Scottish Industry* (Edinburgh, 1980) [hereafter Campbell, *Rise and Fall*], pp. 133–64; P. L. Payne, *Growth and Contraction: Scottish Industry 1860–1990* (Dundee, 1992), pp. 25–36; D. H. Aldcroft, *The European Economy 1914–1980* (1980), pp. 43–80.

2 See C. Harvie, *No Gods and Precious Few Heroes* (1981) [hereafter Harvie, *No Gods*], pp. 88–117.

3 *The History of Scottish Literature*, ed. C. Craig (4 vols., Aberdeen, 1989), iv. 5.

4 *Scots Magazine*, August 1926, 397.

5 Charles Graves, *Scots Magazine*, May 1926, 120–4.

6 Lady Margaret Sackville, *Scots Magazine*, April 1927, 14.

7 G. M. Thomson, *Caledonia or the Future of the Scots* (1927) [hereafter Thomson, *Caledonia*], p.63.

8 James Kidd, Coalition Member for Springburn, *House of Commons Debates, 5th ser.* [hereafter *H. C. Debs.*], vol. 127, col. 2044, 16 April 1920.

9 Thomson, *Caledonia*, p. 10.

10 M. Keating and D. Bleiman, *Labour and Scottish Nationalism* (1979) [hereafter Keating and Bleiman, *Labour and Scottish Nationalism*], pp. 58–101.

11 R. J. Finlay, 'For or Against? Scottish Nationalists and the British Empire, 1919–1939', *Scottish Historical Review*, lxxi (1992), 45–67.

12 G. M. Thomson, *Scotland: That Distressed Area* (Edinburgh, 1935) [hereafter Thomson, *Distressed Area*], p. 34; A. Ernest Glen, *Scotland and Her Railways* (Glasgow, 1934). The number of workers in the railway construction industry in Scotland dropped from 10,000 to 2,000 in the period 1920–32.

13 Quoted in *Scots Independent,* May 1932, 104.

14 Thomson, *Distressed Area*, pp. 26–9; J. A. Bowie, *The Future of Scotland* (Edinburgh, 1939), [hereafter Bowie, *Future of Scotland*], pp. 100–11. Scottish unemployment figures tended to be massaged by comparing them with overall British figures, rather than English figures.

15 Statistics taken from the annual *Survey of Production*, published by the Board of Trade (1932–7).

16 Official answer given by Walter Elliot, Scottish Secretary of State, in the House of Commons, *H. C. Debs.* vol. 328, cols. 1145–6, 4 Nov. 1937.

17 Thomson, *Distressed Area*, pp. 34–46.

18 Ibid., pp. 21–65; James Dunlop (formerly of the Scottish Board of Agriculture), 'Scottish Nationalism and Scottish Agriculture', *Scots Independent*, June 1933, 120; *Statistical Abstract of the United Kingdom*, 1932 (Cmd. 3991).

19 *Glasgow Chamber of Commerce Journal*, Aug. 1932.

20 Ibid., Sept. 1927.

21 *Daily Record*, 31 Dec. 1929.

22 A. D. Gibb, *Scotland in Eclipse* (1930) [hereafter Gibb, *Eclipse*]; G. M. Thomson, *The Re-Discovery of Scotland* (1928); A. M. MacEwen, *The Thistle and the Rose* (Edinburgh, 1932) [hereafter MacEwan, *Thistle*]; The Duke of Montrose, *Scottish Self-Government* (Glasgow, 1933); C. M. Grieve, *Albyn: Scotland and the Future* (London, n.d.).

23 Thomson, *Caledonia*, pp. 18–23. Edwin Muir, *Scottish Journey* (1935; Edinburgh, 1980, ed. T. C. Smout) [hereafter Muir, *Scottish Journey*], pp. 100–62.

24 Quoted *Glasgow Herald*, 27 Nov. 1931.

25 Speech at the West of Scotland Iron and Steel Institute Annual Dinner, Feb. 1931.

26 *Daily Record*, 18 Aug. 1931.

27 *Edinburgh Chamber of Commerce Journal,* 8 Nov. 1932.

28 *Glasgow Chamber of Commerce Journal*, Sept. 1933.

29 *Daily Record*, 23 Oct. 1931.

30 *Glasgow Evening Citizen*, 14 Oct. 1931.

31 Thomson, *Distressed Area*, p. 85.

32 *The Scotsman*, 25 Nov. 1932.

33 *H. C. Debs.*, vol. 272, col. 293, 22 Nov. 1932.

34 Ibid., vol. 272, col. 238, 22 Nov. 1932.

35 Ibid., vol. 272, col. 262, 22 Nov. 1932.

36 *Glasgow Herald,* 27 Aug. 1928.

37 *Revenue From Government Salaries*, Cmd. 4196, Inland Revenue Department (1931).

38 *Report of the Committee on Scottish Administration*, Cmd. 5563 (1937).

39 *Glasgow Herald*, 28 Jan. 1931.

40 Sheriff J. R. N. MacPhail, Scottish Records Society, quoted in *The Scotsman*, 26 April 1932.

41 *Glasgow Herald*, 17 and 18 May 1932.

42 John Buchan, speaking at the annual meeting of the Scottish History Society, reported in *The Scotsman*, 7 Dec. 1930.

43 *Daily Express*, 14 July 1932.

44 *Daily Record*, 8 June 1932.

45 H. C. Milne, *H. C. Debs.*, vol. 272, col. 301, 22 Nov. 1932.

46 MacEwen, *Thistle*, pp. 65–76.

47 Thomson, *Distressed Area*, pp. 79–84.

48 Ibid., pp. 21–9.

49 Gibb, *Eclipse*, pp. 49–55.

50 John Torrence, *Scotland's Dilemma: Nation or Province* (Edinburgh, 1939), p. 15.

51 S. J. Brown, 'Outside the Covenant: The Scottish Presbyterian Churches and Irish Immigration, 1922–38', *Innes Review*, xlii (April 1991), 19–46.

52 *H. C. Debs.*, vol. 272, cols. 237–92, 22 Nov. 1932.

53 Ibid., vol. 272, col. 261, 22 Nov. 1932.

54 Ibid., vol. 272, col. 245, 22 Nov. 1932.

55 Muir, *Scottish Journey*, p. 2.

56 *H. C. Debs.*, vol. 272, col. 238, 22 Nov. 1932.

57 Thomson, *Caledonia*, p. 67

58 *H. C. Debs.*, vol. 272, col. 262, 22 Nov. 1932.

59 Ibid.

60 Ibid., vol. 272, col. 264, 22 Nov. 1932.

61 Keating and Bleiman, *Labour and Scottish Nationalism*, pp. 109–25.

62 R. J. Finlay, 'Pressure Group or Political Party? The Nationalist Impact on Scottish Politics', *Twentieth Century British History*, iii (1992) [hereafter Finlay, 'Pressure Group?'], 274–97.

63 *H. C. Debs.*, vol. 272, cols. 292, 307, 22 Nov. 1932.

64 Harvie, *No Gods*, p. 97.

65 Finlay, 'Pressure Group?', 283–9.

66 Elliot speaking at Cambuslang, quoted in *Daily Record*, 12 Feb. 1932.

67 *Glasgow Herald*, 20 June 1931.

68 *H. C. Debs.*, vol. 272, col. 312, 22 Nov. 1932.

69 The Scots Guards were stationed in London, the Scots Greys in York, and out of twenty battalions of infantry, seldom more than two complete battalions were stationed in Scotland at any one time.

70 The Unionist Association, *The Campaign Guide* (1922), p. 829.

71 Quoted in *Scots Independent*, Jan. 1930, 120.

72 *The Nation*, 9 March 1929.

73 *The Scotsman*, 29 June 1934.

74 Walter Elliot, 'The Scottish Heritage in Politics', *A Scotsman's Heritage*, ed. The Duke of Atholl et al. (1932) [hereafter Elliot, 'Heritage in Politics'], 64–5.

75 Lord Maclay, letter to *The Times*, 15 Nov. 1932.

76 *Daily Record*, 20 Oct. 1932.

77 *Morning Post*, 19 Nov. 1932.

78 *Daily Record*, 26 Nov. 1932.

79 For example, Viscount Younger of Leckie was a director of Lloyds Bank and English Southern Railways, while Sir Robert Horne was a director of Lloyds Bank and the Great Western Railway Company.

80 Campbell, *Rise and Fall*, pp. 164–84.

81 *H. C. Debs.*, vol. 272, col. 341, 22 Nov. 1932.

82 Ibid., vol. 272, col. 265, 22 Nov. 1932.

83 Elliot, 'Heritage in Politics', p. 64.

84 Open letter by the Council of the Royal Incorporation of Architects in Scotland, quoted in *Scots Independent*, April 1930, p. 64.

85 Quoted *Daily Record*, 29 Nov. 1932 (emphasis added).

86 See H. J. Hanham, 'The Development of the Scottish Office', *Government and Nationalism in Scotland*, ed. J. N. Wolfe (Edinburgh, 1969), 51–71; J. Mitchell, 'The Gilmour Report and Scottish Central Administration', *Judicial Review* (1989), 173–89.

87 See Thomas Burns, *The Real Rulers of Scotland* (Glasgow, 1940).

88 *Special Areas Report, 1934–35*, House of Commons Papers, Cmnd. 4958. For example, £60,000 was allocated for the whole of Scotland, compared with £58,000 allocated for Sheffield alone.

89 Lt-Col. T. C. R. Moore MP, quoted in Thomson, *Distressed Area*, p.114.

90 Quoted in R. H. Campbell, 'The Economic Case for Nationalism: Scotland', *The Roots of Nationalism: Studies in Northern Europe*, ed. R. Mitchison (Edinburgh, 1980), p. 151.

91 See Bowie, *Future of Scotland; Annual Surveys of Economic Conditions in Scotland*, issued by the Clydesdale Bank.

92 C. Harvie, 'Labour and Scottish Government: The Age of Tom Johnston', *Bulletin of Scottish Politics*, ii (1981), 1–20.

The Politics of Highland Land Reform, 1873–1895

James Hunter 1974 *Scottish Historical Review* 53, 45–68.

In the 1880s the peace which had prevailed in the Highlands since the clearances was shattered by the rise of a tenants' movement which aimed at reforming the existing agrarian system in the crofters' interests. The response of successive governments to the unrest was a dual one. On the one hand, strenuous attempts were made to restore law and order by strengthening police forces and deploying troops. On the other, a Liberal government passed a Crofters Act while subsequent Conservative and Unionist administrations launched the first of a continuing series of attempts to solve the crofting problem by means of officially sponsored economic development. Although the modern legislative and administrative history of the Highlands stems, therefore, from the 1880s, little is known of the crofters' movement of that decade[1] and still less of its political wing, the organisation eventually known as the Highland Land League.[2] It is with the rôle and significance of the latter body that this article is mainly concerned.

In the political world of the 1880s the Highland Land League was not an isolated phenomenon. The period was one of agricultural depression. Rural unrest was widespread and land reform much in vogue.[3] In Ireland the decade opened with the triumph of the Irish Land League and the Land Act of 1881 which conceded to Irish smallholders fair rents, free sale and greater security of tenure.[4] In Britain land reform was canvassed by individuals ranging from Joseph Chamberlain to Henry George, the former attempting to capture the new rural vote for the Liberal party,[5] the latter propounding land nationalisation as a panacea for all social and economic ills.[6] The Irish Land League, Chamberlain and Henry George all took an active interest in crofting affairs,[7] and the Highland Land League drew some of its founders and leaders from the land reformers' ranks. From the beginning, however, the League had a distinctively highland character as is illustrated by its links with the Gaelic literary movement of the 1870s.[8]

Primarily concerned with linguistic and cultural matters, the Gaelic movement acquired something of the status of a political pressure group by conducting concurrent campaigns for the creation of a chair of Celtic at

Edinburgh University and for an enhancement of the status of Gaelic in highland schools,[9] the latter issue being repeatedly raised in parliament by Charles Fraser-MacIntosh, who had been elected MP for Inverness Burghs in 1874.[10] As farmer's son, businessman, lawyer, and landowner, Fraser-MacIntosh – later to be a Land League MP – was far removed socially from the crofters of the north-west,[11] a characteristic he shared with most of those who made the transition in the 1880s from the politics of Gaelic revivalism to those of highland land reform. Apart from Fraser-MacIntosh, the most important members of this group were John Stuart Blackie, professor of Greek at Edinburgh and an incurable romantic with a passion for all things Celtic; Dr Roderick MacDonald, president of the Gaelic Society of London; John MacKay, a member of that society; Angus Sutherland, president of the Glasgow Sutherland Association; and Alexander MacKenzie, a founder member of the Gaelic Society of Inverness and editor of *The Celtic Magazine*, the leading literary manifestation of the Gaelic movement.[12]

Unlike Fraser-MacIntosh and Blackie, MacDonald, MacKay, Sutherland, and MacKenzie were crofters' sons – Sutherland's grandfather had been evicted from Kildonan and MacKenzie's childhood experience of his father's eviction from a Gairloch croft is reflected in the bitterness which pervades his book about the clearances.[13] All of them, however, had left home as boys – MacDonald was a doctor, MacKay a civil engineer, and Sutherland a teacher – and though they instinctively sympathised with crofters their links with them were not at first very strong. As was pointed out in a Gaelic periodical in 1875, the 'awakening of interest in Celtic matters' was very much a southern, middle-class affair. It had 'not . . . extended to the Highland peasantry'.[14] The corollary was that the Gaelic movement's adherents tended to neglect crofting questions, a situation transformed largely by the efforts of one man, John Murdoch.[15]

Born in Nairnshire in 1818, Murdoch spent his boyhood in Islay where he acquired a deep and enduring interest in Gaelic culture and an equally enduring hatred of highland landlordism. In the course of a long career in the revenue service he observed, and was influenced by, a variety of radical political movements – the Chartist agitation in northern England and the Young Ireland rising in Dublin, for example. In Ireland Murdoch discovered Fintan Lalor's analysis of the Irish land problem – an analysis which gave pride of place to the peasantry as the main agent of agrarian change[16] – and when, in 1873, he retired to Inverness to found a weekly newspaper, *The Highlander,* in order to propagate his political ideas among crofters, it was the task of creating a highland land reform movement rooted securely in the crofting population that was uppermost in his mind.[17] His objective was twofold: to encourage crofters to work towards the overthrow of 'the vicious land system' which he believed to be the cause of most highland ills;[18] and to ensure that southern Gaels actively involved themselves in the crofters' struggle. 'They must all act together in future', he told the Glasgow Islay Association in 1873, 'and solve "The Land Question" which was now coming to the front.'[19]

With some assistance from J. S. Blackie – who advised the Gaelic societies to cease 'vapourising about Ossian whom they never read, and eulogising Duncan Ban whom they do not sing' and 'buckle themselves to serious action in the practical world'[20] – Murdoch's campaign for the amalgamation of the urban Gaelic societies and highland associations into a single organisation with 'social, political, and economic purposes'[21] bore fruit in the formation in 1878 of the Federation of Celtic Societies.[22] A loose amalgam of existing and exceedingly disparate bodies, the Federation was subsequently shown to be of little value as far as highland land reform was concerned. It did, however, represent the first step along the road mapped out by Murdoch, and it is ironic, therefore, that its appearance coincided with the beginning of the end of *The Highlander* as a result of its editor having been successfully sued by a Skye landlord about whom the paper had been particularly scathing.[23]

By 1881 *The Highlander* was dead and Murdoch increasingly involved in Irish and Labour politics.[24] His achievement, however, had been considerable. In 1874 a violent clash between crofters and the Lewis estate authorities, the so-called Bernera Riot, had been virtually ignored in the south.[25] Unrest among Skye crofters in the spring of 1882 was, in contrast, followed by a rash of meetings organised by expatriate highlanders.[26] The president of the Federation of Celtic Societies, Dr Charles Cameron, owner of the Glasgow radical news-paper, *The North British Daily Mail*, and one of Glasgow's Liberal MPs,[27] declared that he would take up 'the land question as the most pressing in Highland politics'[28] and he and Fraser-MacIntosh at once raised the issue in the Commons.[29]

For some, however, this was not enough. John MacKay, for example, thought the time had come to launch an independent highland land reform movement if only to stop what he saw as an evident trend towards the domination of highland radical politics by Irish politicians and organisations.[30] In the Commons, he pointed out, Donald H. MacFarlane, the Parnellite member for County Carlow, was emerging as the crofters' principal parliamentary spokes-man.[31] At the same time, the Glasgow branches of the Irish Land League were showing an increasing interest in the crofting question.[32] MacFarlane, who had been born in Caithness in 1830 but had spent most of his life in Australia and India,[33] soon became so interested in his homeland's problems that he gave up his Irish connections and plunged wholeheartedly into highland politics. And the Irish Land League, whose emissary to Skye was coolly received by crofters –

his meetings were poorly attended and he was widely referred to as 'trusdair', a filthy fellow[34] – quickly ceased to be actively involved in highland affairs. MacKay's fears of an Irish takeover were thus proved groundless. Nevertheless, the concept of a crofters' political party had begun to take shape.

In the country at large, meanwhile, pro-crofter feeling – subsequently described by the Liberal lord advocate, J. B. Balfour, as a 'vague and floating sentiment in favour of ameliorating the crofters' condition' – was steadily growing, largely because of the press publicity given to the Skye crofters' case.[35] In Westminster, radical Liberals began to press for some sort of government initiative on the crofting question and, in January 1883, 21 Scottish Liberal MPs – of whom only one, Fraser-MacIntosh, sat for a northern constituency – signed a commons motion calling for a royal commission of enquiry into crofters' grievances.[36] Two months previously, Gladstone had told D. H. MacFarlane that 'no such question' was 'under the consideration of Her Majesty's Government'.[37] In February, however, mounting political pressure, coupled with the impact of renewed violence in Skye, forced a change of policy. On the 26th of that month the government announced the setting up of a royal commission under the chairmanship of Lord Napier.[38]

Although the commission's appointment was something of a victory for crofters and their southern allies, many of the latter thought it biased in favour of landlordism[39] and suspected that its activities would be confined to the few areas where violent outbreaks had already occurred.[40] John MacKay, for instance, believed that the only way to make the commission effective was 'to commence a vigorous agitation in every parish in the Highlands'.[41] And since the Federation of Celtic Societies had lapsed into inactivity – MacKay remarked that it was 'asleep at this important crisis in crofting affairs'[42] – there was an obvious need for an organisation to supersede both the federation and the motley collection of *ad hoc* pro-crofter groups which had sprung up in Inverness, Glasgow and Edinburgh in 1882.[43] On 31 March 1883 such an organisation appeared in the shape of the Highland Land Law Reform Association of London.[44]

In the chair at the HLLRA's first meeting was Gavin Brown Clark, a Glasgow doctor who had lived for some years in London where he was involved in the activities of a number of socialist and land reform groups.[45] The association's programme, drawn up under his direction, followed that of the Irish Land league in calling for 'fair rents, durability of tenure, and compensation for improvements', but departed from the Irish model in demanding 'such an apportionment of the land as will promote the welfare of the people throughout the Highlands and Islands'. (The demand for more land was a minor matter in Ireland but a major motive in the crofters' agitation because of the essentially pastoral nature of crofting agriculture and the fact that the sheep farming system had deprived crofters of a great deal of hill pasture.) D. H. MacFarlane was elected president of the association,[46] and among its numerous vice-presidents were prominent Gaelic revivalists such as Blackie, Fraser-MacIntosh, Roderick MacDonald and John MacKay, as well as land reformers like Clark and a miscellaneous collection of Liberal and Lib-Lab MPs with a special interest in the land question, notably Jesse Collings and Henry Broadhurst.[47] Donald Murray, a London solicitor who was also a Gaelic-speaking highlander from Shieldaig, Wester Ross, became the HLLRA's secretary[48] and its headquarters were established at his chambers in Westminster.

Declaring its membership 'open to all who approve of its objects and subscribe to its funds',[49] the HLLRA entered highland politics by sending Alexander MacKenzie to help crofters to prepare their evidence to the Napier Commission.[50] The commission itself, by forcing crofters who had been previously uninvolved in agitation to meet, discuss grievances, and elect delegates to it, expedited the emergence of an effective political organisation in the Highlands.[51] In August crofters at Fraserburgh for the summer herring fishings resolved to set up local 'Land Law Reform Associations' on their return home.[52] And the *Oban Times* which, under its new, young and intensely radical editor, Duncan Cameron,[53] was emerging as *The Highlander's* successor, advocated a similar course: 'The opposing force is thoroughly and efficiently organised and it is only by thorough and efficient counter-organisation that it can be successfully coped with.'[54]

The HLLRA was of the same opinion and in November 1883 began to issue Gaelic and English circulars urging crofters to organise themselves within its constitutional framework.[55] 'The object of the HLLRA', a typical circular declared, 'is to effect by unity of purpose and action such changes in the land laws as will promote the welfare of the people . . . The cause has many friends . . . but the success of the movement must ultimately depend upon the unity and determination of the highland people . . . Unity is might, and with might on their side the people will soon succeed in obtaining their rights.'[56] The HLLRA's first highland branch was set up on 5 December, in Glendale, one of the principal centres of the agitation in Skye.[57] Two months later the *Oban Times* reported that 'branch societies of this new mode of agitating crofter grievances are now in full swing in most parts of Skye.'[58] There were similar developments in other parts of the north-west Highlands and Islands, and in June 1884 the HLLRA was able to boast of a paid-up crofter membership of around 5,000.[59]

That summer the tide of events was flowing strongly in the HLLRA's favour. New branches were springing up throughout the Highlands.[60] The Napier

Commission which proved, as G. B. Clark admitted, 'more sympathetic . . . and more advanced in its recommendations than was generally expected',[61] tacitly conceded the validity of the association's case by recommending a reform of the highland land system. And in August Gladstone pledged his government to legislate on the crofting question.[62] It was therefore in an atmosphere of enthusiasm bordering upon euphoria that the HLLRA convened its first annual conference at Dingwall in September 1884, attended by delegates from all over the Highlands. The conference, while welcoming the Napier Report, rejected its proposed restructuring of existing tenurial arrangements in favour of a more radical approach, involving not only the granting to crofters of security of tenure and compensation for improvements but also the establishment of 'a Land Court with judicial and administrative functions' – a measure incorporated in the Irish Land Act of 1881 but rejected by the Napier Commission.[63] Such a court, it was envisaged, would determine fair rents and be empowered 'to enlarge crofting townships and to form new townships . . . on any land which [it] may consider suitable'. In other words, it would redistribute the land in the crofters' favour.

The HLLRA programme adopted at Dingwall[64] was, in short, a very radical document which in its compulsory land settlement proposals went far beyond Gladstone's Irish legislation of 1881 – itself widely condemned as a revolutionary interference with the rights of landed property.[65] Nor did the programme stop at the promulgation of a plan for radical agrarian change in the Highlands. It announced that at the next general election the HLLRA would 'only support Parliamentary candidates for the northern constituencies who approve of this programme and promise to support a Bill to give it full legislative effect'. In a Ross-shire by-election held a month before the Dingwall conference, the HLLRA's candidate, Roderick MacDonald, had been beaten into third place by Liberal and Tory opponents.[66] He had, however, received an enthusiastic reception from crofters[67]; and it was clear that, in conjunction with the imminence of the Third Reform Act which gave crofters the vote for the first time, the HLLRA's Dingwall declaration amounted to a knell of doom for landlordism's long domination of highland politics.

Before the HLLRA's appearance on the scene, the realities of social and economic power in the Highlands were reflected in a parliamentary representation made up of what the association called 'landlords and Whigs'.[68] At the general election in 1880 Inverness-shire returned a Conservative, Cameron of Lochiel, owner of 125,574 acres in that county and in Argyll.[69] The Liberals sent to Westminster by the other highland counties were of the same social class, their party allegiance being determined largely by their families' whiggish traditions. They were: for Argyll, Lord Colin Campbell, son of the duke of

Argyll, whose estates extended to 168,315 acres; for Ross-shire, Alexander Matheson, owner of 220,433 acres in Wester Ross; for Sutherland, the marquis of Stafford, heir to the duke of Sutherland's 1,176,343 acres; and for Caithness, Sinclair of Ulbster, that county's second largest landowner with 78,053 acres to his credit. As landlords these men, not excepting Munro-Ferguson of Novar, the Liberal who held Ross-shire in 1884,[70] had decidedly un-radical views on the subject of land reform. Their mentor was the duke of Argyll who had resigned from Gladstone's government in protest against the Irish Land Act[71] and had subsequently become the leading exponent of what the *Times* called 'the more economical and less sentimental view of the crofters' position and grievances.'[72]

By 1884, however, the highland members were unpleasantly aware that their days were numbered. Such was the influence of the HLLRA, the duke of Argyll warned Gladstone in December, that an election fought under a reformed franchise would result in the replacement of the existing highland Liberalism by 'a Scotch Parnellite Party embracing some 5 county members'[73] – a prediction which the HLLRA was doing its best to fulfil. In September 1885, with a general election only three months away, the association nominated its five candidates: for Argyll, D. H. MacFarlane; for Inverness-shire, Fraser-MacIntosh, who resigned his burgh seat to fight the county; for Ross-shire, Roderick MacDonald, seeking to avenge his 1884 defeat; for Sutherland, Angus Sutherland, who was, like Fraser-MacIntosh, contesting his native county; and for Caithness, G. B. Clark.[74] The association's members were instructed to campaign and vote only for these candidates, and the outcome – the election of all of them except Angus Sutherland – was an undoubted triumph for the movement. 'The enemy have left the spoils and fled before the conquering hosts of land reform', proclaimed the *Oban Times* on 12 December 1885, 'From the Mull of Kintyre to the Butt of Lewis the land is before us.'

Liberal and Tory discomfiture in the Highlands, the *Scotsman* informed its readers – whom it had previously assured of the certain defeat of HLLRA 'carpet-baggers'[75] – was attributable to the fact that crofters, who knew 'nothing of politics' had been 'deluded with promises of nearly everything they desire.'[76] The real explanation lay in the strength and effectiveness of the HLLRA's highland organisation. The majority of mainland crofters were members of the association; in the islands its strength was even greater. In parts of Skye, for example, it was 'probable that every man of the crofter and cottar classes . . . [was] an enrolled member.'[77] The arrival of a 'Crofters' Party'[78] at Westminster in January 1886 is attributable, therefore, to the HLLRA's success in harnessing the sort of militancy which had appeared in Skye in 1882 and had subsequently spread to other crofting areas. It was the fact that they represented a mass movement which by means of rent strikes and land

raids had plunged the north-west Highlands and Islands into its most severe
social and administrative crisis since the demise of Jacobitism that gave the four
crofters' MPs a political significance out of all proportion to their numbers, and
ensured that they took their seats in a parliament preparing to devote more time
to highland affairs than any of its predecessors since the 1740s.

In 1885 it had become apparent to Gladstone's government that the only
possible solution to the crofting question was a legislative reform of the
highland land system.[79] Logically, such legislation should have been based
on the Napier Commission's recommendations. The commission, however, had
rejected current ideas on land reform and had attempted to devise a specifically
highland solution to the crofting problem.[80] Although laudable in theory, the
practical result of this attempt was, as the home secretary, Sir William Harcourt,
remarked, that the commission's proposals did not meet with acceptance in any
quarter.[81] One landlord thought the report 'hardly worth discussing.'[82] Another dismissed it as 'full of inconsistencies and anomalies.'[83] Crofters, for their
part, indicated a strong preference for a measure more akin to the Irish Land Act
than to the proposals of Lord Napier and his colleagues,[84] something to which
the cabinet were not averse. The act in question was Gladstone's own creation,
and one of which he was inordinately proud. Besides, the prime minister, like
Harcourt and Joseph Chamberlain, felt a great deal of sympathy for crofters and
was anxious to do something for them.[85] It was consequently resolved, in
Gladstone's words, to endorse 'the substantial application of the Irish Land Act
to the Highland parishes',[86] and a bill to that effect was introduced in the
Commons in May 1885.[87]

That particular bill fell with the government in June.[88] By the New Year,
however, a new Liberal administration was in power; there were four crofter
MPs in the commons; and so effective had the agitation in the Highlands
become that Liberals and Conservatives alike concluded that remedial legislation of some sort was urgently required.[89] A refurbished version of the previous
year's bill was hastily introduced and met with little opposition. Even the duke
of Argyll agreed not to oppose it, 'not because it was a good bill' but because 'he
could not deny that they were in a position that compelled them to agree to
something being done.'[90] Arthur Balfour, the Conservatives' principal spokes-
man on highland affairs, took a similar line,[91] and on 25 June the bill passed
into law.

The Crofters Act of 1886 – the only major piece of legislation to be
successfully enacted by Gladstone's short-lived third administration[92] – went
a long way towards meeting HLLRA demands, for the simple reason that it was
modelled, like the HLLRA's programme, on Irish land legislation. Security of
tenure and compensation for improvements were guaranteed to crofters. A land

court, the Crofters Commission, was established to fix fair rents and otherwise administer the act.[93] By the standards of the time, therefore, the 1886 act was a very radical measure. The *Scotsman* thought it a 'great infringement on the rights of private property'[94] and at least one highland landlord discovered in it an indication of 'communism looming in the future.'[95] In one crucial respect, however, the act fell seriously short of meeting crofters' wishes: it made little provision for making more land available to crofters.[96] At crofters' meetings throughout the Highlands the bill was consequently condemned as completely inadequate.[97] In the Commons the crofter MPs labelled it a 'sham and delusion'[98] and, supported by the Parnellites, who recognised the crofters' struggle against landlordism to be analogous to that of their own peasant constituents,[99] they opposed the bill through all its parliamentary stages.

The 1886 act did not, therefore, inaugurate an era of tranquillity in the Highlands. Unrest continued – within a few weeks of the bill receiving the royal assent 250 troops were despatched to restore order on Tiree[100] – and at the HLLRA's annual conference at Bonar Bridge in September 300 delegates representing 110 branches[101] resolved to continue their campaign for the compulsory breaking-up of sheep farms and deer forests and, in recognition of this decision, to reconstitute the association as the Highland Land League, the principal task of which was 'to restore to the Highland People their inherent rights in their native soil.'[102]

By the autumn of 1886, however, the political situation had altered radically. Gladstone's government had fallen on the Irish home rule issue; the Liberal party had split on the same question; and a Conservative administration, headed by Lord Salisbury, had been elected. Arthur Balfour, Salisbury's nephew, had taken over the recently created Scottish Office and had at once made clear his intention of forcibly restoring law and order in the Highlands.[103] And as if these were not problems enough for it, the Land League was experiencing its first internal crisis – over home rule.

In the general election which followed the Liberal government's fall in the summer of 1886 D. H. MacFarlane lost his Argyll seat to a Tory landlord, Malcolm of Poltalloch.[104] And though his defeat was partially offset by Angus Sutherland's eventual victory in his native county,[105] the Argyll campaign, in which much was made of MacFarlane's catholicism and Irish connections,[106] showed that the Irish dimension could not be kept out of highland politics. That the Irish question loomed so large in the Highlands was principally due, however, to the Land League's decision to come out strongly in support of Irish self-government. In the context of the history of highland land reform, this was a natural development. The Land League's president, D. H. MacFarlane, had been for five years a member of the Irish parliamentary party; another of its

MPs, G. B. Clark, had been campaigning for Irish home rule since the 1870s;[107] and, most important of all, recent events had shown that the crofters' MPs had few allies outside the Parnellites' ranks. 'These MPs who roar the loudest against Home Rule for Ireland roared quite as loud against the Crofters' Bill', remarked a Lewis crofter in July 1886, adding that 'Crofters are as true as steel and won't forget their friends the Irish MPs'.[108] Such an argument had an irresistible appeal. It was taken up by Roderick MacDonald[109] and appeared over and over again in the resolutions in favour of Irish home rule adopted by practically every one of the Land League's local branches.[110] At the league's conference in September 1886 a resolution in favour of home rule for Ireland was carried almost unanimously.[111] In the following spring Michael Davitt, ex-fenian, founder of the Irish Land League and the Irish nationalists' most radical leader, toured the Highlands and received a wildly enthusiastic welcome from crofters – an effusive but not untypical example of the addresses presented to him welcomed him as 'the martyr Patriot of Ireland, the harbinger of a bright day for the sea-divided Gael.'[112]

The one flaw in this show of Celtic solidarity, which transcended the gulf between the extreme presbyterianism of most crofters and the catholicism of their Irish counterparts, was the attitude of Fraser-MacIntosh. As something of an imperial idealist he had voted against Gladstone's home rule bill.[113] His action at once aroused the ire of his crofting constituents. The member for Inverness-shire, declared the Portree branch of the Land League, had 'acted against the best friends of the Highland people'.[114] And though his opponents had no time to find a rival candidate before the 1886 elections,[115] it became clear in the spring of 1887, when crofters in the Uists, Barra and parts of Skye asked Davitt to stand as their candidate in their next election,[116] that Fraser-MacIntosh's association with the Land League was coming to an end. That autumn, in fact, he failed to be re-elected to the league's executive.[117]

The home rule controversy, though it found most of the league's members on one side, had wider implications than those raised by the casting into outer darkness of Fraser-MacIntosh, John MacKay and a few other Unionists. Fraser-MacIntosh's defence had been based on that clause in the HLLRA's original constitution which held that the association, 'disclaiming any political bias, will endeavour to carry on its work irrespective of party politics.'[118] The league, he had argued, 'should subserve everything else to the interests of Highlanders.' It need not – indeed should not – have a policy on home rule or, for that matter, anything else of no direct relevance to crofters.[119] In 1886 Fraser-MacIntosh's case was lost sight of in the spontaneous swelling of pro-Irish feeling. Within a few years, however, the essence of his argument – that the league should steer clear of party political affiliations – was to be raised again and again, for having once adopted the home rule cause as its own, the league never regained its old status as a uniquely highland political party. After 1886, in fact, it came to be more and more identified with Gladstonian Liberalism.

Many of the league's leaders – men like MacFarlane, Sutherland and MacDonald – had always been middle-class radicals with personal predilections for Liberalism of the Gladstonian brand. In the Highlands, however, they had been confronted with a Liberal establishment dominated by the landlords who were their bitterest adversaries. After 1886, that situation changed. In the Highlands, as in the rest of Britain, the home rule crisis of 1886 'marked the withdrawal from the Liberal party of the aristocratic element.'[120] The consequent socio-political position was well, if emotively, summed up by the secretary of the Argyll Reform League, which was an alliance of the county's Land League and Liberal associations formed to promote a joint radical candidature. 'The Tories', he declared in 1887, 'are composed of landlords and their flunkies, the minister as a rule, some big farmers, and every other blockhead in the place. The Liberals are composed of crofters, fishermen, some farmers, tradesmen, labourers, and every other manly and intelligent person who has a mind of his own, and who will go through thick and thin for the cause of justice and right.'[121] In these circumstances, a Liberal-Land League courtship developed rapidly. By 1888 the league's county associations were affiliated to the Scottish Liberal Association.[122] By 1889 Angus Sutherland was publicly revealing his ambition 'to attach the Highlands to the Liberal party'.[123] And in these years the Land League's conferences took to endorsing most of the Liberal programme and passing resolutions of 'unabated confidence' in Gladstone.[124]

At first the new strategy seemed successful. In 1888 Rosebery, one of the more prominent members of the Liberal hierarchy, admitted the need for 'further legislation' on the crofting question.[125] Two years later, Sir George Trevelyan, former Liberal secretary of state for Scotland, announced that a future Liberal government would meet crofters' demands for more land.[126] Partnership with the Liberals brought its own particular problem however: was more to be gained by an ostentatious show of loyalty to the party or by the maintenance of an aggressively independent posture?[127] It was soon clear that the league's MPs had chosen the first course, and the dangers inherent in it at once became apparent. In November 1888, for example, they voted with the Gladstonians in opposing the granting of treasury loans to Irish smallholders, despite the fact that they had long advocated such loans for crofters.[128] The crofter members were clearly coming to regard themselves as Liberals – a state of mind well calculated to lead them into an ambiguous position where Tory concessions to crofters were concerned. For the moment they were saved from such a fate by the fact that Lord Lothian, Balfour's successor at the Scottish Office, was pinning his hopes for a solution to the highland problem not on a programme of agrarian reform such as that being instituted by his government in Ireland[129] but on 'an attractive and well financed scheme of State-aided emigration'[130] – something which was anathema to crofters.[131] As long as Conservatism was identified with emigration rather than with land reform the crofter vote was bound to go to the Land League-Liberal alliance. As the 1880s advanced, however, the incorporation into the league's programme of Liberal policies which had nothing to do with the highland land question began to bring about the fragmentation of the movement built up between 1883 and 1886. Of these policies, the most important and most controversial was that which involved the disestablishment of the Church of Scotland.

Disestablishment, then becoming the rallying cry of Gladstonian Liberalism in Scotland, was opposed by the Church of Scotland itself, by Liberal Unionists and Conservatives, and by a group of Free Churchmen who, though in a minority in Scotland as a whole, constituted a majority in the Free Church in the Highlands.[132] Since most non-catholic crofters had belonged to the Free Church since 1843, a Land League commitment to disestablishment would force them to choose between loyalty to their ministers and loyalty to the league. In the mid-1880s, when the almost universal opposition of the protestant clergy to the crofters' movement had engendered a fairly high degree of anticlerical feeling in the Highlands,[133] disestablishment might have gained some popular support. In 1888, however, the Free Church's highland clergy had come out strongly in favour of almost all the Land League programme, including the crucial demand for more land.[134] Crofters were henceforth reconciled to their ministers – to the extent that in 1890 a number of Land League branches adopted Free Church ministers as their candidates in local elections.[135] In these circumstances it seemed to many of the league's members that they were being asked to endorse disestablishment merely to appease southern Liberal opinion, a belief which Angus Sutherland, the league's leading pro-Liberal, did nothing to diminish. They should support disestablishment, he told delegates to the league's conference in 1890, because 'they would be false to their Liberal principles if they did not.'[136]

To Alexander MacKenzie, whose ideal was a highland political party which would, like the Parnellites, maintain 'an independent position in the House of Commons',[137] the introduction of disestablishment into Land League politics was a sign that the league was, as a result of the Liberal connection, in danger of completely losing its identity.[138] Among the rank and file too there was growing dissatisfaction with the league's parliamentary representatives.[139] At first, however, criticism was directed not at the Liberal alliance but at the fact that the league was still controlled from London.[140] In 1888 and 1889 the London executive was swept from office and an entirely highland executive, based in Dingwall, was elected. [141]

Although the fact that the struggle for control of the league was conducted in public did nothing to dissipate the growing suspicion that it was no longer 'bound together by anything like the feeling of determination which animated it during the first few years of its existence',[142] the new executive was able to claim some credit for the league's remarkable success in the local elections – the first to be staged in Scotland – held in February 1890. In the Outer Isles crofter candidates were returned en masse; in Skye the league won a majority of two-to-one over its opponents; and in Sutherland it gained 14 of the 16 seats it contested:[143] an achievement made all the more significant by the complete failure of attempts to politicise the elections elsewhere in Scotland.[144] These successes enabled the league to use highland county councils as political platforms. All of them – except Argyll, which returned a pro-landlord majority – petitioned parliament to implement the Land League programme.[145]

In the wider political arena, however, the new executive proved even more committed to the Liberal party than the old. Nothing was done to bridge the divisions which had developed. As a result, the general election of 1892 saw one of the league's founders, John MacKay, standing as a Liberal Unionist against Angus Sutherland, the Land League and Liberal candidate; and another, Fraser-MacIntosh, being opposed on behalf of the Land League and the Gladstonians by Donald MacGregor, a London doctor.[146] Alexander MacKenzie, still campaigning for a Land League 'independent of all cliques and official wire-pullers',[147] backed Fraser-MacIntosh,[148] an action which cost him his seat on the league's executive[149] and did nothing to prevent the league's candidates from winning all five highland constituencies.

Although the league's electoral success was considerable, it was achieved not as in 1885 in the face of opposition from both main parties but with strong Gladstonian support. Crofters voted for the league's nominees as the men most likely to press for further land reform, but no longer was the league the embodiment of a crofters' mass movement. Since 1889, when Lothian had toured the west Highlands and Islands to find out, as he put it, what could be done 'to ameliorate the condition of the inhabitants',[150] and had, on his return, proposed that £150,000 should be spent on developing the fisheries and on building roads, railways and piers,[151] the Conservative government had been more interested in highland development than in emigration. A royal commission had reported on the subject,[152] and £237,291 had been assigned to development schemes in crofting areas.[153] The Land League had warned crofters 'not to allow themselves to be caught in the Unionist snares',[154] but the inevitable effect of development grants, coupled with the workings of the

Crofters Commission, which had everywhere enforced large reductions in rent and helped to restore 'more harmonious relations . . . between Landlords and Crofters',[155] was a virtual cessation of the violent agitation of the 1880s.[156] The highland land question was by no means solved but, as Alexander MacKenzie subsequently remarked, most crofters were for the moment at least 'satisfied with their position, improving their holdings and houses under the protection of the Crofters Act'.[157] Rent strikes and land raids ceased and the Land League, in the words of a Barra crofters' leader, was reduced to the status of 'a mere political Association'.[158] A 'mass-meeting' organised by the league in Skye in 1892 was attended not by thousands of crofters as would have been the case in the 1880s but by 50 people.[159] By the end of that year crofters' contributions to league funds had dried up almost completely.[160] And, in the local elections held in December, scores of landlords and factors were returned unopposed.[161]

In the summer of 1892, in the euphoria induced by the return to power of a Liberal government and the election of five Land League MPs, the league's leaders seemed unaware of these developments. The league's annual conference in September was marked by speeches heralding the dawn of a new era of reform in the Highlands and by a letter from Sir George Trevelyan in which the reinstated Scottish secretary spoke of 'the desire of the Government to fulfil the just wishes and views of the Highland people.'[162] Two months later Trevelyan set up a new royal commission, the Highlands and Islands (or Deer Forest) Commission, whose task it was to report upon the amount of land which, though then under sheep or deer, could be utilised for land settlement purposes.[163] At first the commission's appointment was seen by crofters as a guarantee of good intentions on the part of the Liberals.[164] Within a few weeks, however, Alexander MacKenzie was predicting that the commission would 'be used as an excuse to hang up any crofter legislation for an indefinite period.'[165] His prophecy was verified by events. The commission did not report until April 1895,[166] and by that time the Liberal government was tottering towards defeat and the league was fragmented beyond repair.

Liberal vacillations had the effect of making the concept of an independent land league more attractive. By the end of 1892 G. B. Clark was openly regretting the league's loss of an 'independent capacity',[167] and at the conference in 1893 he launched a passionate attack on the Liberal connection.[168] His proposal to elect a new executive pledged to a more independent line forced the quarrel into the open and, amidst an unedifying wrangle about the *bona fides* of some branch delegates, the pro-Liberal faction secured the election of their presidential nominee, J. G. MacKay, a Portree shopkeeper, by a majority of one vote. Headed by Clark, the dissentients promptly withdrew from the conference and from the league.[169]

The movement was now irrevocably split. On one side was the Land League, with its aim, in Angus Sutherland's words, 'simply to carry out what was embodied nowadays as the Liberal programme. That was . . . the strength of their position . . . they did not differ essentially from the Liberal party.'[170] On the other side was the HLLRA, reconstituted by the rebels and supported by Clark, MacFarlane – re-elected MP for Argyll in 1892 – and J. Galloway Weir, a founder member of the old HLLRA who had replaced Roderick MacDonald as the league's MP for Ross-shire in 1892.[171] Accusing the league of being 'passive, inactive, and too susceptible of inconveniencing the government,'[172] the HLLRA at once declared for an independent policy; its contention, as summed up by Galloway Weir, was 'that no Government, either Tory or Liberal, cared two straws for the Highlands, and it was only as they brought pressure on the government and made their wants known that legislation would be given.'[173] This was, in effect, a return to the strategy of 1885–6. But, though Clark and Galloway Weir began a campaign of parliamentary obstruction which culminated in the summer of 1894 in their putting down hundreds of amendments to government measures,[174] the new HLLRA was unable to overcome its basic weakness: its lack of the united and well-organised mass membership which had ensured the success of its predecessor. Consequently, a series of HLLRA deputations to Trevelyan in the early months of 1895 elicited only a refusal to do anything until the publication of the Deer Forest Commission's report.[175]

When it finally appeared in April 1895 the commission's report scheduled 794,750 acres as suitable for new holdings and a further 439,188 acres as suitable for extensions to existing holdings.[176] Rosebery's government, its majority crumbling and its nerve failing, refused, however, to take the bit between its teeth. Instead of the sweeping land settlement measure expected by crofters, it introduced a lukewarm bill which did not even mention the creation of new holdings.[177] In the Commons, D. H. MacFarlane – perhaps because of his having received a knighthood in 1894[178] – accepted the bill 'as a small instalment towards the payment of a larger debt.'[179] Clark and Galloway Weir rejected the bill and threatened to vote against the government in crucial divisions.[180] And Donald MacGregor, who in 1892 had told a Land League conference that 'they hoped in the Liberal party, they trusted in them, and they had the pledges and promises of the Liberal party to give them what they wanted',[181] resigned his seat in protest against the government's highland policy.[182]

MacGregor's resignation was received more enthusiastically by crofters than anything their parliamentary representatives had done for some years. 'Proud of MacGregor's manly action', a group of Skye crofters declared in a telegram to Galloway Weir, 'Would there were more like him.'[183] The subsequent by-election in Inverness-shire, however, brought out all the contradictions which had developed in the land reform movement. The Scottish Liberal Association, well aware that another by-election set-back would be a serious blow to a government already reeling under a series of defeats and perhaps influenced by Skye crofters' resolution to 'shun party hacks',[184] gave official recognition not to the candidate favoured by their allies in the league but to Donald MacRae, highland organiser of the HLLRA.[185] Having accepted Liberal support, Mac-Rae found himself out of favour with the higher echelons of the HLLRA,[186] a disadvantage which Liberal endorsement did little to off-set. The more socially elevated members of the Inverness-shire Liberal party did not approve of MacRae, who had once faced criminal charges on account of his involvement in land raids in Lewis in 1887.[187] The league for its part felt betrayed, while HLLRA professions of political independence jarred somewhat with the reality of MacRae being accompanied around the county by Munro-Ferguson of Novar, the Liberal landlord swept out of Ross-shire by Roderick MacDonald in 1885 and Liberal MP for Leith since 1886.[188] To make matters worse, Liberal support firmly identified MacRae with disestablishment – which he, in any case, supported. And though he promised not to vote for disestablishment if elected, his gyrations on the church question contrasted strongly with his Unionist opponents' 'emphatic and outspoken' opposition to disestablishment and had a lot to do with his 'chilling reception' in Skye, an anti-disestablishment stronghold.[189] Finally, by accepting the mantle of official Liberal candidate, MacRae at least implicitly endorsed the government's highland policy. That policy, enshrined in a new Crofters Bill introduced in the Commons two days before the by-election,[190] was widely regarded by crofters – as it had been by MacGregor – as little more than a confidence trick. It is not altogether surprising, therefore, that the Unionist candidate, an Inverness-shire landlord, Baillie of Dochfour, was elected by a majority of 650.[191] As Alexander MacKenzie ruefully remarked, 'it must be admitted that Inverness-shire was lost because the Government did not implement, or until recently try to implement, their repeated promises to the Highland people on the subject of land law reform.'[192]

Events in Inverness-shire demonstrated the political bankruptcy of both Land League factions. Their only achievement was to open the way for the Unionist candidate, who based his campaign on his advocacy of a programme of highland land reform similar to that carried out by the Conservatives in Ireland between 1886 and 1892.[193] 'The real solution of the question', declared Baillie's election address on the land problem, 'lies in the intervention of the government with financial assistance on the principle of the Irish Land Purchase Acts – first, to take up suitable tracts of land and utilise them for crofters' holdings; and, secondly, to enable these crofters who are capable and desire to do so, to become owners of their land'.[194] Infinitely more radical than anything offered by the Liberal-HLLRA candidate, these proposals were welcomed as such by, among others, the crofters of Glendale, one of the places where the crofters' agitation had begun thirteen years before.[195] And in 1897 a Unionist government which had come to power a few weeks after Baillie's victory implemented the policy he had advocated by establishing a Highland Congested Districts Board on the lines of the one set up in Ireland in 1891. Its tasks included that of making more land available to crofters and among its achievements was the conversion of the Glendale crofters into the owners of their holdings.[196]

As a movement with any pretensions to political independence, the Land League did not survive the events of 1895. The previous autumn had brought Angus Sutherland his reward for loyalty to the Liberals – the chairmanship of the Scottish Fisheries Board.[197] The general election of 1895 brought about Sir Donald MacFarlane's defeat in Argyll and, although Clark hung on to his seat until 1900 and Galloway Weir until the election in 1906 of another Liberal government pledged to further highland land reform, their status was that of radical Liberals rather than Land Leaguers. The HLLRA disintegrated in 1895, abandoning its annual conference 'in consequence of the crofter vote having gone to the Tories' in the general election.[198] And though the Land League met as usual in 1895 and 1896 it did so only to demonstrate that it was the highland embodiment of official Liberalism.[199]

Recent writers on the Land League have tended to emphasise its role as a precursor of the Labour party.[200] That there is something in this view is undeniable, if only because the league has some claim to the title of first mass party in modern British politics. It should not be forgotten, however, that the league had no connections with organised labour and was intensely suspicious of the quasi-socialist or Georgite solution to the land problem canvassed by groups like the Scottish Land Restoration League. The latter body, founded in Glasgow in 1884 and dedicated to state ownership of land,[201] attracted the support of, among others, John Murdoch, and in 1888 provided a number of the founder members of Keir Hardie's Scottish Labour Party.[202] There was very little love lost between the Land Restoration League and the HLLRA. The Land Restoration League attacked the HLLRA's policy as 'a miserable, unscientific compromise' with landlordism;[203] while the HLLRA dismissed land nationalisation as 'a delusion, an impossibility.'[204]

Of the Land League's leaders only G. B. Clark had any socialist convictions.[205] Moreover, at a time when Labour was severing its connections with Liberalism the league was moving closer to the Liberal party – and those within it who, like Alexander MacKenzie, favoured a more independent line, did not support the adoption of socialist policies in order to achieve it.[206] Both in its political behaviour and in its derivation of support from small agricultural tenants the league was, in fact, more akin to the Irish parliamentary party of the 1880s and 1890s than to the early Labour party. That is not to say that the league was not important. Its significance is to be found, however, not in its impact on the British political system, which was very slight, but in its effect on the Highlands, which was considerable.

The Land League's success was to force the highland question to the forefront of British politics; to compel reluctant governments to investigate its every recess as a preliminary to instituting a whole series of reforming measures; and to ensure that the attitude of British politicians to the Highlands would never be quite the same again. Not all the league's objectives were won in the 1880s, the years of its greatest influence. But in the end all that it advocated was conceded to crofters: security of tenure, compensation for improvements and fair rents in 1886; a system of government grants and a land settlement programme in 1897, 1911 and 1919. The economic, legal and administrative frameworks of modern crofting society are in a real sense, therefore, the league's creations. They constitute, in their ending of a situation in which crofters had neither rights nor security, something of a monument to the Highland Land League and they testify perhaps to the validity of the League's most effective slogan, the old Highland proverb 'Is treasa Tuath na Tighearna', translated by the league as 'The People are mightier than a Lord'.

NOTES

1 For some information about this see J. G. Kellas, 'The Crofters' War', *History Today*, xii (1962), 281–8; H. J. Hanham, 'The Problem of Highland Discontent, 1880–1885', *Roy. Hist. Soc. Trans.*, 5th ser., xix (1969), 21–65.

2 The one article on this subject – D. H. Crowley, 'The "Crofters' Party", 1885–1892', *ante*, xxxv (1956), 110–26 – is marred by a lack of information and many errors of fact. H. J. Hanham, 'Highland Discontent', is more dependable but does not give a great deal of space to Land League politics.

3 For agrarian troubles elsewhere in the British Isles see N. D. Palmer, *The Irish Land League Crisis* (New Haven, 1940); P. Jones-Evans, 'Evan Pan Jones – Land Reformer', *Welsh History Review*, iv (1968), 143–59; J. P. D. Dunbabin, 'The "Revolt of the Field": The Agricultural Labourers' Movement in the 1870s', *Past and Present*, xxxvi (1963), 68–97.

4 N. D. Palmer, *Land League Crisis*, passim; J. E. Pomfret, *The Struggle for Land in Ireland, 1800–1923* (Princeton, 1930), 158–71.

5 J. L. Garvin, *Life of Joseph Chamberlain* (London, 1932), I, 385–8, 461–4; F. M. L. Thomson, 'Land and Politics in England in the Nineteenth Century', *Roy. Hist. Soc. Trans.*, 5th ser, xv (1965), 39.

6 George's influence on British politics was quite considerable – especially on the emerging labour movement. See E. P. Lawrence, *Henry George in the British Isles* (Michigan, 1957); J. Saville, 'Henry George and the British Labor Movement', *Science and Society*, xxiv (1960), 321–33.

7 George visited Skye in 1884 and 1885 (*Oban Times*, 16, 23 Feb., 1 Mar., 1884; 10, 17 Jan., 1885). Chamberlain toured the north-west Highlands and Hebrides in 1887 (*Oban Times*, 30 Apr., 1887; *Times*, 19, 25, 27, 29 Apr. 1887). Irish involvement is dealt with below.

8 See H. J. Hanham, 'Highland Discontent', 38 ff.

9 A. M. Stoddart, *John Stuart Blackie* (Edinburgh, 1895), ii, 93–4, 111 ff, 212–7; *An Gaidheal*, v (1876), 124–8, 343–52.

10 *An Gaidheal*, vi (1877), 155–8.

11 For biographical details see C. Fraser-MacIntosh, *Antiquarian Notes*, ed. K. MacDonald (Stirling, 1913), xiii-xxxi; *Times*, 2 July 1892. Fraser-MacIntosh owned the 390–acre Drummond estate near Inverness (*Return of Owners of Lands and Heritages, Scotland*, P[arliamentary] P[apers], 1874, lxxii).

12 For Blackie's life see Stoddart, *J. S. Blackie*. For the others see *Oban Times*, 14 Nov., 5 Dec. 1885; *The Crofter*, March-Sept. 1885; *Times*, 2 July 1892, *Scottish Highlander*, 28 Sept. 1893, 27 Jan. 1898. The *Scottish Highlander* was a weekly newspaper published and edited in Inverness from 1885 to 1898 by Alexander Mackenzie. Its files are preserved in Inverness Public Library.

13 A. MacKenzie, *The Highland Clearances* (Inverness, 1883 and other editions).

14 *An Gaidheal*, iv (1875), 250.

15 For some account of Murdoch's life and ideas, see J. D. Young, 'John Murdoch: A Scottish Land and Labour Pioneer', *Society for the Study of Labour History Bulletin*, xix (1969), 22–24; *Devoy's Post Bag, 1871–1928*, ed. W. O'Brien and D. Ryan (Dublin, 1948), I, 332–3. Murdoch's partially completed MS autobiography is preserved in five notebooks in the Mitchell Library, Glasgow. It is referred to below as J. Murdoch, Autobiography.

16 See N. D. Palmer, *Land League Crisis*, 108 ff.

17 J. Murdoch, Autobiography, 4.

18 *The Highlander*, 24 May, 12 July 1873.

19 *An Gaidheal*, iii (1874), 351.

20 J. S. Blackie, *Gaelic Societies, Highland Depopulation, and Land Law Reform* (Edinburgh, 1880), 2.

21 *The Highlander*, 27 Feb. 1875; also 9, 23 May 1874, 14 Nov. 1875.

22 Ibid., 16 Nov. 1878. For a list of the constituent bodies see H. J. Hanham, 'Highland Discontent', 38, n. 2.

23 The landlord in question was Fraser of Kilmuir. In 1877 Fraser's mansion had been swept away by a flood, an event which, it was suggested in *The Highlander*, could be construed as a divine judgement on its owner's rack-renting activities. See *The Highlander*, 30 Mar., 13 Apr., 23 Nov., 1878; J. Murdoch, Autobiography, 4; D. Nairne, *Memorable Floods in the Highlands in the Nineteenth Century* (Inverness, 1895), 87–92.

24 J. Murdoch, Autobiography, 5; J. D. Young, 'John Murdoch', 23.

25 The Highlander, 23 May 1874, 14 Nov 1875; Scotsman 21 July 1874; J. S. Blackie, The Scottish Highlanders and the Land Laws (London, 1885), 192–200; D. MacDonald, Tales and Traditions of the Lews (Stornoway, 1967), 147–52.

26 Oban Times, 22, 29 Apr., 6, 13, 20 May 1882. For events in Skye see H. J. Hanham, 'Highland Discontent', 24–30.

27 T. Wilkie, Representation of Scotland (Paisley, 1895), 143; D. C. Savage, 'Scottish Politics, 1885–86', ante, xi (1961), 119. Cameron was not, as Dr Savage suggests, the owner of the Oban Times.

28 Oban Times, 17 June 1882.

29 Hansard, 3rd ser., cclxviii (1882), col. 1032; cclxix (1882), col. 227.

30 N[ational] L[ibrary of] S[cotland] MS 2634, Blackie Papers, fo. 315, J. MacKay to Blackie, 12 Aug. 1882.

31 Ibid. See also Hansard, 3rd ser., cclxxiii (1882), col. 766.

32 Scotsman, 22 Apr 1882; Oban Times, 29 Apr. 1882.

33 See the Crofter, March 1885.

34 S[cottish] R[ecord] O[ffice], GD 1/36/1, Ivory Papers, Police Reports, Glendale, 5 Aug. 1882; Kilmuir, 6 Aug. 1882. This was despite the fact that the emissary, Edward McHugh, was referred to by Michael Davitt as 'a man of remarkable ability and an ideal propagandist' (M. Davitt, The Fall of Feudalism in Ireland [London, 1904], 228).

35 SRO, RH4/9/6, Cabinet Papers, Balfour to Harcourt, 13 Jan. 1885. (The reference is to microfilm copies in the SRO. Original P[ublic] R[ecord] O[ffice] ref.: CAB37/14/7. The same PRO ref. applies to all cabinet papers cited below.)

36 Celtic Magazine, viii (1883), 284.

37 Hansard, 3rd ser., cclxxiv (1882), col. 1206; also cclxxv (1882), cols. 227–8.

38 Hansard, 3rd ser., cclxxvi (1883), col. 853.

39 Celtic Magazine, viii (1883), 317–9. Apart from Lord Napier, himself a landowner, the commission consisted of Cameron of Locheil and Sir Kenneth MacKenzie of Gairloch, both of whom owned large highland estates; Fraser-MacIntosh, who sympathised with crofters but was a landlord nevertheless; and two Gaelic scholars – Alexander Nicolson, sheriff of Kirkcudbright and son of a Skye proprietor, and Donald MacKinnon, the newly appointed professor of Celtic at Edinburgh University, a Tory who had never shown any interest in crofting questions.

40 NLS MS 2635, f. 51, J. MacKay to Blackie, 7 Apr. 1883. When the commission was first mooted by the cabinet it was, in fact, proposed to confine it to Skye. A. Ramm (ed.), The Political Correspondence of Mr. Gladstone and Lord Granville, 1876–1886 (Oxford, 1966), ii, 19, 23, Granville to Gladstone, 6, 9 Feb. 1883.

41 NLS MS 2635, f. 51, MacKay to Blackie, 7 Apr. 1883.

42 NLS MS 2635, f. 57, MacKay to Blackie, 14 Apr. 1883. See also Oban Times, 26 Apr. 1884.

43 These included the H[ighland] L[and] L[aw] R[eform] A[ssociations] of Inverness and Edinburgh, in which Alexander Mackenzie and Blackie played leading parts, and the Skye Vigilance Committee, a Glasgow body under the effective direction of Angus

Sutherland. See *Celtic Magazine*, vii (1882), 461; *Oban Times*, 1 July 1882; D. H. Crowley, 'Crofters' Party', 112. These bodies eventually merged with the larger and more influential HLLRA of London (*Oban Times*, 12 July 1884; *Scotsman*, 3 Sept. 1885).

44 The following account is based on a contemporary report in *Oban Times* and on extracts for the HLLRA's first annual report (*Oban Times*, 7 Apr. 1883, 29 Mar., 28 June 1884).

45 These included the First International and the Social Democratic Federation. Clark subsequently wrote a series of autobiographical sketches, 'Rambling Recollections of an Agitator', which appeared in *Forward*, June-Oct 1910.

46 Though MacFarlane retained this office until 1888, D. H. Crowley remarks that he 'does not appear to have been closely associated with the Highland Land League' (Crowley, 'Crofters' Party', 117). Both Crowley and Hanham assign the leadership to Clark (ibid.; Hanham, 'Highland Discontent', 42). This is typical of the confusion surrounding the subject. (Incidentally, the HLLRA did not adopt the name of Highland Land League until 1886.)

47 Neither Collings or Broadhurst played any real rôle in the HLLRA, their vice-presidencies being virtually honorary.

48 See *Scottish Highlander*, 22 Dec. 1887. His father was Church of Scotland minister at Lochcarron.

49 *Oban Times*, 7 Apr. 1883.

50 *Oban Times*, 12, 19 May 1883; *Report and Minutes of Evidence of the Commission of Inquiry into the Condition of the Crofters and Cottars of the Highlands and Islands of Scotland [Napier Commission]*, PP 1884, xxxii-xxxvi, Q. 41097.

51 A Skye factor subsequently condemned the commission as one of the principal 'means by which discontent has been fostered' (SRO, GD40/16/32, Lothian Papers, p. 29, M. MacNeill, Confidential Reports to the Secretary for Scotland on the Condition of the Western Highlands and Islands, 1886).

52 *Oban Times*, 25 Aug. 1883.

53 In 1881 the paper had changed hands and Cameron was the son of its new owner. For the history of the paper see the centenary edition, 8 July 1961. I am grateful to Mr Allan Cameron, Duncan Cameron's son and the present editor, for allowing me to consult the files of the paper and for lending me a scrapbook kept by his father in the 1880s.

54 *Oban Times*, 8 Sept. 1883.

55 *Oban Times*, 1 Dec. 1883.

56 SRO, GD1/36/1 (2), HLLRA tract, *Shoulder to Shoulder*, enclosed in Police Report, Colbost, 4 July 1884.

57 *Oban Times*, 29 Dec. 1883.

58 *Oban Times*, 2 Feb. 1884.

59 *Times*, 14 June 1884; *Oban Times*, 28 June 1884. Control of each branch was vested in an eight-man committee elected by the members. Each member paid an annual subscription of 1s. to central funds (SRO, GD 1/36/1 (2), HLLRA; Rules for Local Branches, enclosed in Police Report, Colbost, 14 Aug. 1884). Subscriptions were erratic and the HLLRA was persistently short of funds.

60 *Oban Times*, 3, 17 May, 14 June, 6, 27 Sept., 4 Oct. 1884.

61 G. B. Clark, *Highland Land Question* (London, 1885), Preface, p. 3.

62 *Times*, 1 Sept. 1884.

63 *Napier Commission, Report*, 50–51.

64 For the full programme see *Oban Times*, 7 Feb. 1885, *Times*, 5 Sept. 1884, *Scotsman*, 5 Sept 1884.

65 See J. L. Hammond, *Gladstone and the Irish Nation* (London, 1938), 240 ff.

66 T. Wilkie, *Representation of Scotland*, 257.

67 *Oban Times*, 15, 29 Mar. 1884; *Scotsman*, 19 Aug 1884.

68 *The Crofter*, Sept 1885. *The Crofter* was an HLLRA magazine which flourished briefly in 1885.

69 Parliamentary representation from T. Wilkie, *Representation of Scotland*; estate ownership from *Return of Owners of Lands and Heritages, Scotland*.

70 He owned a 15,000–acre estate in Ross-shire.

71 J. L. Hammond, *Gladstone*, pp. 216–7.

72 *Times*, 16 Jan. 1885. For the duke's views on the subject see, inter al., *Nineteenth Century*, xiii (1883), 173–98; xiv (1886), 681–701.

73 Argyll to Gladstone, 4 Dec. 1884, quoted by D. C. Savage, 'Scottish Politics', 125–6.

74 The nominations were made at the HLLRA's annual conference in Portree (*Times*, 3 Sept. 1885; *Scotsman*, 3 Sept. 1885).

75 *Scotsman*, 6 Oct. 1885.

76 *Scotsman*, 12 Dec. 1885.

77 SRO, GD40/16/32, Lothian Papers, p. 3 and passim, M. MacNeill, Confidential Reports, 1886.

78 The phrase was first used in *Oban Times*, 2 Jan. 1886.

79 See SRO, RH4/9/6, Cabinet Papers, J. B. Balfour to W. Harcourt, 13 Jan. 1885; Harcourt to Gladstone, 17 Jan. 1885.

80 For example, the commission set great store on giving legal recognition to the traditional institutions of the crofting township (Napier Commission, *Report*, 17 ff.).

81 *Hansard*, 3rd ser., cclxxxix (1884), col. 1750; ccxcviii (1885), col. 845.

82 SRO, RH4/9/6, Cabinet Papers, Lochiel to Harcourt, 20 Dec. 1884.

83 Lord Colin Campbell (*Hansard*, 3rd ser., cclxxxix [1884], col. 1624).

84 See reports of the crofters' meetings which greeted the publication of the commission's report, *Oban Times*, April-May 1884; *Hansard*, 3rd ser., cclxxxix (1884), col. 1750; G. B. Clark, *Highland Land Question*, Preface, p. 3.

85 SRO, RH4/9/6, Cabinet Papers, Gladstone to Harcourt, 19 Jan. 1885; A. G. Gardiner, *The Life of Sir William Harcourt* (London, 1923), I, 531–4; J. Chamberlain, *A Political Memoir, 1880–1892*, ed. C. H. D. Howard (London, 1953), 123, 133, 270–1.

86 SRO, RH4/9/6, Cabinet Papers, Gladstone to Harcourt, 19 Jan. 1885.

87 *Hansard*, 3rd ser., ccxcviii (1885), col. 556.

88 *Scotsman*, 21 July 1885.

89 *Hansard*, 3rd ser. ccii (1886), cols. 1305–6, cccv (1886), col. 1468; *Annual Register, 1886*, 83; *Scotsman*, 1 Feb., 21 May 1886; *Blackwood's Magazine*, cxxxix (1886), 560.

90 *Hansard*, 3rd ser. cccv (1886), cols. 1481–7.

91 *Hansard*, 3rd ser. ccciii (1886), cols. 217–8; B. E. C. Dugdale, *Arthur James Balfour* (London, 1936), I, 108; S. H. Zebel, *Balfour* (Cambridge, 1973), 45, 56.

92 *Annual Register, 1886*, 82.

93 For an account of the act and subsequent crofting legislation see D. J. MacCuish, 'Origins and Development of Crofting Law', *Transactions of the Gaelic Society of Inverness*, xliii (1962), 181–96.

94 *Scotsman*, 4 Apr. 1886.

95 Fraser of Kilmuir, *Times*, 13 Mar. 1886.

96 The government were not unaware of the demand for more land but shirked the implications of compulsory land settlement. See SRO RH4/9/6, Cabinet Papers, J. B. Balfour to Harcourt, 13 Jan. 1885. The act contained one limited gesture towards facilitating voluntary settlement, but in practice this proved almost valueless (Mac-Cuish, 'Crofting Law', 190; Crofters Commission, *Final Report, 1913*, pp. xxv-xxvi).

97 *Oban Times*, Apr.-June 1886.

98 *Hansard*, 3rd ser., ccciv (1886), col. 1747.

99 For Irish declarations of solidarity with crofters see, for instance, *Hansard*, 3rd ser cccviii (1886), cols. 930, 935, 977.

100 *Times*, 2–7 Aug. 1886.

101 *Times*, 23–24 Sept. 1886.

102 For the League's constitution see *Oban Times*, 1 Jan. 1887.

103 SRO, Scottish Home and Health Dept. Records, HH1/711, A. J. Balfour, Memo., 15 Sept. 1886; *Hansard*, 3rd ser., cccviii (1886), col. 995; Dugdale, *Balfour*, i, 112.

104 Wilkie, *Representation of Scotland*, 51.

105 Ibid, 278.

106 See *Oban Times*, 3, 24 July 1886.

107 See *Forward*, 3 Sept. 1910.

108 *Oban Times*, 3 July 1886.

109 *Glasgow Herald*, 12 July 1886.

110 See *Oban Times*, May-July 1886.

111 *Times*, 24 Sept. 1886.

112 *Oban Times*, 7 May 1887. See also *Oban Times*, 30 Apr., 14 May 1887; *Times*, 2 May 1887.

113 Fraser-MacIntosh, *Antiquarian Notes*, p. xxvi.

114 *Oban Times*, 19 June 1886.

115 Fraser-MacIntosh was returned unopposed.

116 *Oban Times*, 7 May 1887. He refused.

117 *Oban Times*, 24 Sept. 1887.

118 *Oban Times*, 7 Apr. 1883.

119 *Oban Times*, 26 June 1886; *Scottish Highlander*, 29 July 1886.

120 J. Morley, *Life of Gladstone* (London, 1903), 293.

121 *Oban Times*, 17 Sept. 1887.

122 *Scottish Highlander*, 6 Dec. 1888.

123 *Ibid*, 12 Dec. 1889.

124 E.g. *Scotsman*, 28, 29 Aug. 1890; 21 Aug. 1891.

125 *Oban Times*, 23 June 1888.

126 *Scottish Highlander*, 25 Sept. 1890.

127 This problem faced all the sectional interests operating within or on the fringes of the Liberal party (D. A. Hamer, *Liberal Politics in the Age of Gladstone and Rosebery* [Oxford, 1972]), 7.

128 *Scottish Highlander*, 22, 29 Nov. 1888. See also, 'The Dingwall Programme', *Oban Times*, 7 Feb. 1885.

129 See L. P. Curtis, *Coercion and Conciliation in Ireland, 1880–1892* (Princeton, 1963), 331 ff.

130 SRO, GD40/16/27, Lothian Papers, Memo., 10 May 1887.

131 For crofters' reactions to the emigration plan see *Oban Times*, Jan.-Apr. 1888. For the plan itself see J. P. Day, *Public Administration in the Highlands and Islands of Scotland* (London, 1918), 122–5.

132 Savage, 'Scottish Politics', 122; J. G. Kellas, 'The Liberal Party and the Scottish Church Disestablishment Crisis', *Eng. His. Rev.* lxxix (1964), 31–46.

133 See e.g. *Oban Times*, 14 Mar., 22 Aug., 16 Sept. 1885; *Scotsman*, 2 Feb. 1885; *Scottish Review*, xii (1888), 124–5.

134 *Scottish Highlander*, 1 Mar. 1888; *Oban Times*, 3 Mar. 1888.

135 *Oban Times*, 16 Jan. 1890. In those elections the Land League had unanimous Free Church support.

136 *Scotsman*, 28, 29 Aug. 1890.

137 *Scottish Highlander*, 22 Nov. 1888.

138 See ibid., 20 June 1889; 2 July 1891.

139 Ibid., 27 Sept. 1888.

140 See *Oban Times*, 10 Sept. 1887.

141 *Scottish Highlander*, 4 Oct. 1888; *Oban Times*, 21 Sept., 28 Dec. 1889.

142 *Glasgow Herald*, 9 Nov. 1888.

143 *Scottish Highlander*, 13 Feb. 1890; *Oban Times*, 15 Feb. 1890.

144 *Times*, 7 Feb. 1890; *Scotsman*, 11 Feb. 1890.

145 *Scotsman*, 20 Aug. 1891.

146 *Times*, 2 July 1892. For a brief biography of MacGregor see *Celtic Monthly*, i (1893), 97.

147 *Scottish Highlander*, 8 Jan. 1891.

148 See ibid., Jan.-July 1892.

149 *Scotsman*, 29 Sept. 1892.

150 *Oban Times*, 15 June 1889.

151 SRO, GD 40/16/45, Lothian Papers, Lothian to Goschen, 10 Aug. 1889.

152 *Reports of the Royal Commission on certain matters affecting the Interests of the Population of the Western Highlands and Islands*, PP 1890, xxvii; PP 1890–1, xliv.

153 SRO, GD 40/16/53, Lothian Papers, Treasury Statement, 1892.

154 *Oban Times*, 22 June 1889.

155 Crofters Commission, *Fifth Report* (1891), p. xxiii.

156 See, e.g., SRO, AF 67/112, Crofting Files, Ivory to Under Secretary of State for Scotland, 24 Apr. 1891.

157 *Scottish Highlander*, 1 Oct. 1896.

158 Michael Buchanan, ibid., 25 Feb. 1892.

159 Ibid., 6 Oct. 1892.

160 Ibid., 17 Nov. 1892.

161 Ibid., 15 Dec. 1892.

162 *Scotsman*, 30 Sept. 1892.

163 *Report of the Royal Commission on the Highlands and Islands*, PP 1895, xxxviii, p. v.

164 See, e.g., the reaction of Glendale crofters, *Scottish Highlander*, 12 Jan. 1893.

165 Ibid., 8 Dec. 1892.

166 *Times*, 3 Apr. 1895.

167 *Scottish Highlander*, 17 Nov. 1892.

168 *Scotsman*, 21 Sept. 1893.

169 Ibid., 21, 22 Sept. 1893; *Times*, 21 Sept. 1893.

170 *Scotsman*, 14 Sept. 1894.

171 For biographical details see *Scottish Highlander*, 27 Sept. 1894.

172 Ibid., 7 Dec. 1893.

173 *Scotsman*, 22 Sept. 1894.

174 *Scottish Highlander*, 23 Aug. 1894.

175 *Times*, 29 Jan., 7 Feb., 6 Mar. 1895; *Scottish Highlander*, 7 Feb. 1895.

176 *Report*, p. xxii.

177 See Bill to Amend the Crofters Holdings (Scotland) Act, 1886, PP 1896, I.

178 *Scottish Highlander*, 4 Jan. 1894.

179 *Hansard*, 4th ser., xxxiv (1895). col. 920.

180 Ibid. xxxii (1895), col. 1644; xxxiv (1895), col. 944; *Scotsman*, 20 May 1895.

181 *Scotsman*, 30 Sept. 1892.

182 *Scotsman*, 21 May 1895.

183 *Times*, 27 May 1895.

184 Contained in the telegram already quoted.

185 See *Scotsman*, 25, 27, 30 May 1895; *Times*, 25, 30 May 1895.

186 Clark and Galloway Weir had promised to finance his campaign. On his becoming official Liberal candidate they reneged on their promise. MacRae consequently found himself in serious financial difficulties. For this aspect of the affair see *Scottish Highlander*, 16 Apr. 1896.

187 See *Times*, 31 May, 7 June 1895; *Scotsman*, 4 June 1895; *Scottish Highlander*, 20 June 1895.

188 *Scotsman*, 17 June 1895.

189 *Times*, 7, 17 June, 1895; *Scottish Highlander*, 20 June 1895.

190 *Scotsman*, 17 June 1895.

191 *Scottish Highlander*, 20 June 1895.

192 Ibid.

193 For Irish land reform see Curtis, *Coercion and Conciliation in Ireland*, 135 ff.

194 *Scotsman*, 3 June 1895.

195 Ibid.

196 Congested Districts Board, *Seventh Report*, 1905, App., pp. 15–22. The Glendale crofters paid the last instalment of their fifty-year purchase annuity in 1955 and are now the owners of the entire Glendale estate.

197 *Times*, 13 Oct. 1894.

198 *Scottish Highlander*, 31 Oct. 1895.

199 *Scotsman*, 24 Sept. 1896; *Scottish Highlander*, 24 Sept., 8 Oct. 1896.

200 See, e.g. Crowley, 'Crofters' Party', 110; Kellas, 'Crofters' War', 281; J. G. Kellas, 'Highland Migration to Glasgow and the Origins of the Scottish Labour Movement', *Society for the Study of Labour History Bulletin*, xii (1966), 9–11.

201 *Scotsman*, 25 Feb. 1884; *Oban Times*, 15 Mar. 1884; E. P. Lawrence, *Henry George*, 37.

202 W. Stewart, *J. Keir Hardie* (London, 1921), 37–55.

203 J. M. Cherrie, *The Restoration of the Land to the State* (London, 1884), 43–46.

204 *Scotsman*, 29 Aug. 1884. See also *Celtic Magazine*, x (1885), 325.

205 Clark subsequently maintained that the Liberals had destroyed the Land League and in 1902 he became president of a new and Labour-orientated Highland Land League founded in Glasgow by Tom Johnston (*Forward*, 4 Sept. 1909, 8 Oct. 1910).

206 MacKenzie's newspaper carried several attacks on socialism (e.g., *Scottish Highlander*, 12 Sept. 1895, 10 Mar. 1898).

'They Will Listen to no Remonstrance': Land raids and land raiders in the Scottish Highlands, 1886 to 1914

Ewen A Cameron 1997 *Scottish Economic & Social History* 17, 43–64.

Protests concerning the land issue in the Scottish Highlands between 1882 and 1886 have received a great deal of attention. Similarly, the series of land raids which occurred in the years immediately following the end of the Great War have been studied at length.[1] Aside from Dr Hunter's bold attempts to link these two periods, the important series of protests which occurred in the period from 1886 to 1914 have not received sufficient attention.[2]

This article has two objectives; first, to provide some detail on these events and second, to analyse the objectives of the raiders. However, prior to an exploration of these points it is necessary to make some general comments on land raids. Some were demonstrations of a general grievance with the structure of land holding or the perceived inadequacies of government policy. Others were directed towards a specific piece of land, the occupation of which was desired by the raiders. Thus incidents of widely differing scale can be included under the general label of land raids. For example, alongside the large scale events which form the bulk of this article, there were incidents such as the act of crofters from Kilmuir who put 40 of their horses to graze on the farm of Monkstadt.[3] Most land raids were directed against private proprietors, however, with the growing involvement of the government in the land issue, it is interesting to find raids on estates owned by the Congested Districts Board. The latter was the institution established by the government to create a system of peasant proprietorship in the crofting community.[4] Common to all land raids is the underlying notion that the claim to land was neither novel nor legalistic, but historic and traditional.[5] Thus, land raids involved a fundamental clash between rival justifications for the occupation of land. However, it is interesting to note that the land raiders' fundamental belief in the righteousness of their claims was limited in geographical space and confined to very specific pieces of land. It is debateable whether this stemmed from deep historical awareness, or merely from contemporary political convenience.

TABLE 1: LAND RAIDS 1886–1914

	1886–1896		1897–1914	
	RAID	THREAT	RAID	THREAT
Barra & Vatersay	0	0	8	4
South Uist	0	1	7	2
North Uist	0	0	2	0
Harris	0	0	2	0
Lewis	5	2	4	1
Skye	1	0	1	7
Sutherland	3	0	1	2
Elsewhere	0	1	0	1
TOTALS	9	4	25	17

Source: Scottish Record Office AF67, AF42.

I

One author has argued that raids and threatened raids in the Hebrides became 'a part of the accepted order of things'.[6] This raises two issues; first, to what extent were raids confined to the Hebrides? and second, how many raids took place and how many threats were made? Table 1 makes an attempt to do this. However, given the difficulties encountered in defining a raid the figures are far from conclusive. The count has been undertaken using official government sources in an attempt to make the coverage as wide as possible and to avoid rumour and counter rumour.

This table reinforces a number of points; first, raiding was almost entirely confined to the Hebrides, with the exception of some isolated incidents in Sutherland. However, even within the Hebrides there is a clear concentration of incidents in the Uists and Barra. Overall, raids took place in areas where there was a strong tradition of agitation from the 1880s or areas where government institutions such as the CDB were active. Second, there is a clear time pattern to the raids; most of the raids in the first period took place in the immediate aftermath of the Crofters Act. The establishment of the Congested Districts Board in 1897 proved to be the signal for a new cycle of expectation and frustration which produced a concerted series of raids. Threats of raids were mostly tactics to influence very specific situations. For example, the large number of threats made on Skye after 1897 emanate from the Kilmuir estate during the period of negotiation between the CDB and the inhabitants over the issue of land purchase.

This article will focus on specific examples of land raids. In particular, the celebrated raid of the Park Deer Forest in Lochs, Lewis, the lengthy series of raids on Barra and Vatersay from 1900 to 1909 and the raid at Scuddaburgh, on the CDB's Kilmuir Estate, in 1910. These raids were not isolated incidents of protests, they were linked to the wider politics of the land question. It has been noted that each succeeding piece of land legislation in the period between the 1880s and the 1920s served to stimulate demand for land.[7] It is noticeable that the raids discussed here took place at times when new legislation was being considered, or had just been placed on the statute book. Legislation raised expectations, often to unrealistic heights, and the resulting frustration was often expressed in the form of a raid.

The continuity which links the 1880s to the 1920s can best be appreciated by a brief examination of the issues at stake in the Crofters' Wars and the deficiencies of the *Crofters' Holdings (Scotland) Act* of 1886. From the initial sparks of protest, most notably at Bernera in Lewis in 1874 and Braes in Skye in 1882, the principal grievance articulated by crofters was shortage of land.[8] The root of this grievance was held to be landlord appropriation of crofters' grazing land for their own purposes. Only in isolated areas, such as North Skye, Caithness, the Ross of Mull and Iona, was the issue of rack renting prominent.[9] The Crofters' Wars can best be described as a campaign aimed at the restoration of grazing rights, regardless of the antiquity of their loss, and the provision of more land for crofters. It is as well to bear this in mind when one comes to consider the Crofters' Act of 1886. Although an important statute in many ways, it was derided by the crofters' movement due to its failure to deal with this central issue. It provided security of tenure on existing land, the right to have the fair rent of that land adjudicated and the right to compensation for improvements. Thus, it was only a partial settlement for the majority of crofters and it gave no assistance whatsoever to the large class of landless cottars. These facts provide the basis for the land raids in the period after 1886, as well as the legislation of 1897, 1911 and 1919 which attempted in various ways to deal with the crofters' shortage of land.

The immediate aftermath of the Crofters' Act saw outbreaks of agitation in several areas of the newly defined crofting counties. Marines had to be despatched to Skye, Sutherland and Tiree, in the latter case in response to the seizure of Greenhill farm. This raid is interesting as it involved a split in the ranks of the crofting community in Tiree. A prominent member of the HLLRA was held to

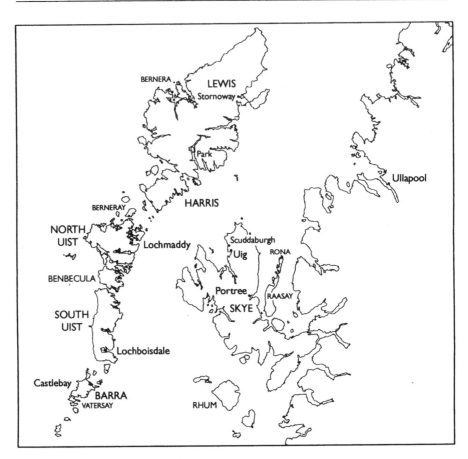

have broken a 'boycott' of the farm when it fell vacant and considerable bitterness ensued. The raiders were sentenced to six months in October 1886, not the last time 'salutory' sentences would be handed down to land raiders.[10]

The chronically congested island of Lewis demonstrated most clearly the inadequacies of legislation lacking provision for extending crofters' lands. Thus, it is no surprise that Lewis was the site of agitation in 1887 and 1888 which focused on the need for more land for the large class of cottars on the island. The principal event in this phase of the agitation was the raid on the Park Deer Forest in late 1887. This former sheep farm had been vacant between 1883 and 1886 and thereafter it was devoted to sporting purposes. During the vacancy the estate had ignored requests from crofters that they should be allowed to take over the tenancy. The estate's reluctance was perhaps encouraged by the growing arrears of a club farm tenanted by six crofters on 4,500 acres of the Deer Forest.[11] Nevertheless, on 22nd November 1887 the farm was raided by a crowd of over 200 men who were equipped in such a manner as to suggest that they intended to initiate a lengthy occupation. The Lord Advocate, acting on information he had received from Stornoway, reported to Lord Lothian, the Secretary for Scotland:

> Today a crowd of men numbering about 200, with rifles, tents, banners and provisions have entered the Deer Forest and intend to remain until all the deer are exterminated. They will listen to no remonstrance.[12]

However, by the 25th of November, the raid had collapsed after prompt action by Sheriff Fraser from Stornoway, and a 'miserably wet night' camped out in the Deer Forest.[13] This action had demonstrated just how nervous the government was in despatching a body of troops from Glasgow to the island. However, the frayed nerves of the government can partly be explained by the contemporaneous disorder at Clashmore, Lochinver and Durness, in Sutherland, and the raid at Greenhill on Tiree, which had elicited a military response from the government. The combination of events led to worries that a major resurgence of the Crofters' War was imminent.[14] Further unrest on Lewis manifested itself in disturbances at Aignish and Galson in January 1887, after the Park raiders were acquitted of mobbing and rioting.[15] Thomas Shaw, for the defence, was able to demonstrate that, at the most, they were guilty of trespass in pursuit of game, which carried a much lighter sentence. He later speculated that the reason why the Crown 'overshot the mark' was:

> . . . that conviction could be followed by such swingeing sentences, even of penal servitude, as might stamp out land agitation for a generation.[16]

The Park Deer Forest Raid attracted some lurid press coverage at the time and much of this has been uncritically recorded by historians.[17] Reports of massive numbers of deer slaughtered and scare stories of rifles being imported from Ireland were products of a growing paranoia in official circles.[18] The information provided by local officials provides a more sober account of proceedings. Official estimates of the number of deer killed amounted to six and the weapons in the hands of raiders were described as 'of the most ancient description'.[19] More important than speculation on these minor details is the nature of the raid itself. Was it a manifestation of a desire to gain possession of the land which had been raided, or a more general demonstration designed to seek publicity for the grievances of the Lewis cottars? The rather rapid withdrawal of the raiders from the deer forest does not say much for their resolution in the face of authority, the kind of resolution demonstrated by later land raiders. At the height of the climate of fear about renewed agitation in late 1887 the raid was being talked up by some newspapers; the *Glasgow Herald* claimed:

> The most striking thing about the raid is the complete organisation and grim determination with which it has been conducted. [20]

On the other hand, the Inverness newspaper the *Scottish Highlander,* edited by Alexander MacKenzie and both well informed and well disposed towards the crofters' movement, had a very different comment on the raid:

> The raiders acted in a most manly and open manner throughout. They declared their object to have been to secure publicity for their condition. Having obtained this they are now surrendering to the authorities, perfectly prepared to suffer any punishment that may be inflicted upon them.[21]

Even leaving aside the likelihood of the paper trying to put the best construction on events, this is an interesting admission.[22] Donald MacRae, the schoolteacher at Balallan, and a leading figure in the recently constituted Highland Land League, emphasised the issue of the prevailing destitution in Lewis in a speech made on his acquittal. The raid was successful in drawing attention to the cottar problem on Lewis and it stimulated the government to make an enquiry into conditions on the island.[23]

The Park raid was a demonstration, seeking publicity for the particular grievances of Lewis cottars, rather than a fundamental claim for the land in question. The publicity of the raid was augmented by that surrounding the trial and acquittal of the raiders in January 1888. The later history of raids would show that where such a fundamental objective was involved, raiders were resolute in their occupation of the land. However, although this was not the last raid which can be seen as a demonstrative publicity stunt, it was certainly one of the biggest and most successful. The Park raid was not the last incident of agitation in Lewis in this period. In December 1887 and January 1888 crofters intimated to the tenant farmers at Galson and Aignish that their farms were to be raided. The raids duly took place on the appointed days, considerable trouble ensued at Aignish and several arrests were made. In contrast to the good fortune of the Park raiders in their encounter with the Courts, heavy sentences were handed down to the 'Aignish rioters'. Most historians accept that the combination of heavy sentences, improved economic conditions and the fact that the agitation had brought little obvious gain, discouraged further instances.[24]

III

The period from 1888 to 1901 saw a very different atmosphere in the Highlands. The long term benefits of the Crofters' Act for certain elements of the crofting community slowly became evident, especially in the shape of improved housing conditions. However, the impression should not be given that the traumas of the 1880s were entirely dissipated. Two recent attempts to catalogue incidences of protest in the Highlands have noted that this period was characterised by agitation of markedly lower intensity.[25] The Congested Districts Board was established in 1897 in an attempt to try to make more land available to crofters. However, the rationale of the Conservative party in doing this was to break the mould of classic crofting involving small pieces of land supplemented by wage labour. So, despite the fact that the Board provided hope that some more land would be brought under the crofting regime, it also had an implied threat to traditional crofting practices. Thus, 1897 can be seen as another significant date in the cycle of expectation and frustration which created the conditions for land raids.

The estates of Lady Gordon Cathcart in Benbecula, South Uist and Barra saw this series of events being played out in dramatic fashion. All the ingredients were present; chronic congestion, a large class of expectant crofters and government awareness that it was a problem area, towards which the Board should direct its attention. Despite being an absentee, the proprietor had very definite ideas about the running of her estates. This involved a prejudice against crofting, which she argued perpetuated congestion and prevented the people from taking full advantage of the fishing industry. Her attempts to encourage young crofters to move away, to be educated and trained for urban employments, had little impact. A report by the Crofters' Commission in 1902 into the condition of the islands of Uist reported that her estate, in contrast with that of Sir Arthur Campbell Orde in North Uist, was teeming with cottars and that the estate took a less than constructive attitude to the idea of granting more land to the crofters and cottars.[26] The roots of the agitation in this area can be traced to the method of estate management and the extent to which it excluded crofters from the general advances of the 1890s.

The culmination of insensitive estate management and unconstructive opposition to demands for more land was a land raid at Northbay, Barra, in September 1900. This helped to put pressure on the estate and the CDB to become involved. After a protracted and complex series of negotiations involving the farms of Eoligarry and Northbay, 25 crofter holdings and 33 smaller fishermen's holdings were created. However, these proceedings had an unsettling influence on cottars throughout Barra, creating a climate of expectation and disappointment. The cottars around Castlebay were unhappy that the CDB was not turning its attention to the island of Vatersay, which had been scheduled as fit for use by crofters by the *Royal Commission (Highlands and Islands) 1892*. The unsatisfactory situation led to more raids at Eoligarry and Vatersay in February and April 1901. This was the beginning of a cycle of raids which would continue until 1909. There were three clear phases to this dispute; the first lasted from the first raid in the spring of 1902 to the election of the Liberal government in December 1905. The second began with the series of raids in the spring of 1906 and continued until the purchase of the island by the CDB in February 1909. The final phase was characterised by tension within the crofting community as the CDB attempted to implement a settlement on the island. This tension would be the chief characteristic of the raid at Scuddaburgh, in the north of Skye, in 1911.[27]

IV

The Island of Vatersay was arranged as a sheep farm extending to 3400 acres, rented at £400.[28] The Vatersay raids were very different to the Park deer forest raid. The longevity of the dispute and the behaviour of the raiders during it, suggests that a much more fundamental claim to the land was being expressed here. The raid was unusual in the respect that the raiders' sense of the legitimacy of their claim was not entirely discounted by the estate management. This claim rested not only on the recognition of the *Royal Commission, 1892*, but also on the recommendation of a Committee of Inverness-shire County Council that it should be let under the Allotments Act of 1892. A third source of legitimacy was the fact that there had been a long-standing arrangement with the tenant of Vatersay that the cottars of Castlebay could use a portion of the island to grow potatoes. When this privilege was withdrawn in the spring of 1902, it induced the cottars to raid the land.[29] In an early indication of the determined approach of these raiders they began to prepare it for cultivation.[30] Lady Gordon Cathcart's solicitors recognised that the case was exceptional:

> It must also be kept in view that this is not a case of a mob taking possession of land with which they had no previous connection. There undoubtedly has been a usage of long standing by which the cottars were allowed potato ground on Vatersay.[31]

Against the background of renewed threats of raids in the autumn of 1902 the estate and the tenant of the farm came to an agreement to sell 60 acres of potato ground to the CDB for the use of Castlebay cottars.[32]

This arrangement proved unsatisfactory. Growing complaints were made about the quality of the ground which had been purchased. It later became clear, after a second survey of the land, that these complaints were justified. However, in the spring of 1905, the cottars' dissatisfaction reached such proportions that a new land raid occurred. In February 1905, 30 cottars went to Vatersay and once again indicated the seriousness of their claims by marking off lots of land. This raid induced the CDB to ask the estate if a more suitable piece of ground on Vatersay could be found for the cottars. The estate gave the appearance of co-operation but by May nothing had transpired and the season for planting potatoes had passed.[33] A third raid occurred in the spring of 1906, this time with 47 cottars going to Vatersay, and once again marking out lots of land on the South East side of the island. The police in Inverness took a relaxed attitude to the repetition of the raid and its objectives, remarking:

> . . . this is a sort of annual proceeding at this season . . . a repetition of the acts of the past two years . . . by cottars with the view of obtaining potato ground.[34]

However, the local policeman in Castlebay had a different opinion of the seriousness of the raid and the objectives of the raiders, he commented of the cottars:

> . . . they are determined to get possession of the whole farm of Vatersay and to remove their dwelling houses to Vatersay as quickly and as early as possible.[35]

The incidence of raids on North Uist, at Bornish and Ormiclate, in February 1906, gave some cause for worry that a more general cycle of raids was about to begin.[36] One important element to the background of this raid was the change in government at Westminster. The Conservatives had been in office for ten years and had been devoted to the notion of persuading crofters to become owner occupiers wherever possible. In the immediate context of Vatersay this was important as there was a close personal relationship between Lady Gordon Cathcart and Lord Balfour of Burleigh, the Secretary for Scotland. This situation changed in 1905 with the advent of a Liberal government devoted to the notion of dual ownership as the central plank of their land policy.[37] While the *Scotsman's* comment, that the raid was no more than a 'dramatic scene intended to impress . . . our new rulers', underestimated the seriousness of the situation, it emphasised the political awareness of the raiders. This was also evident on the Kilmuir estate in North Skye, where the change of government and policy destroyed the credibility of the CDB's attempts to have the crofters buy their holdings.[38]

The next phase of the Vatersay dispute lasted from the third raid of spring 1906, to the sale of the island to the CDB in February 1909. Before examining the tactics of the raiders it is necessary to make a brief comment on the impact of the raid on the negotiations between the government and the estate management. These had a number of elements; first, who should take responsibility for dealing with the raiders, the government through the criminal law, or the estate management through a civil action?[39] The second element of the debate concerned the future of the island. The government argued that the proprietor should retain ownership of the island and co-operate with government agencies in establishing new holdings. This was the substance of the *Small Landholders (Scotland) Bill* which they were having such difficulty getting through parliament, and would not be able to do so until 1911. The position of the estate on this question was simple; the government should buy the estate if it wanted to extend crofting. This was a common position for landlords who merely wanted to shift the burden of responsibility for crofting communities entirely onto the government. In the Vatersay dispute the estate won out on this matter and the island was purchased by the CDB for £6250.[40]

The situation began to escalate in the early summer of 1906 with the raiders transporting their cattle to the island, thus clearly indicating that they would not be happy with a further grant of potato ground but had set their sights on the island as a whole. Further indication of this fact was provided when the raiders began to build huts on Vatersay and permanently occupy and cultivate the land. This phase of the dispute had been reached by the middle of 1907.[41]

The remainder of 1907 saw attitudes harden on all sides. The raiders began to cultivate land all over the island; Reginald MacLeod felt that the raiders were being encouraged by the lack of action against them. Lady Gordon Cathcart's attitude hardened significantly. This was primarily due to her antipathy towards the government becoming personalised by the rhetoric of Thomas Shaw, the Lord Advocate. When the Vatersay raid was discussed in Parliament in August 1907 Shaw described the raid in the following downbeat manner:

> These poor tenants of Barra stepped across to the Island of Vatersay and on the shore they planted a few potatoes, hoping to return in the spring to reap what little crop there was . . . they were interfering with no human soul.[42]

Not the least interesting of the links between the Park raid and the Vatersay raid was personified by Shaw, the defence counsel for the Park raiders, who was now Lord Advocate. He was described by Lady Gordon Cathcart's solicitors as an 'extreme radical' and (probably correctly) as 'hostile to landowners'.[43] The attitude of the estate management hardened further when John Wilson, the Sheriff of Inverness, on a fact finding mission to Vatersay, contrived to give the impression that he had some sympathy with the raiders. Wilson's report is interesting for this reason and for the light it casts on the attitude of the raiders. Wilson met 'the leading man amongst the raiders' Duncan Campbell and other raiders, including Neil MacPhee from Mingulay. All the raiders expressed the difficulty of their former situations in Castlebay or Mingulay; indeed, Wilson visited some of these and concurred with their views. Wilson's report referred often to the 'respectable' nature of the raiders but he failed to persuade them to 'go back on the illegal course on which they had entered'. Wilson's conclusion reinforced a number of notions; first, the raiders were not acting lightly; ultimately they believed that if they endured they would be vindicated. Wilson reported:

> It seemed to me that there were influences at work which were not fully disclosed and which I could not effectually deal with. I was assured that Lady Gordon Cathcart in the end would not use the lash of the law. Their firm conviction, based on past experience, was that she would not be a party to imprisoning them or evicting them; further, that the government would not allow them to suffer. From time to time one or other of the men in the most emphatic language, vowed that he would suffer imprisonment or death rather than yield. I was assured that if they were put down, there were scores of others who would take up the struggle and continue.[44]

Two important points can be made using the evidence gathered by Wilson and embodied in this passage. First, there is here, and throughout the actions of the raiders, a paradoxical relationship between the fundamental nature of the raiders' claim to the island of Vatersay and the ultimately limited nature of that aim. They were not seeking to overturn the institution of landlordism; indeed, they articulated to Wilson the fact that they were trying to influence their own landlord, in whom they had faith not to consign them to prison. Their aim was to gain a foothold on the land on Vatersay, in the form of the establishment of a crofting community. Second, they were clearly trying to influence government and were sufficiently well informed about the frustrated Liberal land policy as to know that they were pushing against an open door in this regard.

The rest of this phase of the Vatersay raid was taken up by tortuous negotiations between the government and the estate management about the details of the purchase of the island. The estate management attempted to put pressure on the government by taking the government's long standing advice and taking a civil action against ten of the raiders in June 1908. This forced a concession from the government and the action was dropped.[45]

The third phase of the Vatersay raid took place after the government concluded the purchase of the island in February 1909. This involved the settlement of the island, the allocation of holdings and the thorny problem of what to do with the raiders if they were found not to be suitable people to take up one of the holdings. The government, in the shape of the CDB, did not want to be seen to be giving in to the raiders, but they did not want to exacerbate an already volatile situation by excluding them from consideration. They made it clear that a person's status as a raider did not affect them, positively or negatively, in the matter of the allocation of holdings. However, in an interesting hint as to the internal tension in the incipient Vatersay crofting community, some of the leading raiders refused to take up their holdings and were given notice to quit. Among those in this category were Duncan Campbell and Neil MacPhee, whom Wilson had met in 1908, along with the father and brother of the latter. These four men had engaged the services of Donald Shaw, an Edinburgh solicitor who specialised in such cases. His representations of his clients' views hinted at their unhappiness that people who had not been involved in the raid were to receive land:

> . . . they do not consider that after the sufferings they have undergone they ought to be called upon to take the chance of allotment with such an overwhelming number of newcomers.[46]

The Vatersay raid was a very different event from the Park raid in 1888. The longevity of the dispute and the much more resolute attitude of the raiders signified a much more fundamental claim to the land in question. This was a land raid where the raiders took physical possession of the land they coveted and fought a political campaign to have their claim recognised. However, this was the extent of their aim. It is interesting to note that the aims of the Park raiders had been much more general and wide ranging. They did not seek to establish permanent possession of the land but to draw attention to a general grievance, that of land being used for sport in the vicinity of chronic congestion. The Vatersay dispute sparked off a series of raids throughout Barra and the Uists, notably at Ardmhor on Barra and Glendale in South Uist.[47] Reginald MacLeod, the *Scotsman*, and the proprietrix felt that these were caused by the government's failure to take a firm hand with the Vatersay raiders.[48] Raids did seem to be infectious within the confines of a circumscribed locality. The Park raid was followed in January and February 1888 by disturbances at Aignish and Galson, near Stornoway, before the heavy sentences handed out to those involved put an end to such events in Lewis for the time being. In this context it is interesting to note that the post-Vatersay raids were largely confined to the Uists.

V

The circumstances behind the raid at Scuddaburgh on the CDB's Kilmuir estate in North Skye, displays many of the same characteristics; a legacy of bitterness from the 1880s, onto which had been grafted a climate of expectation with the purchase of the estate by the CDB in 1904. The holdings on the estate were restructured and the intention was to sell the modified crofts on to the crofters. This plan came unstuck with the reluctance of the crofters to buy, and the reluctance of the Liberal government to push the matter after 1906.[49] Part of the difficulty with this estate was the number of tenant farms which the CDB had inherited. As the leases lapsed, these farms had to be dealt with within the overall strategy for the estate. The CDB had long been critical of the standard of crofting agriculture and husbandry. While they recognised that these had roots in longstanding shortages of capital and land, and made significant efforts to educate crofters in this matter, they were reluctant to hand over good grazing farms to crofters. When this became evident to the crofting communities in the vicinity of the farms it caused some unease. Crofters from Heribusta in the far north of the estate threatened to take possession of the farm of Duntulm in March 1910. Nothing came of this threat, but it served as a warning to the CDB of what was to come.[50]

The farm of Scuddaburgh lies immediately above the township of Idrigill, which is itself on the periphery of the village of Uig. The crofters of Idrigill had first formally made known their wish to add the farm to their common grazings in 1908, when they applied to the Crofters' Commission for 460 acres of the farm. In February 1910, the Commission granted 397 acres as a grazing extension. The Commission argued that the crofters possessed neither the skill nor the capital to make the best use of the 63 acres in question, which was the arable portion of the farm.[51] The Idrigill crofters informed the Scottish Offfice that a meeting of the township had resolved:

> . . . that they could not agree with the decision of the Crofters' Commission in allocating the rocks and heather part of Scuddaburgh to them; that they

must get the whole farm before it would be of any use to them and unless this was granted by your Board within ten days from this date, the meeting unanimously resolved to take possession of the whole farm and till the land for this season.[52]

This did not disconcert the CDB who took out and served interdicts on the Idrigill crofters in an attempt to stave off the threatened raid. This proved to be of no avail, the raid duly took place on the 23rd of April 1910 and the raiders began to till the land. The CDB could scarcely have been surprised; nevertheless, they felt that they had to stand by the decision of the Crofters' Commission and not yield to the demands for an independent valuation of the farm. Further raids took place in June 1910, which involved the raiders bringing their cattle to the farm. The Secretary for Scotland began to make much more resolute noises about the necessity of stamping out lawlessness when it was government property which was being raided. However, he was soon to find out what many other landowners already knew, namely the difficulty of applying the civil law in such remote areas as the North end of Skye.[53]

The local police were reluctant to get involved in a civil matter, and the onus fell on Angus MacKintosh, the CDB's long suffering 'land manager' in Kilmuir. There is some significance in MacKintosh's appellation in that ever since his appointment he had been reluctant to become known as a 'factor', a term which was highly loaded in the Highlands in the late nineteenth century.[54] However, future events were to damage his reputation, regardless of his job description. After a deforcement in August 1910, the onus fell on the CDB to identify the guilty parties. Later in the month MacKintosh was sent to do the dirty work, despite a recognition by the CDB officials that; 'his residence at Uig will be made extremely difficult and his work among the crofters marred'.[55]

In attempting to serve the notices MacKintosh encountered a premeditated and organised riot. With the women of the township in the forefront of the action, the Sheriff Officer was deforced and the party was chased from the village by a 'howling mob' of men, women and (as the crowd passed the school) children. MacKintosh was not surprised to be personally blamed for the failure to secure the whole farm and roundly abused for aiding the Sheriff Officers but was clearly taken aback by the vociferous nature of the proceedings. The language in his report to his CDB superiors in Edinburgh suggests this strongly:

The whole crowd seemed to be perfectly crazy and were hardly responsible for their actions. The men took no active part but they urged on the women, some of whom behaved like furies.[56]

The eventual arrest and imprisonment of the raiders, and those involved in the riot, brought forth ritual condemnation from the crofters and induced an interesting response from the government.[57] The Secretary for Scotland went to Uig and met with the Idrigill crofters in the Free Church to thrash out a solution.[58] The compromise which was eventually reached was that the 63 acres of arable land should be placed at the disposal of the crofters to work in a communal fashion. Pentland was rather proud of his personal input to this outcome. It was, after all, one of his few practical contributions to the Crofting Counties during his troubled tenure as Secretary for Scotland. William Mac-Kenzie, the Principal Clerk of the Crofters' Commission, in an indiscreet aside, remarked; 'Personally I am glad that these men are getting the land after having fought so well for it'.[59]

The Scuddaburgh raid, although not on the same scale as the Park or Vatersay events, is significant. There is evidence of the same attitude of permanence taken up by the raiders who tilled the land on the farm of Scuddaburgh and took their cattle to graze on it. There is also the same limitation of objectives, in this case the acquisition of 63 acres of arable land. However, the tilling and grazing aspects of the raid were purely tactical. The raid was not motivated by the same chronic poverty, congestion and squalor which lay behind the Vatersay raid. As in Vatersay, the raid was a source of tension in the crofting community; Sinclair commented that at his meeting in Uig the prospect of trying to allocate the land to individuals was impossible due to 'jealousy'. It appears that the Scuddaburgh raiders were aware of the details of the Vatersay raid. The CDB solicitor commented:

> I understand they cite the case of the Vatersay men who seized land, were interdicted, imprisoned, allowed to return to the interdicted land and finally given holdings on the land, as a justification of their action at Scuddaburgh.[60]

Events on the Kilmuir estate suggest that the crofters were politically aware, if not politically motivated. In April 1908 they argued in a petition sent to the Scottish Office:

> Our Small Holders Bill was rejected by the House of Lords. And as any legislation you propose to make to get land for us under the Crofters' Act will be likely to be treated by the Lords in the same way, the only weapon for us is to take forcible possession of the land which was bought for us by public money and allocated to us by the Crofters' Commission.[61]

Finally, it was noted in discussion of the Vatersay raid that certain members of the crofting community emerged as ringleaders of the raiding activity. This also seemed to be the case in Scuddaburgh. Angus MacKintosh, who had considerable local insight, identified one individual whom he felt to be behind much of the trouble and said of him:

> . . . he considers himself so full of wisdom and understanding that anyone who refuses to agree with him is either a rogue or a tyrant and the others seem to think that they have only to follow him to get everything they want on their own terms.[62]

The Scuddaburgh raid was unusual in a number of its characteristics. Other raids were characterised by stoic determination rather than outright violence. Indeed, in many ways the incident was more reminiscent of the Crofters' Wars, with its highblown political rhetoric and self conscious publicity. Further, studies of the Crofters' War have noted the role of women at the forefront of protest, as they were at Scuddaburgh.[63]

VI

The period from 1906 to 1911 had seen land raids and threats of land raids throughout the Southern Hebrides in particular. This was born out of frustration at the slow progress of Liberal land legislation. The Scuddaburgh land raid of 1911 is characteristic of a pattern of demand, expectation and disappointment, which followed each succeeding piece of legislation from 1886 to the 1920s. Similar frustration boiled over at Reef in the West of Lewis in late 1913 and early 1914. The Scottish Office was under no illusions that the raid was directed towards the BoAS, as the body who had the facility to grant more land, rather than the landowner. The most senior of the Board's field officers argued that the problem was one of exaggerated expectation of what the Board could do for the crofting community. The raiders were subsequently jailed but released after giving an undertaking not to encroach on the farm again.[64]

The political environment of the years following World War One was very different from the years in which the land raids discussed here took place. The 1911 Act had been a failure due to its own internal inconsistencies and because the outbreak of the Great War led to a suspension of activity on land settlement. Although it has been established that the post war raids were the latest in a long series of protests which had continuity back to the 1880s at least, the new environment in which they took place was significant. The immediate post war period had seen the passage of the *Land Settlement (Scotland) Act* which ironed out many of the irregularities of earlier legislation. Close examination of the results which flowed from it reveal it to be a much more efficient piece of legislation.[65]

The increased rate of settlement under the 1919 Act, however, did not mean that land raids were a thing of the past. A number of factors contributed to their continuation. The first of these was the continuing high level of demand for land. Such was the extent of this that at its peak, and creating very small holdings, the Board of Agriculture for Scotland was only able to settle about one quarter of the applications for land.[66] There was a symbiotic relationship between the nature of land settlement and land raids in this period. Land raids created political pressure and led to a policy of the maximum quantitative settlement of demand. This merely served to exacerbate congestion in the long run and maintain the conditions which had led to raids in the first place. The second important factor in this period was the existence of the ex-serviceman qualification, which stemmed from noble objectives but caused more problems than it solved. Until 1926 ex-servicemen were given preference by the Board of Agriculture; typically, they formed between half and three quarters of the demand for land in this period.[67] This was an additional emotional factor for the Board to conjure with, but they soon found that the ex-service qualification was the only one many of these applicants possessed.

Significant series of raids in the post war period took place on the Island of Lewis in the years from 1919 to 1923, at Balranald in North Uist in 1921, on Raasay in 1922, at Strathaird in Skye in 1923 and 1924, and in many other locations.[68]

VII

The incidents considered in this article took place in diverse political environments. The Park raid was a part of the crofters' agitation which had been continuing since 1882. Thus, in contrast to the other raids discussed here, political objectives were at the forefront. However, it took place when a Conservative government was in power, the approach of that government was to combine firm action to defeat lawlessness, with an information gathering exercise to aid the process of its eradication. These factors, combined with the political emasculation of the Crofters' movement, led to the end of major incidences of agitation until the early years of the twentieth century.

The Vatersay raids took place in a very complex political environment. The newly elected Liberal government encountered great opposition in attempting to pass a bill which was a nationwide application of the Crofters' Act of 1886. This fact clouded the negotiations between the CDB and the estate management over the island of Vatersay. However, what is important is that what was at the forefront of the raiders' minds was to gain possession of the land. It has been demonstrated that crofters were politically aware, but it is equally clear that in this period, as opposed to the 1880s, their motivations were not primarily political. This is but one aspect of the limited objectives of most land raiders. Despite this the cause of the Vatersay land raiders was taken up by the Independent Labour Party newspaper *Forward*. Its editor, Tom Johnstone, was a key figure in developing a rhetoric of anti-landlordism with which to challenge the Liberal party.[69]

The Scuddaburgh raid is difficult to interpret. It took place in the highly politicised period between the two general elections of 1910 and those involved were aware of the controversies surrounding Liberal Land legislation. Feelings were running high, as was demonstrated by the exceptional violence of the raiders in their act of deforcement. Importantly, Scuddaburgh was a raid carried out by crofters rather than cottars as in the cases of Park and Vatersay. This raid provides a link with the post war period, in that government intervention in the Highland land issue tended to increase and frustrate expectations. Nevertheless, what is striking are the limited stakes involved, in this case 63 acres of arable land.

It has been argued that land raids were 'not expressions of radicalism but demonstrations of loyalty to the orthodoxy established in 1886'.[70] It is noticeable that in a number of raids, that orthodoxy was threatened. Lady Gordon Cathcart was fundamentally opposed to the crofting system. Even the Congested Districts Board was conceived as a vehicle for the transformation of traditional crofting practice.

The limited objectives of the raiders can be contrasted with their determination to gain possession of the land which they coveted. This is clearly evident in raids which were motivated by extreme poverty, Vatersay and Raasay in particular. The raids may have presented a challenge to the authority of landowners but they did not present a challenge to their position. This is in clear contrast to the situation in Ireland after 1879, where land agitation and political nationalism were inextricably linked.[71] The agitation of the 1880s, culminating in the 'Plan of Campaign', was more proactive, self sustaining and politically motivated than the crofters' agitation in Scotland. The objective was the expropriation of the landowning classes and one of the results was a wholehearted embrace of the concept of land purchase. This had been conceded in 1885 and was steadily refined in the period down to 1909. In a later stage of the Irish Land War, the so called 'ranch war' from 1906 to 1910, the aims of those involved were also more radical. The ranching system and the associated eleven month tenure of land was being challenged. As well as the obvious tension between graziers and peasants due to the use of land which had been the site of evictions in the aftermath of the famine, there was tension due to the fact that many graziers were capitalists who had emerged from the peasant class.[72] Although the former source of tension existed in Scotland, the latter was not widespread, as most tenant farmers were recent arrivals from the Lowlands, or further afield. However, the instances where tenant farmers had emerged from the crofter class ensured particularly bitter proceedings. This was the case at Greenhill in Tiree in 1886 and at Northbay in Barra in 1900.[73]

Land Raids in the Highlands were far from straightforward expressions of political opposition to landlordism. They often created as much tension within crofting communities as they did between crofter and landlord. At a time when raids are being commemorated publicly for the first time it is imperative that historians explore these complexities to a greater extent than hitherto.[74]

NOTES

1 For the 1880s see J Hunter, *The Making of the Crofting Community*, (Edinburgh, 1976), Chaps 8–10; IMM MacPhail *The Crofters' War*, (Stornoway, 1989) I Fraser Grigor, *Mightier than a Lord*, (Stornoway, 1979); for the 1920s see; L Leneman, *Fit for Heroes: Land Settlement in Scotland After World War One*, (Aberdeen 1989); L Leneman, 'The Last Successful Scottish Land Raid', *Northern Scotland*, 10, (1990), pp. 73–76. Versions of this article were presented as seminar papers at the Open University History Society in Edinburgh and at the School of Scottish Studies in the University of Edinburgh. I am grateful to colleagues for their questions and comments on these occasions.

2 Hunter, *Crofting Community*, pp. 184–206, esp, pp. 188–95.

3 S[cottish] R[ecord] O[ffice], Crofting Files, AF 67/50, Police Report, Staffin, 6 June 1893.

4 For a detailed study of the CDB see EA Cameron, 'Public Policy in the Scottish Highlands: Governments, Politics and the Land Issue, 1886 to the 1920s' (unpublished PhD thesis, University of Glasgow, 1992) chaps 4–5; C Stewart, *Highland Experiment in Land Nationalisation*, (London, 1904).

5 For an exploration of the historical roots of these concepts see; AI Macinnes, 'Scottish Gaeldom: the first phase of Clearance', in TM Devine & R Mitchison (eds), *People and Society in Scotland, Volume I, 1760–1830*, (Edinburgh, 1988), p. 70; AI Macinnes, 'Crown, Clans and *Fine*: the 'Civilizing' of Scottish Gaeldom, 1587–1638', *Northern Scotland*, 13, (1993), pp. 31–2.

6 Hunter, *Crofting Community*, 192.

7 'Land Settlement in Scotland – I', *Scottish Journal of Agriculture*, 15, (1932), 245.

8 *The Highlander*, 25 April 1874; MacPhail, *Crofters' War*, pp. 12–17 & pp. 127–45; CWJ Withers, *Gaelic Scotland: The Transformation of a Culture Region*, (London, 1988), p. 367; Hunter, *Crofting Community*, p. 134.

9   Cameron, 'Public Policy', p. 49; EM MacArthur, *Iona: The Living Memory of a Crofting Community* (Edinburgh, 1990), p. 131.

10   MacPhail, *Crofters' War*, pp. 188–192.

11   W Orr, *Deer Forests, Crofts and Landlords*, (Edinburgh l982) pp. 19, 77, 136.

12   AF 67/35, Telegram, Lord Advocate to Secretary for Scotland, 22 November 1887.

13   SRO, AF 67/35, Lord Advocate to Secretary for Scotland, 25 November 1887; Orr, *Deer Forests*, pp. 137–38; D MacDonald, *Lewis: A History of the Island*, (Edinburgh, 1983 ed), cp. 174.

14   Cameron, 'Public Policy' 68 & Appendix No l; *Glasgow Herald*, 28 November 1887; *Inverness Courier*, 10 January 1888.

15   MacPhail, *Crofters' War*, p. 205; *Northern Chronicle*, 25 January 1888; *Glasgow Herald*, p. 18 January 1888.

16   Lord Shaw of Dunfermline, *Letters to Isabel*, (London, 1921) p. 60.

17   I Bradley, "Having and Holding': The Highland Land War of the 1880s', *History Today*, p. 37, (December 1987), pp. 23–27; Hunter, *Crofting Community*, pp. 172–3.

18   M Davitt, *The Fall of Feudalism in Ireland*, (London, 1921), p. 228, includes the following unsubstantiated and sardonic comment, 'the indignant sporting brewers and lords of Cockneydom were unaware of the fact that the guns which enabled the crofters to kill some venison for their own use were bought for them by the wicked Land League of Dublin'.

19   SRO, Lothian Muniments, GD 40/16/12/39–40, Charles Innes to Francis Sandford, 20 December 1887; SRO, AF 67/35, Sheriff Cheyne to Lord Lothian, 26 November 1887; this point also emerged at the trial of the raiders, *Scotsman*, 17 January 1888.

20   *Glasgow Herald*, 24 November 1887.

21   *Scottish Highlander*, 8 December 1887.

22   Cameron, 'Public Policy', Chaps 3 & 4.

23   *Report on the Condition of the Cottar Population of the Lews*, PP 1888 LXXX.

24   MacPhail, *Crofters' War*, p. 210; Hunter, *Crofting Community*, p. 177; the Park raid seems to have had an unsettling influence on some crofters in Skye who had renewed thoughts of agitation, but little came of these, see SRO, AF 67/95, P.C. John MacRae, Staffin to Chief Constable, Inverness, 14 January 1888.

25   Withers, *Gaelic Scotland*, pp. 373–76, 383; Cameron, 'Public Policy', pp. 81–2 & Appendix No 1.

26   SRO, AF 67/351, Report to the Secretary for Scotland by the Crofters' Commission on the social condition of the island of Uist as compared with 20 years ago, cxxv; MC Storrie, 'Two Early Resettlement Schemes in Barra', *Scottish Studies*, 6, (1962), pp. 71–83.

27   Cameron, 'Public Policy', pp. 111–12.

28   SRO, AF 42/1254, Negotiations to buy Potato Ground at Vatersay, May 1902; Cluny Castle MSS, Bundle 15, Skene Edwards and Garson, to Ranald MacDonald, 16 October 1902.

29   Cameron, 'Public Policy', p. 138; *Return of the Report of a Special Committee of the County Council of Inverness Upon Applications for Allotments in North Uist and Barra, made in September 1897, together with any relative papers.* PP 1908 96.

30 SRO, AF 67/130, Telegram for the Chief Constable, Inverness to the Scottish Office, 25 March 1902.

31 Cluny Castle MSS, Bundle 15, Skene, Edwards and Garson, to Lady Gordon Cathcart, 1 April 1902.

32 SRO, AF 67/130, Police Report, Barra, 28 October 1902; AF 42/1549, Memo on Vatersay by RR MacGregor, (Secretary to the CDB), 19 January 1903.

33 See, SRO, AF 42/2412; AF 67/132, Police Report, Barra, 27 February 1905; Telegram from Chief Constable, Inverness, 7 February 1905.

34 SRO, AF 67/132, Police Report by The Chief Constable, Inverness, 7 February 1906.

35 SRO, AF 67/132, Police Report, Barra, 15 February 1905.

36 SRO, AF 67/132, Telegram from Inspector Henderson, Lochmaddy, 23 February 1906; *Scotsman*, 8 February 1906.

37 EA Cameron, 'Politics, Ideology and The Highland Land Issue, 1886 to the 1920s', S[cottish] H[istorical] R[eview], 72, (1993) pp. 60–79; J Brown, 'Scottish and English Land Legislation, 1905 to 1911', *SHR*, 47, (1968) pp. 72–85; See Cluny Castle MSS, Bundles 17 & 22 and SRO, AF 42/717 & 742 for correspondence between Lady Gordon Cathcart and Lord Balfour of Burleigh.

38 Cameron, 'Public Policy', p. 135.

39 SRO, AF; 42/3129, Skene, Edwards and Garson, to the Secretary for Scotland, 14 March 1906; Minute by the Lord Advocate, 17 March 1906.

40 EA Cameron, 'The Political Influence of Highland Landowners: A Reassessment', *Northern Scotland*, 14 (1994) pp. 27–45, esp, p. 36; for a detailed examination of the politics of the Small Landholders (Scotland) Bill see Cameron, 'Public Policy', chap 6.

41 SRO, AF 42/3325, Skene Edwards and Carson to RR MacGregor, 27 June 1906; AF 42/3914, Reginald MacLeod to Sheriff John Wilson of Inverness-shire, 7 May 1907; AF 42/5318, Scottish Office Engineering Department to the CDB, 7 September 1908; this file contains remarkable photographic evidence of the huts constructed by the raiders.

42 *Parliamentary Debates*, 4th Series, Vol 179, Col 1894, 6 August 1907.

43 Cluny Castle MSS, Bundle 79, Skene Edwards and Garson to Ranald MacDonald, 16 March 1906.

44 *Return of the Correspondence between Lady Gordon Cathcart and the Secretary for Scotland and the Lord Advocate, with reference to the seizure and occupation of the Island of Vatersay*, PP 1908 [91], 35; Lady Gordon Cathcart was so keen to put her own case that she had the same correspondence privately printed with the addition of her own strident introduction. One copy can be found in the Skene, Edwards and Garson Papers, Edinburgh, Deed Box A8, Lady Gordon Cathcart No 3, Bundle 18.

45 Cameron, 'Public Policy', p. 144.

46 SRO, AF 42/6137, Donald Shaw to Reginald MacLeod, 30 April 1909.

47 SRO, AF 67/138, Police Report, Lochmaddy, 9 Feb 1909; AF 67/141, Police Reports, Barra, 4 & 10 March 1909.

48 SRO, AF 42/4127, Minute by the Under Secretary for Scotland, 24 & 25 April 1907; AF 42/5141, Statement By Lady Gordon Cathcart with reference to seizures of Land in Vatersay; *Scotsman*, 29 January 1908.

49 For a full discussion of these proceedings see; Cameron, 'Public Policy', pp. 129–137.

50 SRO, AF 42/7047, Heribusta Crofters to the CDB, 5 March 1910.

51 *Crofters Commission Annual Report, 1909–1910,* Appendix, 50; *CDB Annual Report 1910–1911,* vii; SRO, AF 42/7282, Scottish Office to Idrigill Crofters, 7 May 1910.

52 SRO, AF 42/7195, Idrigill Crofters to the CDB, 11 April 1910.

53 SRO, AF 42/7371, Angus MacKintosh to the CDB, 7 June 1910; Scottish Office to CDB, 8 June 1910.

54 Cameron, 'Public Policy', p. 117.

55 SRO, AF 42/7570, H Cook to RR MacGregor, 24 August 1910.

56 SRO, AF 42/7574, A MacKintosh to the CDB, 23 August 1910.

57 SRO, AF 42/7624, Resolution passed at a meeting in Idrigill, 6 September 1910.

58 I MacDonald, *A Family in Skye, 1908–1916,* (Stornoway, 1982), pp. 15, 64.

59 SRO, AF 42/7652, Minute by William MacKenzie, 27 September 1910.

60 SRO, AF 67/367, H Cook to the Under Secretary for Scotland, 4 May 1910.

61 SRO, AF 67/139, Petition from Kilmuir Crofters, 14 April 1908; for similar rhetoric see, AF 42/7624, Resolutions passed at a meeting in Idrigill, 6 September 1910.

62 SRO, AF 42/7829, Minute by Angus MacKintosh, 7 January 1911.

63 MacPhail, *Crofters' War,* 43; Hunter, *Crofting Community,* p. 136.

64 SRO, AF 67/61, Memo for the Secretary for Scotland, 4 December 1913; Colin MacDonald to John Sutherland, 20 December 1913; see also AF 67/62; *Scotsman,* 20 March & 2 April 1914.

65 For a full discussion of these points see, Cameron, 'Public Policy', Chap 8.

66 Cameron, 'Public Policy', pp. 237–8.

67 Cameron, 'Public Policy', pp. 215–6.

68 See, Leneman, *Fit for Heroes,* pp. 113–15, 119–25, 133–36, 137–41; Hunter, *Crofting Community,* pp. 196–206; Cameron, 'Public Policy', chapter 8; IJM Robertson, 'The Historical Geography of Social Protest in Highland Scotland, 1914–c1939', (unpublished PhD thesis), University of Bristol, 1995.

69 *Forward,* 8 February 1908, 22 February 1908, 11 July 1908 & 23 April 1910.

70 Cameron, 'Politics Ideology and the Highland Land Issue', p. 79.

71 These issues have been explored explicitly by J Hunter, 'The Gaelic Connection: The Highlands, Ireland and Nationalism, 1873–1922', *SHR,* 54, (1975), pp. 178–204; CWJ Withers, 'Rural protest in the Highlands of Scotland and in Ireland, 1850–1930', in SJ Connolly, RA Houston & RJ Morris (eds), *Conflict, Identity and Economic Development: Ireland and Scotland, 1600–1939,* (Preston, 1995) pp. 172–188.

72 For the Plan of Campaign see; FSL Lyons, *John Dillon,* (London, 1968) pp. 82–110; S Warwick-Haller, *William O'Brien and the Irish Land War,* (Dublin, 1990) pp. 81–158; for the implementation of land purchase see A Gailey, *Ireland and the Death of Kindness: The Experience of Constructive Unionism,* (Cork, 1987); P Bew, *Conflict and Conciliation in Ireland, 1890–1910,* (Oxford, 1987); for the 'ranch war' see; DS Jones, 'The Cleavage between graziers and peasants in the land struggle, 1890–1910', in SJ Clarke & SJ Donnelly, *Irish Peasants: Violence and Political Unrest, 1780–1914,* (Dublin, 1988) pp. 374–417.

73 MacPhail, *Crofters' War,* pp. 199–201; Inveraray Castle MSS, Hugh MacDiarmid (Tiree Factor) to the Duke of Argyll, 14 & 17 June 1886; Cameron, 'Public Policy', p. 111.

74 CWJ Withers, 'Place, Memory, Monument: Memorializing the Past in Contemporary Highland Scotland', *Ecumene,* 3 (1996), pp. 325–344.

Concentration and Fragmentation: Capital, Labor, and the Structure of Mid-Victorian Scottish Industry

Richard Rodger 1988 *Journal of Urban History* 14 (ii), 178–213.

In an effort to convey the essence of dynamic growth and technological development, and not least in an endeavour to retain readers' interest, surveys of Scottish industry have concentrated on the spectacular story line. An educated business elite, a reservoir of merchant capital, overseas contacts, and advantageous factor endowments were the ingredients from which nineteenth-century Scottish industrialization emerged with textiles, iron and steel, and ultimately heavy engineering successively transmitting the growth impulse, the whole process lagging the modernization of English industry by at least a generation.[1] Consequently, the blue-ribbon companies have formed the skeleton of the customary accounts of Scottish industrialization and the potential for productivity gains among the smaller entrepreneurial fraternity has rarely been acknowledged. Entire industries have become synonymous with the names of the principal entrepreneurs and their firms, as for example with the Baxters and Coxes of Dundee linen and jute fame; Tennant in chemicals; Neilson, Baird, Dixon, and Colville in iron and steel; and the magnates of shipbuilding whose names even now are closely identified with Clydeside – Denny, Beardmore, Elder and Thomson to name a few. Conceivably, more is known about the business community as a whole in seventeenth- and eighteenth-century Scotland[2] than in the nineteenth century, where the preoccupation with the vanguard of Scottish Victorian businesses has consigned the wider industrial, and thus workplace and social, experience to historical oblivion.

The early historiography of Scottish industrialization stressed a two-phase sectoral advance.[3] For example, Hamilton in an attempt to chart the course of industrial expansion established 1830 as a pivotal point in the course of economic modernization. The conventional view was that from about 1780 to 1830 the engine of growth was the cotton industry, itself the progeny of an established eighteenth-century linen industry.[4] Steam-powered cotton mills, mainly concentrated in the west of Scotland, carried the momentum of Scottish growth from about 1800, while simultaneously the previously dominant linen industry was in decline, as was the cottage-based spinning and weaving of flax, wool and cotton.[5] While textiles gave a new impetus to the chemicals industry, the iron founding and engineering sector initiated a second industrial front from 1830. For the textile industry, cast and wrought iron components, engines, gearing, casings and shaftings were required; and the metal-working interests responded with vigor to continue the momentum of industrialization. By the 1880s the iron and steel sector had matched and surpassed the contribution of textiles to Scottish industrial performance. To the expanding engineering interests in textile machinery was added locomotive construction in the 1850s, and with the adoption of screw propellers in the 1840s and iron-hulled ships in the 1860s, further engineering diversification was nourished by the marine and shipbuilding sectors. By 1871 the Clyde launched 48 percent of British shipping tonnage and was to continue that national and world leadership until the First World War. Accounts of Scottish industrialization then traditionally turned attention to other industrial developments – the crescendo of mid-Victorian jute expansion centered on Dundee, the revitalization of the late-Victorian Aberdeen economy on the basis of fishing and fish processing, linoleum in Kirkcaldy, woolens in the Border towns and the consumption and service industries in white-collar-dominated Edinburgh. Factor endowments, conspicuously iron and coal deposits, it should be said, were not overlooked and it was these that contributed significantly to the urban concentrations that eventually became Motherwell, Coatbridge, Airdrie, and a host of smaller towns in the central lowlands. But the effect of attributing a principal product to, and identifying a particular industry with, a specific urban location skewed the perception of economic progress, elevated the major industries, pinpointed the spectacular achievements of the west of Scotland, and relegated other industries to inferior positions. By the 1960s, and in contradistinction to the emphasis attached by Rostow to the impact of leading sectors, Hamilton himself, Campbell, Smout, and others, in reexamining the process of industrialization, preferred to stress the more gradual and integrated nature of Scottish economic development, this evolutionary emphasis being given further support from the likelihood that, until the 1820s at least, agriculture remained the principal contributor to Scottish national income.[6]

While the simplicity of the sectoral advance approach has been rejected in favor of a more balanced growth model, the logical outcome, the interconnectedness and mutual dependence of Scottish industry, has remained largely confined to accounts of eighteenth-century mercantile and industrial complementarity – smelting-boiling interests in sugar, glass, brewing, iron, soap, and other chemicals – each with its dependence on coal. Most accounts have steadfastly refused to acknowledge what the censuses emphatically record, a nineteenth-century occupational diversity that underscored the contribution of the industrial leviathans. Still the textbook index references to earthenware, brick making, nonferrous metalworking, woodworking, paper products, and food processing – to mention only a few – are rarities; yet their resilience in the urban occupational structure cannot be denied. Wage and employment experiences in these less flamboyant industries were at variance with the major manufacturing concerns, and for this reason alone, though also because they formed a significant element of demand for urban goods and services, these less-noted industries deserve attention.

Behind this textbook perspective of the pinnacles of urban and industrial expansion with their presumed inevitability and desirability are the precepts of classical economic theory to which the historiography of Scottish economic development has in large measure subscribed. Increasing productivity and specialization linked through machines, and the reorganization of production into larger units, which themselves incorporated related stages of production, meant that the logical extension of the division of labor was ever more automated plants.[7] Certainly there were some mighty early nineteenth-century industrial complexes. Compared with their antecedents, the work force and scale of plant must have assumed almighty proportions. Yet the notion, often promoted in such florid phrases as the 'power and intoxication of new industrial possibilities,'[8] that productivity increases and technological frontiersmanship took place only in the predominant firms is on theoretical, empirical, and historical grounds doubtful. Indeed, one of the consequences of heavy capitalization was technological rigidity, a vested interest in preventing alternative production systems because of the substantial capital commitment to a given mode of production.[9] To this end the industrial giants arguably geared their own research and developments along preconceived principles, stifled alternative lines of development, quashed rivals by takeover or attrition. That efficiency and the onward march of economic progress were synonymous with the increasing concentration of nineteenth-century industry remained axiomatic in optimistic textbook accounts of Scottish industrialization. That some sectors remained stubbornly small scale was viewed, when considered, as economic dualism – the sluggish vestige of pre-industrial urban structure, and a counterpoint to the dynamic, technologically conscious and large-scale business concentrations of the modern wing of Scottish industry. Whether medium- and small-scale interests could themselves contribute to the modern sector or sustain their own momentum was never conceived, for the potential productivity gains among this smaller industrial brotherhood – though evident in the longevity of consumer goods and service-based firms, among others – was never systematically considered.[10] Focused on convenient and conspicuous industrial pinnacles, simplistic explanations of Scottish development depended on a comfortable linearity, a historical determinism that stressed the seemingly inexorable transmission of the growth impulse without pausing to notice that between the industrial summits was a series of lesser peaks and connecting ridges that provided the means of access to the heights of industrial performance.

For economic historians the year 1851 has long been associated with a high watermark in the Victorian economy. However, even greater fascination with the years surrounding 1850 has been exhibited by labor historians since the Webbs's contention that this marked a 'watershed' in trade union history and, more recently, with inquiries into whether there was any substantive shift from the working-class radicalism and the Chartism of the 1830s and 1840s to the more conciliatory, collaborative stance after 1850.[11] The role of the 'aristocracy of labour' in this appeasement of class antagonisms has been of central significance.[12] My study examines the numerical importance, vitality, and persistence of small-scale business reliant on skilled artisanal production in mid-Victorian urban Scotland and considers that the occupational experience of significant numbers of workers was by 1851 quiescent and remained so in immediately succeeding decades. As the symbiosis of industrialisation and urbanisation perhaps sustained as much as it smothered labor-intensive skilled handicraft production, long since acknowledged in the textile industry and an obstinate survivor in a wide array of productive spheres considered in this study, a distinctive labor identity was dependent more on residential, church, or cultural affinity than on occupational association.[13]

The attempt here is to draw on a unique survey of employers in an effort first, to demonstrate in mid-Victorian Scotland the coexistence of small firms with their larger brethren; second, to evaluate the degree of concentration of production in Scottish industry and thus of the typicality of the factory as the common workplace experience, and, third, by examining a broad range of manufacturing areas, ultimately to reassert a view of economic dualism, modernity versus traditionalism, in which labor organisation and identity could both prosper and stagnate.

Technical sophistication and the attendant escalation of capital investment requirements were powerful forces in the long-run trend toward larger nineteenth-century firms in Scottish industry, as elsewhere, and so the impetus to cultural solidarity offered by factory-based production was also present in Scotland. But two factors served to reinforce the dependence of Scottish industry on labor rather than capital inputs and consequently on a smaller firm size. First, Scottish real wage levels were lower than in comparable English trades. Indeed, according to Campbell, Scottish industrialization was itself based on 'a low wage economy'.[14] With advanced product and market development already established by English industrial concerns, how else could Scottish industry secure a toehold in either domestic or international markets? Where they were available, cheap raw material supplies were a help, but even as late as 1886 Scottish cotton-workers' wages were only 78 percent of their English counterparts, a position rendered all the more unfavourable by higher price and rent levels operative in Scottish burghs.[15] In woolens (89 percent), worsteds (68 percent), and hemp (94 percent), Scots obtained wages appreciably lower than those of exactly equivalent workers in English industry. Though parity existed in certain metal-working trades, across twenty-seven principal industrial classifications in 1886, Scottish wages averaged only 94.8 percent of English wages.[16] Two exhaustive board of trade studies in the Edwardian period, and a recent examination of comparative real-wage income levels in the 1919–1939 period, confirm the enduring, if narrowing, disadvantage of Scottish urban pay.[17] Earlier in the century the differential had been much greater. In the 1870s it had already narrowed to 10 percent to 15 percent, and in building it had been as wide as 25 percent in the 1830s and 1840s.[18] Although the evidence is of a more fragmentary nature, the pattern of gradual erosion in the Scottish wage disadvantage, commencing in the 1850s and 1860s and accelerating thereafter, while remaining in an inferior position to English wage levels before 1914, was borne out among numerous specific occupations in textiles, iron founding, shipbuilding, boiler making, mining, and engineering.[19] Labour- and capital-intensive production structures in Britain and America, Habakkuk has argued, reflected relative abundance, and thus costs, of these factors.[20] Habakkuk's analysis rests ultimately on marginal rates of factor substitution, that is, on employers' preference schedules for additional labor and capital inputs. In British industry the rationality of labor-intensive production has been vindicated in detail in cotton and coal mining for the post-1870 years,[21] and by extension the reliance of other industries on additional labor rather than capital inputs has subsequently been justified.[22] This emphasis on labor intensity was the more pronounced in Scottish industry due to the enduring availability of labor at rates below those operating nationally. The understandable business response, to employ more labor rather than capital, generated short- and medium-term benefits; long-term structural damage, the misalignment of the twentieth-century Scottish economy, and the 'retardation' of the industrial sector with its heavy reliance in Scotland on the staple industries, was the price for cheap, abundant labor in the nineteenth century.[23]

The second influence on the structure of Scottish firms was the legal frame-work within which they operated. It was not, according to Campbell, incor-poration itself that conveyed particular rights to Scottish business but 'the more tolerant and liberal attitude adopted by the law in Scotland toward unincorpo-rated concerns'[24] The attitudes of the courts – combined with a robust law of partnership that conveyed the right to sue, transfer shares, and elementary limited liability – had been significant influences encouraging the expansion of unincorporated joint stock companies since the late eighteenth century in Scotland. Arguably, then, the law of partnership and its interpretation in the Scottish courts was conducive to the formation of small enterprises. At the other end of the business spectrum, Payne's intriguing observation[25] that when the Limited Liability Act was rendered applicable to Scotland in 1856, the initial size of Scottish firms seeking such status, as reflected in their paid-up capital, was larger than in London suggests an already established concentration of large companies and an early dualism in the Scottish industrial structure.

To what extent were these underlying forces for a small-scale labor-intensive mode of industrial production borne out in mid-Victorian Scotland? A unique survey of urban employers in 1851,[26] together with the number of employees engaged by them, provides a clear indication of the overwhelmingly modest business scale in mid-Victorian Scotland. The survey covered nine principal burghs – Aberdeen, Dundee, Edinburgh, Glasgow, Greenock, Inverness, Leith, Paisley and Perth. Though the survey was also conducted in England and Wales, it is not comparable with Scottish data because, London excepted, the admin-istrative unit of data collection was the county and consequently it failed to distinguish between urban and rural areas. In Scotland, the town or burgh was the basis of recording data.[27] The census schedule required 'masters and employ-ers of workpeople to describe themselves as such and to state the number of hands in their employ.'[28] The survey covered manufacturing principally, though transport and distribution, wholesaling, and retailing were also represented. Excluded were professional employment, government and local officeholders, the armed forces, dealers, domestic servants, agriculture, and related employ-ment. The number of employers in the nine burghs who replied was 9,126, though 3,182 (35 percent) did not specify how many workers they employed. As there was no appropriate category it is probable that a large proportion of these 3,182 employers were in fact self-employed, more particularly as it was among shoemakers, tailors, watchmakers, and especially among retailers where the scale of business operations could most easily be conducted by one person that the returns of unspecified numbers of employees was most heavily concentrated. The 5,994 employers who stated the size of their work force engaged 92,656 hands, of whom 17,306 or 19 percent were women and children. (Some 80 percent of female labor was in textiles and 8 percent in retailing). If the unspecified employers were all self-employed,[29] the addition of a further 3,182 workers would bring the numbers included in the survey to 95,838. The study covered 33 percent of the occupied male work force of the nine principal burghs and accounted for 37 percent of males involved in manufacturing, transport, and trading. Because the schedules applied only to householders and omitted employers who leased property, because the survey neglected a sizeable casual element in the work force estimated at 20 percent to 25 percent of all male workers at the end of the century and not regarded as part of the employers' regular work force,[30] and also because not all of the many employers who failed to specify the numbers in their employ were self-employed, it is impossible to account for the workers not included in this survey. Even so, some 6,000 employers of almost 100,000 employees represents a significant sample by any standards.

Even overlooking the absence of a self-employed category, the overwhelming conclusion of Table 1 is of the small firm as the dominant business unit. Firms employing just one or two workers (column [2]) were the most common form of business organisation; 30 percent of all firms (column [3]) were of this type. Half the firms in mid-Victorian Scottish industry employed four or fewer workers; more than two-thirds of businesses employed seven or fewer workers and three in every four firms engaged fewer than nine workers. Only 10 percent of Scottish businesses engaged more than twenty workers. The frequency of the small firms as the typical unit of production calls into question any need for the vast majority of mid-Victorian employers to 'counter-attack against trade unions and government interference' as suggested by Yarmie.[31] Given the prevalence of firms with a handful of workers, the cooperative, interdependent workplace relationship between employer and employee was more akin to the traditional and paternalistic master and servant roles than to confrontational industrial relations. In a number of occupations, for example in cabinetmaking, saddlery, glove, and dressmaking, but also in soap and tallow manufacturing, nonferrous metalworking, and even textiles, employers participated as workers in an integrated unit of production, while preserving their ultimate entrepreneurial role. Such businesses were unaffected by government factory legislation.[32] Regulation of the workplace was, for most of the century, immaterial outside textile factories, inapplicable in the main workshops, and irrelevant to work forces that employed men only or numbered fewer than fifty. This is not to say that friction did not occur in smaller business units; the recurrent strikes and lockouts, for example, in the building industry bear ample testimony to disagreements.[33] But the notion of endemic class confrontation based on workplace conflict is misleading in the case of a majority of business units.[34] Moreover, as approximately 30 percent of male employment in the Scottish cities between 1841 and 1911 was in nonindustrial areas where professional, domestic, artistic, teaching, administrative, and an element of commercial occupations were conventionally discharged on an individualistic or small group basis,[35] none of them with a record for strike action or even modest unionization, the level of employer-employee harmony or acquiescence exposes the limitation of the workplace experience as a springboard for class action. More valid would be explanations of cultural solidarity based on the place of residence or worship of the type advance by Thompson.[36] Tenement dwelling produced a density of housing and overcrowding unrivaled elsewhere in Britain.[37] Similar consumption, leisure, and wider behavioral patterns – including cultural and political values based on a peculiarly Scottish residential concentration – may well have been more important in a way that the workplace experience, by its very fractured nature and close associations with the employers, was not.

TABLE I: STRUCTURE OF SCOTTISH INDUSTRY: PRINCIPAL BURGHS 1851[a]

NUMBER IN WORKFORCE	EMPLOYERS			EMPLOYEES		
	NUMBER	%	CUMULATIVE FREQUENCY	NUMBER	%	CUMULATIVE FREQUENCY
	(1)	(2)	(3)	(4)	(5)	(6)
1	730	15.0	15.0	730	0.8	0.8
2	727	14.9	29.9	1454	1.6	2.5
3	524	10.8	40.7	1572	1.8	4.2
4	487	10.0	50.6	1948	2.2	6.4
5	293	6.0	56.7	1465	1.7	8.1
6	330	6.8	63.4	1980	2.2	10.3
7	133	2.7	66.2	931	1.1	11.4
8	186	3.8	70.0	1488	1.7	13.1
9	137	2.8	72.8	1233	1.4	14.5
10–19	611	12.5	85.3	8860	10.0	24.5
20–29	226	4.6	90.0	5537	6.2	30.7
30–39	119	2.4	92.4	4105	4.6	35.3
40–49	69	1.4	93.8	3071	3.5	38.8
50–74	98	2.0	95.8	6125	6.9	45.7
75–99	48	1.0	96.8	4200	4.7	50.4
100–149	62	1.3	98.1	7750	8.7	59.2
150–199	26	0.5	98.6	4550	5.1	64.3
200–249	15	0.3	98.9	3375	3.8	68.1
250–299	9	0.2	99.1	2475	2.8	70.9
300–349	8	0.2	99.3	2600	2.9	73.9
350+	35	0.7	100.0	23154	26.1	100.0
Totals	4873	100.0	100.0	88603	100.0	100.0

Source: P.P. 1852–53 LXXXVIII (2), 1022–1024.
a. Retailing, professional and service activities recorded in the census have been removed.

The modest scale of the typical Scottish firm was counter-balanced by some sizable undertakings (Table 2). The largest thirty-five firms in 1851 employed 23,154 workers, equivalent to 25 percent of the industrial and related occupations covered by the survey of employers, and alone accounting for 3 percent of total employment in the nine burghs concerned. The mean work force size in this group of major firms was 662 and, as shown in Table 2, by sector textiles was the most conspicuous. Two-thirds (twenty-four) of the thirty-five largest firms were in textiles though among the largest 300 businesses this dominance was reduced to only 31 percent. Among these largest employers the subdivison of the stages of production and the combination of several interests under the control of one employer frequently produced a dispersion of the work force within the urban area. In reality some larger firms were themselves a series of workshops, with the emergence of foremen and supervisors a recognition of the independence of production units and of the need to develop an embryonic management structure to cope with the integration of the component parts of these large firms. Age, status and skill levels, and gender – 80 percent of women in industrial work were in textiles – all drove additional wedges between elements of the work force, so that numbers alone were no guarantee of employee solidarity.[38]

TABLE 2: THE THIRTY-FIVE LARGEST SCOTTISH FIRMS 1851

RANK	SECTOR	NUMBER OF EMPLOYEES	RANK	SECTOR	NUMBER OF EMPLOYEES
1	IRON	1600	19	COTTON	520
2	MUSLIN	1300	20	COTTON	500
3	FLAX, LINEN	1200	21	SHIPBUILDING	454
4	WOOLLEN CLOTH	1100	22	ENGINEERING	450
5)	SILK	1000	23	SHIPBUILDING	447
6)	COTTON	1000	24	SILK	422
7)	FISH CURING	1000	25	EARTHENWARE	420
8 ·	COTTON	900	26	CARPETS	400
9	IRON	850	27)	COTTON	400
10)	COTTON	800	28)	COTTON	400
11)	SHAWL	800	29)	COTTON	400
12	SILK	786	30)	COTTON	400
13)	ENGINEERING	700	31)	COAL	400
14)	ENGINEERING	700	32	COTTON	395
15	COTTON	640	33)	COTTON	360
16	COTTON	600	34)	IRON	360
17)	COTTON	550	35	MUSLIN	350
18)	COTTON	550			
				TOTAL	23154
				MEAN WORKFORCE SIZE	661.5

Source: P.P. 1852–53 LXXXVIII (2), 1022–1023.

Thus industrial dualism in the Scottish economy was present at an early juncture. Approximately 90 percent of firms employed fewer than twenty workers; yet 1 percent of employers hired more than a quarter of the work force. The workshop mode of production, based on traditional work relations and mainly dependent on labor-intensive production with modest conversions to powered machinery, formed the potential entrepreneurial and technological seedbed for expansion in the industrial interstices left by the business giants. Yet it proved only modestly fertile. At a very early state, abundant, cheap Scottish labor facilitated the continuation of both small-scale producers and labor-intensive large-scale manufacturing; and while low-cost labor was desirable in the initial phase of industrialization, it contributed to the fossilization of the production structure even as early as 1851. Recent support for this interpretation is also available from the history of Scottish education. The generalist qualities of the Scottish curriculum, so conducive to the basic technological advances of the eighteenth and early nineteenth centuries, were by the second half of the nineteenth century regarded as 'irrelevant to modern problems and developments.'[39] As a consequence the inappropriateness of education instruction failed to allow the narrow Scottish industrial base at midcentury to diversify and respond to accelerating technological complexity. As 'science teaching in schools in Scotland . . . [was] deplorable,'[40] a criticism from which English education was not exempt either, it constricted the base for industrial expansion, though an already established mid-Victorian supremacy in mechanical engineering was an offsetting influence. But cheap labor reduced the willingness to shatter the mold of early nineteenth century growth by inhibiting the level of capital investment consistent with a more sophisticated, scientific approach.[41] Long-term capital investment in chemicals, electrical engineering, and alloys, for example, with their wide-ranging industrial and commercial applications, was impeded as early as the 1840s by the negative effects of cheap labor that had proved so decisive to early mechanization in textiles, transportation, and metallurgy.

Hence Tables 1 and 2 show early dualism of Scottish businesses. At a very early stage, in fact by 1851, Scottish firms were already distributed around the twin poles of a fragmented, traditional workshop mode of production or, alternatively, heavily concentrated on factory production based on labor-intensive unskilled and semiskilled manual inputs. Even in the 'modern' branches of the economy, large-scale enterprises coexisted with a proliferation of small-scale producers. The middle range of business organization – firms with twenty to fifty workers capable of developing a future base for industrial development – formed only 8 percent of Scottish firms, and almost half of these were in the building and woodworking, textile and clothing sectors, hardly the harbingers of high technology. Neither committed to a particular production technology nor reliant solely on handicraft skills as in the smallest workshops, the adaptability of this middle stratum of business activity, it has been claimed,[42] was crucial to sustaining new industrial ideas with commercial prospects upon which the momentum of the economy could be maintained. Though comparative data for England or elsewhere are lacking, that only 8 percent of Scottish firms came within this scale of operations may well have had a seriously prejudicial effect on later nineteenth-century economic growth.

The relative number and frequency of employers in the Scottish burghs suggest a number of hitherto unexplored lines of inquiry. First, for example, in retailing, grocers and bakers were equally numerous in the nine burghs, but by comparison, butchers (42 percent), dairies (33 percent), confectioners (20 percent), greengrocers (8 percent), and tobacconists (4 percent) were much less common and their relative occurrence was itself an indication of urban consumption patterns. Second, though retail outlets were predictably most numerous, the variation in the numbers of employers in the branches of industrial production merits further analysis to illuminate the structure of the urban economy. The percentages of firms in printing and publishing (Table 3) was greater than in iron manufacturing, an indication of the importance of the written word, handbills, and the book trade in Victorian society as articles of information, communication, and consumption. There were as many goldsmiths as woolen manufacturers: watchmakers outnumbered nonferrous metal manufacturers. There were fifty-three iron manufacturers within the nine principal Scottish burghs; yet general economic histories of the period make almost no mention of this urban phenomenon concentrating as they do on the more isolated and visible ironworks found in Lanarkshire.[43] Even excepting nailers, cutlers, and blacksmiths, understandably more numerous in urban centers, other metal-working employers based on brass, lead, copper, and tin were virtually as numerous as woolen manufacturers and not so far behind the dyeing, bleaching, and scouring firms so vital to the principal employment sectors of textiles. There were more shoemakers than any other category of employer in 1851, and twice as many cabinetmaking as engineering and toolmaking firms. Indeed the entire area of woodworking affirmed the resilience of this traditional material from the onslaught of metal manufacturing. Clearly the substitution of iron for wood was far from universal or as instantaneous as the accounts of dramatic technological breakthrough in metallurgy might suggest. If this was the case in the principal urban areas, how much more did it apply to the lesser burghs where still lower wages prevailed? In fact the structure of businesses as revealed by the 1851 survey was consistent with the extended retention of generalist economic functions in each burgh. Shoemaking, cabinetmaking, metal working, and a range of service industries were common denominators and remained so, while relatively low wages nurtured the continuation of handicraft production and transport costs canceled out the cost-reducing potential of specialist machine production. The vigorous survival of pre-industrial economic functions and occupational divisions into the machine age is in itself a revealing aspect of this survey of employers.

Third, some indication of the basic business structure of the Scottish urban economy is provided in Tables 3 and 4 by means of both the relative and proportionate number of entrepreneurs in the industrial subdivisons. For example, toolmakers, whom Saul has identified as a vital ingredient in the development of a broad front of engineering opportunities in the second half of the nineteenth century,[44] were equivalent to only one-third of the number of mechanical engineers in the nine Scottish burghs. In 1851 there were only seven firms identifying themselves as civil engineers, though no doubt a few of the builders assumed such constructional activities and there were seven firms of contractors too. There were, however, only one stocking manufacturer and three glovers recorded in the survey of employers; yet just seven years earlier a survey of the hosiery trade identified 150 frames in Edinburgh and 108 in Perth, with 280 in Glasgow and Kilmarnock combined.[45] This suggests a rapid decline by any standards. Had Hawick, Dumfries, and other border centers suffered similarly, had they subverted the trade of the central belt, or had English east midlands producers usurped the position of Scots manufacturers in this area? In a similar vein, the 1851 survey identified thirteen earthenware and eleven glass manufacturers in the principal Scottish burghs. A high degree of business concentration in the nine burghs and the continuity of productive units would not be unreasonable conclusions. Nor was the number of bankrupts in this sector likely to be high, particularly as the level of exports through Scottish ports in this sixteen-year period increased substantially.[46] Did exports in glass and earthenware, valued together in 1876 at 0.25 million, point to Scottish self-sufficiency in these products? What was the extent of cross-border traffic and dependence on imports from Staffordshire and Lancashire?[47] Though not specifically addressing such issues, the statistical analysis of the distribution of employers suggests a number of previously unasked questions about the precise characteristics of urban economic structure.

Fourth, the dependence on and change over time of casual labor deserves attention. The continuing Victorian dependence on animate rather than mechanical power was reflected in the transport sector, where haulage, carting, coach, and cab firms provided entrepreneurial roles for 143 persons. Indeed, the fact that the average size of these concerns was just 9.4 men, and that only 23 percent of those occupied in road transport in the nine burghs were engaged by these 143 firms, indicates a previously unsuspected scale of casual employment in portering, carting and haulage.[48] Certainly it was far more extensive than at the end of the nineteenth century and further research on this basis might reveal a greater degree of irregular work in the mid-Victorian urban economy and a declining incidence over time.

Finally, the data on employers provides an interesting panorama on the urban elite in Victorian society. As individuals described themselves as entrepreneurs, the 1851 survey permits an analysis of the manufacturing and commercial group that accounted for 4.8 percent of adult males in the nine burghs. The diversity of small manufacturing and shop-owning interests, overwhelming more important numerically than the industrial magnates, was evident with retailing, shoemaking, and the clothing trades providing 44 percent of the representatives of employers in the nine burghs. Though by no means immune to the fortunes and favors of local industrial magnates, the influence of shop owners and small businessmen as electors, taxpayers, and officeholders could not be lightly disregarded, and they were disproportionately represented in the council chamber.[49] It is therefore possible to identify the sectoral compositon (Table 3) and quantify the significance of these entrepreneurial groups who provided the urban economic base as well as largely determining urban morphology 'being the dominant claimants for sites.'[50] In a modest fashion this adds a further dimension to the composition of urban politics and power. No doubt the values of these 'fit and proper persons' in local government owed a considerable amount to the economism, small scale, and limited horizons of the shopkeepers whose careful accounting, tight margins and personal involvement overflowed in their approach to council business.[51]

Attention has so far been focused on the structure of Scottish businesses and the typical size of firms. For employees the experience in 1851 was rather different (Table 1, columns [4]-[6]). According to the survey of employers in 1851, approximately one-quarter of the industrial labor force was engaged in firms of fewer than twenty workers, another one-quarter in firms with twenty to 100 workers, another quarter in workplaces with 100 to 350 employees, and a final 25 percent in firms with more than 350 employees. Hence as early as 1851 the employment experience of half the Scottish manufacturing work force was concentrated in concerns of more than 100 workers. Even allowing for the physical separation and logistical subdivisions of the productive process, and for the areas of nonindustrial employment that predominantly engaged labor in small-scale activities, for significant numbers of Scots the workplace experience by 1851 was the factory. Outside textiles, however, where the logic of subdividing the production process and subjecting each stage successively to some degree of automated production was not extensively developed, the degree of concentration in plants with 100 or more workers should not be overstated.

TABLE 3: SCOTTISH MANUFACTURING EMPLOYERS 1851[a]

	%		%
SHOEMAKER	12.41	SILK	1.33
TAILOR	8.64	BRASS, COPPER, LEAD	1.32
MISCELLANEOUS[b]	5.93	PLASTERER	1.18
FOOD PROCESSING	5.16	COAL MERCHANT	1.18
CARPENTERS, JOINERS	5.02	ENGRAVER	1.07
CABINET MAKER	4.73	SLATER	1.06
COTTON	4.09	COOPER	1.03
PAINTING, PLUMBING, GLAZING	3.99	BRUSH, BROOM MAKER	1.00
BLACKSMITH	3.15	TINPLATE	0.93
IRON	2.50	HAIRDRESSER	0.89
ENGINEERING TOOLMAKING	2.43	STATIONER	0.78
TRANSPORT	2.17	EARTHENWARE, GLASS	0.76
HOSIER, GLOVER, HABERDASHER	2.08	WHEELWRIGHT, MILLWRIGHT	0.72
BUILDER	1.92	DRUGGIST	0.68
LEATHER	1.82	PROFESSIONAL[c]	0.68
DYER, SCOURER	1.81	BREWER	0.65
WOOLLENS	1.53	SHIPBUILDING	0.60
DRAPER	1.50	ROPEMAKER	0.57
PRINTER	1.50	COACHMAKING	0.53
WATCHMAKER	1.47	BRICKMAKER, QUARRIER	0.53
GOLDSMITH	1.46	FLAX, LINEN	0.51
PUBLISHER	1.42	SOAP, TALLOW	0.50
CORK, WOODWORKING	1.40	CHIMNEY SWEEP	0.49
MASON	1.38	BRICKLAYER	0.36

Source: P.P. 1852–53 LXXXVIII (2), 10–22–1024.
a Based on 7,195 employers in nine principal burghs.
b Includes comb, matress, chandlery, musical instruments, oil, miscellaneous mineral and vegetable production.
c Includes dentists, architects, veterinary surgeons.

Only 25 percent of employees in firms with 350 or more workers were in nontextile plants; only 45 percent and 52 percent of employees in firms with 100–plus and 50–plus workers, respectively, were engaged in nontextile plants.[52] Specialization, automation, and concentration had not been so widely diffused through industry by 1851. While only 39 percent of the manufacturing labor force came within the factory inspectorate's definition of a workshop, that is fewer than fifty employees, 94 percent of firms did so; consequently no more than 6 percent of firms in 1851, nearer 2 percent given the exclusion afforded to certain manufacturing sectors, were subject to monitoring under the Factory Acts. Among women, few outside textiles were employed in factories, and even those who were represented a small proportion of the industrial work force – and an even smaller percentage of the overall female work force in view of the numbers in domestic service.

TABLE 4: STRUCTURE OF SCOTTISH INDUSTRY 1851: NUMBER OF EMPLOYEES

BUSINESS SECTOR	1-4		5-9		10-19		20-49	
	(1)	(2)	(1)	(2)	(1)	(2)	(1)	(2)
Iron	1.8	33.6	2.0	15.6	6.2	20.5	9.6	13.9
Blacksmith	27.5	71.5	18.3	16.9	22.9	8.7	8.8	1.7
Brass, copper, lead	2.9	31.2	4.8	19.5	11.2	20.8	19.8	16.9
Tinplate	23.6	63.6	19.6	18.2	31.1	12.7	25.6	5.5
Goldsmith	21.8	55.4	36.2	31.3	29.0	10.8	13.1	2.4
Earthenware, glass	1.9	25.8	4.8	25.8	5.2	12.9	15.8	19.4
Brickmaker, quarrier	0.2	3.0	3.4	18.2	7.6	21.2	26.1	33.3
Coal merchant	2.8	55.0	2.8	20.0	–	–	2.9	5.0
Builder	0.8	10.6	3.5	18.7	7.2	18.7	23.9	29.3
Carpenter, joiner	15.5	53.5	20.1	24.8	23.7	13.2	28.4	7.6
Painter, plumber, glazier	4.6	52.5	19.0	25.6	23.9	14.5	18.4	4.5
Mason	3.9	34.2	7.5	21.1	14.4	19.7	16.3	10.5
Slater	14.4	40.9	39.6	43.9	22.8	10.6	23.3	4.5
Bricklayer	19.4	66.7	14.1	16.7	14.1	8.3	21.8	4.2
Plasterer	10.6	39.0	21.7	28.6	37.5	23.4	21.1	7.8
Timber merchant	4.0	17.6	41.7	55.9	29.2	20.6	7.1	2.9
Woollens (inc carpets, felt)	2.3	38.9	2.8	16.7	5.6	15.3	16.3	20.8
Cotton (inc thread, muslin)	0.7	31.1	0.8	14.9	1.0	7.5	3.6	12.4
Flax, linen	0.1	10.7	0.6	10.7	0.9	7.1	9.2	28.6
Silk	0.8	27.4	1.9	21.0	1.9	9.7	6.3	14.5
Tailor	26.7	63.6	28.9	23.6	23.9	8.9	20.6	3.9
Hosier, glover, other clothing	16.8	72.2	9.7	13.9	11.0	6.3	17.1	3.8
Draper	12.4	51.5	16.0	25.8	21.9	15.2	11.9	3.0
Shoemaker	20.5	62.2	21.8	21.5	25.7	11.5	15.8	3.9
Paper, box and stationery	36.4	78.3	8.2	6.5	39.6	13.0	15.7	2.2
Cabinet maker	12.2	45.8	21.6	31.8	20.9	13.7	18.7	5.8
Cooper	15.1	58.7	13.3	17.5	12.2	7.9	48.8	14.3
Cork cutter, woodturner	30.8	71.7	19.3	15.4	21.2	7.7	28.8	5.1
Ropemaker	2.1	28.6	3.8	20.6	8.7	20.6	11.8	12.7
Brush, broom, basket maker	27.8	67.9	22.9	21.4	8.8	3.6	40.6	7.1
Skinner, currier, tanner	6.5	39.6	10.3	20.8	23.6	22.6	27.4	13.2
Saddler, harnessmaker	28.8	64.3	29.8	23.2	24.7	8.9	16.6	3.6
Soap, tallow	17.6	47.8	22.9	21.7	59.5	30.4	–	–
Dyer, scourer	4.6	36.9	6.5	17.5	12.6	16.5	29.5	18.4
Watchmaker	55.7	83.3	21.6	11.1	22.7	5.6	–	–
Engine & tool maker	1.1	20.3	3.2	22.6	4.3	14.3	12.8	19.5
Wheelwright, millwright	16.0	59.5	12.9	21.6	20.8	14.3	8.3	2.4
Ship, boat builder	1.0	19.4	2.6	27.8	1.7	8.3	6.4	13.9
Coachmaker	1.4	12.1	7.1	24.2	12.5	18.2	57.4	39.4
Printer, binder	5.7	30.0	16.7	37.0	13.7	13.0	27.7	14.0
Publisher, bookseller	14.4	58.0	15.2	20.3	19.2	13.0	10.9	4.3
Engraver, lithographer	10.8	44.6	20.6	32.3	15.6	10.8	30.1	9.2
Carman carrier	26.5	75.3	15.1	16.9	10.2	4.5	4.3	1.1
Other transport	7.0	33.3	24.6	33.3	38.2	25.0	30.3	8.3
Chimney sweep	82.4	94.7	17.6	5.3	–	–	–	–
Druggist	36.1	77.3	18.5	13.6	13.4	4.5	31.9	4.5
Dentist, architect, vet	48.3	8.7	25.2	14.8	9.9	3.3	16.7	3.3
Hairdresser	60.6	87.9	20.6	9.1	18.7	3.0	–	–
Brewer	9.6	48.7	10.6	17.9	16.7	12.8	48.6	17.9
Food-processing	4.7	43.8	7.8	23.6	8.6	12.5	21.8	15.3
Butcher	75.1	90.6	24.9	9.4	–	–	–	–
Baker	63.7	82.5	28.9	15.8	7.4	1.6	–	–
Grocer	50.1	82.2	24.4	13.2	18.2	3.9	7.3	0.7
Shopkeeper	32.9	75.0	20.6	16.7	13.7	4.9	16.0	2.8
Miscellaneous	20.2	41.0	14.8	17.8	24.1	7.0	13.9	1.6
Total	8.3	56.0	8.7	20.9	10.1	10.8	14.0	7.1

Source: Census of Scotland 1851, P.P. 1852–53 LXXXVIII (2), 1022–1024.

Note: The 1s in parentheses indicate the percentage of employees in businesses with work forces of one to four, five to nine, and so on. The 2s in parentheses indicate the percentage of employers in businesses with work forces of one to four, five to nine, and so on.

TABLE 4, CONT.

	50–99		100+		TOTAL EMPL-OYEES	EMPL-OYERS	MEAN WORK-FORCE
	(1)	(2)	(1)	(2)			
Iron	14.4	9.8	65.9	6.6	5887	122	48.3
Blacksmith	9.2	0.6	13.2	0.6	949	172	5.5
Brass, copper, lead	17.6	6.5	43.6	5.2	2063	77	26.8
Tinplate	–	–	–	–	326	55	5.9
Goldsmith	–	–	–	–	451	83	5.4
Earthenware, glass	19.0	9.7	53.2	6.5	1118	31	36.0
Brickmaker, quarrier	23.4	15.2	39.3	9.1	1338	33	40.5
Coal merchant	–	–	91.4	20.0	848	20	42.4
Builder	28.7	14.6	35.8	8.1	4611	123	37.5
Carpenter, joiner	5.1	0.7	7.2	0.3	2446	303	8.1
Painter, plumber, glazier	24.1	2.9	–	–	2124	242	8.8
Mason	49.7	13.2	8.3	1.3	1511	76	19.9
Slater	–	–	–	–	445	66	6.7
Bricklayer	30.6	4.2	–	–	205	24	8.5
Plasterer	9.1	1.3	–	–	696	77	9.0
Timber merchant	18.0	2.9	–	–	348	34	10.2
Woollens (inc carpets, felt)	–	–	73.0	8.3	2877	72	40.0
Cotton (inc thread, muslin)	6.1	9.3	87.7	24.8	17289	161	107.4
Flax, linen	8.0	14.3	81.1	28.6	3113	28	111.2
Silk	7.3	8.1	81.8	19.4	4624	62	74.6
Tailor	–	–	–	–	2367	440	5.4
Hosier, glover, other clothing	18.9	2.5	26.4	1.3	662	79	8.4
Draper	18.9	3.0	18.9	1.5	662	66	10.0
Shoemaker	3.4	0.4	12.9	0.5	3673	563	6.5
Paper, box and stationery	–	–	–	–	220	46	4.7
Cabinet maker	17.1	2.2	9.5	0.7	2633	277	9.5
Cooper	10.6	1.6	–	–	596	63	9.5
Cork cutter, woodturner	–	–	–	–	410	78	5.3
Ropemaker	8.7	4.8	64.8	12.7	2160	63	34.3
Brush, broom, basket maker	–	–	–	–	170	28	6.1
Skinner, currier, tanner	8.5	1.9	23.7	1.9	738	53	13.9
Saddler, harnessmaker	–	–	–	–	295	56	5.3
Soap, tallow	–	–	–	–	171	23	7.4
Dyer, scourer	34.0	8.7	12.8	1.9	1950	103	18.9
Watchmaker	–	–	–	–	255	72	3.5
Engine & tool maker	14.5	9.8	64.0	13.5	6445	133	48.5
Wheelwright, millwright	–	–	41.9	2.4	418	42	9.9
Ship, boat builder	9.4	8.3	78.9	22.2	2536	36	70.4
Coachmaker	21.6	6.1	–	–	695	33	21.0
Printer, binder	18.1	4.0	18.1	2.0	1381	97	14.2
Publisher, bookseller	22.0	2.9	18.3	1.4	681	69	9.9
Engraver, lithographer	22.9	3.1	–	–	655	65	10.1
Carman carrier	–	–	43.9	2.2	570	89	6.4
Other transport	–	–	–	–	114	12	9.5
Chimney sweep	–	–	–	–	34	19	1.8
Druggist	–	–	–	–	108	22	4.9
Dentist, architect, vet	–	–	–	–	147	37	4.0
Hairdresser	–	–	–	–	78	33	2.3
Brewer	14.4	2.6	–	–	435	39	11.1
Food-processing	9.1	2.8	48.0	2.1	3022	144	21.0
Butcher	–	–	–	–	373	159	2.3
Baker	–	–	–	–	1572	487	3.2
Grocer	–	–	–	–	479	152	3.1
Shopkeeper	–	–	16.9	0.6	740	144	5.1
Miscellaneous	3.1	0.5	23.9	0.7	1942	259	7.7
Total	11.3	2.5	47.6	2.6	92656	5944	15.6

How far, however, was this aggregate picture valid according to the manufacturing subdivisions of the Scottish economy? Table 4 summarizes almost 200 occupational classifications covered by the census schedule of 1851. Several mid-Victorian business characteristics are immediately apparent. For example, flax and linen manufacturers narrowly exceeded cotton enterprises as the largest Scottish business units as reflected in the mean size of the work force. Averaging over 100 employees these areas of textile production were approximately 50 percent larger than silk manufacturers and shipbuilders with their average of 74.6 and 70.4 employees, respectively. Below this top tier of producers and with thirty to fifty employees came, successively, engineering and toolmaking firms, iron manufacturers, brick, glass, and woolen manufacturers, builders, and rope makers with work forces approximately 35 percent to 45 percent of those in the cotton and linen industries. Understandably the level of capitalization generally required in these industrial processes inclined entrepreneurs to a larger scale of production and so increased manning levels; yet size of work force alone was no guarantor of uniform workplace experience. Class consciousness as reflected in labor activism was, in the second half of the nineteenth century, significantly more highly developed among engineers, tool-makers, and ironworkers than it was among the brick, glass, and woolen workers in correspondingly sized productive units. Or was it? Studies of these branches of Scottish industry and of their labor forces are virtually nonexistent. Interest in the major pinnacles of Scottish industrial achievement has obscured the lesser peaks; consequently testable hypotheses such as the importance of the size of the unit's production in relation to the formation of workers' identity and consciousness have been overlooked, thereby confining conclusions to generalizations based on a narrow selection of industries.

In the next group of industries, with a mean work force size of between one and two times the national average, came nonferrous metalworking, food processing, coach making, chemicals, and printing, areas of employment that were to expand appreciably in the second half of the nineteenth century. Finally, there was another group of manufacturing activities in which the firm functioned with only a handful of employees. Employees in precious metal-working and watchmaking, woodworking, brush, broom, and basket making, in soap, engraving, leather working, and the various subdivisons of the clothing industry could be numbered on the fingers of one hand; and in retailing normally only two or three sales assistants were engaged who, together with the employer, would be sufficient to serve the customers.

The obdurate nature of traditional modes of production was also reflected in the absolute number of employees according to the various occupational subdivisions in Table 4. There were as many workers in the shoe and tailoring branches of employment as in woolens, flax, and linen combined, and the labor force in the building industry was larger than the combined strength of those in iron and engineering. The relative size of the components of the industrial labor forces is also instructive – as for example with shipbuilding, which was ranked only eleventh in 1851 and was equivalent to only 38 percent of the engineering work force and 84 percent of food processing. Those occupied in rope making formed a larger work force than those in chemicals. Blacksmiths outnumbered tanners by 33 percent and were two-and-a-half times more numerous than butchers; druggists employed a total of only 108 people in the nine largest burghs but even this exceeded those occupied as hairdressers, who numbered just seventy-eight. The comparisons, the relativities, are infinite. The general point, only briefly examined here, is that occupational and business data for 1851 permit a sensitive and quantifiable analysis of the urban economic structure; and although the nine burghs are not treated separately, this was the only systematic and comprehensive survey of the urban economy outside London before the twentieth century censuses of production, which themselves do not permit an urban scale of analysis.

For British urban historians the level of economic analysis has remained steadfastly macroeconomic. Sectoral, industrial, or national aggregates have been grafted onto the city in a manner sufficiently uncomfortable to move Checkland to accuse urban historians of being 'soft at the core' in terms of fundamental economic analysis.[53] This microeconomy of the city has therefore been saddled with frequently inappropriate macroeconomic trends and developments. Remarkably, the implications of substantive amendments to generalist economic theories, such as inverse cycles in home and foreign investment,[54] on the basis of local variations in economic structure have not been taken up and the economic base of cities has largely been neglected, save where it has related to particular issues of social structure and labor relations, or to studies of individual industries. Generalized notions of liberalism and laissez-faire and assumptions about perfect competition in mid-Victorian Britain have been brandished as the context of business activity, whereas in fact the pragmatic conduct of daily business was often much more closely circumscribed due to hand-to-mouth considerations. The theory of the firm has therefore been largely absent from urban historical analysis, and the dualism evident in this study suggests that universal statements regarding business policies, credit rating, and other issues need considerable refinement to take account of the number, size, and distribution of firms in the local urban economic structure.

Because the mean work force size of Scottish firms as presented in Table 4 takes into account extremely large- (and small-) scale producers, comparisons of all work forces around their individual means is improved by using the percentage coefficient of variation (Table 5, column [2]). Adjusted for absolute

TABLE 5: BUSINESS SIZE, RANGE AND DISTRIBUTION IN URBAN SCOTLAND 1851

BUSINESS SECTOR	MEAN FIRM WORKFORCE (nos.)	COEFF OF VARIATION (%)	MEDIAN FIRM WORKFORCE (nos.)	SKEWNESS β_1 COEFF	PEAKEDNESS β_2 COEFF
	1	2	3	4	5
Iron manufacture	48.3	351.9	14.04	7.41	62.02
Blacksmiths	5.5	220.9	2.64	7.53	65.80
Brass, copper, lead	26.8	194.8	9.33	3.75	14.67
Tinplate	5.9	116.3	3.25	2.25	5.56
Goldsmiths	5.4	102.8	3.75	2.61	9.28
Earthenware, glass	36.0	220.2	8.38	4.20	19.36
Brickmaker, quarrier	40.5	127.9	24.42	3.28	13.09
Coal merchant	42.4	224.4	4.00	3.17	11.07
Builder	37.5	123.3	24.13	2.36	6.01
Carpenter, joiner	8.1	165.1	4.17	7.44	83.04
Painter, plumber, glazier	8.8	156.2	4.28	3.74	15.84
Mason	19.9	136.9	8.25	2.00	3.38
Slater	6.7	106.2	5.05	2.80	8.54
Bricklayer	8.5	170.8	3.50	3.06	9.26
Plasterer	9.0	100.7	6.29	3.02	14.67
Timber merchant	10.2	102.5	8.70	3.99	19.47
Woollens (and carpets)	40.0	347.8	7.75	6.71	49.49
Cotton (inc thread, muslin)	107.4	199.7	14.54	3.10	10.67
Flax, linen	111.2	203.4	44.50	4.42	21.55
Silk	74.6	230.1	14.17	4.02	17.81
Tailor	5.4	113.6	3.27	2.80	9.75
Hosiery	8.4	267.4	2.54	5.88	40.34
Draper	10.0	187.5	4.33	4.41	22.72
Shoemaker	6.5	207.2	3.31	10.35	142.29
Chimney sweep	1.8	75.8	1.29	2.06	4.37
Druggist	4.9	148.5	3.02	3.57	13.98
Dentist, vet, architect, etc	4.0	108.3	2.46	3.55	14.99
Hairdresser	2.3	111.5	1.37	3.43	14.50
Paper, box and stationery	4.7	130.5	2.50	2.97	10.95
Cabinet maker	9.5	167.1	4.96	*	*
Cooper	9.5	135.7	3.85	2.26	5.21
Cork cutter, woodturner	5.3	125.3	2.75	2.81	8.84
Ropemaker (inc sails, sacks)	34.3	186.9	14.04	3.34	12.36
Brush, broom, basketmaker	6.1	140.8	3.21	2.93	8.19
Skinner, currier, tanner	13.9	151.3	7.25	*	*
Saddler, harnessmaker	5.3	101.3	3.50	2.13	4.79
Soap, tallow	7.4	71.3	6.00	−0.38	1.52
Dyer, scourer	18.9	136.2	8.00	2.31	5.50
Watchmaker	3.5	91.2	2.67	2.28	5.36
Engine & tool maker	48.5	207.8	14.50	4.79	27.02

TABLE 5, CONT.

BUSINESS SECTOR	MEAN FIRM WORKFORCE (nos.)	COEFF OF VARIATION (%)	MEDIAN FIRM WORKFORCE (nos.)	SKEWNESS β_1 COEFF	PEAKEDNESS β_2 COEFF
	1	2	3	4	5
Wheelwright, millwright	9.9	269.7	4.00	5.99	37.38
Ship, boat builder	70.4	164.9	14.33	2.30	5.05
Coachmaker	21.0	90.0	14.75	−1.69	3.76
Printer, binder	14.2	147.5	7.25	−3.65	15.75
Publisher, bookseller	9.9	195.2	3.82	4.51	22.50
Engraver, lithographer	10.1	148.5	5.08	3.30	12.72
Carman carrier	6.4	288.4	2.63	6.18	38.42
Other transport	9.5	98.0	7.00	−1.92	4.47
Brewer	11.1	126.1	5.00	2.01	4.45
Food-processing	21.0	415.9	5.86	10.23	113.00
Butcher	2.3	67.7	1.94	1.73	3.47
Baker	3.2	66.5	4.61	2.77	10.83
Grocer	3.1	122.1	2.07	4.68	30.67
Shopkeeper	5.1	222.9	2.80	8.54	85.81
Miscellaneous	7.7	244.5	3.51	8.18	80.84
Total		402.9	3.91	12.87	215.99

Source: Census of Scotland, P.P. 1852–53 LXXXVIII (2), 1022–1024.
Note: * : bimodal distribution

sizes in this way the variation around the mean work force is directly comparable for each manufacturing activity. Relatively speaking, therefore, the variation in firm size (Table 5) was greater among hosiery employers (267.4 percent) than nonferrous metal manufacturers (194.8 percent). The range of firms according to size of the work force was, in the textile sector, greatest in woolens (347.8 percent), with silk (230.1 percent), flax (203.4 percent), and cotton (199.7 percent) substantially lower. Surprisingly, relative variation of firm size in the cotton industry was superseded by blacksmiths (220.9 percent), shopkeepers (222.9 percent), and shoemakers (207.2 percent). Least variation in relative firm size was experienced among employers in retailing (such as bakers, butchers, and grocers), in the service industry (employers in hairdressing, chimney sweeping, and professional services), and among firms in precious metals, coach making, leather working, slating, plastering, and tailoring. Put another way, the homogeneity of the productive unit was much greater in those areas than among employers, for example, in food processing, haulage, and iron manufacturing or, more surprisingly, in cabinetmaking, coopering, or plumbing. The significance of this type of analysis is that it permits for the first time an elaboration of the industrial structure for the principal Scottish burghs in 1851 and is, arguably, appropriate for the adjacent decades of the 1840s and 1860s. Furthermore, the degree of variation in the size of manufacturing firms is directly comparable. Work forces in iron manufacturing ranged almost identically to those in the woolen industry and both were three times more widely dispersed than, for example, tinplate-manufacturing businesses. Hence the smaller the value for the coefficient of variation the greater the concentration of firms around the typical (mean) producer. Significant interindustry and intersectoral variations in typical productive units are therefore apparent in the mid-Victorian Scottish industrial structure, thereby permitting a more sophisticated level of urban economic analysis.

Another comparative dimension of urban economic structure can be viewed through the median firm in each line of production. Values in Table 5 (column [3]) indicate the size of firm in which exactly 50 percent of workers were engaged; half the ironworkers were employed in firms of less than 14.04 workers and half in firms of more than 14.04 workers. Half the work force in the cotton industry were in firms of less than 14.54 workers, and similarly in nonferrous metal manufacturing less than 50 percent were in establishments of 9.33 or fewer workers. Although this tends to confirm the pattern of Tables 1 and 4, it does allow direct comparisons of the size of productive units in each industry at the 50 percent level of employment and thus identifies, for example, that iron, cotton, silk, rope making, sailmaking, engineering, shipbuilding, and coach making shared a common feature – namely, that 50 percent of their work forces were in firms with fewer than fourteen to fifteen workers, and of course the other 50 percent were in firms above that level. Again the interindustry level of comparison suggests further lines of inquiry, indicates comparisons and contrasts previously overlooked, and particularly highlights features of mundane manufacturing activity such as cabinetmaking, engraving, tinplate manufacturing and working, and shoemaking that have been regarded as insufficiently remarkable in previous studies to attract attention but which are essential explanatory elements in the local employment structure in mid-Victorian Scotland.

Divergences in the structure of productive units can be seen in Figure 1.[55] These cumulative frequency distributions for a sample of manufacturing and transport activities illustrate the marked variations in their dependence on small- and large-scale businesses. Four key features are worth noting. Where the curve closely follows the horizontal axis and then abruptly surges upwards – that is, the closer the distribution approximates a J shape, then the greater the polarization between small and large firms in the industry or sector. Such is the case in iron, most textiles, food processing, and shipbuilding. Where this exponential characteristic is less emphatic, as in paper, brick, or brushmaking

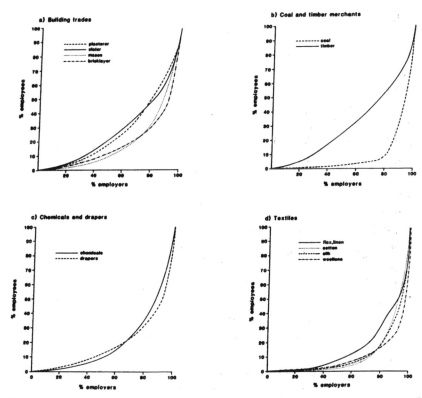

Figure 1: Divergence in the Structure of Productive Units.

and printing, for example, so medium-size firms were more conspicuous. By contrast, where the curve approaches the 45° line then dualism in the industry was largely absent; the percentages of employers and employees rise by roughly equal amounts, indicating greater homogeneity in the corporate and work force experience. Such identity of business experience in urban Scotland was most pronounced in the retailing and service industries, and in certain branches of transport. Perhaps, understandably, it was observable among the more 'traditional' industries – leather, watch and coach making for example – though not exclusively confined to them. Thus the distribution of chemical and drapery firms, remarkably, differed little, and among paper and soap manufacturers and brewers, the distribution of enterprises approximated that of grocers and goldsmiths more than that of iron or textile manufacturers. The graphical analysis, only very partially covered here, also highlights intra-industry differences, as shown in Figure 1 (quadrants a and d) for textiles and the building industry. Variations in the array of firms within such similar product or market ranges identifies a series of questions regarding logistical considerations and factors influencing optimal firm size. Under what conditions – business, urban, technical, or other – would medium-size firms be more conspicuous in flax and linen than in other textiles; why should cotton and silk firms rather than any other other textile pairing be almost identically distributed in 1851? Builders, plumbers, and joiners were very similarly distributed in terms of the composition of firms and work forces; yet these differed when compared with slating, mason, and plastering firms for which a given scale of business operations appeared more appropriate than in the more variably sized building joinery and plumbing firms. In a similar vein, the radically divergent distribution of coal and timber merchants identifies fundamentally different wholesaling and distribution patterns in these commodities. More generally, the common and dissimilar business scale in mid-Victorian Scotland presents just one tool by which the urban economic fabric can be explored.

In 1851 the structure of production in Scottish manufacturing was highly asymmetrical. The skewed distribution of firms as presented in Table 4 demonstrated as much. But the extent to which each branch of employment was skewed remains unclear. Whether ironmasters, though widely dispersed as seen in Table 5 (coefficient of variation 351.9 percent) were also asymmetrically distributed, to what extent, and how this compared with other areas of production, can be viewed through a measure of skewness, β_1, and the direction of that skewness adds a further dimension to the pattern of production in mid-Victorian Scottish industry. A symmetrical or normal distribution of firms according to their payroll size would produce a β_1 coefficient of zero; the more uneven the spread of firms the higher the β_1 value. In all except five areas of production – plastering, cabinetmaking, saddlery, coach making, and various transport activities – the skewness was positive; that is, the principal concentration of firms was to the lower work force size with a scattering of employers with larger work forces. In general an even distribution of firm sizes in an industry would be denoted by a zero coefficient, and a value of 2.0 regarded as high.[56] In fact, therefore, Scottish producers in virtually every classification were highly skewed, with coefficients substantially above 2.0, the most extreme being in joinery, iron manufacturing, shoemaking, and in the food-processing, shopkeeping, and miscellaneous manufacturing categories. Productive units were far from evenly distributed in other areas of production. For manufacturers of woolens, hosiery, glass and pottery, silk and flax, in engineering, paper manufacturing, and publishing, and among firms of wheelwrights and coopers the distribution of productive units was highly skewed with β_1 coefficients in the 4.0 to 6.99 range. Least skewed were coachmaking and brick-making firms with a β_1 coefficient of just under 2.0. A little above this came a group of building, wood- and leather-working firms, shipbuilders, brewers and watch-makers, goldsmiths and tinplate manufacturers (see Table 5). Again direct comparisons of each industry can be made because of the β_1 coefficient, namely, that it measures relative skewness. Not only is it possible to say that the size distribution of firms was more skewed in earthenware compared with brick making, but by how much – 28.0 percent; or that the distribution of firms in woodturning and cork cutting was identical to that in tin-plating, albeit distributed around a different mean work force size, 9.5 in woodworking and 5.9 in tin-plating.

A further window on the production structure of mid-Victorian Scottish industry can be provided by an analysis of the degree of 'peakedness' or the clustering of firms around a particular level of production as reflected by the work force. Thus, rather than normally distributed throughout an array of firm sizes the relative degree of business concentration is measure by the β_2 coefficient for kurtosis. Values of β_2 greater than 3.0 would indicate a heavy concentration of business around a particular firm size.[57] In fact, no β_2 values of 3.0 or less were recorded. Throughout Scottish manufacturing and distribution the concentration of the scale of business activity was therefore very pronounced. Nowhere was this more obvious than in retailing, but in textiles, in the clothing and footwear industry, and in engineering, ironworking, and joinery, the degree of concentration on a particular scale of business operations was more emphatic. Insofar as any industrial sector was evenly distributed across the range of firm sizes, masons (β_2 = 3.38), brewers (β_2 = 4.45), transport (β_2 = 4.47), saddlers (β_2 = 4.79), shipbuilders (β_2 = 5.05), and dyers (β_2 = 5.50) experienced a lesser divergence in the size of business units, though even here there were observed concentrations. As a measure of relative concentration or peakedness, comparisons between industries can be made simply by reference to the numerical values of β_2. Hence the clustering of business units among brush, broom, and basket manufacturers (β_2 = 8.19) was 74.8 percent of that among paper, box, and stationary manufacturers, though similar to that of slating or cork-cutting firms. Brewers, transport firms, and saddlers, though roughly similar, were relatively 31.7 percent, 32.2 percent, and 41.7 percent more concentrated around a particular scale of production than masons, and, perhaps surprisingly, the degree of 'peakedness' among blacksmiths and iron manufacturers was very similar.

Comparative degrees of concentration in the production structure and respective coefficients of variation indicate considerable divergences in the experience of Scottish firms, as indeed does the asymmetry reflected in the analysis of skewness among Scottish producers. Although each cell of Tables 4 and 5 has not been described individually, the analytical approach to manufacturing interests does proceed some way in response to Checkland's accusation that 'business history and urban history have largely failed to come together.'[58] Certainly, as far as the principal mid-Victorian Scottish burghs are concerned, reference to the urban economic structure need not be confined to the principal industries. Dovetailed into any historical analysis of urban economic structure is a much wider array of industries, with the range and distribution of their constituent firms and work force sizes more completely understood. Added to this, the statistical analysis provided in Tables 4 and 5 ensures direct comparability. A sharper analytical edge should result. For example, the range of nonferrous metalworking firms was much less widely distributed than in ironworking (Table 5, column [2]). Yet though the size spectrum of iron manufactures was very wide, wider in fact than almost any other area of production, they were less evenly distributed than brass, lead, and other nonferrous firms (β_1 [iron] = 1.41; β_1 [non-ferrous] = 3.75), and with a significant concentrations of operations four times more pronounced than among nonferrous producers (β_2 [iron] = 62.02; β_2 [non-ferrous] = 14.67).

Under what operating conditions can such a wide array of producers of iron coexist? Were the producers competing or were there elements of very specialized manufacturing? Does a greater concentration of firms suggest optimal operational levels were perceived and that these differed in iron from nonferrous production? Such issues emerge from the comparative statistical analysis and could be replicated both within and between the constituents of the urban economic structure. For example, though shipbuilders registered the fourth largest mean firm size, the medium-size firm was not dissimilar to coach making or rope making, and the relatively modest skewness and kurtosis coefficients indicate that there must have a considerable number of modest ship-repairing and boat-building operations. From a scrutiny of the various textile subdivisions, the character of production in each was evidently different (see Figure 1). What was it about woolens that made for greater concentration around a particular level of operations even though average firm size was well below other fibers? Though the mean work force was similar in flax and cotton industries, why should there be greater unanimity among flax firms as to the level of business operations? The stark comparison of fragmentation and dispersed distribution of soap producers and the concentrated, skewed pattern of dyers confirms the alliance of textile firms with the latter and indicates the different type of market that confronted soap and candle makers. Assuming some degree of business common sense prevailed over irrationality, it is now possible to analyze the essential characteristics of urban economic structure and to pose questions that will illuminate areas previously consigned to backstage as well as those with leading parts in the *dramatis personae* of Scottish economic development.

Although the intention has been to map out the contours of the mid-Victorian Scottish urban economy, certain conclusions have emerged. For example, first, the presence, durability and quantitative importance of traditional modes of production in areas such as woodworking, building, shoemaking and leather working, printing, and clothing was pronounced. Low wage costs, normally associated with labor processes introduced by early factory production and mechanization also conveyed considerable long-term advantages to a host of long-established manufacturing and distributive activities. Second, the traditional mode of production, small-scale units of workshop activity, frequently entailed direct entrepreneurial involvement in the labor process; a majority of firms (56.7 percent) were so small (one-five employees) that they could not have functioned otherwise. Third, this fragmentation and the basis of employer-employee workplace relations was not as conducive to the development of a labor consciousness, identity, and politicization as often advanced, and while not rejecting the contribution of the workplace experience to emergent labor organization, alternative avenues of explanation should be emphasized. Examples include associations of tenants and other informal groups based on shared residential experiences or based on leisure institutions such as the pub, both of which cut across occupational skills and provided a deeper sense of identity than that simply of the workplace. Indeed conflict and coercion in the workplace needs amendment to encompass compliance and cooperation in the workshop. Fourth, economies of scale were clearly developed as early as the 1840s, judged by the 1851 returns. More than 60 percent of the industrial labor force was concentrated in plants of 100 or more workers in iron manufacturing, engineering, rope, sack and sail making, while in textiles and shipbuilding approximately three-quarters to four-fifths of the labor force was hired in such large-scale enterprises. While the torchbearers of late-Victorian industrial growth therefore figured as substantial undertakings at an early stage, firms of these proportions, if less numerous, were by no means unknown in other less prestigious areas of manufacturing. In earthenware, nonferrous metals, and food processing almost half and in leather, hosiery, and a miscellany of manufacturing industry, a quarter of the work force could be found in firms of more than 100 employees. Thus, judged on scale of business operations and size of work force, mid-Victorian Scottish industry, in its various subdivisions, exhibited an early and highly developed degree of dualism though the small-scale element of production was not necessarily a low-productivity backwater. Fifth, while there were few employers of large work forces, the frequency of small manufacturing and especially of retailing employers gave them a disproportionate presence in the council chamber, though not in the Palace of Westminster.[59] Accordingly, the size, number, and composition of employers contributes to an understanding of the underlying stance of economism so widely adopted by mid-Victorian councils in relation to their muncipal responsibilities. The power of the Victorian 'shopocracy' is the more plausible for this quantification of the structure of Scottish employers.

Finally, though in no way approximating the matrix of input-output relationships sought by Checkland, the presentation of business operations in fifty-five manufacturing, distributive, retail, and allied subdivisions of the urban economy goes some way to fleshing out a production structure previously confined to the high peaks of Scottish industrial achievement. To implicitly assume that textiles, iron manufacturing, engineering, and shipbuilding were proxies for overall urban economic performance is illogical; it overlooks the life cycle of expansion and decay within these prominent sectors themselves, attributes an unwarranted parallel experience to, for example, tanning, comb and basket making, and supposes that economic growth was preordained in certain industrial sectors. This is not to say that the experience of businesses in building, consumption industries, and retailing was unconnected to the harmonics of the trade cycle as it related to coal, cotton, or iron but that there were independent and complementary forces simultaneously operative. Hence this preliminary analysis of the comparative range and distribution of firms according to size of work force, and of the skewness and peakedness of the distribution of firms within each manufacturing activity, provides a much more comprehensive view of the urban economic structures than previously available. Direct, systematic, and relative comparisons of the array of firms in each branch of employment also suggest avenues for further analysis – why were business operations clustered at one level among plumbers, painters, glaziers, and carpenters, yet more evenly distributed among masons? Why were the productive units differently skewed in the subdivisions of the textile industry? Were the seeds of industrial stagnation sown so early by undue concentration of labor intensity in both small- and large-scale enterprises? Both inter- and intraindustry levels of analysis are therefore suggested by subjecting mid-Victorian Scottish industry to a more systematic analysis and thereby redirecting attention from the 'Munros'[60] of Scottish industry to the no less important, if less precipitous, industrial heights.

NOTES

Author's Note: *I am indebted to Professor D. H. Aldcroft, Tony Adams, D. K. Bhattacharyya, John Beckett, Nick Morgan, Sylvia West, and Charlotte Kitson for their helpful advice and comments. Members of the Urban History Seminar at Strathclyde University offered many useful observations, some of which have been incorporated in this article. For the*

suggestions of an anonymous referee, and encouragement from the editor, I am also
indebted. A particular intellectual debt is to the late Professor S. G. Checkland for the
stimulus to undertake this type of research and his stimulating and enthusiastically
encouraging remarks on an earlier draft of this article. It is a matter of personal regret
that he did not live to see this work published.

1 See, for example, A. Slaven, *The Development of the West of Scotland, 1750–1960*
(London, 1975), chaps. 4, 5, and 7; S.G.E. Lythe and J. Butt, *An Economic History of*
Scotland, 1100–1939 (Glasgow, 1975), 161–195, 214–218; S.G. Checkland and O.
Checkland, *Industry and Ethos: Scotland 1832–1914* (London 1984), 14–33; R.H.
Campbell, *Scotland Since 1707* (Edinburgh, 1985), chaps. 6, 7 and 12; I.H. Adams,
The Making of Urban Scotland (London, 1978), chap. 7; B. Lenman, *An Economic*
History of Modern Scotland, 1660–1976 (London, 1977). The same approach, albeit from
different disciplines, is followed by T. Dickson, ed., *Scottish Capitalism: Class, State and*
Nation from Before the Wars to the Present (London, 1980), 181–243 and D. Turnock,
The Historical Geography of Scotland Since 1707 (Cambridge, 1982), though the latter
notes a wider array of industries, 119–123; and D. Bremner, *The Industries of Scotland*
(Edinburgh, 1869) remains exceptional in this respect. W. Forsyth, 'Urban Economic
Morphology in Nineteenth Century Glasgow,' in A. Slaven and D.H. Aldcroft, eds.,
Business, Banking and Urban History (Edinburgh, 1982), 166–192 is a conspicuous
exception to the traditional approach to Scottish industrialization and urbanization. See
especially Table 2 and Figures 1 and 5.

2 T.M. Devine, 'The Merchant Class of the Larger Scottish Towns in the Later Seventeenth
and Early Eighteenth Centuries,' in G. Gordon and B. Dicks, eds., *Scottish Urban History*
(Aberdeen, 1983), 92–111; 'An Eighteenth Century Business Elite,' *Scottish Historical*
Review 57 (1978), 40–63; and 'The Social Composition of the Business Class in the Larger
Scottish Towns 1680–1740,' in T.M. Devine and D. Dickson, eds., *Ireland and Scotland*
1600–1850 (Edinburgh, 1983); T. Donnelly, 'The economic activities of the Aberdeen
Merchant Guild 1740–90.' *Scottish Economic and Social History* 1 (1981), 25–41.

3 H. Hamilton, *The Industrial Revolution in Scotland* (Oxford, 1932).

4 See references in note 1 above and J. Butt, 'The Scottish Cotton Industry During the
Industrial Revolution, 1780–1840,' in L.M. Cullen and T.C. Smout, eds. *Comparative*
Aspects of Scottish and Irish Economic and Social History 1600–1900 (Edinburgh, 1977),
116–128; A.J. Durie, *The Scottish Linen Industry in the Eighteenth Century* (Edinburgh,
1979).

5 N. Murray, *The Scottish Handloom Weavers* (Edinburgh, 1978), 4–5.

6 W.W. Rostow, *The Stages of Economic Growth* (Cambridge, 1971), 52–57; H. Hamilton,
An Economic History of Scotland in the Eighteenth Century (Oxford, 1963); R.H.
Campbell, *Scotland Since 1707*, parts 1 and 2; T.C. Smout, *A History of the Scottish*
People (London, 1969) part 2; Murray, *Handloom Weavers*, 1.

7 M. Berg, *The Machinery Question and the Making of Political Economy 1815–48*
(Cambridge, 1980); A. Smith, *The Wealth of Nations* (London, 1776, Book 1) 4–15;
F. Engels, *The Condition of the Working Class in England in 1844* (London, 1936),
Introduction. I am grateful to an anonymous referee who drew my attention to an article

that appeared while this article was under consideration and with which the views expressed here closely correspond. The article is by C. Sabel and J. Zeitlin, 'Historical Alternatives to Mass Production: Politics, Markets and Technology in Nineteenth Century Industrialization,' *Past and Present* 108 (1985), 133–176.

8 Checkland and Checkland, *Industry and Ethos*, 19.

9 C. Sabel and J. Zeitlin, 'Historical Alternatives,' 137–141.

10 Ibid., 142–156.

11 J. Foster, *Class Struggle and the Industrial Revolution: Early Industrial Capitalism in Three English Towns* (London, 1974; principally concerned with the decline of a revolutionary class consciousness 1820–1850); A.E. Musson, 'Class Struggle and the Labour Aristocracy, 1830–60,' *Social History* 3 (1976), 333–356; and comments by J. Foster in the same volume, 357–366; P. Joyce, *Work, Society and Politics: The Culture of the Factory in Later Victorian England* (Brighton, 1980); G. Crossick, *An Artisan Elite in Victorian Society* (London, 1978); R. Harrison, *Before the Socialists: Studies in Labour and Politics 1861–1881* (London, 1965), see especially pp. 1–39; R.Q. Gray, *The Labour Aristocracy in Victorian Edinburgh* (Oxford, 1976).

12 For a penetrating summary of the debate, see N. Kirk, *The Growth of Working Class Reformism in Mid-Victorian England* (London, 1985), 1–31.

13 R. Samuel, 'The Workshop of the World: Steam Power and Hand Technology in Mid-Victorian Britain,' *History Workshop Journal* 3 (1977), 1–72; N. Murray, *Handloom Weavers;* P. Corfield, 'Slopmen and Specialists: Urban Occupations in the Early Industrial Revolution' (paper delivered to the Urban History Group Annual Conference, Cheltenham, 1986).

14 R.H. Campbell, *The Rise and Fall of Scottish Industry 1707–1939* (Edinburgh, 1980), 80.

15 Ibid., 190.

16 *P.P. 1887, LXXXIX,* Returns of Wages Published Between 1830 and 1886; *P.P. 1893–94 LXXIII (ii),* Wages of Manual Labour Classes; Industrial Remuneration Conference, *Report* (London, 1885), 142, 515; R.G. Rodger, 'Employment, Wages and Poverty in the Scottish Cities,' in G. Gordon, ed., *Perspectives of the Scottish City* (Aberdeen, 1985), Tables 6, 7 and 8.

17 *P.P. 1908 CVII Cd.3864* and *P.P. 1913 LXVI. P.P. 1913, LXVI,* Report of an Enquiry by the Board of Trade on Working Class Rents, Housing, Retail Prices and Standard Wages in the United Kingdom. P. xxxvi concluded 'The index numbers for the Scottish towns . . . are considerably higher on the whole than for those English and Welsh towns'. N.K. Buxton, 'Economic Growth in Scotland Between the Wars: The Role of Production Structure and Rationalization,' *Economic History Review* 23 (1980), 538–555.

18 A.L. Bowley, 'The Statistics of Wages in the United Kingdom in the Last Hundred Years,' *Journal of the Royal Statistical Society* 62 (1899), 708–715; 63 (1900), 297–315; 64 (1901), 102–112; 68 (1905), 563–614; E.H. Hunt, *Regional Wage Variations in Britain 1850–1914* (Oxford, 1973).

19 A.L. Bowley 'Wages in the United Kingdom', R.G. Rodger, 'The 'Invisible' Hand: Market Forces, Housing and the Urban Form in Victorian Cities' in D. Fraser and A. Sutcliffe, eds., *The Pursuit of Urban History* (London, 1983), particularly 194–206.

20 H.J. Habakkuk, *American and British Technology in the Nineteenth Century: The Search for Labour-Saving Inventions* (Cambridge, 1967) 1, 142; 'since labour in England [sic] was abundant it was hostile to labour-saving inventions.'

21 A.J. Taylor, 'Labour Productivity and Technological Innovation in the British Coal Industry, 1850–1914' *Economic History Review* 14 (1961), 48–70; L. Sandberg, *Lancashire in Decline* (Columbus, 1974).

22 D.N. McCloskey and L.G. Sandberg, 'From Damnation to Redemption: Judgements on the Late-Victorian Entrepreneur.' *Explorations to Economic History* 9 (1971), 89–108; L.G. Sandberg, 'The Entrepreneur and Technological Change' in R. Floud and D. McCloskey, *The Economic History of Britain Since 1700* (Cambridge, 1981), II, 99–120.

23 N.K. Buxton, 'Economic Growth in Scotland.'

24 R.H. Campbell, 'The Law and the Joint-Stock Company in Scotland' in P.L. Payne, ed., *Studies in Scottish Business* (London, 1967) 142, notes that Scottish law provided three attractions unavailable until the middle of the nineteenth century in England. These were the transferability of shares, a separate legal entity for the company and limited liability for shareholders. Six nineteenth-century acts of Parliament, largely inapplicable to Scotland 'where there was much less need for them' were therefore aimed 'at remedying the defects in English law.' A succession of statutes – the best known were the Bubble Act, 1825; the Joint Stock Companies Act, 1844; and the Limited Liability Act, 1855 – provided the benefits of incorporation, actions for damages and protection for shareholders under limited liability, share transfers, and other rights that had been available in Scotland from the eighteenth century.

25 P.L. Payne, *The Early Scottish Limited Companies 1856–1895* (Edinburgh, 1980) 77.

26 *P.P. 1852–53, LXXXVIII (2),* 1022–1024.

27 *P.P. 1852–53, LXVIII (1).*

28 *P.P. 1852–53, LXXXVIII (2).*

29 This was in fact adopted in the English survey, see *P.P. 1852–53, LXVIII (1).* lxxvii-lxxviii.

30 J.H. Treble, 'The Market for Unskilled Male Labour in Glasgow, 1891–1914' in I. MacDougall, ed., *Essays in Scottish Labour History* (Edinburgh, 1979), Appendix, column 6, and 'The Seasonal Demand for Adult Labour in Glasgow, 1980–1914,' *Social History* 3 (1978), 60; R.G. Rodger, 'Employment, Wages and Poverty,' Tables 9, 10.

31 A.H. Yarmie, 'British Employers' Resistance to 'Grandmotherly' Government 1850–80,' *Social History* 9 (1984), 141; for a critique see R.G. Rodger, 'Mid-Victorian Employers' Attitudes,' *Social History* 11 (1986), 77–80.

32 J.T. Ward, *The Factory Movement 1830–1855* (London, 1962); A.E. Peacock, 'The Successful Presentation of the Factory Acts, 1833–55,' *Economic History Review,* 37 (1984), 197–210.

33 *The Builder* April 30, 1864; April 21, 1866; April 2, 1870; March 2, April 6, May 11, June 1, 1872. R. Price, *Masters, Unions and Men: Work Control in Building and the Rise of Labour* (Cambridge, 1980), 34–65, 200–220.

34 R. Price, 'The Labour Process and Labour History,' *Social History* 8 (1983), 62 refers to 'a mutual and dialectical relationship . . . between resistance and subordination.'

35 R.G. Rodger, 'Employment, Wages and Poverty,' 29.

36 E.P. Thompson, *The Making of the English Working Class* (London, 1968) 456–485.

37 *P.P. 1917–18, XIV,* Royal Commission on Housing in Scotland, 1971, *Report,* paras. 716–717.

38 See, for example, the work and references contained in J. Melling 'Non-Commissioned Officers and 'The Foreman': A Forgotten Figure in the Social History of the Workplace? Superiors and Industrial Labour in Britain 1850–1914,' *Social History* 5 (1980), 183–221, and P. Joyce, *Work, Society and Politics.*

39 G.E. Davie, *The Democratic Intellect: Scotland and Her Universities in the Nineteenth Century* (Edinburgh, 1961), 150, quoted in R.H. Campbell, 'Introductory Essay' in Scottish History Society, *Scottish Industrial History: A Miscellany* (Edinburgh, 1978), xxxiii. Even the generalist qualities of Scottish education have come under attack; see R. Anderson, 'In Search of the 'Lads of Parts': The Mythical History of Scottish Education,' *History Workshop Journal* 19 (1985), 82–104.

40 T. Purdie, *The Relation of Science to University Teaching in Scotland* (St. Andrews, 1885), 10.

41 P.L. Payne, *British Entrepreneurship in the Nineteenth Century* (London, 1974), and references therein.

42 C. Sabel and J. Zeitlin, 'Historical Alternatives,' 142–151.

43 See for example, A. Slaven, *Development of West Scotland,* 114.

44 S.B. Saul, 'The Machine Tool Industry in Britain to 1914,' *Business History* 10 (1968), 22–43.

45 D. Bremner, *Industries of Scotland,* 177–178.

46 Ibid., 393.

47 Even allowing for the problems associated with the method of recording trade with England, business and industrial histories have added very little to an understanding of an essential element in the business operations of large numbers of Scottish firms, namely, the price, composition, and direction of cross-border traffic in industrial products.

48 J. Treble, 'The Seasonal Demand for Adult Labour' and *Urban Poverty in Britain 1830–1914* (London, 1979), 61–62.

49 B. Elliott, D. McCrone and V. Skelton, 'Property and Political Power: Edinburgh 1875–1975' in J. Garrard et al, *The Middle Class in Politics* (Edinburgh, 1978), 108 and Tables 6.2–6.5.

50 S.G. Checkland, 'An Urban History Horoscope,' in D. Fraser and A. Sutcliffe, eds., *The Pursuit of Urban History* (London, 1983), 455.

51 See, for example, J. Garrard, *Leadership and Power in Victorian Industrial Towns, 1830–1880* (Manchester, 1983) for an extended discussion of these points.

52 Calculated from *P.P. 1852–53, LXXXVIII (2),* 1022–1024.

53 S.G. Checkland, 'Urban History Horoscope,' 459; and 'The City and the Businessman', Seventh H.J. Dyos Memorial Lecture, Leicester, May 1985, published as *The City and the Businessman Viewed Historically: An Aspect of the Performance of Capitalism* (Victorian Studies Centre publication, University of Leicester, 1985).

54 See A.K. Cairncross, *Home and Foreign Investment 1879–1913* (Cambridge, 1953); B.

Thomas, *Migration and Economic Growth* (Cambridge, 1954); and responses of H.J. Habakkuk, 'Fluctuations on Housebuilding in Britain and the United States,' *Journal of Economic History* 22 (1962), 198–230; and S.B. Saul, 'Housebuilding in England 1890–1914,' *Economic History Review* 15 (1962), 119–137.

55 Full graphical and statistical analyses of each manufacturing category are available on request from the author.

56 F.E. Croston and D.J Cowden, *Applied General Statistics* (New York, 1948), 256. Note that 'values as great as ± 2 . . . indicate marked skewness.'

57 Ibid., 259.

58 S.G. Checkland, 'Urban History Horoscope,' 455.

59 M. Dyer, ' "Mere Detail and Machinery": The Great Reform Act and the Effects of Redistribution on Scottish Representation, 1823–1868,' *Scottish Historical Review* 62 (1983), 31 and Table 2.

60 Sir High Munro classified Scottish mountains of 3,000 feet and above into 538 tops and 283 distinct mountains. The term *Munro K* became associated with these peaks with the publication of his tables of heights. See J.C. Donaldson and W.L Coats, *Munro's Tables of the 3,000 Foot Mountains of Scotland and Other Tables of Lesser Heights* (Edinburgh, 1969).

Scotland in the International Economy, 1860–1914

Extracted from M Gray 1990 *Scots on the Move: Scots Migrants 1750–1914*, Dundee, 33–40 (Studies in Scottish Economic & Social History 1).

For long the main source of Scottish migration was a countryside that remained populous in spite of the departure of so many of the country-born. Such were prevailing rates of natural increase that the universal tendency for part of the rural population to move away did not bring decline over most of the rural Lowlands or, until the fourth decade of the nineteenth century, in the Highlands. The forces that produced the seepage from the countryside were many and changing, and in the last quarter of the century, as the rural exodus continued, or even increased, new factors were at work.

In the early seventies agriculture generally ran into severe problems of falling prices, particularly of grains. The main change that international pressures forced upon the agriculture of the Scottish Lowlands was to make farmers turn to less intensive rotations and to increase the period of years in which land would lie under rotation grass; little land went down to permanent pasture or fell into complete neglect (Orwin and Whetham, 1964, 268). The core work of the farm, the ploughing and the fertilising of the land, was somewhat diminished. But there were greater economies in harvesting, in threshing and in transport. The consequent shedding of casual and less skilled labour was reinforced by an autonomous revolt by women against much of the agricultural work they had for long undertaken. More varied tasks were forced upon the skilled workers, the ploughmen, who in the past had acted as aristocrats with well-defined and highly skilled work. Farmers, too, were forced by the rise in the real earnings of these skilled workers into economising even in the types of skilled labour that remained essential. Altogether, then, there were cuts in the farm labour force in all branches but most of all in subsidiary and seasonal labour. Apart from the movement of the labourers for whom there was now no demand the loss of their incomes tended to the diminution of purchasing power in the rural community and to a drift affecting all in any way connected with farming.

One of the factors that perplexed employing farmers was the rise of the real wages of their employees. They were facing scarcity rather than superfluity in the labour market. That scarcity cannot be explained by any faltering in the underlying tendency of the rural population to grow. Both birth- and death-rates were falling from 1870 but the fall in birth rates was slightly steeper to give a very slow fall in the rate of natural increase which certainly never sank below 10 per cent per decade in Lowland rural areas. In this time of little change between 1861 and 1911 the rate of natural increase was higher in the Western Lowlands and the North-East than it was in the Eastern Lowlands and Borders. But in all rural areas out-migration began to exceed natural increase, commonly at some time in the second half of the nineteenth century, and once decline had begun it was irreversible (Collett, 1977, 49–59; Walton, 1960, 40–1; Snodgrass, ed.,1953, 69).

While the rural areas were almost all, decade by decade, shedding population, towns as a whole were gaining by a small margin over natural increase. Between 1861 and 1901, towns, defined as centres of 1,000 inhabitants and over, were in aggregate growing at about 13 per cent per decade. Such an increase represented at very most a gain of 3 per cent over natural increase, while the remaining rural areas were losing in gross terms something over 15 per cent of their people decade by decade. Such figures, which probably understate rural loss and overstate urban gain, would mean that the towns were taking in less than half the number of those leaving the country areas. This apparent failure to match is partly explained by the fact that the net figures for gain by the town sector do not indicate the gross numbers entering towns. Net gain or loss by migration was always the difference in scale of two considerable streams (Flinn, ed., 1977, 313–5).

Continuing heavy migration of country people into the towns is indicated by the totals of country-born people recorded within town populations as late as the 1930s. In Aberdeen, for example, in 1931, 38 per cent of the inhabitants had been born in the rest of the North-East, that is, came from nearby rural settlements (Mackenzie, 1953, 197). Glasgow continued to take in large numbers from Renfrewshire and Lanarkshire, even while the lesser towns of the area were growing relatively to the main centre (Slaven, 1975, 233–4). Immigrants into the towns of the Western Lowlands also included significant number from the Continent of Europe, notably from Italy, Russia and Poland, to add to a steady but small influx from England (Flinn, ed., 1977, 458).

The urbanised counties of the central belt still, in 1891, contained, proportionately to their total populations, as many incomers from the rest of Scotland as they had done in 1851 (Campbell, 1984, 55–9). Yet, while towns were absorbing a continuing stream of incomers, the population of the urban sector as a whole increased by very little more than the natural rate of increase, and some of the towns that were clearly taking in numbers of migrants were, in net terms, losing by migration (Flinn, ed., 1977, 312–5).

The figures for regional growth tell the same story of an apparent slackening in net switches of population. Throughout the nineteenth century there was a continuous re-distribution of population between regions. In part this was caused by the manner in which the immigrant Irish chose to settle, giving a differential boost to the population of the Western Lowlands. To a slight degree, too, the Western Lowlands may have gained by a particularly high rate of natural increase. But in the main it was the migration of Scots that explained the tendency for the regions of central Scotland to expand more rapidly that those to the north and south. After 1861, with the benefit of figures showing rates of natural increase, the movement across regional boundaries can be seen more clearly, at least in net terms. Net migration figures show a continuing but undramatic concentration in the Eastern and Western Lowlands. But it was only through net migration rates differing by tiny percentages that readjustment proceeded. The days of headlong movement into any region were past. In fact, all regions except Western Lowlands were showing loss by net migration from 1861 onwards with the Far North, North-east and Borders losing the greater part of their natural increase or even running into actual decline, while Eastern Lowlands retained all but a small proportion of natural increase. Western Lowlands continued to gain by net migration until 1900 (with the exception of the one decade 1881–90) but after 1901 this region along with all others was a net loser by migration (Flinn, ed., 1977, 304–5).

The figures for net migration across the national boundary indicate emphatically that Scotland was losing, decade by decade, part of its natural increase. But, taken as a sequence, the decades at least from 1871 show an intriguing, regular and well-defined pattern of alternative episodes of relatively high and low rates of loss. Thus the decades of the seventies and the eighties show losses of no more than 20 per cent, while those of the nineties and 1900s were 43 and 47 per cent respectively (Robertson, 1954, 13). In fact the figures based on the rigidly-spaced decennial count capture and reflect the effect of the peaks and troughs of regular swings in the total of emigrants in which numbers were continuously changing from year to year. Within each decade, it is true, there were short-term oscillations but smoothing of these short-term movements reveals in clear form successive cycles in the emigration total, each of a duration of around twenty years. Peaks were reached in the eighties and 1900s with troughs roughly located in the alternating decades. From this results the very marked differences in the averaged migration patterns of successive decades (Thomas, 1973, 86–90). Each cycle, of course, was an individual affected by non-recurring events whether it was railway construction in the USA, prairie expansion in Canada or investment in the budding electrical industry.

The influences determining these swings were increasingly complex, with investment in diverse types of development on both sides of the Atlantic playing a part. But forces long at work were still strong. The push from the land was a factor in external as well as in internal migration and we have seen it strengthen as agriculture moved into the crisis of the last quarter of the century. The rural outflow went in part towards the towns, in part overseas, and the strict balance between these two components came under the influence of developments all around the Atlantic world. Certainly, the emigration process increasingly departed from the simple model of troubled agriculturists seeking cheap and plentiful land in the New World, a model which had never in fact expressed the full complexity of emigration experience. The record of the receiving countries shows that emigrants were now predominantly non-agricultural. Indeed, sampling of Scottish immigrants to the USA indicates that some 77 per cent came from towns rather than rural areas, a higher proportion than that held by towns within the total Scottish population (Flinn, ed., 1977, 454). The attraction of favourable terms of employment known to apply in particular occupations played a large part. In fact the figures for gross emigration include parties moving temporarily to seasonal employment in specific skilled crafts. A notable example of temporary emigration is found in the Aberdeen granite trade. Workers with skills learnt in Aberdeen found seasonal employment in the granite workings of New England; generally they would return within the year (Harper, 1984, 526-7).

The involvement of industrial and craft labour in the trans-Atlantic migration points to the influence of long cycles in investment discernible in the Atlantic countries. The phases of boom and depression, associated with periods of heavy and of lesser investment, were inversely correlated in Britain and America. Thus a phase of high investment in America, resulting in good wages and high employment, would coincide with a period of heavy unemployment and general depression in Britain (even though there might be minor booms within the long depression). The factors both of push and of pull would then move in favour of high emigration. A period with reverse characteristics would not only damp down emigration but also, with heavy investment at home, would stimulate migration into British towns (Thomas, 1973,109-13).

These phases in development, with interactions of investment and migration, encompassed the whole of Britain. The Scottish components seem to follow the general patterns, indeed in some sectors strongly influence the British figures. In building and construction the Scottish activity fits in well with the sequence of investment in the United Kingdom as a whole (Cairncross, 1953, 12-22). It was much influenced by the rate of growth of the towns, which in turn is linked to the scale of migration within Scotland. There are signs, admittedly fragmentary, that the volume of emigration was in inverse relationship with that of internal migration. It appears that part of the mobile force from the countryside was moving now overseas, now to the Scottish towns. In the decades 1881–90 and 1901–10, respectively 43 and 47 per cent of natural increase left the country while migration into Glasgow and suburbs fell to low levels; there was also net out-migration from the Western Lowlands in both decades. The decades of comparatively low emigration of the seventies and nineties saw positive net in-migration to the Western Lowlands. Migration into Glasgow shows a similar pattern of increase to higher levels in the nineties between the two decades of low in-migration, but the decade of the seventies breaks the alternating pattern being a time of failing in-migration as was the following decade (Cairncross, 1953, 23).

Relations between Canada and Britain, and particularly Scotland, in the period 1901–13 show vividly how boom on one side of the Atlantic, coinciding with secular stagnation on the other, affected migration. This was a time of protracted boom in Canada associated with the opening of prairie land to wheat farming. The rapid expansion of prairie agriculture was accompanied by intense activity in all sectors of the Canadian economy – in railroad building, construction, manufacturing, mining and lumbering. The signs of boom were most evident in the west but the east also participated in large measure. Shortages of labour occurred in all areas and wages rose sharply. Only two short-lived checks in 1903 and 1907 occurred to hold back expansion (Cairncross, 1953, 37–42, 62–3). For Britain the period was one of relatively modest investment except in export trades and of a faltering of the increase in real wages. Agriculture, on the other hand, was in a period of modest recovery. But there is no doubt that, compared with Canada, Britain was stagnating.

The result of these contrasting developments on the two sides of the Atlantic was to raise British emigration totals through annual increments to their highest recorded levels. The peak year for the UK was 1913 and for Scotland 1911. The slight drop in the Scottish figures in the last two full pre-war years may have been due as much to a change in method of recording as to a real drop. Significantly, both UK and Scottish figures recorded their only undoubted fall within the general period in the years immediately following the rundown in Canadian activity in 1907. Even so the numbers of emigrants whose permanent home was recorded as being in Scotland (the criterion for inclusion after 1912) was greater than had been the number of emigrants born in Scotland (the earlier definition of 'Scottish') in any year between 1900.

Between 1860 and 1914 the main theme in the Highlands continued to be of unremitting loss by migration and, for the most part, of actual decline in population. Some of the force that had caused so many to leave, the vast over-crowding of the land, was spent but new influences assembled, also tending towards decline.

The problems of poverty and land scarcity were still a force even after the mass migrations of the forties and fifties. It is true that many of the poorest had gone and that the exodus did significantly diminish the number of cottars. But this left the recognised land-holding population – the crofters – much as it had been even while much of the available arable land had been turned over to large-scale sheep farming in the massive clearance of the turbulent decades (Devine, 1988, 277). Thus, there remained in place a society of small-holders many of whom had insufficient land for full subsistence or any form of fully independent farming. The legislation of 1886, while it alleviated the conditions under which the crofter held his land, effectively froze the existing system of division into small holdings. It also did little to blunt the feelings of grievance and of loss, the sense that restriction was imposed by men rather than nature.

It was not merely the shell of the land-holding system that determined the living conditions of the crofters. They became more and more involved in the market economy and, in particular, turned to the purchase rather than the production of basic foodstuffs. The earlier use of the arable land of the croft was to produce a subsistence supply of food in the shape of oats and potatoes. Now, with the purchase of breadstuffs coming from elsewhere, of necessity the crofts had to be turned wholly towards the generation of cash income. The obvious move was to devote all the resources of the arable land to the support of animal production in the shape either of cattle or, increasingly, of sheep. Oats might continue to be produced for animal fodder but, more commonly, grain-producing land was put into rotation grass or set in permanent pasture. Undoubtedly, too, some of the croft land fell into neglect. But animal production was beset with difficulties. Demand for the traditional type of Highland cattle, sold as store beasts at three or four years old, was falling both because of the import of chilled or frozen meat and because a change of taste favoured slaughter of younger cattle. The yield from sheep-rearing, to which many crofters turned, fell with the depression in the price of wool. Again the partial substitution of sheep for cattle led in conjunction with other factors to deterioration of hill pastures (Collier, 1953, 68–75).

In short, the risks of crop failure and shortage of subsistence now gave way to those of involvement in a world economy of fluctuating prices. The points at which the movement of prices pressed on the personal economy of the crofter were many. Paramount perhaps was the cost of the foodstuffs, and particularly bread, that were now purchased. Probably the fall in the price of breadstuffs after 1880 did secure a rising and more dependable standard for the crofters but another factor was of great importance: there were now rising expectations of being able to purchase a diversity of goods. In itself, the small-holding system that continued to prevail was unlikely to fulfil such expectations.

However, the mystique of holding land was still potent. A good part of the population continued to cling to holdings that remained tiny, helped to a reasonable livelihood by the greater freedom that was conferred by the newer system of husbandry to seek work elsewhere while holding on to the croft as a base. For others, however, the scarcity of land was a crucial limitation. It might stand in the way of the young man seeking a holding within the tightly controlled system so as to start a married life; or it might prevent the ambitious from enlarging an existing farming business. For all the benefits of security of tenure and fair rents accruing from the Act of 1886 there was still discontent enough to keep the stream of migration moving. With land scarcity imposing its limitations, with the increased vulnerability to external price fluctuations, with rising expectations and increasing propensity to make comparisons with life in other parts, and the teasing lure of the known success of Highland settlements across the Atlantic, every Highland parish continued to lose its natural increase in part or in whole.

But change in the rate of natural increase was itself affecting the demographic situation with peculiar force in the Highland area. Crude birth rates were showing an uncertain decline from 1861 and after 1881 uncertain wavering turned to a definite and continuing fall, carrying the average rate for the Highland counties from 27 per 1,000 in 1861 to 18.4 in 1911 (Flinn, ed., 1977, 340). This decline was more severe than in any other part of the country and seems to have been due more the increasing tendency for Highland women to marry late than to any fall in fertility within marriage. It is uncertain, then, whether the root cause was distortion in the sex ratio or, quite possibly, limits on the opportunity to set up family. Both the range of employment opportunities which might be relatively good – for example, where fishing was well established as a by-employment – and the ease with which land was to be had might be influential. In any case there were considerable differences in the levels to which the birth-rate fell in different parts of the Highlands and Islands, as evidenced by figures for the decade 1901–10. Rates were 18 per 1,000 or less in Wester Ross, Western Inverness and most of Argyll. They were similarly low in Mull and the Small Isles, rather higher in southern Argyll and over 20 per 1,000 in Kintyre and Islay. The greatest deviation was in the North Hebrides where the rate stood at 26.9 per 1,000 (Barclay and Darling, 1956, 121). These differences in birth-rates led to similar differences in annual rates of natural increase which ranged between 11.3 per 1,000 in North Hebrides to less than 1 per 1,000 in parts of Wester Ross.

The fall in the rate of natural increase did not diminish the propensity to migrate out of the Highland area. There were variations in the rate of out-migration between parishes and between wider districts but they do not correlate with differences in the rate of natural increase (Barclay and Darling, 1956, 119–21). Over the whole Highland area the rate of net out-migration remained high, probably at over 10 per cent per decade, between 1861 and 1911. The fluctuations from decade to decade were minor although the rate was perceptibly lower in the decade 1901–10 than over the previous forty years (Collier, 1953, 135).

In every decade, and probably in most years, since the beginning of the nineteenth century the Highlands and Islands in all their parts had been sending away part of their natural increase, a possible exception being Orkney and Shetland before 1861 (Smith, 1984, 157–9). From 1861, even with the falling birth-rate, the stream continued unabated with Orkney and Shetland conforming to the general pattern of loss by migration and, in the main, of decline of population. But the direction of movement was changing. By 1880 there had ceased to be much difference between Argyll and the more northerly areas in the tendency to seek jobs elsewhere in Scotland. The migrants from all over the Highlands and Islands were now dividing more equally between domestic and foreign destinations (including England and Wales) (Collier, 1953, 138; Flinn, ed., 1977, 476–7; Thomson, ed., 1960, 121). On the whole, however, these 'foreign' parts took a proportion which tended to diminish through the period from 56 per cent in the decade 1861–70 to a mere 33 per cent in the decade 1901–10. This last figure shows the Highlands continuing to be widely aberrant from the rest of Scotland in migration habit. While emigration from Scotland as a whole was soaring in the period of Canadian boom the Highland emigration total was declining, in spite of the strong historic links between the Highlands and the Maritimes. Nor is there any indication of a tendency for the balance between migration to the Scottish towns and emigration to move in the pattern of change, decade by decade, that we have seen for Scotland as a whole. The implication must be that the ten-yearly alternations were even more dramatic for the Lowlands of Scotland than for the country as a whole (Collier, 1953, 138). The Highlands remained an area on its own with its migrants insensitive to the surges of economic activity in the Atlantic world which virtually dominated migrant behaviour in the rest of Scotland.

REFERENCES

R.S. Barclay and F. Fraser Darling, 'Population', in F. Fraser Darling, ed., *West Highland Survey* (Oxford, 1956).

A.K. Cairncross, *Home and Foreign Investment* (Cambridge, 1953).

A.K. Cairncross, ed., *The Scottish Economy* (Cambridge 1954).

R.H. Campbell, 'Inter-county migration in Scotland and the experience of the South-West in the nineteenth century', *Scottish Economic and Social History*, 4, 1984.

J.A.V. Collett, 'Population and employment' in W.A. Illsley, ed., *Third Statistical Account. The County of Angus* (Arbroath, 1977).

A. Collier, *The Crofting Problem* (Cambridge, 1953).

T.M. Devine, *The Great Famine: Hunger, Emigration and the Scottish Highlands in the Nineteenth Century* (Edinburgh, 1988).

M.W. Flinn ed., *Scottish Population History* (Cambridge, 1977).

H. Hamilton, ed., The Third Statistical Account of Scotland, Vol. VII, The County of Aberdeen (Glasgow, 1960).

M. Harper, 'Emigration from the North-East of Scotland, 1830–1880', Unpublished Ph.D. Thesis, Aberdeen, 1984.

H. MacKenzie, *The Third Statistical Account of Scotland. The City of Aberdeen* (Edinburgh, 1953).

C.S. Orwin and E.H. Whetham, *History of British Agriculture*, 1846–1914 (London, 1964).

D.J. Robertson, 'Population growth and movement', in Cairncross ed., *Scottish Economy*, 1954.

A. Slaven, *The Development of the West of Scotland* (London, 1975).

H.D. Smith, *Shetland Life and Trade* (Edinburgh, 1984).

C.P. Snodgrass, *The Third Statistical Account of Scotland. The County of East Lothian* (Edinburgh, 1953).

B. Thomas, *Migration and Economic Growth* (Cambridge, 1973).

G. Thomson, ed., The Third Statistical Account of Scotland. The County of Lanark (Glasgow, 1960).

K. Walton, 'Population', in Hamilton, ed., *County of Aberdeen*, 1960.

Infant Mortality Rates and Housing: Twentieth Century Glasgow

RA Cage 1994 *Scottish Economic & Social History* 14, 77–92.

The decline in general death rates in Britain from the mid nineteenth century has received considerable attention from historians as an indicator of improvements in the standard of living. However, few have examined the pattern of infant mortality rates, which, as argued by the late R.S. Neale, would be a more accurate reflection of living conditions.[2] Recent work by Woods, Watterson, Woodward, Thompson and Lee helps to overcome this deficiency.[3] Lee examines Britain on a county basis, whereas Woods, Watterson, and Woodward compare selected urban and rural areas, and Thompson concentrates on the experience of Bradford. Definite patterns emerge from these studies. First, average infant mortality rates were higher in urban than in rural areas. Second, considerable regional variation was present. Third, within urban areas and counties the rates varied widely. Fourth, there was a dramatic secular decline in infant mortality rates in the late nineteenth and early twentieth centuries. Fifth, climatic changes and population density influenced the pattern of infant mortality rates. To a large extent similar conclusions were reach by contemporaries, with all studies placing emphasis upon population densities in terms of population per acre. In this article I conclude that density per room is the crucial component in explaining local variations and trends in infant mortality rates.

Public health officials at the turn of the century were concerned about the high infant mortality rates. Detailed studies were undertaken to try to discover the causes; probably the best were those undertaken by Arthur Newsholme, the Medical Officer for the Local Government Board.[4] The conclusions derived by these studies indicate that (a) infant mortality was higher in urban than in rural areas; (b) towns with the highest populations did not necessarily have the highest infant mortality rates; (c) there were widely divergent rates between areas within counties and towns; (d) infant mortality rates exhibited definite seasonal variation, being the highest in the third quarter of the year, which generally was warmer and drier, increasing the risk of diarrhoeal infections; (e) rates were highest in areas with inadequate sanitary conditions, such as the lack of an effective sewage system, unpaved streets, lack of clean water; (f) amongst the poor, infant morality rates were higher for large families than for small ones; (g) poverty was an indirect cause in that it contributed to poor diets, over-crowding, uncleanliness, drunkenness; (h) the abandonment of breast-feeding contributed to higher rates; (i) the infant mortality rate for males was sig-nificantly higher than for females; (j) deaths under one month of life formed almost one third of total infant deaths during the first year of life, with those occurring within the first week of life accounting for half of the first month's total.

Even though contemporaries recognised that infant mortality rates had been falling, from their studies they were able to make a series of recommendations which they felt would bring about further decreases. Given that a very high proportion of deaths occurred within the first month, it was felt that better provision should be made for both neo- and post-natal care; it was especially argued that this was essential for women in the lower income groups, as they were less likely to be aware of proper nutrition and hygiene standards. Emphasis should be placed upon the necessity of breast feeding, and when not possible, there should be an adequate, safe supply of milk. Thus, without directly saying so, the experts were stressing the importance of education as a tool for helping to reduce infant mortality rates. It was also felt that more work would have to be done to ensure the elimination of the use of ashpits and their replacement by water-closets properly attached to sewers. Similarly, convenient supplies of safe water should be made available to all households. These types of recommenda-tions were a reflection of the fact that most causes of death were from infectious diseases, whether air or water borne.

Infant mortality rates had fallen prior to 1900. It is probably safe to conclude that their decline was a result of sanitation improvements which reduced the incidence of water-borne and diarrhoeal diseases. The 1860s and 1870s witnessed the introduction of safer sources of water not dependent upon polluted rivers and wells, the establishment of more effective sewer systems designed to carry the effluence away from population centres and sources of water, and the clearance of slums and the expansion of public housing. The effectiveness of these measures was limited, however, as piped water and sewerage disposal did not generally extend into the poorer areas, and slums were cleared at a faster rate than new housing was constructed, thus creating overcrowded conditions elsewhere. Infant mortality rates were not as respon-sive to sanitation improvements as was the general death rate; the latter fell at a much faster rate between 1870 and 1900 than did the former.

The data presented in Fig. 1 enable comparisons to be made between Glasgow, Liverpool, and Manchester for the period 1855–1938.[5] The rates

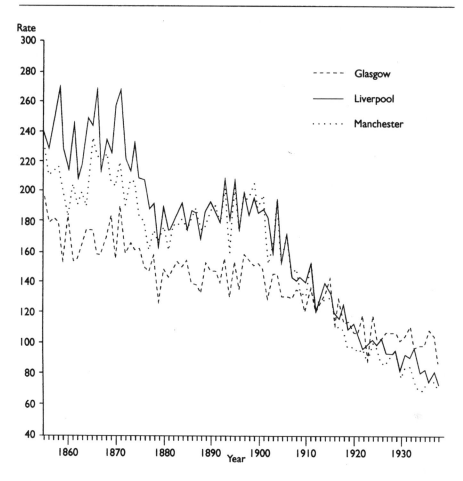

Figure 1: Infant Mortality Rates per 1,000 Live Births: Glasgow, Liverpool, Manchester, 1855–1938.

for Liverpool and Manchester were substantially higher than those for Glasgow until about 1908; after about 1920 Glasgow's rates were higher. It should also be observed that the rates for Liverpool and Manchester actually increased between 1880 and 1900, whereas for Glasgow they remained stable. For the period as a whole the improvements were more impressive for the two English cities than for Glasgow partly because they started from much higher levels, giving them more room for improvement. Clearly, something was causing infant mortality rates to decline throughout the whole of Britain, with the differences between cities becoming less striking. Part of the explanation must lie with sanitary improvements; for example, in the 1870s, there was extensive slum clearance in Glasgow undertaken by the City Improvement Trust which cleaned up the worst slum areas of the city, and in Liverpool there was an extensive campaign against common privy middens.[6] In spite of the extensive improvements in sanitation, water supply, housing, the quality of food, the introduction of fever hospitals occurring in most major British cities, the Pooleys argue that economic, social, and environmental changes outside the control of public health authorities were also instrumental. Such changes would have caused a decrease in the virulence of infectious diseases as a result of diets and general living standards improving due to higher real wages.[7]

From the Annual Reports of the Glasgow Medical Officer of Health it is possible to make some brief comparisons between Glasgow, Edinburgh, Aberdeen, Dundee, Birmingham, Manchester, Liverpool, and London at various points in time.

Until about 1910 the Scottish cities on average had lower infant mortality rates than the English cities; indeed, until about 1910 infant mortality rates for England and Wales were higher than for Scotland; Ireland had the lowest rates, a reflection of its rural nature.[8] Furthermore, with the exception of Edinburgh, Glasgow had lower rates than the other Scottish cities until about 1925–30. Finally, in all cities the infant mortality rates improved at a faster pace than in Glasgow.

TABLE I. INFANT MORTALITY RATES PER 1,000 LIVE BIRTHS

	1905	1911	1927	1931	1937	1963	1967
Glasgow	131	139	107	105	104	32	25
Edinburgh	133	118	80	69	70	23	21
Dundee	133	156	138	92	87	20	19
Aberdeen	140	139	105	90	72	19	23
London	131	129	59	65	60	N/A	N/A
Birmingham	154	164	75	71	61	24	20
Manchester	157	154	86	84	76	29	23
Liverpool	153	154	94	93	82	27	22

Source: Annual Reports, Medical Officer of Health, Glasgow.

This paper concentrates on Glasgow; information for the twentieth century, unless otherwise stated, was obtained from the Annual Report of the Medical Officer of Health. Even though data prior to 1855 is extremely sketchy, the evidence that is available indicates that infant mortality rates peaked during the 1840s; in fact it would appear that in the early stages of industrialisation caused

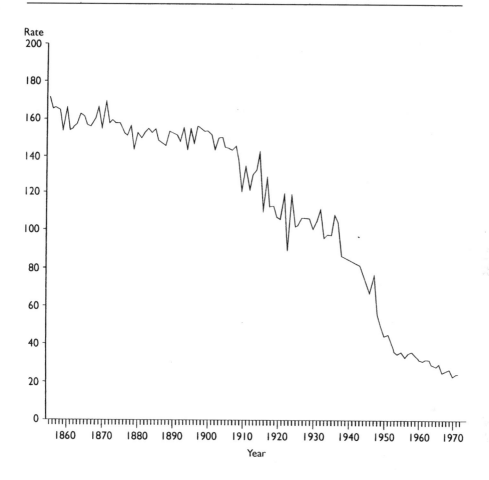

Figure 2: Infant Mortality Rates per 1,000 Live Births: Glasgow, 1855–1972.

a rise in the rate due to excessive overcrowding and appalling sanitation conditions; indeed, mortality rates for all age groups in Glasgow rose between 1831 and 1851 as a result of fever and cholera epidemics.[9] The overall trend of infant mortality rates after 1855 was downward (Fig. 2), and several distinct periods can be detected. The first is a drop from higher pre-1860 rates to a levelling off during the 1860s. The second period of improvement was the 1870s, and was very dramatic. By 1880 infant mortality rates were again levelling off. From about 1900 until the 1940s there was a steady decline. Finally, the period with the most dramatic drop in infant mortality rates was that after 1944. A number of factors can account for these patterns.

One variation in infant mortality rates is that between legitimate and illegitimate births. Not surprisingly, the rate for illegitimate births was considerably higher than for legitimate. The reasons should be obvious, given the attitudes of society to children born out of wedlock, and the fact that many of the mothers would have been from economically disadvantaged backgrounds. A.K. Chalmers was aware of this problem, stating that unlike general infant mortality rates, those for illegitimate children demonstrated no influence of locality.[10] For the period in question the biggest drop in mortality rates for illegitimate children came after 1908, with the passage of the Infant Life Protection Act, an extension of the previous Acts of 1872 and 1897. For the first time the government required supervision of persons fostering or adopting a child, besides making such persons legally liable for maintaining them with adequate food, clothing, medical aid, and lodging, thus giving abandoned babies better protection.[11] In 1950 for the first time, the Medical Officer of Health was able to report that the infant mortality rate for illegitimate babies was the same as for the legitimate.[12] From then on, the rates for the two categories were similar, with at times that for illegitimates lower than for legitimates. To some extent, no doubt, this situation was more a reflection of a change in social attitudes, than of medical improvements.

An examination of infant mortality rates by sex also produces expected results; the rate for males is consistently higher than for females, given the fact that the rate of male births is higher than for female births. The ratio, however at 129:100 on average, is higher than one would expect, given that about 52 per cent of births were males. At one time it was felt that the higher rate for males was due to the fact that they have larger heads at birth, which may had led to injuries during birth. However, this was discounted.[13] Thus, no explanation has been provided as to the difference. The fact that the infant mortality rates for both males and females followed the same pattern means that the two sexes faced the same causes of death and with about the same degree of incidence; prematurity and congenital defects were the major cause of death. These were followed by respiratory diseases (such as pneumonia), then digestive diseases (such as diarrhoea), then infectious (such as measles). Interestingly, in England, the order was different, with digestive diseases being the second most important, followed by respiratory ones. It was known that respiratory diseases were more prevalent and severe in the northern parts of Britain than in the southern areas.[14] However, the greatest difference between urban areas as to the cause of infant death was that for infectious diseases.

TABLE 2. INFANT MORTALITY RATE PER 1,000 LIVE BIRTHS, 1927

Cause	GLASGOW	BIRMINGHAM	LIVERPOOL	MANCHESTER
Immaturity	37.9	34.4	31.8	32.5
Respiratory	30.0	15.8	25.9	20.3
Digestive	13.4	10.6	15.2	10.7
Infectious	14.0	3.7	7.7	8.7
Other	11.8	10.8	13.0	13.7
Totals	109.2	75.3	93.6	85.8

The incidence of both respiratory and infectious diseases was higher in crowded conditions where child to child contact was increased. In this respect the housing conditions of Glasgow were such that there was much more intimate contact.[15]

Data on the percentage of infants who died within the first month, months two and three, months four to six, and months seven to twelve of the first year of life exhibit definite patterns. The first month of life was clearly the most hazardous. This remained the case throughout the period under review, and most deaths within the first month were attributed to premature births. As a result, by the early 1940s more emphasis was placed upon the care of premature babies in both hospitals and at home. This action brought about a decrease in the number of deaths from this cause.[16] There are a number of reasons for this, but two of the most important were the nutritional level of the mother and whether or not the infant was breast-fed. A number of studies indicate that mothers' diets in the poorer districts were inadequate, and that bottle-fed babies in these same areas received inferior quality milk.[17] These factors are directly related to the social conditions of the mother. The following table illustrates the infant mortality rate per 1,000 live births for males and females within the first four weeks of life for mothers from three areas.[18]

TABLE 3: INFANT MORTALITY RATES, BY SEX AND DISTRICT, 1909–12

	MALES	FEMALES
Poor districts	48.01	36.56
Artisan districts	30.25	25.71
Residential districts	24.76	18.36

Similar patterns hold for later years.[19] Studies into the physique of Glasgow school children further emphasised dietary deficiencies, causing the Medical

Officer to recommend that the Education Authority introduce within its cooking courses the teaching of food values. Another recommendation was that new born infants in the poorer district should be regularly visited to help to ensure proper care. This led to the establishment of voluntary organisations, such as the Ladies Child Welfare Association, and to the city-sponsored Maternity and Child Welfare Scheme.[20] The city also established milk depots and put considerable effort into ensuring safer milk and impressing upon mothers the importance of breast-feeding whenever possible. These programmes reaped benefits, for by 1946 the Medical Officer of Health was able to report that few infants died of digestive diseases under the age of three months, and that most deaths from that cause occurred after the child was weaned.[21]

If Glasgow is divided into districts, several important trends emerge. There was a high correlation between general death rates and infant mortality rates. When each rate is ranked by district, there is almost a direct match.[22] Therefore, at all ages of life, some districts had features which were threats to life. Ironically, those districts with the highest infant mortality rates were not necessarily those with the highest population densities in terms of population per acre. However, all were working class, most were central, and all but two had a higher than average proportion of small houses, indicating a high density per room. Thus, in these districts factors were prevalent which contributed to high morbidity rates for infectious and diarrhoeal diseases. This conclusion is strengthened by the following information for 1911:

TABLE 4. INFANT MORTALITY RATES CAUSED BY INFECTIOUS AND DIARRHOEAL DISEASES, BY SEX AND HOUSE SIZE, 1911

| Size of house | PERSONS/ROOM | POPULATION SHARE | INFANT MORTALITY | |
			MALES	FEMALES
1 room	3.2	13.8	210.3	163.6
2 rooms	2.4	48.4	163.9	123.3
3 rooms	1.7	21.1	128.3	101.1
4+ rooms	1.9	16.8	102.6	72.9

Sources: *Annual Report, MOH*, 1912, Appendix II, p. 182, and A.K. Chalmers, *Census 1911: Report on Glasgow and its Municipal Wards* (Glasgow, 1912), pp. 35–36.

This same pattern existed for each type of cause of death.

In order to demonstrate that persons per room was a more crucial variable than persons per acre, 1911 will be analysed in detail. The following table shows the infant mortality rates and persons per acre for seven British cities for 1911.

TABLE 5. INFANT MORTALITY RATES AND DENSITY PER ACRE, 1911

	INFANT MORTALITY	PERSONS PER ACRE
Glasgow	139	60
Edinburgh	118	29
Dundee	156	35
Aberdeen	139	26
Birmingham	164	28
Manchester	154	33
Liverpool	154	45

Sources: Annual Report, MOH, 1911 and A.K. Chalmers, Health and Housing (1912), p. 7.

As can be seen, there is no correlation between population density per acre and infant mortality rates; Glasgow had the highest density rates, but one of the lowest infant mortality rates. If we concentrate on Scottish cities, it can be seen that the number of rooms per house and the number of persons per room are more important in determining the level of infant mortality rates.

TABLE 6. SELECTED HOUSING STATISTICS, 1911

	ROOMS/ HOUSES	PERSONS/ HOUSE	PERSONS/ ROOM
Glasgow	2.55	4.66	1.83
Edinburgh	3.82	4.59	1.20
Dundee	2.53	4.27	1.69
Aberdeen	3.24	4.53	1.40

Source: A.K. Chalmers, Census 1911: Report on Glasgow and its Municipal Wards (Glasgow, 1912), p. 32.

The above data indicate that density per room played a major role in the determination of the level of infant mortality rates for all cities, not just Glasgow. To cast additional light on the above figures for Glasgow,

It is to be remembered further, that in the population we are dealing with 66 per cent. of the houses are of not more than two rooms, and that 62 per cent. of the population inhabit them – that in six only of our city Divisions (or Wards) is the proportion of one-apartments below 10 per cent.; that in nine wards they form from 10 to 20 per cent., and in six wards vary from 20 to 30 per cent. of the total houses, while in five wards the proportion is above 30 per cent. The smaller-sized houses are, therefore, distributed throughout the City in varying proportions, and their room density reaches a high average.[23]

The 1925 Annual Report of the Glasgow Medical Officer of Health made a detailed analysis of infant mortality rates by district and cause of death.[24] The city's wards were grouped into four categories: residential (I), residential and industrial (II), mainly industrial (III), and industrial and poor (IV); density per room increased with the movement from group I to group IV. These categories also reflect the magnitude of infant mortality rates, with them being lowest in the residential districts and highest in the industrial and poor ones. When the cause of death is compared for each group, it becomes obvious that room density was the crucial variable. Three major categories of death (diseases of the respiratory system, diseases of the digestive system, and infectious diseases) were the only ones to display any variation between the ward groupings, as illustrated in the following table, which shows the percentage of deaths by each disease type:

TABLE 7. INFANT DEATHS, BY DISEASE TYPE AND WARD GROUP, 1925 (PER CENT)

Disease	WARD GROUP			
	I	II	III	IV
Respiratory	3.7	12.2	18.7	23.0
Digestive	3.7	6.2	10.5	12.3
Infectious	2.7	7.1	13.2	15.1

Source: Annual Report, MOH, 1925, p. 41.

The higher the density per room, the greater the mortality rates.[25]

In order to assess the impact of room density upon infant mortality rates, cross section regressions were estimated for the 26 districts of Glasgow.[26] The first stage is reported in equation 1 (see Table 8), where a simple two variable regression is estimated using a natural log-linear specification. The result is clearly statistically significant with $\overline{R}^2$ of 0.468 and a highly significant F statistic. The estimated coefficient on room density is strongly significant. The result suggests that a one per cent rise or fall in room density caused a one per cent rise or fall in the infant mortality rate.

The next stage was to examine whether house size mattered. Hence, separate room densities were entered for each house size ranging from one to five rooms. These, of course, vary in importance across districts so, in each case, the room density in a particular size of house was weighted by the proportion of such houses in the district in question. The summation of these yields the average room density per district used in equation 1. If house size did not matter, the explanatory power of the disaggregated equation would be unchanged. Initially, all the house size room densities were entered as explanatory variables and the insignificant ones were eliminated. Only two were significant, one room and four rooms, although experimentation showed that the four room and five room variables reported very similar coefficients. Thus, they were grouped together into one four/five-room house variable. The results are reported in equation 2, Table 8, and suggest that differentiation of room densities by house size leads to a rise in the $\overline{R}^2$ from 0.468 to 0.766. The most powerful explanatory variable is room density in one-roomed houses, the 'single ends.' In other words, it is room density in these small houses which has the most powerful effect on overall infant mortality. The significant large house effect is surprising until it is appreciated that, in some areas, these constituted multiple occupancy residences with very poor living conditions.

TABLE 8. ORDINARY LEAST SQUARES ESTIMATES, 1911

	$\overline{R}^2$	F
Eq1 lnIMR = 4.06 + 1.03lnRD (22.76) (4.59)	0.47	21.09
Eq2 lnIMR = 5.70 + 0.40lnRDI + 0.22RD45 (35.21) (7.97) (4.01)	0.77	37.65
Eq3 lnIMR = 5.62 + 0.40lnRDI + 0.19RD45 + 0.48BLY (36.59) (8.54) (3.69) (2.23)	0.81	31.12

Notes
t statistics in parentheses
IMR Infant mortality rate per 1,000 live births per district.
RD Average room density per district.
RDI Room density in one-roomed houses weighted by the proportion of such houses in each district.
RD45 Room density in four- and five-roomed houses weighted by the proportion of such houses in each district.
BLY Dummy variable with a value of one for the district of Blythswood and zero for all other districts.

The third stage was to introduce the factor which appears to be the most popular explanation of mortality in past studies, namely geographical location. To do this, dummy variables for the four district groups were added to the specification in all permutations of three (we cannot have four dummy variables in the presence of a constant). It was discovered that only Group 4 was a significant explanatory variable, and only marginally so. However, this can be explained by the unusual concentration of large multiple occupancy dwellings, in one district in Group 4, namely Bythswood. When we substitute the Blythswood dummy for the Group 4 one, the overall explanation is marginally improved, as shown in equation 3. The evidence in Table 8 is clear and the regression diagnostics are robust (in addition to the reported explanatory power, there is no evidence of either heteroscedasticity or non-normality in the residuals). What matters for infant mortality is not district, but room density. Furthermore, it is room density in small, one roomed houses and large, multiple occupancy houses which matters most.

Inadequate housing remained a major problem for Glasgow; the 1951 Census highlights this. Between 1931 and 1951 Glasgow had the lowest increase of houses amongst the Scottish cities at 14.61 per cent, compared with 26.81 for Edinburgh, 23.23 for Aberdeen , and 14.89 for Dundee. Between the same years the percentage decrease in the number of one room houses for the same cities was respectively, 13.06, 27.38, 39.81, and 29.40. Thus, density levels for Glasgow remained high. In fact, in 1951, for Glasgow as a whole 8.5 per cent of the population lived in houses with more than three persons per room, as compared to 2.6 per cent for Edinburgh and Aberdeen, and 2.9 for Dundee. Those areas of Glasgow which had the highest infant mortality rates in 1951 had the highest percentage of people living in rooms with more than three people; for example, Gorbals had the highest infant mortality rate at 54 per 1,000 live births and 17.2 per cent of its population lived in rooms with more than three people. Overcrowding in Glasgow was much worse than in England. In 1951, 48 per cent of Glasgow's population lived in houses of two or less rooms, while in Birmingham the corresponding figure was 2.0 per cent, Manchester 2.0 per cent, and Liverpool 3.4.[27] It is interesting to note that in 1871, 80 per cent of Glasgow's population lived in houses of one or two rooms.[28]

In 1951, 37.5 per cent of Glasgow's households shared a water-closet. Shared facilities were even more common in some districts; in Dalmarnock, which had an infant mortality rate of 51 (city average was 41), 75.5 per cent of the population shared a water-closet. The type of housing constructed in Glasgow made it more difficult to introduce sanitary improvements within them, thus perpetuating problems associated with high infant mortality rates.

The existence of detailed studies and statistics allowed the authorities to pinpoint and concentrate on problem areas. With the passage of the Notification of Births Act in 1907 and extended in 1915, Glasgow established a department of two female doctors and ten health visitors to visit all births not medically attended to ensure that proper care was being undertaken. To assist these workers, the Glasgow Infant Health Visitors' Association was formed in 1908, consisting of volunteer female visitors who made follow-up checks. Moreover, dispensaries were established within selected districts, and they held weekly consultations.[29] In 1919 two country homes were opened to house delicate infants.[30] Milk depots were set up, and greater emphasis was placed upon the care of premature babies, especially after 1940. Finally, the public health officials placed great reliance upon the role of education as a means of helping to reduce infant mortality rates; in other words, they did not assume that motherhood comes naturally to all women.

Similar measures were put into operation throughout Britain. Why then did Glasgow's infant mortality rates not fall as rapidly as elsewhere, causing it to have the highest rates during the twentieth century amongst the cities examined? The answer lies in the number of persons per room. In terms of housing density measured by persons per room, Glasgow's was the worst in Britain. Ironically, in the city whose economic growth and wealth so heavily depended upon its human capital, improvements in housing were slow in coming, especially in the predominantly working class areas. Thus, in terms of the standard of living debate, the fact that room densities in Glasgow remained much higher than elsewhere for a longer period of time indicates that the working classes in Glasgow experienced a slower rate of improvement in their standard of living relative to other British cities.

Room densities varied considerably within cities, and Glasgow was no exception. The place of birth did have an impact on the ability to survive. An infant born in Gorbals in 1952 was 3.6 times as likely to die within its first year of life as one born in Cathcart.[31] And, an infant born in Glasgow in 1952 was more likely to die during its first year than if born in another British city. Moreover, regardless of the geographic area of birth, this paper demonstrates, beyond doubt, that an infant born into a one room dwelling faced the highest chance of dying within infancy than if born into a larger dwelling. Glasgow's single-ends were death traps, and as long as they existed, medical advances were unable to provide further reductions in infant mortality rates. Such was a fact of life, and death.

University of Queensland.

NOTES

1 I wish to thank Professor John Foster, Economics, University of Queensland, for his comments and assistance. I would also like to thank the Department of Economics, University of Queensland for financial assistance, and Professor Tony Slaven, Economic and Social History, University of Glasgow, for putting up with me on my numerous visits.

2 R.S. Neale, 'The Standard of Living, 1770–1844: A Regional and Class Study', *Economic History Review*, 2nd ser., 19 (1966), pp. 590–606. See also R.S. Neale, *Writing Marxist History* (Oxford, 1985), pp. 109–141.

3 R.I. Woods, P.A. Watterson, and J.H. Woodward, 'The Causes of Rapid Infant Mortality Decline in England and Wales, 1861–1921' Part 1, *Population Studies*, 42 (1988), pp. 343–366; Part II, *Population Studies*, 43 (1989), pp. 113–132. Barbara Thompson, 'Infant Mortality in Nineteenth-Century Bradford' in: Robert Woods and John Woodward (eds.), *Urban Disease and Mortality in Nineteenth-Century England* (1984), pp. 120–147. C.H. Lee, 'Regional Inequalities in Infant Mortality in Britain, 1861–1971: Patterns and Hypotheses', *Population Studies*, 45 (1991), pp. 55–65.

4 See for example, Supplements to the Local Government Board Annual Reports for 1909–10 [Cd. 5263], 1912–13 [Cd. 6909], 1915–16 [Cd. 8496], 1917–18 [Cd. 9169].

5 All graphs were compiled from data contained in the published Annual Reports of the Medical Officer of Health of Glasgow, 1898–1970.

6 *Annual Report of the Medical Officer of Health of Glasgow,* (hereafter *Annual Report, MOH),* 1905, p. 34.

7 Marilyn E. Pooley and Colin G. Pooley, 'Health in Manchester' in: Woods and Woodward, *Urban Disease and Mortality* p. 175.

8 Supplement to the Report of the Local Government Board for 1909–10, [Cd. 5263], p.7.

9 See R.A. Cage, 'Health in Glasgow', in R.A. Cage (ed.), *The Working Class in Glasgow, 1750–1914* (1987), pp. 56–76.

10 A.K. Chalmers, *The Health of Glasgow, 1818–1925* (Glasgow, 1930), p. 194.

11 Chalmers, *Health of Glasgow,* p. 195.

12 *Annual Report, MOH,* 1950, p. 48.

13 *Annual Report, MOH,* 1909, p. 16.

14 *Annual Report, MOH,* 1928, p. 28.

15 *Annual Report, MOH,* 1928, p. 31.

16 *Annual Report, MOH,* 1949, p. 38.

17 Chalmers, *Health of Glasgow* p. 199.

18 Chalmers, *Health of Glasgow* p. 212.

19 See for example *Annual Report, MOH,* 1925, p. 40.

20 *Annual Report, MOH,* 1904, pp. 30–35, and Olive Checkland, 'Maternal and Child Welfare', in: Olive Checkland and Margaret Lamb (eds.) *Health Care as Social History: The Glasgow Case* (Aberdeen, 1982).

21 *Annual Report, MOH,* 1946, p. 28

22 *Annual Report, MOH, 1906,* p. 37.

23 *Annual Report, MOH,* 1912, Appendix II, p. 182.

24 *Annual Report, MOH,* 1925, pp. 38–42.

25 The appendix expands on this concept. It gives the districts included in each ward grouping, along with the following information for 1911: the infant mortality rate, the percentage of houses by number of rooms from one to five, and the average number of people in each house according to the number of rooms.

26 I am indebted to Professor John Foster, Department of Economics, University of Queensland, for his advice and assistance concerning the statistical analysis.

27 The above information was computed from the *Annual Report, MOH,* 1952, pp. 142–153.

28 Robert Baird, 'Housing', in: J. Cunnison and J.B.S. Gilfillan (eds.), *The Third Statistical Account of Glasgow* (Glasgow, 1958), p. 454.

29 *Annual Report, MOH,* 1914–1919, pp. 15–16.

30 *Annual Report, MOH,* 1920, p. 28.

31 *Annual Report, MOH,* 1952, pp. 142–153.

APPENDIX

Infant Mortality Rates, Per Cent of Houses of Various Room Sizes, Average Number of People per Room, By Group and Districts, Glasgow, 1911

DISTRICT	INFANT MORTALITY RATE	ONE ROOM HOUSE		TWO ROOM HOUSE		THREE ROOM HOUSE		FOUR ROOM HOUSE		FIVE ROOM HOUSE	
		% OF TOTAL HOUSES	AVERAGE PEOPLE PER HOUSE	% OF TOTAL HOUSES	AVERAGE PEOPLE PER HOUSE	% OF TOTAL HOUSES	AVERAGE PEOPLE PER HOUSE	% OF TOTAL HOUSES	AVERAGE PEOPLE PER HOUSE	% OF TOTAL HOUSES	AVERAGE PEOPLE PER HOUSE
City	136	20.1	3.2	46.3	4.9	18.9	5.2	6.6	5.0	8.1	5.6
GROUP 1											
Dennistoun	99	8.7	2.8	44.2	4.1	31.9	4.7	9.5	5.2	5.8	5.5
Park	85	2.2	2.4	13.4	4.0	19.0	4.5	30.7	4.5	34.7	5.5
Langside	59	0.7	3.1	21.8	3.6	38.9	3.9	18.9	4.3	19.7	5.1
Pollockshields	86	1.2	3.2	7.3	4.2	5.9	4.2	20.9	4.0	64.6	5.1
Kelvinside	29	0.3	2.3	3.9	4.4	21.7	3.5	15.3	3.8	58.7	5.0
GROUP 2											
Springburn	117	27.7	3.5	58.6	5.1	10.0	6.2	1.9	5.5	1.8	5.3
Cowlairs	130	21.5	3.3	58.7	5.0	17.6	5.7	1.3	5.7	0.9	6.5
Maryhill	106	14.5	3.3	54.7	4.8	16.9	5.1	5.5	4.4	8.5	4.9
GROUP 3											
Townhead	161	20.5	3.0	53.8	4.9	17.7	5.7	5.3	5.8	2.7	7.0
Sandyford	145	15.1	3.1	38.1	4.8	24.9	5.2	8.2	5.3	13.8	5.2
Woodside	144	18.5	2.9	53.0	4.6	18.0	5.2	5.4	5.3	5.1	5.6
Hutchesontown	145	33.3	3.2	58.7	5.2	7.2	6.5	0.5	5.6	0.2	7.9
Govanhill	76	13.7	3.3	56.8	4.5	22.0	5.3	5.3	5.5	2.2	5.6
Kinning Park	145	30.7	3.5	54.6	5.4	12.3	5.8	1.0	6.1	1.5	6.5
GROUP 4											
Dalmarnock	152	37.3	3.4	54.3	5.4	7.3	6.1	0.7	6.5	0.4	7.9
Calton	155	30.9	3.0	45.8	5.0	16.8	5.6	3.4	5.9	3.2	8.1
Mile-end	159	34.7	3.4	56.8	5.3	7.4	6.5	0.8	6.0	0.4	6.8
Whitevale	151	24.3	3.3	52.1	4.9	19.3	5.7	3.2	6.2	1.1	7.0
Blackfriars	180	26.2	3.0	47.1	4.9	18.6	5.9	4.7	6.4	3.4	10.9
Exchange	200	15.4	2.5	27.4	4.4	25.2	5.1	17.9	5.2	14.2	10.4
Blythswood	160	4.3	1.9	14.2	3.5	14.6	4.4	26.6	4.7	40.4	7.4
Broomielaw	234	15.9	2.8	47.3	4.9	23.3	5.7	10.1	6.7	3.4	13.3
Anderston	126	19.9	3.1	53.2	4.7	20.1	5.7	4.3	5.7	2.5	6.8
Cowcaddens	163	24.8	2.9	47.5	5.1	18.9	5.4	5.5	5.8	3.4	7.1
Gorbals	145	15.7	2.9	40.4	4.6	30.8	5.5	7.9	6.2	5.3	6.9
Kingston	145	16.1	3.2	42.2	4.7	31.2	5.3	8.0	5.8	2.5	6.8

Death, Chambers Street and Edinburgh Corporation

R J Morris 1992 *History Teaching Review Year Book 6*, 10–15.

At the end of the nineteenth century, Chambers Street was one of the great institutional streets of Europe.[1] In the centre of the street was the Museum of Science and Art, foundation stone laid by Prince Albert in 1861, and with an architecture taken straight from the Italian Renaissance just to remind passers by of the mixture of wealth and good taste that Edinburgh represented. On the other side of the road was the Heriot Watt College with the names of professors of theoretical mechanics, engineering and electrical engineering on the door. Nearby was the Medical College for Women, the Edinburgh Dental Hospital and School and the Edinburgh Eye Dispensary. Going west along the street, the observer can still pass the building of the Normal Training College of the Church of Scotland (the precursor of Moray House Teacher Training College) and reach the quadrangle of Edinburgh University. Fifty years earlier the University was the only one of this collection to be recorded on the first large scale Ordnance Survey map of Edinburgh which was surveyed in 1854. This map showed a huddle of crowded closes, squares and wynds leading down to the Cowgate. What was the meaning of this spectacular change?

The first clue stands in the middle of the street. A slightly larger than life statue of William Chambers Lord Provost with the following inscription,

> William Chambers of Glenormiston
> Lord Provost of Edinburgh 1865–69
> Erected by the Lord Provost, Magistrates and Council 1891

William Chambers was not quite a renaissance prince outside his palace. He had come to Edinburgh in the early 1830s with his brother Robert. They became booksellers and then publishers and printers. There is a rather pleasant *Memoir* by William which portrays this process as a rather heroic self help struggle by the penniless lads from the Borders. In fact they were men of very modest means

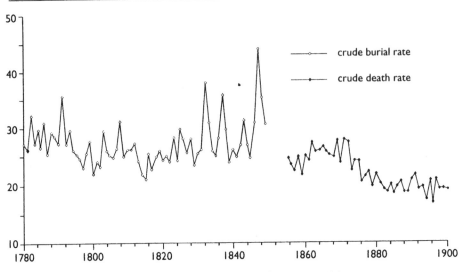

Figure 1: Crude Burial/Death Rates, Edinburgh 1780–1900.

with a few connections and a little credit. They spotted the new market in improving and educational literature which grew rapidly in the 1830s and 1840s. They published *Chambers Edinburgh Journal,* a mixture of morality, entertainment and 'facts'. They rapidly moved to encyclopaedic and educational publications and made a small fortune. Indeed anyone old enough to have used log tables for doing multiplication and division at school probably had them printed by Chambers. They headed for a mass market, mass production and steady profits. Having made money Robert retired to St Andrews but William wanted to make his mark on history; the result amongst other things was Chambers Street.

As always the story was not quite so simple as that. The story begins with the rapid rise in Edinburgh's population during the nineteenth century. The population of the burgh and its suburbs rose from 69,000 in 1801 to 161,000 in 1851. They came to work in the expanding brewing industry around Holyrood and Fountainbridge, in the insurance and legal offices of the new town and in the expanding printing and publishing industry of which Chambers was a part. Although Edinburgh's image as a professional and white collar city contains much truth it also had a varied and important often forgotten industrial sector. Growth was not as rapid as Glasgow but some of the results which accompanied this growth were familiar to many cities. Scotland had developed a tradition of statistical enquiry since the late eighteenth century and this enables us to get a glimpse of what was happening through the work of Dr James Stark, medical man of Edinburgh. In the 1840s, inspired by the interest in sanitary improvement, he made a careful check of the burial registers of Edinburgh.[2]

The results were startling. Two features stand out. There were substantial year to year fluctuations caused by epidemics and the ill health brought by periods of high food prices and unemployment. Underlying these fluctuations were clear trends. From the early 1820s, the 'death rates' of Edinburgh began to climb. They were driven forward by a series of major epidemics; cholera in 1832 and 1849, influenza and typhoid in 1837 and the famine fever, typhus brought by the refugees from the Irish famine in 1847. These figures need to be treated with care. They are burial figures. Thus they included people brought into Edinburgh for burial and excluded those who died in Edinburgh and were buried elsewhere. They were also crude 'death' figures, which means that they can be influenced by the age composition of the population. For example the migrants who made the rapid growth of urban populations possible were mainly young adults. Young adults marry and have children. The death rate amongst young children, especially in the first five years of their life was massive. Thus this migration in itself could be one basis of the increase in deaths without any worsening of conditions. These figures can and should be argued over but there can be little doubt that something very threatening was happening in Scottish cities in the 1830s and 1840s.

Medical men, administrators and politicians argued over the action which should and could be taken. Surveys and statistics were piled one upon another. By the late 1840s many were convinced that there was a clear link between these high death rates and certain areas of the great towns. These areas were crowded, ill drained, ill supplied with water and inhabited by the poor. These observations were linked to the so-called miasmatic theory of disease. Although this theory has been crudely summarized as bad smells cause disease it was more sophisticated and subtle than this, suggesting that when certain predisposing causes were linked with certain environmental conditions, then disease was the result. Predisposing causes could include drink, poverty, immoral habits or even contact with the sick. The environmental conditions were linked with the smells and vapours from rotting waste and sewage. The solution in the minds of many reformers was to provide piped water and sewage disposal and reduce the number of crowded unhealthy houses.[3] Action was slow and contested for three reasons. It was expensive but this was not all.[4] The so called dirty party was not totally motivated by meanness. The evidence was not very convincing. No one knew anything about germs. They did know that many in crowded and dirty conditions never caught the epidemic diseases whilst cholera and typhoid could appear in the best regulated housing. Indeed by the 1850s there had been noted examples of medical disasters created by the reformers. Newcastle fitted a brand new sewage system which discharged the waste into the river without calculating that the tide would bring it up river again ready to be sucked into the brand new piped water system. It was a perfect means of spreading diseases like cholera as well as a way of putting the rates up. The debate has much in common with the current debate over smoking and cancer. There are many smokers who live to a ripe old age but . . . Criticism of the Victorian politicians should compare their actions against twentieth century action against smoking.

Edinburgh moved slowly on all this. In the 1850s, the debate was characterized by two pamphlets by George Bell.[5] Trained in medicine he was interested in the links between poverty, lack of religious faith and the conditions he found in the closes and tenements around the High Street. His was the voice of fear. His reactions were those of a man of evangelical faith horrified at the sight of so many immortal souls in danger. Their squalid conditions were a barrier to faith. He also saw such conditions as a threat to his own way of life. He warned his readers of the disease, violence and disorders that could erupt from the back of the High Street. Advice on policy direction was less obvious. He realized it was little use preaching his religion until conditions improved. He knew that poverty was central to the squalor and disease he observed, yet his faith in political economy with its belief in the free market and the demoralizing effect of state or charitable help to the poor made it very hard for him to discuss poverty. His dilemma has much in common with the problems of those who seek policy directives in the face of the AIDS epidemic[6], except that for George Bell and his like it was attitudes to poverty rather than attitudes to sexuality that provided the challenge.

In a vague and general way Bell and others in Edinburgh called for more power for the local state to regulate sanitation, the disposal of waste and unsafe buildings. The result was the appointment of Dr James Littlejohn as the first Medical Officer of Health in 1862. He was a former police surgeon and had two policemen as his assistants. He used his position to collect more information. His *Report on the Sanitary Condition of the City of Edinburgh* published in 1865 was a careful dispassionate account of conditions in Edinburgh. He used information gathered in the course of his activities as MoH. He pointed to the filth of the town dairies from which stall-fed cows supplied milk to the surrounding population. He drew attention to the filthy crowded back courts of the tenements. He criticized even those which had water closets, for they were in poor repair and ill supplied with water. Above all he attacked the foul burn system which was peculiar to Edinburgh. The sewage of the old town was used to irrigate a series of meadows on the edge of the town, notably one just beyond

Holyrood Palace.[7] The smell must have been appalling, one of the many reasons Queen Victoria so disliked staying in Edinburgh. Littlejohn also had numbers to support his case. Since 1855, Scotland had had its own Registrar General of Births, Deaths and Marriages, who had the power to enforce the systematic recording of these vital events. Information was a vital weapon in this debate. Littlejohn had none of the hell fire threatening language of George Bell. Littlejohn's book was a much more boring read but these dull figures were more effective in getting action . . .

. . . It was at this point that Littlejohn's careful professional work together with the campaigning momentum built up by George Bell and others met with the political ambitions of Williams Chambers who wanted to make his period as Lord Provost a time to remember. The result was the 'Chambers' Improvement Act for Edinburgh passed in 1867. Scotland had a relatively weak series of public health acts in the nineteenth century. As a result many cities, like Edinburgh and Glasgow sought their own private legislation.[8] In Edinburgh several important streets were widened, but the most spectacular result was the creation of Chambers Street, which was driven through the crowded housing that surrounded the University and the site for the new museum. Some of the influences that make Chambers Street what it is have already been outlined. William Chambers wanted to celebrate his own success and prestige as an industrial leader. Littlejohn and his allies wanted to counter the threats to health and to public order posed by the poor of Edinburgh. Those who button their collars against the wind should remember that miasma will pose no threats in such conditions. If bad smells and stale air cause disease, then well ventilated Chambers Street will hold no fears.

Other forces were at work. South of the High Street, Edinburgh had some very good north-south links provided by the South Bridge and George IV Bridges, but the east west links were poor. Chambers Street was located to solve this problem. Fire and Ambulance services still use it gratefully and noisily when in a hurry. In addition, the growth and changing nature of cities in the nineteenth century created a major demand for large institutional buildings near the city centre, banks, theatres, museums, commercial offices, local government buildings and educational establishments.[9] Edinburgh was no exception and the houses of the poor stood in the way. Whole landscapes had to be re-organized and the authority of the market needed to be supplemented by the power of the local Improvement Act.

Did the poor gain? Certainly death rates fell in the areas affected. In the Tron area of Edinburgh, the crude death rate fell from 34.6 per thousand in 1863 to 28.9 per thousand in 1883. The reason was closely related to the fall in

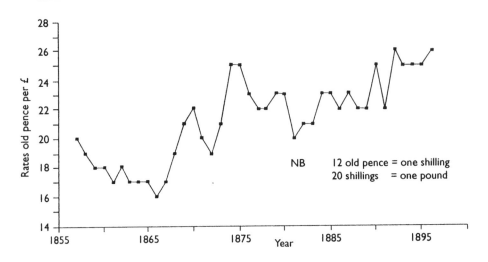

Figure 2: Local Rates old pence per £, Edinburgh 1856–1899.

population density from 314 per acre to 178. However the major drawback of the act for the poor was the failure to replace the housing which was demolished. Under the Chambers Improvement Act 2741 houses were demolished but only 340 were built.[10] With one exception the rebuilding was done by private developers. Urban clearances as extensive as anything that happened in the Highlands were concealed by the sheer size of the great towns. The displaced population simply disappeared into surrounding areas increasing the overcrowding in the rest of the town. The results of Chambers Street and related changes for the poor were mixed. For the ratepayers of Edinburgh the results were clear: rates increased.

The Act of 1867 itself was responsible for some 4d in the pound of the increase in rates which Edinburgh experienced in the last thirty years of the nineteenth century. That increase brought a resistance to further change which was not overcome until after 1900.

Chambers Street and the Improvement Act of 1867 were impressive achievements. Chambers, Littlejohn and subsequent historians relate them to the fall in death rate which took place in the later years of the century. There was an important fall in death rate in the 1870s and early 1880s when the clearances following the Act might be expected to have had an impact, but that improvement seemed to have begun in the 1850s although it suffered a check in the 1860s. In addition, infant mortality remained stubbornly high until the 1890s, although infants drank the same water and breathed in the same air as adults. The same sort of relationship between improved death rates and Improvement

Acts existed in other cities like Birmingham where the building of Corporation Street turned the city into the shopping capital of the English Midlands.[11] As with many historical stories the fall in death rates was not a simple one. Steady improvements in living standards and cleanliness, especially for adults, began in the 1850s as working people began to make real gains from industrialization and the poorer elements like the hand loom weavers disappeared from the scene. The great epidemics of the 1830s and 1804s were not repeated. The cholera epidemics of 1854 and 1866 were less damaging than earlier epidemics. After these factors had started the process, the Improvement Acts of the 1860s arrived to assist the process, to be helped by the falling food prices of the 1870s. Thus the reading of Chambers Street is not a simple matter. It was a story of falling death rates and rising local rates of taxation. It was a story of William Chambers's ambitions and James Littlejohn's campaigning use of statistics, but these were only chapters of a larger more complex story. Improving living standards and the changing geography of cities were others. This was one street in one, albeit important city but the same complex set of processes was at work in other towns. There are many other streets in Scotland which can and should be 'read' in this way.

NOTES

1 There is more on the context of Chambers St. in R.J. Morris, Urbanisation and Scotland, in W.H. Fraser and R.J. Morris (ed.), *People and Society in Scotland*, Vol. II, 1830–1914, Edinburgh 1990, pp. 73–103 and in R.J. Morris, Urbanization, in John Langton and R.J. Morris (eds.) *Atlas of Industrializing Britain, 1780–1914*, London 1986, pp. 164–179.

2 James Stark, *An inquiry into some points of the sanitary state of Edinburgh,* Edinburgh 1847.

3 Anthony S. Wohl. *Endangered Lives, Public Health in Victorian Britain,* London 1983; and M.W. Flinn (ed.) *The Sanitary Report on the Condition of the Labouring Population of Great Britain in 1842,* by Edwin Chadwick, Edinburgh 1964.

4 Christopher Hamlin. Muddling in Bumbledom; on the enormity of large sanitary improvements in four British towns, 1855–1885, *Victorian Studies*, vol. 32, Autumn 1988, pp. 55–84.

5 George Bell, *Day and Night in the Wynds of Edinburgh (1849) and Blackfriars' Wynd Analyzed (1850)*, reprinted Leicester 1973.

6 Susan Sontag, *Aids and its Metaphors,* London 1988. p.55.

7 P.J. Smith, The foul burns of Edinburgh: public health attitudes and environmental change. *Scottish Geographical Magazine,* vol. 91, 1975, pp. 25– 37.

8 G.F.A. Best, Another part of the Island, in H.J. Dyos and M. Wolff (eds.), *The Victorian City,* vol. one. London 1973, pp 389–411.

9 J.W.R. Whitehand, *The Changing Face of Cities,* Oxford 1987.

10 P.J. Smith, The Rehousing/Relocation Issue in an Early Slum Clearance Scheme: Edinburgh 1865–1885, *Urban Studies*, vol. 26, 1989, pp. 100–114.

11 R. Woods, Mortality and Sanitary Conditions in the 'best governed city in the world' – Birmingham, 1870–1910, *Journal of Historical Geography*, vol 4. 1978. pp. 35–56.

Urban Growth and Municipal Government: Glasgow in a comparative context, 1846–1914

Extracted from Tom Hart 1982 *in* Anthony Slaner and Derek Aldcroft (eds) *Business, Banking and Urban History,* Edinburgh (John Donald), 205–16.

'PROGRESSIVISM', POPULISM AND SOCIAL BUREAUCRACY IN GLASGOW

Progressive philosophy supported increases in municipal activity and spending where these gave substantial benefits, not otherwise available, to those making the heaviest contribution to local taxation. On this basis, how far did Glasgow's policy goals fit the 'progressive' model? Clearly, the initiatives to strengthen the police force and to improve the city streets were progressive. They maintained law and order while improving the transport system. The municipalisation of water, gas, tram and electricity services was also strongly influenced by the practical desire to retain effective control over the public streets and by the more theoretical view that direct operation of unified public utilities could yield savings and allow pricing to be adjusted to reflect municipal, not commercial, priorities. Monopoly profits came under direct public control and could be used to reduce charges while taking full advantage of the ability of further investment and economies of scale to lower operating costs per unit of output. Comparisons were constantly made with other authorities and, on a simple cost basis, Glasgow emerged very favourably. After municipalisation in 1894, tram fares were lowered and the quality of service improved yet, despite low fares, the trams still achieved a significant surplus which was transferred to the city's Common Good Fund.[1] Gas prices were reduced from 4/7 (23p) per 1000 cubic feet before municipalisation in 1869 to 2/6 (12½p) by 1893, 2/2 (11p) by 1900 and 1/8 to 2/- (depending on the type of customer) by 1910.[2] A large part of this reduction was due to a 32% fall in coal prices between 1869 and 1895, while average consumers also gained from a reduction in the discounts to large customers. Had private operation continued, price cuts would also have been possible due to cheaper coal and economies of scale similar to those pursued by the city council, but comparisons with private and municipal gas undertakings elsewhere indicated that Glasgow secured even larger gains. Only Newcastle (close to good sources of gas coal), Plymouth and Portsea had cheaper municipal gas in the 1890s, and their gas had a lower illuminating power than that of Glasgow.[3] In 1900, the water undertaking combined the second lowest water rate in Britain (5d (2p) in the £) with an excellent quality and quantity of supply. The industrial use of water in Glasgow was much higher than in any other city and, as a matter of policy, charges for metered water supplies were arranged to permit a lower water rate for domestic users.[4]

TABLE 1: *Taxes imposed by city council on owners and occupiers of property*

Financial Year	TAX INCOME (£ THOUSANDS)	RATEABLE VALUE (£ THOUSANDS)	POPULATION (THOUSANDS)	TAX PER £ OF RENTAL	TAX PER HEAD OF POPULATION
1846/47	35	900	300	4P	12P
1850/51	70	1100	330	6.4P	21P
1860/61	170	1625	396	10.6P	42P
1870/71	270	2126	478	12.9P	56P
1880/81	380	3427	510	11.2P	75P
1890/91	400	3455	566	11.4P	71P
1900/01	769	4953	762	15.4P	101P
1910/11	1067	5961	784	17.8P	137P
1913/14	1402	7473	1050	18.7P	134P

While the total city rate did rise sharply between 1845 and the 1860s (Table 1), a large part of this increase was, in the terminology of the time, 'remunerative'; it was related to the benefits of improved and expanded services.[5] For example, the levying of a 1/2d (6p) water rate in the 1850s made a large contribution to the rate increase but, against this, the benefits of an improved system were gained and consumers avoided the payments which would have been due to the water companies. The softer Katrine water also produced savings on soap and in other ways for domestic and industrial users.[6] In contrast, the increased rates in rural areas at this time were more heavily concentrated on 'unremunerative' relief of the poor.[7] Most of the increase in urban rates reflected 'progressive' thinking. Some freestanding burghs did have lower rates than Glasgow but, with lower populations, they had less need, and less desire, for the more elaborate services of a large city.[8] The fringe burghs around Glasgow also had rates below those of the city but their inhabitants were seen as temporarily avoiding their proper contribution to a city from which they drew large benefits. 'Progressivism' required a regular extension of the city boundaries so long as there was confidence that the overall policy of the city would be 'progressive'. It was the lack of this condition which made it more difficult to extend the boundaries of the more populist American cities.

From the 1870s, there were fewer instances (apart from education which was being separately rated by the Schools Boards from 1873) where additional rates appeared to give clear benefits to the middle class. The relative stability of the city rate between 1870 and 1895 can therefore be seen as evidence of continuing 'progressivism', with further expansion being concentrated on the municipal trading sector which offered better services and lower costs with little risk of burdening the rates. Much of the interest in public parks, public halls and civic buildings, sewage purification, the prohibition of advertisements on trams, the aesthetic design of wires and poles, street cleansing and the removal of public health eyesores also derived from the middle class desire for an 'improved' city. However, when the rate costs of a large scheme were high in relation to the benefits to principal ratepayers, projects were deferred. This is best illustrated by the long delay in tackling the cleansing of the Clyde. The capital cost of this project, first contemplated in the 1850s, rivalled that of Katrine water but the benefits were less, especially since no easy way could be found of recovering the organic matter in sewage and selling it to farmers. Not until the 1890s did the city feel that it could afford sewage purification and, even then, action was influenced by the prospect of costs being lowered through the integration of intercepting sewers with construction of the Argyle railway tunnel.[9]

Park costs were, however, much lower. Not only was there a direct gain in amenity but costs could be recouped by the sale of parts of the land acquired for high-amenity housing. The same thinking entered the strategy of the City Improvement Trust. There were originally high hopes that the cost of slum demolition could be recouped by the sale of the land for the higher value purposes of an expanding city centre. When these hopes did not materialise, Lord Provost Blackie was rejected by city voters. Such evidence suggests a strong 'progressive' element in Glasgow's policy goals. This element was also well entrenched by 1850, forty years earlier than the peak of American concern about urban corruption and the need for more efficient government . . .

CHANGING PERCEPTIONS OF GLASGOW: 1900–14

In the decade before 1914, euphoric assessments of Glasgow's municipal enterprise underwent significant modification. As in the 1880s, doubts arose about the level of local taxation and the scale of city debt in relation to the

economic prospects of the region. The city was far from being on the edge of
bankruptcy – it had an excellent financial standing – but there was a strong
consciousness that this standing, and a reasonable level of rating, depended
upon sound financial policies. Borrowing was carefully controlled to restrict the
increase in the rate burden and, though the immediate depression was less severe
than in the 1880s, doubts about the longer-term growth prospects were
stronger. Financial prudence was a significant factor in phasing sewage purification plans over a ten-year period, while the major new gasworks at Provan
was designed to be completed in stages. The first phase was completed in 1904
but subsequent spending was slowed down in view of deteriorating prospects.
Worries about local coal supplies, slow progress on boundary extensions, the
contraction of housebuilding from 1902 and a reduction of the growth rate in
locomotive and ship construction made City Treasurers and their officials less
confident about a continuation of nineteenth-century levels of growth.[10]
Economic weakness also revealed itself in a rise in the number of households
with rate arrears from 12,834 in the prosperous year 1895/6 to 35, 671 by
1980/9.[11]

Sound finance became the watchword and there was concern that departmental plans for expansion might take precedence over a more integrated view
of the total objectives of the city in the light of realistic financing policies. By
1908, the *Glasgow Herald* was reporting proposals for the appointment of a
City Manager[12] and, four years earlier, Mabel Atkinson had picked out poor
co-ordination as one of the main weaknesses of even the larger Scottish local
authorities.[13] Confidence in municipal trading was waning with the failure to
sustain earlier performances. Fears about the abuse of monopoly, and socialist
tendencies, became more common as a wider franchise opened up the potential
for destructive impacts on the economy as voters sought special favours from
city councillors.[14] The tram strike of 1911, and the national increase in labour
unrest, were a reminder that cosy assumptions about comparative efficiency and
a tranquil labour force could be rudely interrupted with the passage of time . . .

Until around 1900, 'progressive' and 'social bureaucratic' tendencies could
co-exist in Glasgow. Local ratepayers could tolerate, and even encourage, a
certain amount of social spending which could not be fully reconciled with a
'progressive' philosophy. Some tensions did appear in the moderate depression
of the 1880s, but improved conditions in the 1890s favoured further
enterprise . . .

Glasgow's civil government still deserves commendation for its nineteenth-
century enterprise, but success owed much to the city's strong economy. From
1900 it was becoming impossible to satisfy 'progressives', social bureaucrats
and populists within the city framework, and the conflicting images of Glasgow,

which became more obvious between the late 1890s and 1914, reflected a relative weakening of the regional economy aggravated by the shift of emphasis in public policy and financing from local to national issues. The debate on the merits of public and private enterprise intensified, but it was a debate being conducted at a different level.

NOTES

1 C. A. Oakley, *The Last Tram*, 1962 p. 58.

2 Sir James Bell (Lord Provost, 1892–96) and J. Paton, *Glasgow: Its Municipal Organisation and Administration*, 1896, pp. 267, 271 and 272. W. Smart (Professor of Political Economy, University of Glasgow), 'The Municipal Work and Finance of Glasgow', *Economic Jnl. 5*, 1895, pp. 47–8. *Municipal Glasgow: Its Evolution and Enterprises*, Corporation of Glasgow, 1914, p. 123.

3 W. Smart, *ibid.*

4 J. Colquhoun (Convener of Finance Committee), 'Glasgow Corporation Finance', 1894, p. 15 (paper read at meeting of Glasgow Institute of Accountants Debating Society, 18 January, 1894).

5 Report by Goschen (President of the Poor Law Board) on 'The Progressive Increase in Local Taxation', *HC Paper 470, 1870* - reprinted as *HC Paper 201, 1893*. The 'remunerative'/unremunerative' distinction is also taken up in the Local Taxation (Scotland) Report (Skelton Report), C7575, 1895.

6 Bell and Paton, *op. cit.*, p. 245.

7 The Goschen Report refers to the substantial increase in spending on poor relief to the late 1860s, and the Skelton Report illustrates the high level of Poor and Educational Rate Poundages in rural areas with low rateable values.

8 In 1892/3, several small and poor towns had total rates (including poor and education rates) over 6/- in the £. Glasgow's combined rate, for a much wider and better range of services, was 5/- but the medium-sized towns of Airdrie, Stirling and Kilmarnock had rates as low as 3/7, 3/2 and 3/-, while in the burghs around Glasgow were: Clydebank (3/6), Govan (3/7), Partick (3/5), Pollokshaws (3/8) and Kinning Park (3/5) (Skelton Report).

9 Bell and Paton, *op. cit.*, pp. 140–141.

10 See the following, especially the 1900 paper by A. Murray, pp. 22–25. A. Murray CA (City Treasurer), 'The Glasgow Corporation: Finance, Bookkeeping and Balance Sheet', 1900 (paper read to Students Society of Glasgow Chartered Accountants, 20 March, 1900). A. Murray CA (City Treasurer), 'The Glasgow Corporation Accounts with special reference to Depreciation and Sinking Funds', 1903 (paper read to Economic Science Section of the Royal Philosophical Society of Glasgow, 4 March, 1903). A. Walker (City Assessor), *City Rating*, 1911. T.E. Robinson (City Registrar), 'Municipal Borrowing', 1912. *loc. cit.*

11 A.Walker, *City Rating*, 1911, p. 22.

12 *Glasgow Herald*, 6, 13, 18–20 May, 1908 (quoted in B. Aspinwall, 'Glasgow Trams and American Politics', *Scottish Historical Review 56*, 1977, p. 83).

13 M. Atkinson, *Local Government in Scotland,* 1904, pp. 54–60 and p. 397.

14 J. R. Kellet, 'Municipal Socialism, Enterprise and Trading in the Victorian City', *Urban History Yearbook,* 1978, pp. 36–45.

A Burgh's Response to the Problems of Urban Growth: Stirling, 1780–1880

Finlay McKichan 1978 *Scottish Historical Review* 57, 68–86.

. . . Stirling was an ancient market town which was able to share in the economic 'take-off' of the late eighteenth and the nineteenth century.[1] Its population rose from around 4000 in 1755 to 13,480 in 1881. Such a rate of growth was undramatic compared to industrial boom towns, but it did reflect significant economic success. This success was broad based. Stirling's principal share in the industrial growth of the period came from wool. By the 1860s the most successful of the town's woollen firms, Robert Smith and Sons, was employing 950 hands in its Parkvale and Hayford mills. However, manufacturing industry did not dominate the economy of the town. Agricultural improvement made the carse of Stirling into one of the most fertile farming areas in Scotland and increased the importance of the royal burgh as a market town and regional centre. In the nineteenth century the numbers of bankers, land surveyors, auctioneers, medical practitioners, grain merchants and many types of tradesmen and shopkeepers grew in proportion much more rapidly than did the general population of the town, and reflected the business brought to Stirling from the surrounding area.

Business came also from further afield. Stirling's strategic position, as a gateway to the south and the Scott country and also on the roads and then the railway to the north, allowed it to take advantage of the growing tourist traffic. An important hotel trade was developed. Some of those who came to visit Stirling remained to become residents. As one commentator put it in 1832, 'many respectable families have been induced to settle in Stirling in consequence of the cheapness of living, the beauty of the surrounding country and the society which the town affords';[2] living off landed property, capital or pensions, these families became another important pillar of the town's economy.

Till the end of the eighteenth century Stirling was almost entirely built on the castle rock and the ridge leading from it. Thereafter, the town's growing middle class became less willing to live in the crowded old town and built for itself fine new houses on the open ground to the west and south. The first of the substantial villas were built around the end of the Napoleonic Wars. By 1857 the *Stirling Journal* could report that 'building operations were going on very fast at the west end and in a few years at the present rate of feuing a new town will be formed'.[3] These houses were for men in business on a substantial scale and for lawyers, ministers of the wealthier churches and people living off capital or landed property. To the north of the town were built terraces which were more modest and were clearly intended for the less opulent middle class. As those who could afford to moved out to the suburbs, the old town gradually became the quarter of the poorer inhabitants. For example, in 1851 James Burden, a town councillor and master brewer, still lived in St Mary's Wynd in the heart of the old town, but this was becoming more and more unusual for a man of his standing. In 1851, we find that twenty-two per cent of the house-holders in that street owned their own businesses, were professional men or lived off landed property, capital or pensions. By 1881 only eight per cent were in these categories.[4]

   A graphic account of what it was like to live in the old town in 1841 was given in a report made as part of the enquiry into the sanitary condition of the labouring population, directed for the Poor Law Commissioners by their secretary, Edwin Chadwick. The Stirling report was written by Dr William Hutton Forrest.[5] Forrest was to be a key figure in the improvement of the sanitary state of the town and he was in may ways a provincial Chadwick. He had the same evangelistic dedication to cleansing and sanitation and the same combination of energy, self-confidence and tactlessness. He began his report with a table showing the incidence of typhus fever among cases brought to the dispensary in the period 1831–41. The list of streets with an incidence of more than 1 in 20 is in fact a list of the principal streets in the old town, the highest being 1 in 8.68 in St Mary's Wynd. Of the streets shown to have an incidence of less than 1 in 20, all except one were on the periphery of or outside the old town. In Forrest's mind there was no doubt that the old town was fever-ridden because it was filthy. He wrote that:

> The poor . . . are very much exposed to the effluvia arising from decaying animal and vegetable substances. These, for the most part, are thrown from the houses into abominable recepticles called 'middings'. Many, very many of the poor do not put themselves to the trouble of depositing filth in these recepticles, but use the best place that presents its self, such as common stairs, closes, etc. Many, again, throw it without any ceremony or hindrance from their windows into the public streets and closes.

It is difficult for those who take for granted a system of under-ground water-borne sewerage to imagine how such a town must have looked and smelled. Forrest made it clear that it was not only the poor who were responsible. The filth from the jail was floated away down the ridge leading from the rock every second or third day, makings its way down several of the principal streets. Blood from the slaughter house was also allowed to run down the streets. And how could matters be otherwise? According to Forrest the sewers were open, cleansed only by rain water and (except in the main streets) often blocked. And there was a desperate shortage of water, which had to be drawn from street-standpipes, at which it was not uncommon to see a queue of from 80 to 100 persons. Water was not piped into the houses of even the wealthy inhabitants. The streets were cleaned by a few old men without any apparent attention to time or order.

Forrest was, of course, a propagandist. He sometimes highlighted the worst cases in an attempt to get action and his statistics (like so many nineteenth-century statistics) were derived from incomplete evidence and loosely interpreted. However, there is plenty of corroborative evidence that by at least the 1840s the old town of Stirling had been allowed to accumulate a mass of poverty, filth, disease and misery.[6] How far can the municipal authorities, the town council, be blamed for this state of affairs?

To provide water and sewers and efficient cleansing cost money. It is only fair before assessing the performance of the town council in the late eighteenth and early nineteenth century to examine the financial resources it commanded. Like the other royal burghs, Stirling received by royal grant early in its existence a package of property and rights, known as the common good, which was intended to be sufficient to enable it to carry out its responsibilities. The common good normally included lands, fishings, mills and the right to levy customs on goods entering and leaving the burgh and tolls on articles brought for sale at the burgh's markets and fairs.[7]

Like many royal burghs, Stirling had by the late eighteenth century frittered away most of its lands – lands which would have yielded a rich profit as the town expanded in the nineteenth century.[8] The town council depended now for most of its income on fishings and customs. From 1790 until 1818 the rents of the fishings on the Forth and Teith produced a slightly higher revenue than customs, reaching a peak of £1,444 in 1810–11. Thereafter, however, the yield of fishings declined somewhat, while that of customs greatly increased, so that from around 1820 the yield of customs was usually about double that of fishings. Customs revenue rose consistently, with only two major set-backs, from £508 in 1789–90 to a peak of £2,636 in 1855–6. Stirling's strategic position at the crossing of the Forth meant that a great deal of freight passed through the town and paid customs dues, and industrial and commercial development thus benefited the burgh funds. The common good in the early nineteenth century was, therefore, far from being an unimportant or declining asset. Burgh revenue kept pace with the rapid price rise during the French wars. From 1815 to the 1850s, apart from short term fluctuations, revenue maintained the level of wartime boom while prices were very much lower than in 1808–14. The real value of burgh revenue was therefore considerably higher in the 40 years after 1815 than it had been in the previous 25 years.[9]

What level of municipal services did this make it possible for the town council to provide? In street paving at least it must be granted that it did well. The Buccleuch Commissioners complained in 1845 that many of the streets they inspected, especially in the poorer parts of towns, were quite unmade.[10] But in Stirling most of the principal streets of the old town were paved in the course of a sustained programme from 1834 to 1841. The proprietors in these streets were persuaded to make subscriptions. The portion paid by subscriptions varied from 13 to 41 per cent, and the council was thus prepared to meet the greater part of the cost from the common good.[11]

It must be admitted, however, that the council's reaction to many of Stirling's problems was woefully inadequate. The water supply by 1842 was still providing at best about 2¼ gallons per head per day, whereas Manchester and Liverpool (with much greater population growth) were providing 6–8 gallons per head per day in the 1830s.[12] In Stirling, over the years, many council committees considered the problem. In 1834 one produced a carefully-prepared plan for a stone reservoir at Touch, from where the supply came, but only £9 was spent to bring into the supply pipe the water from a small rill at Touch.[13] The council was unable to translate concern and ideas on the water supply into effective action.

Over the watching of the town there was for years not even much concern. In 1835 the representative of the Municipal Corporations Commission was told that the townspeople were satisfied with the system of watching because crimes were few. An examination of the court reports in the *Stirling Journal and Advertiser* for that year shows that crimes were indeed few and were mostly cases of petty theft. This may have partially excused a system which depended during the day on four part-time (and sometimes broken-down) town officers and at night on a town-guard of householders, a duty which those who could afford to do so escaped when their turn came by sending a substitute (often the cheapest available and therefore the least able).[14] The system made no effective provision for serious disorder. In the event of riot the magistrates invariably called out the military, but once the troops were summoned there was no telling what damage might be done. When troops were used to quell a riot in Stirling in

1823, some of them were drunk and started firing and it was only by good fortune that there were no casualties.[15]

In cleansing and drainage the performance of the town council was particularly poor. In the late eighteenth and early nineteenth century street-cleaning in Stirling (as in most towns) was let out to contractors for most of the time. Carting was the most expensive part of the operation, and contractors who had submitted low tenders to get the contract often left filth lying around in heaps to avoid making a loss on the deal. For several years after 1798 and between 1840 and 1842 the council took the work into its own hands and engaged men for the purpose, yet while it deplored the inefficiency of the contractors, it was unwilling to spend enough to do the job properly itself.[16] The return to contracting in 1842 was a particularly retrograde step, as the trend among progressive authorities in Scotland by then was undoubtedly to employ direct labour and accept that it was expensive.[17] The council seems to have been content to leave the slope on which the town was built to propel the filth through the open sewers. There is evidence that some of the newer streets were hardly drained at all: as late as 1859 there were no sewers in streets in the fashionable West End and sewage was being allowed to flow onto the road.[18] Stirling seems to have delayed longer than most comparable burghs before starting to build covered sewers in its main streets.[19]

Yet it would be unjust to suggest that in the early and mid-nineteenth century Stirling town council ignored these problems. Attempts were often made to find solutions, as in the acrimonious debate in 1834 about the municipally-owned slaughter-house when it was claimed that 'it was owing to this nuisance that Stirling, though occupying the most delightful spot in the country, was called a dirty town'. The council decided to build a cesspool to receive the blood, but seven years later Dr Forrest was complaining that it was still running down the streets.[20]

The real stumbling block was that the council lacked the resources to tackle the town's problems effectively.

The common good was no longer sufficient to meet the needs of an expanding town, but what alternatives were available? The town council could, of course, appeal for voluntary subscriptions, and on a few occasions this was successfully done in Stirling. It worked during the street-paving programme in the late 1830s, when it was clearly in the interests of the subscribers[21] who might expect to have the value of their properties increased by more than the amount of the subscription. But even in this case not all the proprietors fulfilled their promises nor even agreed to subscribe. Appeals for subscriptions also worked during an emergency. An outbreak of body snatching from the churchyard in 1823 caused such indignation that the magistrates were able to persuade a public meeting to agree to the appointment of twelve nightwatchmen, financed by public sub-scription to guard, not only the churchyard but also the rest of the town. The scheme operated for two years until the scare passed and subscriptions dried up.[22] Subscriptions were also used during the cholera epidemic of 1832 to provide an emergency hospital and a soup kitchen, food and clothes for the poor in the hope of building up their resistance, but subscriptions dried up when it began to appear that Stirling would escape the disease. The day after the soup kitchen closed the first case occurred. Not only were subscriptions renewed, but the £12 householders of the burgh even agreed to a compulsory assessment under the Cholera Act. Cholera was a novel and frightening disease which seemed to threaten rich as well as poor.[23] In contrast, during the typhus epidemic of 1847 which killed many more people in Stirling than cholera had done, but which was regarded as mainly a poor man's disease, the council did nothing.[24]

The needs of all sections of the population of a growing town could only be met by a compulsory and permanent assessment of those who could afford to pay. This truth was first recognised by Scottish cities and towns which in the late eighteenth and early nineteenth century obtained local acts of parliament authorising the imposition of an assessment or rate for such purposes as watching, lighting, cleansing and water supply.[25] These assessments were normally levied by *ad hoc* bodies known as police commissions, a majority of whose members were generally elected by the ratepayers, occupiers paying according to the value of their property with exemptions below a certain annual value. These local police acts are the origin of modern burgh rating in Scot-land.[26] Obtaining a local act was, however, a difficult and costly business, and a general statute passed in 1833 made it easier for towns to be assessed for police purposes.[27] This authorised householders of properties worth £10 per annum in royal burghs or burghs of barony to elect commissioners of police with power to assess for lighting, watching, paving, cleaning, water supply, drainage, scaven-ging and the prevention of infectious diseases. The town would thereafter be administered by two bodies – the town council and the new police board. The town councils were not yet trusted to raise an assessment, despite the fact that the same year, 1833, saw the abolition of the close corporations and provided for the election of new town councils by the same £10 householders who were empowered to establish police boards.

Stirling was prompted to take advantage of the General Police Act to levy an assessment in 1835, but the Municipal Corporations Commissioners doubted whether the inhabitants would do so.[28] Their pessimism was justified. The council agreed to appoint a committee to consider which parts of the act might be applied to Stirling and to call the meeting of inhabitants which would have to adopt the act.[29] In the event nothing more was heard of the proposal.

It was of critical importance in the mid-nineteenth century that the prospective ratepayers be convinced in advance that a proposed assessment really was necessary and unavoidable. This was shown by Stirling's reaction to prison assessment. The Act to Improve Prisons and Prison Discipline in Scotland (1839) transferred responsibility for maintaining jails from the royal burghs to county prison boards.[30] Stirling town council had welcomed this measure, thinking it merely meant that the rest of the county would in future have to pay a fair share of the running costs of Stirling jail, but the prison board began to build new jails and imposed levies on the town council which were substantially higher than the amount its own jail had formerly cost – so high that the council could not meet the board's levies from the common good, as it had anticipated, but instead had to impose a prison assessment as authorised by the act. This was quite unexpected by anyone in Stirling[31] and the reaction of the ratepayers was angry and obstructive. A public meeting demanded that the money be raised without resorting to an assessment – in other words that it should all be paid from the common good.[32] This the council could not do, and throughout the 1840s it struggled against adamant resistance to try to collect the assessment, which varied from three pence to sixpence per pound of valued rental. In 1847 the council was almost sued by the prison board for non-payment and in 1848 it was actually sued.[33] Ratepayers could resist an assessment which they resented.

The adoption of a poor rate came to be an important step in the gradual acceptance by the people of Stirling of the need for assessments. Under the old Scottish poor law, the magistrates in royal burghs had responsibility for the management of the poor, but they usually delegated this to the kirk session of the parish church, which provided poor relief out of church door collections.[34] From the late eighteenth century, because of the large numbers of seceders in the town, these had to be supplemented in Stirling by an organised system of voluntary subscriptions called the poor's scheme.[35] However, this system collapsed under the pressure of the acute destitution of the early 1840s and the Disruption of 1843 (which in Stirling dramatically reduced the collections in the Established Church). In January 1844 the kirk session gave up the management of the poor.[36] A debate followed on whether a poor rate should be imposed. The editor of the *Stirling Observer* felt it safe to advise 'Away then with the bugbear of an assessment. We conclude that the Town Council as guardians of the poor of the parish . . . do wrong if any undue stringency be evinced towards them to prevent an assessment on the inhabitants, for which we believe the great majority of them are now quite prepared'.[37] After a delay during the passing of the Poor Law Amendment (Scotland) Act of 1845 and the formation of a parochial board (to which responsibility for the poor now passed), a poor rate was introduced in Stirling in 1846. Although it was levied in its first year at 1s. 3d. in the pound (substantially more than the prison rate) it was accepted without fuss.[38] Resistance to assessments ended if the need was sufficiently pressing.

In one sense, however, poor relief was a special case. It had always been paid out of the pockets of the townspeople and not from the common good. Water was the first service formerly financed from that common good which the householders agreed to support by a rate – but only after three years of controversy. In 1844 when a committee of inhabitants was formed to press for a large new waterworks, it remarked that 'the inhabitants generally are opposed to permanent annual assessments', a conclusion echoed in 1847 by one opponent who claimed that 'the privilege they now enjoyed of little local taxation had been a great mean of bringing respectable inhabitants to the town and they ought to take care how they encroached upon that privilege'.[39] Reluctance to pay a water rate became intertwined with the party feuds of town council politics.

During 1845 the demand for an efficient waterworks was pressed with great energy by the leaders of the water committee, Dr Forrest and Councillor William Rankin who had proposed the adoption of the General Police Act in 1836, whose efforts put the majority group in the town council on the horns of an agonising dilemma. The Liberals had controlled the council since municipal reform in 1833 and owed their power in part to their respect for the electors' dislike of assessments. But a water scheme would need at least £3,000 and probably nearer £5,000. The reaction of the council was to accept the need for more water but to delay taking any effective action. Forrest and Rankin made water the major issue in the municipal elections of November 1845, which brought the defeat of Bailie Robert Smith, the Liberal councillor most closely associated with the policy of delay. The staunchly Conservative *Stirling Journal* commented on this by smugly looking forward to 'the affairs of the burgh being managed without being mixed up with politics, its parties and their crooked ways'.[40]

Another threat in the opposition to the water scheme came to the fore during 1846. Again it was represented by Smith who contrived to be co-opted to the council only three months after his election defeat. When the water scheme came before the council in June 1846 after detailed planning by its supporters, Smith proposed that it be combined with a sewage scheme, the total cost of £7,500 to be met by householders paying at once two-thirds of one year's rent of their properties – a method of financing sure to sink the proposal. Furthermore, some proprietors had already formed their own sewers, and these were in the more fashionable parts of the town where the assessment would be greatest. As the principal wool manufacturer in Stirling, Smith was a leading figure among this social group and represented its sectional interest in opposing a water assessment. The power of this interest was seen in December 1846 when a proposal to adopt the General Police Act (an attempt to finance the water scheme) was defeated in a poll of the £10 householders, who, the water committee complained, 'have . . . virtually declared that a measure, tending more to the moral and physical improvement of the poorer classes than any that can be named shall not be carried into effect . . . they have looked to themselves and forgotten the interests of the poor.' The Conservative *Journal*, which had earlier supported the water scheme as a stick to beat the Liberals with, now opposed the adoption of a police rate as a means of getting the water: class interest had now become as important an element in the resistance to the water scheme as political tactics had earlier. Of course the group represented by Smith also wanted more water, but they wanted it on their own terms. Their ideal was a plan proposed in March 1847 for a water company.[41] Experience elsewhere, publicised by Chadwick's Sanitary Report in 1842, was that water companies tended to concentrate their efforts on those who could afford to pay and were less enthusiastic about supplying the poor, from whom it was more difficult to make a profit.[42]

But the town council now had a majority who favoured a municipal scheme and made a last effort to achieve it without an assessment by canvassing householders in the late summer of 1847 to see if a sufficient number would pay their share in a lump sum. Predictably, very few were willing to do this but a very significant shift of opinion now took place. There seems at last to have been a growing realisation in Stirling in the autumn of 1847 that, every probable and improbable alternative having been investigated, there was now no choice but to accept a compulsory assessment if an improved water supply was to be got. Even Smith accepted this, and in October a meeting of proprietors and householders approved almost unanimously a proposal by the council for a water works to be built by a public trust, to be established by local act and financed by assessment.[43] The Stirling Waterworks Act duly became law in June 1848.[44] Once again, to meet a pressing practical need the inhabitants were willing to drop the opposition to compulsory rating which had been proclaimed in many ringing speeches to be based on fundamental principle.

A new problem arose with the passing of the Police (Scotland) Act, 1857 which placed under the authority of the county's commissioners of supply the task of watching in any burgh which had not obtained a local police act or adopted the general one.[45] As this measure was passing through parliament, the town council realised what this could mean. The county gentlemen might appoint a large number of watchmen for Stirling, whom the townspeople would have to pay for by an assessment but over whom they would have no control. In order to avoid this the council called a meeting of £10 householders on 5 August 1857 to adopt the General Police Act. Typical of the arguments used to persuade the householders were those of Procurator Fiscal Sconce, who formally proposed adoption. He said that

> I know there was a general feeling in this burgh not to have any new assessment imposed upon us. We were contented to go on with things as they were before, and did not think that, although perhaps we might be better off with a regular police, the improvement was worth the additional cost; now, however, the question is not whether there shall or shall not be an assessment at all – we are to have a compulsory assessment by the new bill, and the question comes simply to be, whether the burgh of Stirling should assess itself or whether a committee of the county should assess the burgh. Now I am one of those who think that self-government is a good thing. It is a practice acted upon only by burgesses for many centuries and we should by all means continue it . . . therefore adopt the provisions of the old Police Act, which is the only way to save us from coming under the new one.

There is no hint of enthusiasm for the new sort of municipal government which was emerging, increasingly active, increasingly expensive and increasingly regulated by the state. It was in fact a speech perfectly calculated to appeal to older ideals – self-government and minimum taxation. And it worked. The motion to adopt the General Police Act (in its revised version of 1850)[46] was carried unanimously after very little discussion. Those who advocated adoption (in the local press, at the council board and at the public meeting) spoke almost solely of watching and the need to keep it out of the hands of the county. They completely failed to explain that the householders were authorising the commissioners under the act (the town council) to assess them for a wide range of purposes, not only for watching but also for sewerage, paving, cleansing, fire-fighting and the regulation of lodging houses.[47]

Did the council, then, take advantage of the scare created by the Police (Scotland) Bill, and the need to take quick action before it became law, to gain other new powers by something like a sleight of hand? An interesting comment on this was made by William Drysdale, a well-informed observer of the Stirling municipal scene in this period. He wrote in 1899 that John Sawers set on foot a scheme for laying sewage pipes in the streets during his provostship (1849–58) 'but as a number of proprietors refused to connect their house pipes with the mains and the town council possessed no compulsory powers, Provost Sawers convened a public meeting of the inhabitants by whom the Police Act was adopted in the burgh'.[48] The early 1850s did indeed see the first serious attempt to provide a system of underground sewers in Stirling, and the spur for it was the new water supply, for effective sewers could not have been built without it. But it also meant that the volume of sewage water to be disposed of was certain to increase rapidly and, if nothing was done to build new sewers, the pollution of the town could dramatically worsen. The problem was not merely to get proprietors to build drains from their houses into the sewers. Underground sewers were built down several streets in the old town during the years 1852–6 and while the council was prepared to pay something from the common good, an average of seventy-six per cent of the cost was raised in subscriptions. The council could no longer afford the large proportion it had paid in the 1830s for the street paving projects. There were too few streets in which the proprietors could pay the greater part of the cost of drainage and this made it very difficult to build up a general system of sewers.[49] The problem appeared again in 1855 and 1856 when the council was negotiating the paving of Port Street, fast becoming the new shopping centre of the town.[50] The fact that the council moved fast and energetically to try to use the paving and drainage powers given by the Police Act as soon as it got them makes it likely that it had in mind much more than watching when it recommended adoption of the act in 1857.

The town council met in its new capacity as a police commission for the first time on 5 October 1857. Many householders may have been unaware of the full extent of the powers they had given the councillors, but that the commissioners knew the provisions of the act and wished to make the most of them may be seen from the stream of enquiries made and orders issued during the last months of 1857. By December a full-time paid police force of thirteen men was at work – a superintendent, a sergeant, seven night and four day constables. This was done without public protest. It was clearly understood by the householders who had adopted the act that more was to be spent on watching than hitherto and that this money was to be raised by compulsory assessment. With paving and drainage the situation was very different. After carefully surveying the streets, the commissioners in December 1857 ordered their proprietors in almost every major street to have their foot pavements made up to certain specifications within six weeks.[51] They apparently thought that by waving the Police Act like a magic wand they could transform the pavements of the town. It was not to be. After two years of very slow progress, in 1860 one proprietor firmly refused to take any action. This was seen as a test case, and the commissioners were perplexed to get differing opinions from the two counsel they consulted. The General Police Act of 1850 was ambiguous on many points, and one was whether proprietors or commissioners should pay for making up pavements.[52] The Stirling commissioners decided not to take the case to court and thus capitulated before the weight of public opinion. If the pavements were to be made up, the cost had to be met either by the proprietors or by occupiers through the police assessment. When the act was adopted in 1857 the public was not prepared for its use as a means of raising extra funds and giving new powers for the improvement of the town. The commissioners seem to have decided that they could not enforce the letter of the act when the public of Stirling had still not accepted its spirit. This point was made very succinctly by Bailie Monteath in 1863 when he told his fellow commissioners that 'the moment they extended their power too far, according to the notion of the public, they would be checked, and there was no man who would go in opposition to the public'. Finally, in the early 1870s the climate of opinion changed. The commissioners then felt sufficiently confident of public support again to order pavements to be made up and to sue those who resisted (which other burghs had done successfully a decade earlier, despite the ambiguity of the act).[53] The ratepayers accepted the need for a start to be made on laying paving on the many streets which were still unmade. During the 1860s the police rate remained at ninepence in the pounds since the commissioners thought the public would not allow it to be raised to pay for street paving. But in 1873 the rate went up to one shilling to allow a new paving programme to begin. There was no resistance.[54] The rate-payers were at last convinced that an increased rate was preferable to the continued muddiness of the streets.

The Stirling police commissioners had a similar experience in dealing with drainage. In November 1857 they instructed their improvement committee to arrange for the completion of the system of main sewers. They seem to have thought that the mere adoption of the police act would persuade proprietors to pay.[55] It was not so. Throughout the 1860s the commissioners sheltered behind the weaknesses in the act, using them as an excuse for not compelling payment against the weight of public opinion. As a result, in most parts of Stirling drainage was improved very little in the decade after the adoption of the act. Finally, by the early 1870s, the householders were convinced that an assessment was a lesser evil than continuing to see sewage boiling up from inadequate sewers and in 1872 the commissioners were able to impose a general sewerage rate at one penny in the pound.[56] This was not enough to transform the drainage of the town in a short period, but the way in which this would finally be achieved was now clear. There was little doubt that, once some areas had been improved by means of a general assessment, pressure from other parts of the town would ensure that in time they would get the same treatment. Some problems like unmade streets and bad sewers were regarded as intolerable and justifying municipal action: others were not. For example, the smell from Gaff's vinegar works on Burgh Muir exercised the police commissioners over a three-year period from 1866 to 1869: prosecuted unsuccessfully under the Nuisances Removal (Scotland) Act, 1856, Gaff nonetheless got himself elected to the commission – which was taken as evidence that the electors supported him and that the matter should be dropped.

How far in this period did central government bring pressure to bear on Stirling to deal with the problems created by the town's growth? It is true that the decision in 1857 to establish a force of professional rate-supported police-men would probably not have been taken had it not been for the Police (Scotland) Act, 1857, which threatened that burghs like Stirling would be incorporated in the county for the purpose of watching if they did not adopt the General Police Act. But this does not itself explain why Stirling adopted the General Act in 1857 and, far beyond requirement, trebled the number of its policemen. Nor was this done at the behest of the inspector appointed under the 1857 act in order to qualify Stirling for the government grant for it was not till over a year later that Stirling decided to apply for this.[57] The act provided for a grant of up to a quarter of the cost of pay and clothing for each year a police force was reported to be efficient in terms of numbers and discipline by the inspector of constabulary of Scotland. This device of a treasury grant, depen-dent on the efficient exercise of a local administrative function, was to be of great importance in the future. But in this case, as Professor Burn pointed out, 'it was not applied in a grossly overbearing manner. Indeed it could not be, for the sanction was scarcely adequate'. Since the grant was so small, a town council could refuse to apply for it or threaten the inspector that, if it did not receive the grant, it would give up making any effort to qualify.[58]

An examination of the relationship between the Stirling police commissioners and successive inspectors of constabulary of Scotland confirms that the influ-ence of the inspectors was limited. An extra man was added to the force in 1859 when the grant was first applied for, and a proposal in 1864 to reduce the force by two was scotched[59] but a long campaign to persuade the police commis-sioners to pay higher wages had a very limited effect. The inspector argued that, to get and keep good policemen, it was necessary to pay well and ensure that they regularly received an increase in pay: yet after almost ten years of pressure Stirling in 1869 still paid low wages – 19s. to 21s. per week for sergeants and 16s. to 18s. for constables, compared to 23s.4d. and 17s.6d.-19s.6d. respec-tively in the county of Stirling and 23s.-25s. and 16s.-22s. in Glasgow, so that the burgh suffered from an above average turnover of officers. This the Stirling commissioners did not seem to mind, but they did begin to worry in 1872 when it became difficult to fill vacancies in a period of industrial boom when high wages elsewhere were tempting many Scottish policemen to resign. In 1872 the Stirling commissioners twice raised wages by 1s. per week and removed the limit they had placed on the number of officers who could be paid the top rate; when after 1874 a downturn in trade made it easier to keep policemen there was only one further increase in pay in Stirling in the 1870s – of 1s. a week for sergeants and 6d. for constables in 1877–8. The Stirling commissioners also managed to resist the inspector's advice in 1869 that their police force should be merged with that of the county: in this case they were probably right in claiming that they knew what was best for Stirling, as the county force gave a very poor service to Falkirk, the other major town in the area.[60]

The other agency of central government which attempted to influence Scottish local authorities in this period was the board of supervision for the relief of the poor in Scotland which was given certain powers over the public health activities by the Public Health (Scotland) Act, 1867. Professor Best has suggested that the Poor Law Board was relatively ineffective in forcing authorities to take action because its powers and staff were strictly limited,[61] a view confirmed in its relations with the Stirling police commissioners. One of the powers the 1867 act gave to local authorities was to set up fever hospitals in case of epidemics and in 1871 the board issued a circular urging authorities to use this power. Stirling, like most towns, had been content to wait till an epidemic became serious and then look for emergency accommodation for a hospital and met a fever epidemic in the autumn of 1873 in the usual way. Valley Lodge, a building on open ground below the castle, was pressed into service as a temporary hospital which was then retained on a permanent basis: but under the 1867 act permanent fever hospitals had to be approved by the Board, which in 1874 decided that Valley Lodge was unsuitable and licensed it only for a further twelve months. The town's commissioners ignored this decision and made no attempt to replace Valley Lodge. They knew they were not obliged to provide any fever hospital and seem to have calculated correctly that the Board would consider any hospital better than none and so would not dare to close it down as an unsuitable building.[62]

A power which the Board of Supervision did use regularly was to send an inspector to look at the sanitary state of a burgh or parish and then ask the local authority to comment on his findings. In 1875–6, for example, inspectors reported on over 250 places.[63] Were these inspections successful in forcing improvements? It was indeed after an inspection of the nuisances of the town, ordered by the Board during a cholera scare, that the Stirling commissioners decided in 1872 that a sewer rate was necessary. However, if it was fear which persuaded the commissioners to take action, it was fear of cholera and not fear of the Board. The Board, for example, devoted a lot of attention to the drainage of two outlying villages for which the Stirling commissioners were responsible, over a period of six years form 1872 trying to persuade the commissioners to deal with the Raploch Burn which carried effluent from Robert Smith's Parkvale and Hayford Mills – but with no success, for the commissioners were determined to deny responsibility, presumably because a sewer would be costly (around £800) and the number of sufferers was relatively small. Thus, where a local authority was obdurate, the mere calling for reports and sending comments (which was all the Board could do) achieved little. Yet in the instance of St Ninians the Board was more successful: an inspector twice visited the village and reported it almost undrained, and only two months after the second visit (in 1877) the Stirling commissioners agreed to lay sewers there at a cost of £250.[64] No doubt they were more inclined to listen to the ratepayers of St Ninians than those of Raploch because they were more numerous and were demanding a smaller expenditure yet the St Ninians case suggests that it was possible for the Board at least to accelerate the efforts of the authority.

But the crucial decisions in local government in the 1850s, 1860s and 1870s were in effect still taken locally. In Stirling money was spent on new municipal projects only when the ratepayers were persuaded that that would be a lesser evil than the consequences of continuing to do little or nothing. The adoption, in 1872 and 1873 respectively, of compulsory ratings in order to finance drainage and street paving occurred shortly after the enlargement of the municipal electorate in 1868. It might be surmised that these rates were adopted because of pressure from the new electors, but no hint of this appears in any contemporary comment and a considerable number of those who received the municipal vote for the first time in 1868 had been ratepayers for many years.[65] The ratepayers might proclaim themselves to be supporters of individualism, and continue to demonstrate it by refusing to allow effective action against nuisances like Gaff's vinegar works 'to support a fair field for capital and for enterprise', but when the pressures of living in a growing town became intolerable to them, they were persuaded to pay rates in turn for water, watching, drainage and paving – rates which at one time they would have regarded as an intolerable intrusion on the rights of the individual.

NOTES

1 For a more detailed analysis see Finlay McKichan, 'Stirling 1780–1880: The Response of Burgh Government to the Problems of Urban Growth' (unpublished M.Litt. thesis, Glasgow University, 1972), 20–58.

2 *Reports upon the Boundaries of the Several Cities, Burghs and Towns in Scotland in respect to the election of members to serve in Parliament* (PP 1831–1, xlii), 95.

3 S[tirling] J[ournal] and A[dvertiser], 1 May 1857.

4 In 1851 76 per cent of householders in St Mary's Wynd were manual workers, street

traders or unemployed. By 1881 86 per cent were in these categories. (Registrar General for Scotland's Office, New Register House, Census Schedules, Stirling, 1851, 1881.)

5 *Reports on the Sanitary Condition of the Labouring Population of Scotland* (London, 1842), 261–7. Forrest was medical attendant to the Stirling Dispensary founded in 1831 to give medical attention to some of those who could not afford to pay. (William Drysdale, *Old Faces, [Old Places and Old Stories of Stirling]*, 1st ser. [Stirling, 1898], 94.)

6 E.g. N[ew] S[tatistical] A[ccount of] Stirlingshire (Edinburgh, 1842), 394–6.

7 Mun[icipal] Corp[orations (Scotland)] Comm[ission], General Report (PP 1835, xxix), 21.

8 Ibid., *Local Reports*, ii (PP 1836, xxiii), 507.

9 S[cottish] R[ecord] O[ffice], B66/23/8–13, S[tirling] B[urgh] T[reasurer's] Acc[ounts], 1789–90 to 1857–8. The prices index used is that of E.H. Phelps Brown and Sheila V. Hopkins, 'Seven Centuries of the Prices of Consumables, Compared with Builders' Wage-Rates', *Economica*, xxiii (1956), 313–14.

10 *Comm[ission] on [the State of] Large Towns [and Populous Districts], Second Report* (PP 1845, xviii), 35.

11 SRO, B66/23/11, SBT Acc., 1834–5 to 1840–1.

12 *NSA Stirlingshire*, 394. Midwinter, *Lancashire*, 97.

13 SRO, B66/21/17 S[tirling] T[own] C[ouncil] M[inutes], 21 July, 18 Aug. 1834, 4 May 1840; SRO, B66/23/11, SBT Acc., 1833–4.

14 *Mun. Corp. Comm., Local Reports*, ii, 516–17.

15 S[tirling] J[ournal], 24 Apr. 1823.

16 SRO, B66/21/14 and 17, STC Min., 13 Oct. 1798, 8 June 1799, 21 Nov. 1842; *SJ & A*, 20 Nov. 1840.

17 *Comm. on Large Towns, First Report*, ii, 391–2.

18 [Stirling, Old High School Buildings], Central Region Archives, S[tirling] Police [Commissioners] Min[utes], 14 Feb. 1859.

19 Edwin Chadwick, *Report on the Sanitary Condition of the Labouring Population of Great Britain*, 1842, ed. M.W. Flinn (Edinburgh, 1965), 107, 115. Thomas Ferguson, *Dawn of Scottish Social Welfare* (London, 1948), 160.

20 SRO, B66/21/17 STC Min., 20 Jan. 1834; *SJ & A*, 24 Jan. 1834.

21 See above, p. 72.

22 *SJ*, 24 Apr., 8 May 1823; SRO), B66/21/16, STUC Min., 5 Mar., 3 Dec. 1825.

23 SRO, B66/24/13. Stirling – Minute Book of Board of Health relating to Cholera, 1831–2, 26 Jan.; 2, 9, 23, 27 Feb.; 5 May 1832; *SJ*, 14 June 1832.

24 *SJ & A*, 18 June, 2, 9 July, 24 Dec. 1847; Central Region Archives, STC Min., 6 July 1847.

25 Canongate (1772), Greenock (1773), Glasgow (1800), Edinburgh (1805), Paisley (1806), Gorbals (1808), Kilmarnock (1810), Perth and Dunfermline (1811), Calton (1819), Peterhead (1820), Airdrie (1821), Alloa (1822), Dundee and Bathgate (1824), Anderston (1826) and Aberdeen (1829). Source: *Mun. Corp. Comm., Local Reports*.

26 S. Turner, *History of Local Taxation in Scotland* (Edinburgh, 1908), 183–4, 190.

27 3 and 4 Will, IV, c. 46.

28 *Mun. Corp. Comm., Local Reports*, ii, 517.

29 SRO, B66/21/17, STC Min., 15 Feb. 1836, *SJ & A*, 19 Feb. 1836.

30 2 and 3 Vict., c. 42.

31 SRO, B66/21/17, STC Min., 2 Apr. 1839, 3 Apr. 1841, 21 Feb. 1842; SRO, B66/23/11 and 12, SBT Acc., 1836–7 to 1844–5, 1845–6 to 1850–1.

32 *Stirling Observer*, 7 Oct. 1841.

33 SRO, B66/21/17, STC Min., 25 Jan. 1847; Central Region Archives, STC Min., 21 June 1848.

34 Sir John Sinclair, *Analysis of the Statistical Account of Scotland* (Edinburgh, 1831 ed.), ii, 172–3.

35 *Statistical Account of Scotland*, viii (Edinburgh, 1793), 281–2, 287.

36 SRO, B66/21/17, STC Min., 22 Jan. 1844.

37 *Stirling Observer*, 1 Feb. 1844.

38 *SJ & A*, 19 Sept., 3 Oct. 1845, 19 June 1846.

39 Ibid., 13 Dec. 1844, 8 Oct. 1847.

40 SRO, B66/21/17, STC Min., 17 Mar., 20 Oct. 1845; *SJ & A*, 23 May, 1, 15, 22 Aug., 17 Oct., 7 Nov. 1845.

41 SRO. B66/21/17, STC Min., 18 May 1846; *SJ & A*, 29 May, 12, 19 June, 4, 11 Dec. 1846, 26 Mar., 2 Apr. 1847; Smith was a member of its provisional committee.

42 Chadwick, *Sanitary Report*, 143–4.

43 Central Region Archives, STC Min., 8 June, 27 Sept. 1847; *SJ & A*, 11 June, 2 July, 8 Oct. 1847.

44 11 and 12 Vict., c. 8 (Local and Personal Acts).

45 20 and 21 Vict., c. 72.

46 13 and 14 Vict., c. 33.

47 Central Region Archives, STC Min., 6 July 1857; *SJ & A*, 10, 17, 31 July, 7 Aug. 1857; *Stirling Observer*, 30 July 1857.

48 Drysdale, *Old Faces* (2nd Ser., 1899), 132.

49 SRO, B66/23/12, SBT Acc., 1852–3 to 1855–6; *SJ & A*, 21 Mar. 1856; Stirling Public Library, MS notebook of James Shirra, Statistics and Notes of the Royal Burgh of Stirling, 48.

50 Central Region Archives, STC Min., 23 Apr. 1855; *SJ & A*, 14 Mar. 1856.

51 Central Region Archives, S Police Min., 5 Oct., 8 Dec. 1857.

52 James Muirhead, *The Law and Practice relating to Police Government in Burghs in Scotland* (Edinburgh, 1893).

53 *SJ & A*, 13 Jan., 16 Mar., 17 Aug., 14 Sept., 12 Oct, 1860; 23 Jan. 1863; 14 Apr. 1871; 16 Aug., 13 Sept., 15 Nov. 1872.

54 *SJ & A*, 14 May, 17 Dec. 1869; 14 Feb., 16 May, 11 July 1873.

55 Central Region Archives, S Police Min., 9 Nov. 1857.

56 *SJ & A*, 12 Feb., 14 May 1858: 13 Dec. 1867: 15 Mar., 14 June, 13 Dec. 1872; 15 Feb. 1878. The sewerage rate was technically a general public health assessment levied under the Public Health (Scotland) Act, 1867.

57 *SJ & A*, 31 Dec. 1858.

58 W.L. Burn, *The Age of Equipoise* (London, 1968 edn.), 176.

59 *SJ & A*, 31 Dec. 1858; 13 May, 3 June, 15 July, 12 Aug., 14 Oct. 1864.

60 *Report of H.M. Inspector of Constabulary of Scotland*, 1868–9 (PP 1868–9, xxxi), 206, 208; 1870–1(PP 1871, xxviii), 623, 661; 1871–2 (PP 1872, xxx), 337–8, 382; 1872–3 (PP 1873, xxxi), 455; 1877–8 (PP 1878, xl), 496; *SJ & A.* 14 Oct. 1864; 14 May, 18 June, 13 Aug. 1869; 16 Aug. 1872.

61 Best, 'Scottish Victorian City', 333–4.

62 Thomas Ferguson, *Scottish Social Welfare 1864–1914* (Edinburgh 1958), 485–7; *SJ & A,* 17 Oct., 14 Nov. 1873; SRO, HH26/10, Board of Supervision: Chairman's Minute Book (Public Health), 5 Nov. 1874.

63 *Report of Board of Supervision for the Relief of the Poor and of Public Health in Scotland,* 1875–6 (PP 1876, xxxii), 507.

64 SRO, HH26/7 and 14, Board of Supervision: Chairman's Minutes, 29 Aug. 1872; 30 Aug., 8 Nov. 1877; 17 and 24 Jan. 1878; *SJ & A,* 17 June, 16 Sept. 1870; 15 Sept. 1871; 12 Jan., 18 Oct. 1872; 20 Oct. 1876; 18 May, 16 Nov. 1877; 25 Jan., 15 Feb., 12 Apr. 1878.

65 For example, the rate levied under the General Police Act, 1850, was in effect paid by £5 householders.

Protestant Extremism in Urban Scotland 1930–1939: Its Growth and Contraction

Tom Gallagher 1985 *The Scottish Historical Review* 64, 143–67.

Ultra-protestantism, manifesting itself in a dogmatic hostility to roman catholicism and its adherents, was to remain a distinctive force in Scottish life even as religious devotion declined in the midst of the Industrial Revolution. New developments such as the 1870 declaration of papal infallibility and the 1907 *Ne Temere* decree whereby Rome condemned marriage with non-catholics increased protestant hostility based only in part on roman catholicism's alleged disregard for the bible and the sanctity of the sabbath, its veneration of our Lady and religious images, its belief in transubstantiation and, of course, its abdication before papal authority.

Usually protestant militancy has not gathered sufficient motive-force behind it to be able to express itself – effectively – in the political arena. Religious tension has been more in evidence in the social, recreational, or cultural spheres with disputes over the scale and consequences of Irish immigration, state funding for catholic education, and the perennial rivalry between two Glasgow football teams, accounting for much of the heat and bitterness. Politics were never polarised along clear religious lines in the way that occurred in Belfast and Liverpool (cities comparable to Glasgow in other respects) where catholics from rural Ireland dwelt in uneasy co-existence with a protestant host community.

Only once, in the 1930s, did religious extremism emerge as a force to be reckoned with in Scottish politics. Two new movements, the Scottish Protestant League in Glasgow, and Protestant Action in Edinburgh, scored dramatic victories in municipal politics, the Edinburgh body eclipsing every other British extremist grouping in the percentage of votes it won at local elections in the 1930s. Both movements emerged independently of one another around the same time and their growth and decline was remarkably uniform. This tends to support the view that religious tensions in Scottish society may have been acute enough in the 1930s to trigger off extreme political movements in two cities whose political behaviour usually has been strikingly divergent.

The conditions that enabled parties antagonistic to a specific minority to briefly make the running in the 1930s can be traced back to the beginning of the last century. Irish immigrants flocked to industrial Scotland in such numbers, seeking work, that already by 1841 they comprised a larger percentage of the population than they did in England and Wales.[1] Immediate hostilities did not break out between proletarian hosts and peasant newcomers even though two events in Scottish history, the Reformation, and the Industrial Revolution itself, had created a major cultural and developmental gap between Scotland and most of Ireland which had not existed previously when both had lain outside the English state.

There are a number of obvious reasons why Scotland avoided the degree of sectarian violence associated with the Know Nothing movement of the USA during the 1850s and with Belfast and Liverpool starting in the 1850s: the bulk of immigration to Scotland occurred when the economy was buoyant and usually able to absorb the extra numbers; high emigration from Scotland to the British Empire removed disaffected elements who might have fomented inter-communal strife; north British values were replacing Scottish ones as important symbols in the 1820–60 period when Irish immigration was at its height: so the Irish in Scotland were not treated as an 'outgroup' by a chauvinistic bourgeoisie as their counterparts were in multi-national empires at the opposite end of Europe; and nineteenth-century Scottish protestantism may have been too preoccupied with its own internal schisms to spare energy for properly combating the 'Menace of Rome'.

The immigrants were victimised for their religion, anti-social behaviour, or wretched status but not for their un-Scottishness. The Irish situation may have had an effect on Scottish politics with the emergence of the Liberal Unionist Party in 1886[2] and with increased Catholic working-class backing for the Labour Party after 1910 but political crises in Ireland rarely triggered off communal unrest in Glasgow, Scotland's largest city where up to two-thirds of the Irish settled, in those years when Ireland was a key issue on the British political agenda.[3] Another sign of domestic calm was the manner in which the restoration of the Scottish catholic hierarchy passed off in 1878 with little of the rancour that accompanied this act in England in 1850.

Although the presence of the catholic Irish and their descendants would be resented by large numbers of Scots over several generations, there were signs that by the 1920s, old enmities and suspicions were being broken down. 1922 seemed a particularly hopeful year since it was the last one in which Ireland was a divisive issue in British politics and it appropriately marked the start of the Labour Party's rise to prominence in Scottish affairs.[4]

But it was in the 1920s, when Scotland appeared to be swinging in a radical and secular direction, that sectarianism began to make a political breakthrough. A number of explanations can be offered. World War One certainly had a disruptive effect on Scottish society as it did on other participating European countries where even more extreme forms of political behaviour would quickly emerge in its wake: society became more turbulent as restraints checking disruptive behaviour were disregarded. The cracking of old political moulds also provided opportunities for right-wingers and traditionalists to exploit grievances that they had been unable to articulate effectively in more settled times: the threat to the *status quo* posed by the Scottish left inside and outside parliament, also produced an emphatic response from this quarter.

So the 1920s were a decade of experimentation and opportunity not just for the left: the profound dissatisfaction produced by the slump beginning in the early 1920s in Scotland's manufacturing industries did not redound wholly to the benefit of radical interests and was not merely confined to the working-class or the unemployed. In fact it is to the Scottish middle-class, to the professions and the intelligentsia, that the first clear indication appears that protestant extremism was ceasing to be a marginal affair confined to small areas of urban Scotland, a few working-class hotheads, and certain emotive days of the year.

Probably the first clear sign that religious divisions were hardening came in 1923 when the General Assembly of the Church of Scotland endorsed a report entitled *The Menace of the Irish Race to Our Scottish Nationality*. It demanded that Irish immigration be curtailed and, for over a decade, ministers lobbied parliament or spoke out at the Assembly about the 1918 Education (Scotland) Act which gave Scottish catholic schools more state aid than any others in Britain. In the Conservative Party (known from 1911 to 1964 in Scotland as the Unionist Party) which many ministers of the established church supported, liaison with the Orange Order and with militant protestantism generally, was far more noticeable in the 1920s than hitherto.[5] Sometimes appeals to sectarian prejudice were made by Tory candidates trying to dislodge roman catholic Labour MPs in working-class seats where the Tories hoped to replace the Liberals hitherto the dominant force in Scottish politics. The most serious example occurred in 1924 when John Wheatley, labour's first minister of health and housing got back as MP for Glasgow Shettleston with only a 74–vote majority after his Tory challenger, Major Reid Miller, had waged a campaign against him couched in sectarian terms. Along with other right-wing politicians, he talked with barely concealed contempt about the 'Irish' in Scotland even though the majority of catholics were now Scottish-born and Irish immigration was down to a trickle.

Intellectuals advocating Scottish independence sometimes refused to concede that the descendants of Irish immigrants were true Scots. George Malcolm Thomson (later a notable journalist and longstanding aide to Lord Beaverbrook) and Andrew Dewar Gibb, professor of Scots law at Glasgow University were two nationalists who by the end of the 1920s, were writing about the menace from within posed by the 'Irish' in Scotland.[6] This theme may have had its greatest impact in the popular novels produced by some leading members of the 'kailyard' school of Scottish literature. In the writings of Annie S. Swan and R. W. Campbell, the Irish in Scotland were sometimes targeted as being alien intruders who were subverting the true character of 'Bonny Scotland'. Usually politics as such were downplayed even in the work of the arch-imperialist R. W. Campbell, of whom it has been said that he seemed to 'despise anyone who was not a white, Scottish, Boys Brigade member'.[7]

Campbell's published novels expressed disgruntlement with the fact that times were changing, that new values were displacing old ones depicted as archetypically Scottish and that foreign immigration was threatening the integrity of the race. These attitudes certainly reflected and may have fuelled the bitterness felt in the protestant and middle-class Scottish establishment as a result of the economic depression and the rise of the left which, in their turn, were eroding many old certainties.

The Scottish Protestant League (SPL) was the first of the protestant political movements of the 1930s to make a definite impact. It was founded in Edinburgh in 1920 by Alexander Ratcliffe, a railway clerk who was soon after elected to the Edinburgh education authority. Ratcliffe was born in 1888 in the east coast town of Bo'ness which was known for its dissenting Presbyterian traditions. His father had been a clergyman attached to the Scottish Coast Mission first there and later in Leith, Edinburgh's port.[8]

Dour and obsessional, Ratcliffe was nevertheless a good self-publicist. At the end of the 1920s he moved to Glasgow where, as a full-time lay preacher, he was soon to have his own church building situated near the City Chambers and offices in the commercial district in Bath Street. He steered clear of both the Unionist Party and the Orange Order, both of which he criticised in his paper *The Vanguard* for their reluctance to provide a more trenchant defence of protestant values. At the 1929 general election he had stood as a Protestant and Progressive candidate in the seat of Stirling and Falkirk. The sitting Labour MP, Hugh Murnin was a roman catholic and Ratcliffe gained 21.3 per cent of the vote. He later accused Tories in the Orange Order of having sabotaged an Orange and Protestant Party formed in 1922, because it threatened Tory interests.[9] Being a rank individualist, he was unwilling to cooperate with the Orange Order (and *vice versa*) thus forfeiting an important reservoir of organised support.

[handwritten note: Religion moved in to politics Prodie Ekstreamist aguse Cath]

The SPL's first electoral success occurred in the aftermath of the 1931 general election when the left crashed to defeat in Scotland as in the rest of Britain. Five of the seven seats retained by the Labour and Independent Labour Parties in Scotland were in Glasgow but even here the left was on the defensive. In the constituency of Bridgeton held by James Maxton, leader of the Independent Labour Party (ILP), Labour lost a seat in the 1931 municipal elections to the SPL's Charles Forrester. Forrester's majority was substantial and since he was a former Communist who had spent time in the Soviet Union, he demonstrated the appeal of traditional values on the working-class even in the midst of a severe depression. Ratcliffe was elected in the Dennistown ward where he got more votes than all of his opponents combined. This had hitherto been a safe Tory seat in a lower middle-class area of Glasgow. With two out of three of its candidates being elected, the SPL had done well among contrasting groups of voters and at the expense of both major parties.

On what kind of platform did the SPL go before the voters? After the election, Ratcliffe claimed that 'it was not a matter of politics that made it necessary for the League to seek representation on the Council but one of Protestant principle'.[10] Nevertheless, by studying the voting behaviour of the SPL in the council as well as its election literature, an attempt can be made to locate it on the political spectrum. Rather surprisingly perhaps, a strong case can be made for placing it to the left of the Moderates (as the Tories were known in Scottish municipal politics), on socio-economic issues, which are usually the ones that dominate local politics. The city's leading newspaper, *The Glasgow Herald* had no doubt about the matter: the SPL was 'presenting what is essentially a Socialist case wrapped up in the garments of religion'.[11]

The 'religious' matter which chiefly preoccupied the SPL was the fact that catholic schools were now maintained by the state under Section 18 of the 1918 Education (Scotland) Act. Previously largely financed from the meagre resources of the 650,000 strong (and mainly working-class) catholic community, they were absorbed into the state system after 1918 although still retaining much independence in terms of curriculum, staffing, and the involvement of catholic clergy. The 1918 settlement put the Scottish catholic authorities at an advantage over their English and Welsh counterparts. Much resentment was felt in Scottish protestant circles and the cry 'Rome on the Rates' was not merely taken up by the SPL. This slogan conveniently overlooked the fact that up to 1918, catholic ratepayers had been obliged to subsidise non-catholic schools while having to make other provisions for their own. Much heat and very little light attended the whole debate.[12] The SPL coupled a demand that the relevant clause of the 1918 Act be revoked with one that religious education in Glasgow schools cease to be taught at the ratepayers' expense. The aim of this proposal would seem to have been to stop subsidising the visits of priests to classrooms.

By themselves, these contentious issues were not likely to produce an effective political response from the voters. Ratcliffe shrewdly combined them with more material concerns that a wider circle of voters were likely to be preoccupied with. Thus the SPL made great play about opposing cuts in social services and increases in rents, while advocating reduced corporation rates. These were rather contradictory and populist postures designed to win support from protestant voters in contrasting districts of the city. The SPL also sought to befriend teachers, whose salaries had been cut by the ruling Moderates in 1931 as well as council workers. It argued that savings could be made by cutting back on waste and Ratcliffe made much of the fact that he never availed of special privileges for councillors such as free lunches.

In his bid to woo diverse interests, Ratcliffe had a letter published in the Glasgow-based socialist weekly *Forward*, shortly before being elected.[13] In it, he assured readers that they had nothing to fear from his election to the council: 'The Protestant councillors will support every measure brought forth in the best interests of the working people. And they will oppose any moves by the Moderates to "down" the working man.'[14]

The SPL gained further ground in 1932 when it won another seat and 11.71 per cent of the total municipal vote in Glasgow. It took working-class Kinning Park from the Moderates but in Dalmarnock, scene of an earlier victory, two rival SPL candidates cancelled each other out. This was the first real sign of the fission that would do untold harm to the ultra-protestant cause, not just in Glasgow. But further scope for SPL success still remained with the left divided by the competing Labour, ILP, and Communist parties and, more especially, with the ruling Moderates unpopular due to their austerity measures. Its best year was 1933 when four more protestant councillors were elected in Glasgow, the SPL acquiring 67,000 votes, 23 per cent of the total. The gains were made in the wards of Camphill, Cathcart, Govanhill, and Dennistoun, lower middle-class districts where hitherto the Moderates had been dominant. In some years, Moderate councillors had been returned unopposed in those seats and Ratcliffe may have been able to exploit the complacency and neglect which often accompanied electoral one-party rule. The SPL also took votes from the left whose total vote fell collectively by 9 per cent but its chief victim was the Moderates who were replaced in office by a minority Labour administration.

1933 marked the beginning of Labour's long hegemony in Glasgow politics but it was largely thanks to the spoiling rôle of the SPL that it achieved its breakthrough when it did. Perhaps because of these circumstances, Ratcliffe was not regarded as completely beyond the pale by the left and he was even able to contribute articles to the Labour weekly, *Forward*.[15] In a long piece which the editor, Emrys Hughes, had asked him to write in March 1934 in order to clarify the relations between the SPL and Labour, Ratcliffe made some interesting disclosures.

It was revealed that the five-strong SPL group on the council was free to vote as it chose on purely political questions but a whip applied to any with a religious dimension.[16] With this ruling in force, two SPL councillors usually voted with the Moderates, while the rest joined with Ratcliffe in backing Labour on issues like the need for free school textbooks. Ratcliffe tried to give the impression that he was the most progressive member of the group by citing the time when he had been the only one to back a motion which provided for help to be given to unemployed people suffering ill-health.[17]

Ratcliffe's access to *Forward*, the premier paper of the Scottish left from 1906 to the 1950s can only be described as bizarre when it is realised that he lent his support to a home-grown fascist party in 1933. The Scottish Democratic Fascist Party was founded by W. Weir Gilmour and Major Hume Sleigh in that year and he was attracted by the fact that membership was withheld from roman catholics.[18] In November 1933, William Gallacher, later Communist MP for West Fife, declared in Glasgow at a meeting where the German playwright, Ernst Toller was on the platform that 'in Scotland, the fascists were not anti-Jewish but anti-Irish'.[19] For a short time, Ratcliffe belonged to the Scottish Fascists whose leader, Weir Gilmour, maintained his anti-catholicism well into the post-war years.[20] In the first issue of *Commonwealth*, the Scottish fascist monthly which ran for only two issues in the summer of 1933, the SDFP unfurled a 5–point programme which advocated the expulsion from Scotland of all religious orders, the repeal of Section 18 of the Education (Scotland) Act and the prohibition of Irish immigration to Scotland.[21]

Ratcliffe applauded the arrival on the Scottish scene of this party but it must be admitted that his own anti-catholic stance was not always clear-cut or consistent. In a survey of the religious and occupational backgrounds of the 116 members of Glasgow city council, published in a March 1933 issue of *Vanguard*, Ratcliffe was not unduly concerned that six were roman catholics.[22] He vented more fury at the eleven Orangemen who sat as Moderates for not defending protestant interests. He claimed that five of them were on the education committee of the council and asked why they had not petitioned the government to repeal the Education Act. Later, when the number of catholic councillors had increased to nine, he remarked that 'this is not many' and he tended to refrain from attacking Patrick Dollan, who had been leader of the Labour group for most of the time since 1922.[23] Dollan's faith, politics, and Irish ancestry were anathema to Ratcliffe but more mileage could be obtained from attacking the Moderates, many of whom were directors, stockbrokers, or retired gentlemen who were set apart from their electors.

Perhaps realising that the catholic community was well-entrenched in Glasgow and that protestant-catholic relations were only tense in a few localities or at certain times of the year, Ratcliffe's anti-catholic stance varied and depended on who he was talking to and where. In his newspaper and, no doubt, in his pulpit, his anti-catholic diatribes were fiercer than in the council chamber or on the hustings; in response to the ILP councillor, Joseph Payne, who claimed that 'the whole foundation of the SPL programme was to "Kick the Pope", take that away and there is nothing left . . .', Ratcliffe agreed:[24]

'Yes we *do* kick the Pope! That *is* our job! It *is* our programme'![25]

His newspaper, which first appeared in August 1931, usually carried adverts for SPL publications which included such titles as 'The Life of a Carmelite Nun', 'Why Priests Don't Wed', and 'The Horrible Lives of the Popes of Rome'. In 1930, he had gained publicity in the press for writing and presenting an anti-catholic play called 'The Trial of Fr Diamond' which played to distinctly unenthusiastic audiences in the north east of England before being taken off.[26] But his anti-catholic message could be less crude and more sophisticated. In *Forward*, he took issue with a correspondent who had stated that his object 'in life is to exclude catholics from social and political activity . . .'

> But I must admit that one of my objects in life is to exclude the Catholic Church and her priests from dominating 'Roman Catholics' who desire to take a citizen's part in social and political activity. Moreover, while I am not opposed to Catholics taking a fair share in the administration of the country's affairs, I certainly object to the Catholics being petted and pampered even within the Socialist movement.[27]

One SPL candidate in the Gorbals ward even declared in 1934 that, if he returned, he 'would give the same attention to Roman Catholic voters in the ward as he would do to Protestant voters'.[28]

Ratcliffe had close ties with militant protestants in Northern Ireland where the Unionist Party could have been a possible source of support for the SPL if it had assumed a more permanent shape in Scotland. Ratcliffe held a number of speaking tours in Ulster in the early 1930s and Major J. H. McCormick, a Unionist MP in the Belfast parliament chaired one of his meetings, later travelling to Scotland to speak on behalf of the SPL. But relations between Ratcliffe and his Ulster allies were badly strained after an incident in the newly opened parliament at Stormont on 2 May 1933 when a picture depicting King William of Orange being blessed by an ecclesiastical figure resting on a cloud was attacked by an SPL contingent.[29] Outraged protestant hardliners had assumed the ecclesiastical figure to be the Pope and the painting was daubed in paint by Mrs Mary Ratcliffe and then slashed by Councillor Forrester, both of whom were briefly imprisoned by the Belfast authorities before being fined.[30]

In one issue of *Vanguard*, Ratcliffe posed the rhetorical question, 'If Home Rule works in Ulster, why cannot it work in Scotland?'[31] Later he delivered a sermon in his church bearing the title 'Would Scottish Home Rule Mean Rome Rule'? Ratcliffe's verdict was that a parliament in Edinburgh would not be detrimental to protestant interests in Scotland and he declared himself willing to support Home Rule in principle, if not the nationalist parties then promoting it. Here he was going out on a limb since most militant protestants in Scotland were staunch Unionists. But Ratcliffe was so much at odds with the protestant establishment that he appeared to enjoy promoting ideas like Scottish Home Rule which were totally at variance with protestant conservative orthodoxy. In 1933, he criticised the Tory MP for Ayr, Sir Thomas Moore, for opening a catholic bazaar in Ayr Town Hall and speaking at an Orange day parade in nearby Maybole to 4,000 Orangemen, all in the space of a few hours.[32] This was an indication of Tory flexibility which he could not bear but even sympathetic Tories would find Ratcliffe too quirky and unreliable. Lord Scone, Tory MP for Perth from 1931 to 1935 resigned as honorary president of the SPL in 1934, shortly after Ratcliffe had boasted that four of the Moderate councillors the SPL had helped oust in the 1933 elections were Orangemen.[33]

Eventually Ratcliffe seems to have fallen out with most of his allies. His involvement with the Scottish Fascists ceased when they deleted anti-catholic articles from their charter later in 1933 and then rapidly disappeared into oblivion. Disputes with an organiser of the SPL over cash reached the courts.[34] More seriously, he found it difficult to retain control over the other SPL councillors and, by 1934, four of the six elected had broken with him. Apparently the SPL leader preferred a vertical chain of command and was reluctant to delegate authority to others even as the SPL was enjoying electoral success. No local branches were formed and Ratcliffe gave senior posts to women, perhaps because he thought them less likely to challenge his authority. In March 1933, he had to appeal through his newspaper for readers interested in being SPL candidates to come forward. Candidates 'do not need to be brilliant speakers but sincere, reliable and incorruptible'.[35]

In 1934, with councillors defecting, Ratcliffe was hardpressed to maintain his political offensive and in the run-up to the November council elections, he made a pact with the Moderates. They were prepared to strike a deal with their erstwhile foe so as to unite the non-socialist vote and prevent Labour from consolidating its hold on the council. No terms were published but, in his election address he declared that 'the Moderate Party have entirely changed their view on . . . my appeal for a revision of the 1918 Education (Scotland) Act as they recently in the Council unanimously supported my motion for action'.[36]

Sir Charles Cleland, a leading local Tory, and former chairman of the Glasgow Unionist Association,[37] aligned himself with Ratcliffe on the catholic schools issue when making a speech at the opening of an extension to the top girls school in the city just before the poll.[38] But not all Moderates supported the pact whereby Ratcliffe was given a free run in Dennistoun in return for the SPL not standing in traditionally Moderate seats. Ex-councillor Matthew Armstrong, an elder of the Kirk and member of the Glasgow Presbytery came out of retirement to stand as an Independent Moderate against Ratcliffe whom he regarded as 'a menace who needed to be driven from public life'.[39] As a prosperous businessman, he was able to finance a strong campaign and he even made contact with the Catholic Union,[40] an electoral pressure group whose patron was the Archbishop of Glasgow, which campaigned discreetly for Labour candidates deemed to be favourable to catholic interests.

With Labour and Moderates declining to stand in Dennistoun for separate reasons, Ratcliffe went down to defeat. As a councillor, he had displayed much of the opportunism for which he was so ready to slam professional politicians. The alliance with the Moderates was an effort to repair the damage caused in his anti-Socialist seat by political behaviour which, in no small measure, contributed to Labour's 1933 victory but it failed.

Ratcliffe's demise was welcomed by the press. *The Daily Record* had refused to take SPL adverts and on polling day it had declared that if sectarianism prevailed, 'It may be necessary to plead for the running of Glasgow's affairs by a dispassionate Commission.'[41] *The Glasgow Herald* and *The Evening Citizen* were also hostile but most of the SPL's wounds were self-inflicted and responsibility for its rapid electoral demise can be placed squarely at the foot of its leader who showed himself to be a clumsy and egotistical politician. The SPL gained only 7 per cent of the vote in 1934 and Ratcliffe lost control of all but one of the four councillors (besides himself) elected under SPL colours, three of whom styled themselves Independent Protestants. Thereafter he drifted to the political sidelines. Standing for Campbell ward against a Moderate in 1937, he got 2,500 votes but was still convincingly defeated. Never again would he enjoy the political limelight. Through the medium of his paper, he criticised the first signs of entente between the protestant establishment and upwardly mobile catholics as when Lord Provost Dollan and Sir Alexander Swan, the Provincial Grand Master of the Scottish Freemasons were piped into Glasgow's St

Andrews Hall where a masonic banquet was in progress. A horrified Ratcliffe wrote:

> A papist receiving the honours of the Masonic order, and this when the Masonic order is officially cursed and condemned by the Church . . . No wonder the Pope died a few days afterwards.[42]

Shortly after Ratcliffe returned from a visit to Germany in August 1939, his newspaper was able to appear fortnightly instead of monthly. No evidence survives that he received any help from the Nazi authorities but he was prepared to speak up for Germany, refuting claims that the people there were starving or that they hated Hitler.[43] By 1940, the Jews had replaced roman catholics as his main bugbear and he contemptuously referred to the Gorbals district of Glasgow as 'Jew-land'. An advert in the first issue of 1940, promised articles on 'Our Jewish Usurers', 'The Jews and Crime', and 'Why Germany Put Out the Jews'.[44] Soon after, another edition had a piece entitled 'Britain's Pro-Jew Menace'.[45]

In February 1940, Ratcliffe clashed with Councillor H. D. Longbottom, leader of the Protestant Party in Liverpool who questioned his belief that Hitler was working for the end of 'Popery' in Germany.[46] Later, in June 1940, with Nazi Germany at the zenith of its power, he plaintively remarked in the *Vanguard*, that 'we are very kind to the Roman Catholics in Scotland, of course the reason being seemingly that we have no Hitler in our midst to eject Popery'.[47]

From the tenor of his statements in 1939–40, anyone might be forgiven for thinking that Ratcliffe, a protestant iconoclast to the last, wanted to see the triumph of Hitler. During the rest of the war, he campaigned against it in association with the anarchist pacifist Guy Aldred and he died in relative obscurity in January 1947.[48]

In Edinburgh, where the ingredients for sectarian politics seemed lacking at the beginning of the 1930s, protestant extremists were shortly to enjoy greater political success than in Glasgow and, moreover, their campaigns were laced with anti-catholic violence. Edinburgh was a far more homogeneous city with a much smaller proportion of catholics and no strong Orange or militant protestant tradition. Yet it was here that a religious party called Protestant Action won a series of sensational victories in the mid-1930s.

Protestant Action's manifesto was a negative one but no other religious party has ever done so well in local British politics. It advocated the withdrawal of all state aid from catholic schools, the removal of catholics from the officer corps of the armed forces and the judicial bench, the curtailment of catholic Irish immigration, and the expulsion of all catholic religious orders from Scotland.[49] Its programme specified that just 'as Romanists deal with Protestants in countries where they have full power, so we will deal with Romanists in this country'.[50] At its height, the behaviour of many of its supporters was questionable: catholic functions were attacked, priests assaulted in the streets, and catholic shop assistants threatened. From studying the Edinburgh press, it is apparent that editors were embarrassed that such a party had got loose on the streets of Edinburgh and they were frankly at a loss to explain how this phenomenon had arisen in their tranquil city.

Protestant Action was even more centred on its leader, John Cormack, and its rise would seem to have owed more to his abilities than to the prevailing political situation or previous sectarian unrest. Cormack was born in 1894, the son of Highland parents. He was brought up in a devout Baptist household and, at the age of fifteen, he joined the Argyll and Sutherland Highlanders as a boy soldier. Serving in the trenches in the First World War, he later saw action in Ireland during the 1919–21 War of Independence. Collusion between catholic priests and Sinn Fein separatists made him strongly anti-catholic. Such feelings were not assuaged when he worked in the Edinburgh Post Office (GPO) from 1922 to 1934, after leaving the forces. In his new job, he was suspected of tampering with mail destined for the Archbishop of Edinburgh and, eventually, he was accused of stealing letters and postal orders by a catholic GPO worker. No formal charges were lodged against Cormack but he was suspended from the GPO in 1932. Already he was speaking on Sundays at the Mound, the venue for open-air speakers in Edinburgh. Initially, this was a gesture of solidarity with his father, a lay preacher who was being maltreated by young catholics in the crowd when he spoke.[51]

Cormack and some supporters came along to give him protection and the Mound became the son's regular pitch from the early 1930s until he suffered a heart attack in 1964.[52] He was a slightly-built man who had saturnine features and a superb speaking voice. A limited education detracted from his undoubted intelligence and his clumsy efforts with the written word gave little clue to his great platform ability.

In 1934, Cormack decided to stand for the ward of Leith North in the Edinburgh municipal elections. Leith, Edinburgh's port, was not his home area, nor did it harbour a 'No Popery' tradition. In 1886 it had elected William Gladstone when he was championing Irish Home Rule.[53] From 1918 to 1927, the radical Liberal William Wedgwood Benn was the town's MP. Indeed this working-class port remained in the hands of the National Liberal MP, Ernest Brown, right up to 1945. But on the municipal council, Liberal votes were attainable since the party did not contest local elections.

Moreover the Labour Party had been unable to fill the political vacuum. It languished even as the docks and chemical-making, the chief export trade associated with Leith, ground to a halt in the depression of the 1930s. With its government departments, insurance offices and printing works, Edinburgh avoided the worst of the recession and remained comfortably Tory. So Leith was a place apart that proved receptive to Cormack's populist message. In a rowdy election, he defeated the Moderate, A. H. A. Murray (a future Lord Provost of Edinburgh) and was returned for the north ward. He owed this and future victories to an unusually high poll. In 1934, the average Edinburgh turnout had been 40 per cent but in North Leith, it was 58.4 per cent, the highest in the whole city.

In 1935, Cormack took advantage of this mandate to embarrass and intimidate the catholic authorities in Edinburgh. He gave a warning of the lengths he was prepared to go to shortly before the city council was due to give a civic reception to the Catholic Young Men's Society:

On the 27th day of April, the peaceful, cultured, enlightened city of
Edinburgh, that has never known in my lifetime at least what a real smash-
up means, is going to know it that day, if this civic reception comes off.[54]

Councillors Cormack and James Marr, the latter newly returned for Central Leith at a by-election, duly turned up outside the City Chambers with over one thousand people, many of whom barracked the arriving council guests.[55] When the Archbishop of Edinburgh arrived, his car was surrounded by a hostile mob before the police brought him to safety.[56] Later, on 10 June 1935, Cormack interrupted the ceremony in which Joseph Lyons, the Prime Minister of Australia, and a Roman Catholic, was being given the freedom of Edinburgh along with John Buchan.[57] Still more unruly scenes occurred later when a Catholic Eucharistic Congress was held in Edinburgh. On the evening of 24 June, there was much disorder in Waverley Market where a women's eucharistic meeting was being held and four priests were rescued from a hostile mob.[58]

The worst scenes of all occurred at the climax of the Congress on 25 June at an open-air procession of the Blessed Sacrament. This avoided the city centre and was held in the grounds of St Andrew's Priory, Canaan Lane, in the Morningside district. The next day, *The Scotsman* related how 'as the hour of the gathering approached, tramcar after tramcar brought protestant extremists and others to the scene . . . By seven p.m., there must have been at least 10,000 people in Morningside Road. Gangs of youths and young women shouted "No Popery" . . .' It went on to report that special coaches containing women and young people were stoned, fighting broke out in the crowd, the police were attacked and baton charges were made.[59]

The atmosphere was ugly and the intimidation of catholics continued on and off for the rest of the summer. Catholic activists stood on all-night vigils guarding their churches,[60] worshippers were jeered and taunted as they entered St Mary's cathedral,[61] and years later Edinburgh Catholics can still recall how attempts were made to pressurise shopkeepers to sack catholic employees.[62]

Retired accountant John McLaughlin recalls how at midnight mass on a Christmas Eve in the mid-1930s a few of Cormack's supporters entered St Mary's Star of the Sea church in Leith 'when it was packed to the doors' and 'went to communion simply for the sake of coming out and waving the host saying this is what they believe and it is not true'.[63] A gang called the Blackie Boys (named after their headquarters in Blackfriars Street), sought to defy Cormack's movement and engaged in skirmishes with its militants until its members were caught unawares by a successful incursion of their opponents into their area, the working-class Cowgate, when gang members were taken from their homes and beaten up in the street, without the intervention of the police;[64] catholics would have been hard pressed to resist longer-term violence. Edinburgh was a city that lacked a strongly unionised working-class where socialism could have posed as an alternative magnet of support. It was a financial and merchantile city where class consciousness had developed slowly, where the left had got its worst Scottish results in 1931, and where appeals to atavistic prejudice could be successfully directed at sections of the proletariat.

The Archbishop of Edinburgh was Andrew Joseph McDonald who publicly criticised the press for downplaying the 1935 violence[65] and who privately lobbied the Scottish Office to take strong action against Cormack and his party.[66] At the height of the trouble in June 1935 the future Cardinal Gordon Gray, a Leith man himself, was ordained a priest in the troubled archdiocese he would inherit from the then archbishop. Although a Benedictine monk, McDonald was no cloistered figure but an outgoing prelate who was prepared to give strong leadership to Edinburgh's catholics. *The Scotsman* criticised the archbishop for over-reacting to the threat posed by Cormack but, on 15 July 1935 it warned:

> Let us realise before it is too late, that the credit of our city, our reputation for culture and tolerance, even our peace and personal safety are at stake.[67]

In his heyday, Cormack kept the temperature high by holding meetings on every day of the week and three on Sundays.[68] Thanks to the work of the Hope Trust,[69] which had been giving anti-catholic literature out to Bible classes and the Boys' Brigade for many years, 'he did not have to convert many to his views, they were already latently held'.[70] But in living memory, nobody in Edinburgh had gone quite so far as Cormack whose hostility to 'Popery' was so total that 'he was prepared to see the day when it would be removed from Scotland'.[71] He made no attempt to distinguish between catholicism and individual catholics unlike some fundamentalists who tended to see ordinary roman catholics as dupes rather than conscious enemies.[72] But he later mellowed, adopting the traditional point of view of attacking the system not the individual.

In the 1935 council elections which were then held on the first Tuesday of November, Protestant Action apparently was not harmed by its association with violence. In Leith, the campaign was marred by 'considerable rowdiness'. *The Edinburgh and Leith Observer* which usually supported the Moderates, had a dramatic headline in large black type on the front page of its pre-election issue: 'Sectarianism Dominating Municipal Election, Wild Ward Meetings, "Protestant" Storm Troops Adopt Unchristian Tactics.'[73]

No further Protestant Action members were returned in 1935 but those standing on a protestant ticket got nearly one-quarter of the total vote and, in South Leith, lay preacher George Horne was returned as an Independent Protestant (although Protestant Action did his election work for him).[74] There were also Protestant Parents and Protestant Defence candidates in the field (one of whom lost Dalry by only 4 votes) which demonstrated the volatility of fringe religious politics.

Cormack reached his zenith in November 1936 when Protestant Action gained 30.84 per cent of the total municipal vote. Six of its thirteen candidates were returned, from different parts of the city, and Labour was driven into third place. Protestant Action gained two seats from Labour and three from the Moderates as well as defeating an Independent Catholic; Cormack had now realised his aim of driving all catholics from the council.[75]

Protestant Action supporters were mainly working-class but backing was also forthcoming from small businessmen, a number of shopkeepers providing contributions for the movement's annual bazaar.[76] Mainstream protestants provided stability at the top in its early years, but the movement had unusual characters at its fringes. An early and fleeting collaborator was James Graham, a catholic who had broken with the church after being imprisoned for running guns to the IRA.[77] Another ex-catholic was John P. Fagan who sought to emulate Cormack.[78] The Rev J. C. Trainer was a Protestant Action councillor but no other Church of Scotland ministers openly identified themselves with Cormack and relations with the Orange Order were problematical. Cormack joined in 1936 but he resigned in 1939 and was not re-admitted until twenty years later. The Order in the 1930s was effectively led by Frank D. Dorrian, the deputy grand master, a mining contractor from Bellshill who sought to maintain its still close links with the Unionist Party. Although Cormack was at logger-heads with the hierarchy of the Edinburgh district, he could count on support from the Midlothian district 'which was virtually Protestant Action under a different name' and there is no doubt that he brought the Order many new members in the east of Scotland.[79]

At a time when there were few openings for women in protestant life with membership of the Freemasons and any kind of influence in the Orange Order denied to them, many women emerged as Protestant Action candidates and they would be among Cormack's staunchest supporters for years to come. The same applied to the SPL and one observer has written how Ratcliffe 'and his Edinburgh counterpart poured excitement into lives that were a vacuum of inactivity . . . and frustration'.[80] One of Protestant Action's successful candidates in 1936 was a 53–year-old Jewess, Mrs Esther Henry, the owner of a famous antique shop in the Canongate. Esther Henry was a Rabelaisian figure who is still remembered for her trenchant personality and colourful language. She was keen to enter the council, and once this goal was achieved she drifted away from Cormack and was not as anti-Catholic. Others followed suit and Cormack would be unable to repeat his 1936 success.

Protestant Action rapidly grew unwieldy. In its heyday, Cormack claimed 8,000 card carrying members[81] but 'he had only one big meeting instead of separate branches'.[82] The movement was organised along increasingly authoritarian lines and the constitution and rules were changed to give the General-Secretary increasing power. By 1937 the constitution had been altered to allow the General Secretary to 'hold permanency in office', to 'have authority over all members' and to control all properties and funds along with the Treasurer, John Aitchison, a lifelong follower whom Cormack appointed 'with Members approval'.[83] This tight form of control must have encouraged defections but it might have been impossible for Cormack to decentralise even if he had wanted to because his charisma was probably the main attraction, especially for women. His sister recalled:

> People were not interested in anybody else. He could not be everywhere at once. It was worship, man-worship in a lot of cases; they would have followed him to the end of the world.[84]

The crash came rapidly in 1937 when, unwisely Cormack stood in two seats and was defeated in both. Labour took North Leith from him perhaps because voters were indignant that he would not be giving them his undivided attention if he represented two wards. So, like Ratcliffe, Cormack failed to be re-elected but those on the protestant ticket still captured 25.5 per cent of the Edinburgh vote in 1937. In 1938, he was returned for South Leith, a ward he represented without interruption until his retirement in 1962.

Re-elected on the eve of war, Cormack had disavowed all connections with fascism in an interview which he gave to the press in 1936: 'All our energies will be directed against the Fascists. When I get control, I will put a ban on Fascists on the streets.'[85] But in 1935, this did not prevent him from forming Kormack's Kaledonian Klan, a paramilitary body derived from the Ku Klux Klan which possessed a number of cars and had headquarters in the Lawnmarket.[86] This initiative demonstrated the sway Cormack had over volatile working-class elements. Ratcliffe had been unable to create an equivalent power-base in any of the working-class areas of Glasgow where sectarianism divided voters. Bridgeton, whose cross had been a favourite venue for protestant speakers before the First World War,[87] would have been a suitable point to concentrate on. With the football stadium of the mainly catholic Glasgow Celtic football team being situated near to a district where the Orange Order had many adherents, it witnessed much of the small-scale sectarian violence that affected Glasgow in the 1930s. The Grand Master of the Orange Order in Scotland, A. D. McInnes Shaw, was the Tory opponent of James Maxton MP at the 1935 general election and William Fullerton, the leader of the protestant 'Billy Boy' gang, came from this part of Glasgow and was a section-leader in the British Union of Fascists.[88] But this turbulent area of Glasgow differed from Leith in that the left was sufficiently well-organised to prevent it becoming a launching pad to elective office for either a protestant extremist or a populist Unionist.

Some might think it remarkable that Cormack was not detained under Defence Regulations 18b along with Sir Oswald Mosley and Captain A. H. M. Ramsay, Unionist MP for Peebles and Midlothian in 1940. On two separate occasions at the Mound, in June 1940 he was reported as saying that 'when Protestants went "over the top" with Roman Catholics, the Protestants should shoot them', but no action was taken.[89] Additionally Archbishop MacDonald complained to the authorities that he was behind attacks on Italian property in the city after Italy entered the war on Hitler's side, but this claim was regarded as being without foundation.[90]

By the end of the war, Cormack and his loyal secretary, Miss Watson formed the hardcore of a much depleted movement. At the 1945 general election, he made his one bid for parliament as a candidate for Edinburgh East when he got 2,493 votes, the seat going to Labour. But he was five-times re-elected in what should have been a safe council seat for Labour because the Progressives (as the Tories were then called in local government), declined to oppose him. In return he sided with them on the council and in 1955 he was elected a baillie by his fellow councillors. There is no evidence that, in trying offenders, Cormack showed outright bias against roman catholics which had been the fear of some of his colleagues. Indeed, by the late 1950s, with religious passions cooling off, he was reverting from an ogre to a local institution. In 1959, the *Evening Dispatch* even wrote of him:

> He is held in high regard by the people of Leith as fearless and honest, attributes which, with his record of service on the council may give him the edge over his opponent.[91]

John Cormack retired from politics in 1962, his seat promptly reverting to Labour and he died in 1978 aged eighty-four.

Having long ago sunk roots in Scottish society, protestant militancy was unable to enjoy equivalent success in Scottish politics. The joint experience of protestant parties in the two largest cities of Scotland was remarkably similar: sudden dramatic success in municipal politics, splits, recriminations, inability to formulate a coherent programme, followed by electoral defeat and eventual oblivion. Ironically it was placid Edinburgh, where the catholic community was small and religious strife usually absent, that gave the longest-lease of life to protestant extremism. Perhaps it was not so much anti-catholicism but Cormack's skills as a demagogue and the fact that he provided free open-air entertainment in a Calvinist city where interesting diversions were in short supply, that account for his long-term success. He was also able to exploit the fact that Leith had apparently been neglected by the urban metropolis after it renounced its status as a free burgh in 1920.[92] This was a widely-held grievance and Cormack may have owed his string of victories in Leith South, not so much to religious prejudice (very few catholics lived in the port) but to the fact that at least it could not be wholly overlooked as long as he was representing it.

As protest movements, the SPL and Protestant Action did well because they echoed the prejudices of certain groups of voters at a time when the major parties were exhausted or else unpopular. Third parties once more did well in Scotland in the late 1960s and early 1970s but then the Scottish Nationalists and the Liberals had a set of policies and an organisation and were not just built around a handful of personalities or a bundle of negative attitudes. A party based solely on prejudice can only continue to attract voters in a polarised political atmosphere and politically Scotland was among the calmer European countries of the 1930s. The negativism was on full display in the attitude of Cormack and Ratcliffe to each other. Instead of pooling their energies and forming a nationwide movement, they went their separate ways in the 1930s. Ratcliffe could not bear to be faced with a rival who refused to defer to him and who went on to enjoy much greater political success.[93] Their enmity demonstrated just how difficult it is for protestantism, a faith prone to faction and schism, to participate in electoral politics in the highly successful way its rival has done in catholic Europe.

But in Scotland, if the roman catholic minority had responded to the protestant challenge in the 1930s by setting up its own sectional party, the political battle-lines might have been drawn more firmly and real hostilities might have commenced.[94] However, the response of Scottish catholic leaders to the threat posed by Ratcliffe and Cormack was usually a measured one.[95] Catholics supported a mainstream political party (Labour) or else the ILP and this strong labour movement would have been a formidable opponent for protestant extremism to surmount, even if, politically, it had remained in contention beyond the 1930s.[96]

The indifference of major vested interests in protestant Scotland was another powerful obstacle that the protestant parties were unable to overcome. With its huge membership, the Orange Order could have boosted their prospects but support was never forthcoming, at least from its pro-Unionist leadership. The movement distrusts populists who have emerged outside its ranks and it has tended to be reactive in politics. The Orange Order has not tested its strength in the open political arena although members can participate in politics and it usually prefers to exercise influence from behind the scenes.[97]

At least one industrialist, Sir John Cargill, whose grandfather founded Burmah Oil, had close links with the all-protestant football team of Glasgow Rangers and was active in the Unionist Party as well as being the driving force behind the anti-labour Economic League in the west of Scotland. But neither he nor his economic counterparts appear to have supported the SPL with financial donations in the way that rising authoritarian movements on the continent were backed by economic interests hoping to influence them if they obtained power. If they had, it would have been ironic since many of the Irish arrived in nineteenth-century Scotland, thanks to local entrepeneurs sending their agents to Ireland to recruit them as cheap labour.[98]

The tacit or open hostility of the protestant churches probably was vitally important in limiting the appeal of the SPL and Protestant Action. No doubt the prejudices of Ratcliffe and Cormack were shared, albeit in a diluted form, by many church ministers but they had no desire to collaborate with demagogues. Even a conservative minister like the Rev. D. M. McGregor spoke out against the linking of protestantism with mob violence: 'If protestantism can only be vindicated in such crude ways, its day is nearly done.'[99] Few if any ministers made common cause with the *ultras* and the Rev. F. C. C. Watson, the leading Church of Scotland fundamentalist on catholic education, suffered criticism at the hands of Ratcliffe.[100]

The resilience of the Tories in municipal politics also acted to the disadvantage of the religious parties. In Glasgow, municipal Toryism was going through a crisis of identity in the 1930s as evidenced by the decision of the Moderates to rename their party the Progressives and then revert to the original name, all in the space of four years. But the influx of Liberal supporters into the Tory camp in urban Scotland following the decline of Scottish Liberalism, probably helped to steer the party away from the wilder shores of sectarianism.

Media hostility too in both Edinburgh and Glasgow made it difficult for the religious parties to break out of their electoral ghetto and it would appear to have hastened their demise. Nevertheless, it is worth remembering that Ratcliffe and Cormack did far better politically than the more charismatic Sir Oswald Mosley in the 1930s. In local politics, no member of the far-left ever did as well in the electoral politics of 'Red Clydeside' as Ratcliffe did in 1931–3. He and Cormack headed reactionary movements in what was still a traditionalist country in key aspects of political culture. In many ways, they were merely reflecting existing prejudices which is a far easier task than popularising new ones. But dependent largely on inflamatory leaders and fickle councillors, protestant extremism was unable to break into mass politics, even when conditions seemed to briefly favour it in the 1930s.

NOTES

1 G. C. Gunnin, 'John Wheatley, Catholic Socialism, and Irish Labour in the West of Scotland', unpublished PhD, University of Chicago, 1973, 23.

2 For this movement, there is J. F. McCaffrey, 'The origins of Liberal Unionism in the west of Scotland', ante, 1 (1971), 47–71.

3 For the political behaviour of the Irish in Scotland before the 1930s, see the following: Ian Wood, 'Irish Immigrants and Scottish Radicalism, 1880–1906', in I. McDougall (ed.), *Essays in Scottish Labour History* (Edinburgh, 1979) and his 'John Wheatley, the Irish, and the Labour Movement in Scotland', *The Innes Review*, xxxi (1980), 71–85.

4 Northern Ireland erupted into conflict after 1968 but except for rare intervals, the Ulster question has not subsequently been a divisive one in British politics.

5 During 1923–4, Hugh Ferguson, a hardline Orangeman described by his predecessor as being 'of the stuff of which are made cruder members of Hitler's entourage', was Unionist MP for Motherwell: note that he took the Unionist whip, having been elected as an Orange and Protestant Party representative.

6 See George M. Thomson, *Caledonia or the Future of the Scots* (London, 1927) and his *Re-Discovery of Scotland* (London, 1928). Andrew Dewar Gibb's *Scotland in Eclipse* (London, 1930) is in the same *genre*.

7 R. D. Elliot, 'The Glasgow Novel', unpublished PhD, University of Glasgow, 1977, 329.

8 *The Vanguard*, Apr. 1937. Biographical data about Ratcliffe can be obtained from reading a semi-autobiographical series in his newspaper entitled 'Twenty-Five Year's on the Hustings', published in successive issues starting in April 1937.

9 In *The Vanguard*, Sept. 1937, he wrote: 'The Orange and Protestant Party . . . after

sending one representative to parliament had to surrender to the politicians . . . It did not live very long. It became a menace to the Unionist Party, and so the Unionists in the Orange Order killed it.

10 *Forward*, 3 Mar. 1934.

11 *Glasgow Herald*, 6 Nov. 1933.

12 Two pamphlets defending the catholic schools settlement are *The Education (Scotland) Act 1918*, Catholic Truth Society (Edinburgh, n.d.) and the ironically named *The Catholic Menace*, Catholic Truth Society (Edinburgh, 1935).

13 *Forward*, 21 Oct. 1931.

14 *Ibid.*

15 Ratcliffe published articles in *Forward* on 13 June 1931 and on 3 Mar. 1934.

16 *Forward*, 3 Mar. 1934.

17 *Ibid.*

18 Sir Oswald Mosley's British Union of Fascists made little impact in Scotland and Glasgow and Edinburgh were the only major British cities where Mosley found it impossible to hold a public meeting (in Edinburgh after 1936). The militancy of the left told against him in Glasgow but he was also hampered by his consistent support for a united and independent Ireland. This made him anathema to the Unionist far-right in Scotland and enabled a local fascist movement to compete for support.

19 *Forward*, 4 Nov. 1933.

20 As an aspirant for elective office, Gilmour was the New Party's candidate in Coatbridge in the 1931 general election, Liberal candidate in the Scottish Border constituencies after 1945, and an unsuccessful candidate for the Moderates in the 1962 Edinburgh municipal elections. As late as 1983, he was writing letters to the press, sniping at roman catholicism.

21 The programme is published in full in *Commonwealth*, no. i, 2 June 1933. This issue can be found in the Baille Library collection deposited in the Mitchell Library's Glasgow Room since 1982.

22 *Protestant Vanguard*, 11 Mar. 1933. *The Vanguard* was published either weekly, fortnightly, or monthly between Aug. 1931 and Mar. 1947; it was known as *Protestant Vanguard* from Aug. 1931 to July 1933 and again from Sept. 1944 to Nov. 1946. The British Library at Colindale has almost a complete run while the Mitchell Library in Glasgow has most of the numbers produced up to June 1940.

23 *The Vanguard*, July 1937. Dollan may have escaped Ratcliffe's slingshots because in the SPL leader's own words: 'He is more of a Socialist than he is a practising Roman Catholic', *The Vanguard*, 15 Nov. 1933.

24 *The Vanguard*, 29 Sept. 1934.

25 *Ibid.*

26 *Glasgow Observer*, 22 Feb. 1930.

27 *Forward*, 13 June 1931.

28 *Glasgow Herald*, 5 Nov. 1934.

29 The SPL's version of this incident was published in *The Vanguard* on 20 May 1933. The issue also reprinted an article entitled 'Attack on the Pope's Picture', taken from *The*

Northern Whig, a Belfast daily paper which reported the incident on 3 May 1933 just after it had happened.

30 Graham Walker, 'Painting Framed by Controversy', *The Irish News* (Belfast), 5 May 1983.

31 *The Vanguard*, 3 Jan. 1934.

32 'The Acrobatics of an Orange MP', *Protestant Vanguard*, 4 Jan. 1933. Moore, a retired army officer from Ulster, belonged to the far-Right of the Tory Party, and was sympathetic to the domestic policies of Hitler, whom he met in the 1930s. See Richard Griffiths, *Fellow-Travellers of the Right* (Oxford, 1980), 157–8.

33 *The Vanguard*, 8 Nov. 1933.

34 This was in 1932 and after taking legal action against a former SPL organiser, Ratcliffe had to drop his charges and apologise when he could not substantiate them. See *Forward*, 3 Nov. 1933.

35 *Protestant Vanguard*, 11 Mar. 1933.

36 His election address is quoted in a Memorial of the Archbishop of Glasgow, Donald Mackintosh, 1935, in the Catholic Union Files, Box 11, Archives of the Roman Catholic Archdiocese of Glasgow. One practical outcome of the Moderate-SPL pact was that the SPL was given a free-run in seven working-class wards while the Moderates were unopposed by the SPL in more affluent districts.

37 Sir Charles Cleland (1867–1941), chairman of the Glasgow Unionist Association 1914–25, chairman of the Education Authority of Glasgow 1919–28. One of his daughters became the wife of Sir Richard Dawson Bates, Home Secretary in the Northern Ireland government from 1921 to 1943.

38 Box 3, Catholic Union Files, Archives of the Roman Catholic Archdiocese of Glasgow.

39 Letter from William Spiers, ex-member of the SPL: 14 Mar. 1984.

40 Letter from H. Grace to John Campbell, Hon. Secretary of the Catholic Union, 23 Oct. 1934, Box 9 Catholic Union Files, Archives of the Roman Catholic Archdiocese of Glasgow.

41 *The Daily Record*, 6 Nov. 1934.

42 *The Vanguard*, Mar. 1939.

43 *The Vanguard*, 14 Oct. 1939.

44 *The Vanguard*, 6 Jan. 1940.

45 *The Vanguard*, 20 Jan. 1940.

46 *The Vanguard*, 3 Feb. 1940.

47 *The Vanguard*, June 1940.

48 *The Glasgow Herald* carried a short obituary on 14 Jan. 1947.

49 Constitution of Protestant Action (Edinburgh, n.d.).

50 Constitution of Protestant Action.

51 The personal details about John Cormack's early life were provided by his younger sister, Mrs Dora Wight in an interview on 18 July 1983; additional information about Cormack and the catalyst which brought him to the Mound by McDonald Morris, Dec. 1984.

52 Interview with J. G. MacLean, member of the Protestant Action Society.

53 Alistair B. Cooke, 'Gladstone's Election for the Leith District of Edinburgh in July 1886', *ante*, xlix (1970), 172–94.

54 *The Daily Record*, 18 Apr. 1935. Cormack made this statement at a meeting in the Usher Hall, Edinburgh attended by nearly 3,000 people.

55 *The Scotsman*, 29 Apr. 1935.

56 *Glasgow Observer*, 4 May 1935. *The Bulletin*, 29 Apr. 1935.

57 *Glasgow Observer*, 15 June 1935.

58 *The Scotsman*, 25 June 1935. In its report, the paper mentioned that 'American sailors and marines from the warship in the Forth mingled in the crowds, and one sailor asked, perhaps with less innocent intent than his eyes suggested, "Is this how you Scotch folk usually make whoopee?"

59 *The Scotsman*, 26 June 1935.

60 *Edinburgh and Leith Observer*, 3 May 1935. *The Scotsman*, 26 June 1935.

61 *Edinburgh and Leith Observer*, 3 May 1935.

62 Interview with Mrs. J. McLay: 20 Dec. 1935.

63 Interview with Leith-born catholic, John McLaughlin: 21 Aug. 1984.

   Often John Cormack produced what he claimed to be consecrated hosts at both public and private gatherings, the consecration of the blessed sacrament being a part of the catholic act of worship that was especially repugnant to him: interview with Fr Anthony Ross: 21 Dec. 1981.

64 Interviews with John McLaughlin and McDonald Morris.

65 *The Times* on 19 Aug. 1935 published a letter from the Archbishop in which it was rebuked for referring to 'exaggerated reports of sectarian trouble in the Scottish capital' from the continental press.

   On 11 July 1935, Archbishop McDonald had issued a press statement, the first sentence of which read: 'For some months past, Catholics have been subjected to a campaign of vilification, calumny and savagery that would be difficult to parallel in these days of enlightenment and progress.'

66 The Archbishop's letter to the Scottish Office of 16 July 1935 primarily related to the operational responsibility of the Chief Constable and therefore his representations were passed to the Edinburgh magistrates who considered that the authorities 'had done everything to meet the situation created by the disturbances . . .'. Scottish Record Office HH1/777.

67 *The Scotsman*, 15 July 1935.

68 Interview with J. G. MacLean.

69 The Hope Trust was endowed by John Hope (1807–1893), an Edinburgh lawyer and elder of the Church of Scotland. Funds were set aside for 'the dissemination of knowledge regarding the antiscriptural nature of Popery, in arousing people to a sense of the evils of Popery, in efforts towards the conversion of Roman Catholics . . .'. David Jamie, *John Hope, Philanthropist and Reformer* (Edinburgh, 1900), 531.

70 Interview with J. G. MacLean.

71 J. G. MacLean.

72 J. G. MacLean.

73 *Edinburgh and Leith Observer*, 25 Oct. 1935.

74 However, A. H. A. Murray, Cormack's defeated opponent in 1934 was returned for a Leith ward in this election.

75 Earlier, on 13 Feb. 1936, John Cormack mobilised some of his supporters against an indoor meeting of the Catholic Truth Society in Edinburgh that was addressed by Monsignor Ronald Knox. The police were out in greater force than on some previous occasions when disorder had resulted and the event passed off without serious violent incidents. Nevertheless, Cormack was later arrested and when he refused to pay a fine was sentenced to sixty days in prison. He served only one night in prison as his fine was paid by a well-wisher but his popularity increased and the *Edinburgh Evening Dispatch* of 21 Oct. 1961 later recalled that 'the trial seemed to add strength to the Protestant Action Society', which, at the end of 1936, won its best results.

    Information about this collision with the law was provided by Mrs Dora Wight and details were obtained from a booklet entitled *John Cormack, Some Memories*, Protestant Action Society (Edinburgh, 1978).

76 J. G. MacLean.

77 Letter from Christopher Graham: 8 July 1983.

78 Letter from David A. Watt: 23 July 1983.

79 The information in this paragraph about Cormack's relations with the Orange Order was provided by J. G. MacLean.

80 Colm Brogan, 'Catholics in Changing Social Conditions', *Glasgow Observer and Scottish Catholic Herald, Scottish Survey, 1878–1955*, v.

81 J. G. MacLean.

82 Interview with Mrs Dora Wight: 18 July 1983.

83 But the constitution was altered again in 1939 to read: 'The General Secretary shall hold office unless two thirds of the members called to an Emergency General Meeting decide otherwise.

84 Mrs Dora Wight.

85 *Edinburgh Evening Dispatch*, 5 Nov. 1936.

86 *Glasgow Observer*, 29 Jan. 1938; J. G. MacLean.

87 See John Paton, *Proletarian Pilgrimage* (London, 1935), 70.

88 *The Evening Citizen* (Glasgow), 19 Jan. 1955.

89 SRO, HH1/777.

90 *Ibid.*

91 *Edinburgh Evening Dispatch*, 23 Apr. 1959.

92 Interview with John McLaughlin.

93 Cormack, who had been a member of the SPL in Edinburgh, broke with Ratcliffe who had wanted him 'merely to hold the door' at meetings (information from J. G. MacLean). Ratcliffe sniped at his Edinburgh rival in the columns of his newspaper right through the 1930s. In *The Vanguard* of 6 July 1935, one headline proclaimed, 'Edinburgh's Underworld at Large, The Fruits of Protestant Action'. Later, in the Nov. 1937 issue, Ratcliffe announced that he had written a pamphlet that would 'bring to light the acrobatics of . . . Cormack and his gang of meeting breakers and noisy and ill-behaved females'.

94 The Catholic Union, the self-appointed guardian of catholic interests in Glasgow and

elsewhere had successfully run candidates for local Education boards until these were abolished in 1929. The question of standing candidates in local council elections was discussed internally at different times in the 1930s. Although many activists were in favour of taking this step in Glasgow, the Archbishop was unhappy with the idea and, since he had the final word in the Catholic Union, it was decided to support the candidates of existing parties deemed favourable to catholic interests.

95 The testimony of an ex-SPL member is useful here: Ratcliffe's 'own class were his worst enemies. The Roman Church "took the stick", often ignored the challenge and like the Arabian proverb: the dogs bark but the caravan moves on.' Letter from William Spiers: 14 Mar. 1984.

96 For the political behaviour of Scottish catholics during the period under discussion, see the author's 'Scottish Catholics and the British Left 1918–39', *The Innes Review*, 34, I, Spring 1983, 17–43.

97 Before the Second World War, the statutes of the Orange Order debarred members from being socialists.

98 In a 1932 parliamentary exchange, David Kirkwood, the left-wing Scottish MP reminded Sir Robert Horne, a former Chancellor of the Exchequer and Glasgow Tory MP making anti-Irish remarks, of this fact: 'I want to ask the right honourable gentleman, the member for Hillhead, who brought the Irish to Scotland? Who? Ask the Chairman of the Tory Party, Lord Stonehaven. It was has great-grandfather who brought the Irish to the west of Scotland because they were cheap labour.' *Hansard*, vols 32–3 (272), 329, 29 Nov. 1932.

99 Quoted in Compton MacKenzie, *Catholicism in Scotland* (London, 1936), 169. On pp. 170–2, Mackenzie reproduced a letter from Cormack which the *Glasgow Weekly Herald* published on 22 June 1935. He claimed that the bad grammar and clumsy syntax which Cormack exhibited warned off the respectable protestants who had hitherto endorsed him but the available evidence does not necessarily back up this claim.

As to the identity of his respectable protestant backers, Mackenzie makes a sensational claim on p. 177, for which no evidence has been found; as an example of the fears held by some catholics, it is nevertheless interesting: 'Such ferocity would never have been tolerated but for the base interest one political party has in fostering it with the hope of political advantage. It is difficult to free the mind of the suspicion that the Protestant agitation both in Belfast and Edinburgh have been systematically fed by the secret elements of that same political party.'

100 Ratcliffe denounced Reverend Watson in *The Vanguard*, 3 Jan. 1934.

Women Compositors in Edwardian Edinburgh

Extracted from Sian Reynolds 1989 *Britannica's Typesetters*, Edinburgh (Edinburgh University Press), 72–80.

THE UNION AND THE 'FEMALE QUESTION': THE GATHERING STORM

No very great resistance had been mounted to the employment of women in the early days, partly because the numbers were small, partly because the union had been weakened by the 1872–3 strike, and partly, it must be remembered, because the girls recruited to the trade were often the daughters of print workers. The tangle of hostile and sympathetic feelings towards the new recruits, while hard for the historian to penetrate, must have complicated everyday life in the printing office. In later years, one union member pointed out that there was 'a new generation of printers who have sprung up since the strike. When I say that some of them take [women compositors] to be wives, there cannot be ill-feeling toward them'.[1] (Though of course one of the most efficient ways of removing women from the printing houses was to propose marriage, and this was more than once half-seriously proposed as a deliberate strategy.)

When in the 1880s, anxiety about the question grew more acute, and when exhortation to society members not to instruct 'female learners' or to allow their daughters to take up the trade seemed to have little effect, more organized attempts were made to confront the problem. At the conference held in 1888 by the three compositors' unions, the Typographical Association (English provinces), the London Society of Compositors and the Scottish Typographical Association, specifically to discuss the Edinburgh question, the following resolution was passed:

> That while strongly of the opinion that women are not physically capable of performing the duties of a compositor, the Conference recommends their admission to membership of the various typographical unions upon the same conditions as journeymen, provided always the females are paid strictly in accordance with the scale.[2]

Cynthia Cockburn call this 'studied hypocrisy', arguing that as things stood no woman could expect to earn the same wage as a man, because of the Factory Acts among other things, and links it with the undoubtedly fiercely held view among many compositors that women really had no right to 'leave the home', anyway.

It is possible to nuance this view slightly as regards the Edinburgh union leadership. There may just have been some hope of effecting change through organization, especially when the numbers of women were still low (about 300 at the end of the 1880s), though the means chosen were not welcomed by the rank and file of the men's union. Although unfortunately details of the projects are tantalizingly hard to ascertain, at least two attempts were made after 1888 by the Edinburgh Typographical society to set up a women's union. The first, in the late 1880s, is referred to only in the retrospective 'Statement on the Female Question', published in 1904:

> Miss Black of London [who must have been Clementina Black] a lady who was well-known for her efforts to improve the social condition of her sex, offered to make an endeavour to organise the female compositors in Edinburgh, with a view to remedying the evils complained of by the journeymen. The branch committee favourably entertained Miss Black's assistance, but on it being remitted to a general meeting of the Society, it was rejected on the grounds that if the females were organised, their position would be improved as an industry for females, which would result in great accession to their numbers in the printing trade in Edinburgh.[3]

What seems to have happened here (as on other matters) is a division of opinion between the ETS committee – who may have been quite sincere in trying a long-term solution – and the knee-jerk reaction of the membership against the permanent acceptance of women as compositors which the project undeniably contained.

That some compositors, and not only on the committee, took a more sympathetic view of the problem is suggested by one writer to the *STC*, as far back as 1886, whose attitude seems with hindsight to be the most constructive approach voiced by an Edinburgh man: that the women be treated seriously as colleagues and an attempt made to integrate them into the cultural world of the compositor from which they were decidedly excluded:

> A trade female society should be organised, having in connection a sick etc. fund; a reading-room provided with illustrated and comic papers and magazines; a library of high-class light literature chiefly and encyclopedias,

dictionaries etc.; and an efficient committee to arrange for a grand picnic every summer and social gatherings in winter evenings.[4]

A rather patronising choice of literature perhaps, but the suggestion was a positive one. Such was not apparently the view of the bulk of the membership however, and the chance was lost to try an experiment in creating greater unity while the numbers of women were still comparatively low.

The strategy of continuing to exclude women from the union did not prevent their recruitment in ever greater numbers by the employers. So in the late 1890s, another attempt, this time apparently not vetoed by the membership, was made to organize a women's union. The central figure on this occasion was the more locally known organizer, Margaret Irwin of Glasgow, acknowledged to be an expert on women's trades in Scotland.[5] The delegate meeting of the STA at Dumfries in 1895 had called upon those branches affected by women's employment to 'exercise their influence in every way to secure the standard wages and fair conditions of employment for female compositors'. Accordingly, 'with the praiseworthy assistance of Miss Irwin, Secretary of the Women's Federal Council', and with financial help both from the ETS and the STA, a 'Female Compositors Society' was set up as the *STC* reported in July and August 1898. Margaret Irwin 'paid three visits to Edinburgh to address meetings at the invitation of the Typographical Association', and the STA *Annual Report* of 1898 claimed that the new society 'bids fair to succeed; if it will be the means, as anticipated, of improving the position of the *male comp* [*sic*, my italics] there will be no lack of well-wishers'. The next report however carried the sad news that the 'Female Compositors Society has not survived the ailments of its infancy: it closed at the end of the year'.[6]

The reasons advanced for this failure in the 'Statement' of 1904 were 'the difficulties which female organisers have had to contend with in other trades – apathy and lack of support'. This is familiar language, and Eleanor Gordon and others have argued that much more investigation of the circumstances of setting up women's unions is needed before it can be accepted at face value. Material obstacles made union membership difficult for women: their low pay made it hard to pay dues, while their domestic duties as daughters and sisters, not to mention the question of staying out late, made it hard to attend meetings. These problems have to be weighed along with less tangible factors: what would women (as distinct from 'the male comp') get out of the organization? How far did it address their grievances? How whole-hearted was the men's support?[7] In this case, the lack of details urges us to caution. The literature (especially Macdonald's 1904 account) is full of references to women's 'pessimistic and listless' attitude to the fight for higher wages, but as we have already noted, women were often inclined to agree that they were not doing the 'full job', a view in which they were daily fortified by both masters and men. Margaret Irwin herself accepted that the lack of success was caused by 'the apathy of the women themselves . . . the woman does not take her industrial work as seriously as a man . . . [she] does not regard it as the permanent occupation of her life'.[8] Margaret Irwin's views are not to be dismissed lightly, but it is worth noting that she herself did not approach the question with any blazing convictions about equal pay. She argued that if women were paid the same as men, 'it would result in many women being dismissed from many trades', and also accepted without demur, when giving evidence to the Fair Wages Committee a few years later, the proposition that women were satisfied with less money because they were earning 'pin money' if married, and 'pocket money' if not.[9] With such pessimism about equal pay entrenched in the mind of their organizers, with such low evaluation being set on their work, one might argue that it would have been surprising if a militant women's union could really be organized in the prevailing atmosphere.

While it would be nice to imagine an alternative history in which either Miss Black or Miss Irwin succeeded in organizing the women compositors, who then ended up with a reading-room full of the encyclopaedias they had themselves typeset, it was not to be. Since later events were to show that women compositors were by no means incapable of taking action, we may be sceptical about 'apathy' as the sole explanation for the collapse of the early attempt to form a union. But in the mean time, encouraged perhaps by such apparent signs of weakness, perhaps simply by pressure on their order-books, the Edinburgh master printers began recruiting girl apprentices in larger numbers than ever before during the early years of the century, to the growing despair of the ETS and increasing anger from the male trade-union movement in general.

The Edinburgh 'female question' clearly had repercussions outside the city, as can be seen from the reasons given by the Arbiter who turned down the Glasgow compositors' pay-claim in 1904. Arguing that Glasgow wages were already higher than those in Edinburgh, and pointing out that the Glasgow printers had successfully blacked firms trying to employ women, he went on (in rather clotted prose):

> I am satisfied that the employment of female compositors in Glasgow, while it would increase the total volume of work done there and admit of the natural development of the Glasgow book trade, would not injure the position of the Glasgow men printers, while it would enable the Glasgow printing trade, employed as well as employers, to obtain and retain work which at present ought to come to Glasgow, or at least might come to Glasgow but now goes to Edinburgh.[10]

The Glasgow patriotism of the Arbiter was more to the taste of the employers than the employed, whose irritation showed itself within the STA.[11] Branches without women rivals now sided with Glasgow in demanding a campaign to exclude women for good, while branches such as Edinburgh, who had to contend with the problem, tried to go on arguing for some form of recognition of women workers. The STA delegate meeting of 1905 passed a resolution urging branches to ban any new women entrants to the trade, and over the next year or so Edinburgh became increasingly isolated as first Aberdeen, then Dundee and Perth succeeded in closing the trade to new women recruits (there were far fewer women compositors in these towns anyway). During 1907–8, although a local committee was formed by the ETS to study the 'female question', priority went to the 50 hours campaign, which was finally settled in February 1909, thus leaving the way clear. Moves towards unity within the branch, and towards federation within the printing trades as a whole, strengthened the resolve of the Edinburgh compositors. In 1908, the longstanding split between themselves and the machinemen had been healed: 'a happy consummation' and 'an event full of promise for the future', as the local branch of the Printing and Kindred Trades Federation put it. The NPKTF, which had taken definitive form in 1902, had been pressing for reconciliation within the Edinburgh branch, and was to play a strongly supporting role in 1910.[12]

1910: THE MAIN ISSUES

It was with the new strength born of unity then that the Edinburgh Typographical Society presented the employers with its memorial on women workers in November 1909. For the first time, this took an uncompromising line; there was no more talk of limiting the damage. This time they demanded:

> That from the first of January 1910, there shall be no further introduction of females into our trade in Edinburgh, nor any importation of female compositors from other centres, and that in future, machine composition be solely undertaken by male union labour.[13]

Two things are worth noting at this point. First, the memorial did not call for the dismissal of any women employed in Edinburgh at the time. This was important for relations with the existing women compositors, none of whose own jobs was under threat. The calculation behind the memorial was naturally that most of the women would leave to get married within a few years. Secondly, and this became clear in the negotiations that followed, machines were the real key to the whole question. This was a dispute about future technology as much as about women's labour. The memorial marks a striking turnabout in the men's approach to composing machines, which must have been the result of a fairly recent appreciation of the double threat posed by women Monotype operators. It has already been observed that male compositors had virtually boycotted the machines at first. Now, possibly alerted by advisers from outside (such as C. M. Bowerman, from the London Society of Compositors, chairman of the NPKTF, and member of parliament, who attended the negotiations during 1910), the committee of the ETS on behalf of its members, came into line with compositors everywhere else in claiming the right to work the machines.[14]

It is evident from the progress of the talks between employers and union, that the employers equally recognized this as the heart of the dispute. With hindsight, one can read from their responses that the days of recruiting women as hand-setters were in any case numbered. The master printers readily concurred with 'the desirability of gradually reducing the ratio of female to male labour employed in hand-setting' in their first reply to the ETS committee in January 1910, but 'they did not mention the proposal to replace the monotype keyboard operators by male union labour'.[15] Through the winter months, the larger firms gave further assurances that they were willing 'to take immediate steps for the gradual reduction of female comps'; some it seems went even so far as to dismiss women. The close attention which the union committee gave to every case of a girl being hired in the winter and spring months of 1910 argues that the recruitment had slowed to a trickle . . . whereas large numbers of the women would have been 14–year-olds in 1908–9, hardly any were younger than this. (Two surviving compositors, both of whom began work in 1909 told me that they had been among the last recruits.) The employers did however wish to keep the door open for the future, and proposed a ban of five years on women entrants – something which the union was prepared to accept in the hope that 'natural reductions' over this period would leave the men in a commanding position.

On machines however, a tough rearguard action was fought by the employers. Pressed by the men, they offered various compromises at the April 1910 negotiations of which the minutes have been kept.[16] Still pleading competition and the greater suitability of women for keyboard work, they proposed first that machines henceforward be given alternately to men and women workers; or, a further concession, that all new machines be given to men until there were 50 per cent worked by each sex, and attributed alternately thereafter. Neither of these proposals was accepted by the men who, both in December 1909 and May 1910, voted by two-thirds majorities to reject them.[17] The talks remained in deadlock through the summer of 1910, but following energetic efforts by the compositors and the unions representing kindred trades, pressure was mounting for a confrontation, which took place in the last weeks of the summer.

'NOT FOUND WANTING': THE WOMEN COMPOSITORS WHO JOINED THE MEN

It is during the summer, and before the September dénouement, that the voices of the women compositors for the first time become audible to the historian. Not before time, the reader may think, we can find out something of what the central figures in this dispute thought about it. Until this date, it has been difficult to escape from a picture of the women compositors as the subject of other people's discourse: employers, trade unionists, parliamentary commissioners, commentators like Macdonald, organizers like Margaret Irwin. The 1910 dispute, which is particularly well documented in the press as well as in manuscript sources, enables us to see that on this occasion at least, the women did not stand by and wait for it to be resolved over their heads. They took an active part – but on both sides of the argument. One section of the women backed the men; another formed a separate union for a short while and tried to resist the ban called for in the men's memorial.

The first definite report of women taking the side of the men comes in early August, when it was announced at the quarterly general meeting of the Edinburgh Typographical Society that in the office of Neill & Co, 51 'female compositors had intimated their intention of tendering notices on Friday 5 August' alongside the men. Neill's was one of the largest employers of women and therefore one of the main targets of possible strike action. The same source claims that the 51 women in question 'consisted of the best workers in that department' (presumably this means the most senior).[18] Details of the circumstances at Neill's emerged only slowly and selectively, but the women apparently exacted a price for their support. Not only did they get a promise from the secretary of the men's union that they would be paid full wages by the union if they came out on strike (unusual, if not unprecedented for non-members) but the agreement subsequently signed with Neill's management included some improvements in their piece rates. 'Female comps' were in future to be paid for 'inserting leads [ie spacing material] and justification'. What was more, since 'a deputation from the female compositors [had insisted] upon an agreement anent same', they were to be allowed to do 'upmaking and corrections on machine-set matter until the whole matter is settled'.[19] As a result of the threatened strike – in which the women's participation would have been crucial – Neill's came to a separate agreement with the men, signed the memorial and thus dropped out of the dispute during the month of August. They were quickly followed by another large-scale employer of women, Morrison & Gibb. Less is known about the Morrison & Gibb case, but again it appears that the women indicated their solidarity with the men.

It may seem odd at first sight that women should actively promote their own exclusion from the trade. But it should be remembered that the memorial did not call for the dismissal of a single woman. If in addition promises were made, as it seems they were, of helping to boost wage rates, and if particular grievances were also thrown into the package, it is not necessarily paradoxical that women should have agreed both to the five-year ban on entry (they were not to know that it would really be a permanent one) and to the assigning of all new machines to men. There was no question of taking away their own machines from women already working as Monotype operators in 1910. What is also easily over-looked is the appeal to their class solidarity. When it was put to them that they were taking jobs away from men, many working-class women were prepared to agree that this was 'not fair'.[20] But there may be more to this than comradely debate.

At a subsequent mass meeting, John Templeton, secretary of the STA, referred to these 'two great cases' (Neill's and Morrison & Gibb) and said that women workers in these firms had been 'weighed in the balance and not found wanting'.[21] Jean Symonds, one of the women who organized resistance to the men, retorted that 'the girls he referred to had been weighed against their will. In one firm, the girls had practically been compelled to join with the men'. It appeared that she meant Morrison & Gibb.[22] It is hard to know how to measure this kind of evidence. It is not at all unlikely that some pressure was put on women in these two key firms, but it may have been of a persuasive rather than an intimidating kind. 'A woman worker' wrote to the *Despatch* in late August, claiming that 'persistent attempts are being made by the men to work on the motives of selfishness and self-interest of the women'. Another anonymous woman, 'a looker-on' claimed that 'the men have recently shown a curious and novel diligence in the way of coaxing, bribing or even fighting girls into joining a trade union'.[23] (The union in question was one of the unskilled unions in the NPKTF.) Whatever the tactics used, it soon appeared that the men were having some success in winning women over to their side in other firms as well. The *Despatch* on 9 September, as the dispute was reaching its climax, reported:

> It is claimed by the men that they are receiving a very large measure of support from the women. It is reported that in a large printing office in the city [which can only be R. & R. Clark] where there are about 100 females employed, more than 70 handed in notices to strike yesterday, while correspondingly large proportions of the females employed in other firms are said to have signified their intention of going on strike, failing a settlement.

Only a 'claim', but one that looked quite likely. It was not only the female compositors who were being asked for support. Amelia McLean, who led the resistance to the men, alleged that Mr Alfred Evans, general secretary of the Warehousement and Cutters' Union, was 'trying to organise all the girls in the printing trade, including warehouse, machine room and stationery workers, [to come out] on strike with the men'.[24]

Mr Evans and his union were crucial to the men's strategy. The Warehousemen's and Cutter's Union might not seem the obvious place for compositors – even women – to find a welcome. But within the NPKTF, it was successfully recruiting a number of the unskilled or 'auxiliary' women workers in the printing trade. It was an English union, based in London and not affiliated to the STA, with whom it had dealings only within the NPKTF. Soon Alfred Evans was claiming women compositors as members: 'We have 420 female workers [in Edinburgh], 280 of them comps.' And later, 'we have 280 women comps enrolled in our society and over 100 fresh nomination papers handed in'. Ellen Smyth, an experienced organizer, helped in the recruitment campaign. This was the union which Edinburgh male printers had been 'coaxing, bribing even fighting' women to join.[25] Why did they not rather try to recruit them into the STA in some way, as a separate women's branch for instance, as in the past? Cynthia Cockburn is probably quite right when she refers to this as a way of getting women to recognize that they were inferior beings.[26] The 'looker-on' correspondent of the *Edinburgh Evening News* certainly thought so. She wrote that a woman who had been a comp for eleven years had told her that the subject of a union had never been mentioned to her before. 'Now a special male organiser from the South has been brought in' to get them to join 'not the STA, which by rights skilled workers like compositors should enter, but an inferior English union, composed of unskilled workers'.[27]

Amelia McLean also pointed out that skill was at stake: 'fortunately, the majority of women workers cannot see their way to join that union, as they claim to be skilled workers'.[28] For the first time, perhaps because by now there was a 'critical mass' of older and more experienced women to take a lead, we find some women taking a stand specifically on the definition of skill, and refusing to be absorbed into an 'unskilled union'. The women's resistance movement crystallized around this refusal, drawing hostile comment from Alfred Evans, who praised the 'shoulder to shoulder' solidarity with the ETS shown by his own members, while deploring the aid given to the resisters by 'middle-class women who are on the warpath on behalf of the employers'. For it was known and greatly deplored by male unionists, that the women's resistance movement did indeed have support from middle-class women's suffrage groups in Edinburgh.

NOTES

1 *Royal Commission on Labour* (1893–4), para 23269, Alex Ross's testimony.

2 Sarah Gillespie, *A Hundred Years of Progress, 1853–1932: The Record of the Scottish Typographical Association* (Maclehose, Glasgow, 1953), 106; Cynthia Cockburn, *Brothers: Male Dominance and Technological Change*, (Pluto, London, 1983), 34.

3 *Scottish Typographical Circular* (Dec. 1904), hereafter cited as *STC*. Clementina Black (1855–1923) was a well-known figure in the movement for women's trade-union organizations at the turn of the century, taking a leading role in e.g. the Anti-Sweating League and the Women's Industrial Council. See, Ellen Mappen, *Helping Women at Work: The Women's Industrial Council 1889–1914* (Hutchinson, London, 1985).

4 *STC* (Aug. 1886), 383.

5 Margaret Irwin (d. 1904), the secretary of the Scottish Council of Women's Trades, carried out many investigations into women's industrial work; while on 'cordial terms with the trade union movement', Eleanor Gordon writes, she remained firmly within a philanthropic tradition. Regrettably little is known about her life.

6 *STC* (July and Aug 1898); *Scottish Typographical Association Annual Report* (1898), 28, and (1889), 29.

7 Cf. discussion of this topic in Eleanor Gordon, 'Women Workers and the Labour Movement in Scotland' (Ph.D., Glasgow, 1985).

8 *Fair Wage Committee* (PP 1908), para. 6035, Margaret Irwin's testimony. See, J. Ramsay Macdonald (ed.), *Women in the Printing Trades: A Sociological Study*, (King, London, 1904) 28, 53.

9 *Fair Wage Committee* (PP 1908), para. 6221, Margaret Irwin's testimony.

10 *STC* (Apr. 1904), 267.

11 The Glasgow printers rightly pointed out in reply that the structure of the trade was quite different in the two cities: 'What the average printer in Glasgow would do with the ladies I cannot fathom, for while they may be taught to sling plain dig [i.e. bookwork: straight setting], I am not aware that the lady jobber has yet come along. The very nature of commercial work, which constitutes the general run of Glasgow work, precludes her employment,' *STC* (May 1904), quoted in, Cockburn, *Brothers*, 154.

12 *Scottish Typographical Journal* (1908). On the 'female question' in general, see the sections in, Gillespie, *A Hundred Years* 101–7, 203–8. On the Printing and Kindred Trades Federation, ibid., 128–30.

13 Edinburgh Typographical Society (ETS), minute book, Feb. 1910.

14 C. M. Bowerman (1851–1947), Secretary of LSC, president of TUC 1901, MP for Deptford 1906–31.

15 NLS MS, Acc 4068 (8) minute book for ETS, 19 June 1910.

16 NLS MS, Acc 4068 124 (1), minutes of talks, Apr. 1910.

17 The voting figures are in Acc 4068 (8), minute book of the ETS, 22 Dec. 1909 and 18 May 1910.

18 NLS MS, Acc 4068 (8), ETS minute book, 3 Aug. 1910.

19 Ibid., 10 Aug. 1910. It was clear from the minutes of the talks held on 26 Aug. 1910 (Acc

4068 124 (1) that Neill's and Morrison & Gibb had signed the memorial. Both firms had originally been firmly opposed to any concessions.

20 Cf. the case reported by Macdonald, *Women in the Printing Trades*, 53, of a woman bookbinder being offered a more skilled job: 'I know my place', she replied, 'and I'm not going to take men's work from them.' Powerful loyalties were at work among women of the working class, brought up in respect for the male breadwinner. This is not the same thing as 'apathy'.

21 *Scotsman*, 1 Sept. 1910.

22 *Edinburgh Evening News*, 2 Sept. 1910. See the account in the *Despatch* for the same date. Miss Symonds is quoted as saying 'the conduct that went on during the dispute in that office was something disgraceful'.

23 *Edinburgh Evening News*, 19 Aug. 1910.

24 Amelia McLean, article in *The Vote*, 10 Sept. 1910.

25 *Edinburgh Evening* News, 2 Sept. 1910, and NLS MS, Acc 4068, 124 (1). The union's full title was the National Amalgamated Society of Printers, Warehousemen and Cutters. Alfred Evans wrote to the *Scotsman* on 2 Sept. 1910, saying that there was a total of 5,000 women and girls employed in the printing trade in Edinburgh: they outnumbered men by two to one; most of these were in 'auxiliary' trades, as machine-feeders, folders, envelope-makers and so on. He said they were all, including the compositors, welcome to join his union. Thus women were regarded as a single category, united by their sex rather than defined by their work, at a time when wage and status differentials among men were jealously guarded.

26 Cockburn, *Brothers*, 157.

27 *Edinburgh Evening News*, 29 Aug. 1910.

28 *The Vote*, 10 Sept. 1910.

Women and the Labour Movement in Scotland, 1850–1914

Extracted from Eleanor Gordon 1991 *Women and the Labour Movement in Scotland*, (Oxford University Press), 202–11, 285–91.

DISPUTES IN DUNDEE'S JUTE INDUSTRY, 1906–1914

Dundee was not unaffected by the general upsurge in militancy in the immediate pre-war years, and membership of the DDUJFW accelerated to a peak of 8,560 in February 1914.[1] More significantly the union had to cope with an increasing number of strikes which were initiated at the workplace, and a workforce who were less amenable to arguments persuading them to return to work whilst negotiations were conducted.

Despite the existence of two major textile unions, it was still the case that the mainstream of Dundee jute workers' action occurred outside the folds and influence of formal organizations. In a letter to the management committee of the General Federation of Unions, Sime outlined the case for the union receiving Federation benefits for what he considered would be an inevitable general strike. He noted that, because there was a boom in the jute trade, 'general gossip among the workers' indicated that there would be a strike before long as 'strikes, general and sectional, take place at the will of the unorganised workers'.[2]

Between 1906, when the DDUJFW was formed, and the First World War, there were twenty-one officially recorded disputes in the jute industry, although, as has been suggested, the actual number was higher than this.[3] The issues involved in the disputes covered the range of industrial grievances, but in the years 1908 to 1911 disputes over working conditions were more common and in the two or three years before the war claims for wage increases predominated.[4]

The years 1908 to 1911 were difficult ones for the jute industry as the competition from India became more acute and its share of the world market declined. The employers' attempts to cut costs by intensifying the utilization of labour resulted in speed-ups and productivity schemes which were vehemently resisted by the workers. By contrast the pre-war boom, which began in 1912, ushered in two or three years in which claims for wage increases dominated the industrial scene. Strikes over wages in the immediate pre-war years tended to be more successful than the strikes over working conditions in the earlier period. This was undoubtedly due to the buoyant state of the industry and the demand for labour.

It has been argued that the upsurge in militancy throughout Britain between 1910 and 1911 was not restricted simply to economic grievances, but was a product of a more generalized disenchantment with and resentment towards social and political conditions. Although the prevailing orthodoxy emphasizes the absence of a coherent political challenge to the social order, there is evidence of a climate of discontent which narrowly transcended economic demands.[5] In Dundee this was reflected in 'indignation meetings' organized by various political groups and the labour movement to protest about a number of issues, including rising rents.[6] The employers responded to the crisis by reorganizing their association and also ensuring that it took account of 'all subjects connected with the welfare of their workers, such as the housing of the poorer classes which was not satisfactory in Dundee'.[7]

There were also impressive displays of solidarity across industries. In 1911 there was a general strike of carters and dockers for a minimum wage. The locked-out jute workers, thrown idle by the dispute, expressed their solidarity with the strikers by joining their demonstrations and whole-heartedly embracing their cause. The *Dundee Advertiser* carried an article on the dispute which featured a photograph of mill girls with the caption 'A bevy of millgirls making a triumphal march along Dock Street'.[8] In recognition of this support the carters and dockers pledged to give any assistance they could in future disputes involving jute workers, and indeed only two months later they offered to black the goods of a particular firm where there was a strike.

The DDUJFW's moderation and its inclination to look to outside agencies to resolve industrial problems partly reflected changes which were taking place within the Women's Trade Union League, to which the Dundee union was affiliated. It also reflected the desire of the union for recognition by the employers and to establish formal collective bargaining procedures. There was therefore a reluctance to call strikes, except when pressure from operatives forced their hand. For this reason most strikes involving union members continued to be initiated by rank-and-file members at their workplace, although some of these strikes subsequently obtained union support; and, of course, the 'unorganized' majority persisted with their well-established pattern of wildcat strikes.

It has been argued that action which lacks an institutional form or basis is destined to be ephemeral and of little historical significance.[9] However, this need not involve accepting the contention that the spontaneous strikes of Dundee's textile labour force were a product of its weakness or disunity. The nature of the jute industry was such that for most of its pre-war history there was a shortage of labour. It obviously had to endure periodic bouts of unemployment but they were of very little significance in the sense that they were not protracted. The spontaneous strike, generated and extended by word of mouth, could be an effective weapon when there was a seller's market for those workers whose labour was in demand and whose lack of skill could otherwise have ensured their easy replacement.

The spread of disaffection during the strike of 1906 typified the manner in which strike action was generated:

> In the present labour trouble history repeated itself, inasmuch as matters were precipitated by that section of the operatives described by the union executive as 'thoughtless', leaving their places, and thus precipitating the struggle that it has been the effort of the union to avert since first the agitation for a five per cent advance of wages was begun . . .
>
> At Tay works, the great spinning and weaving establishments of Messrs Gilroy Sons and Company, there was also a gathering of malcontents who 'demonstrated' according to the accepted fashion. The general body of hands seemed undecided, but most of them in the end filed past the porter's lodge. At the dinner hour, however, evidently impressed by the knowledge of what was going on elsewhere, their ranks were largely augmented.[10]

Although protracted disputes were not unknown, the short lightning strike was more common. The brevity of the disputes mean that the backing of an organization which could provide financial assistance was not so necessary as for a lengthy strike. The jute workers had proved themselves capable of organizing and co-ordinating action on numerous occasions and, therefore, union membership may not have seemed to offer any substantial benefits. The absence of permanent trade union organization should not necessarily be interpreted as meaning that workers were lacking the faculty of effective organization, for, given the objective conditions of the jute industry, it is doubtful that formal trade organization could have achieved more than the informal patterns of mobilization.

The spontaneous mode of resistance seemed most appropriate to a workforce lacking the industrial muscle derived from skill or workplace authority but whose labour was often in high demand and indispensable to the production process. Decisions to strike were usually taken at the workplace, although doubtless their resolve was buttressed by informal discussions with workmates in their leisure hours. There was rarely recourse to formal meetings and the usual pattern, after the seeds of discontent had been sown, was for someone to say: 'We're no goin' in. Are you goin' in? Naebody's goin' in!'[11] The absence of a central organization capable of co-ordinating action did not seem to detract from their ability to generalize the action, as disaffection rapidly spread within the work and to other works, in the streets and amongst the community generally.

Mass pickets were typically employed to persuade workers to join a strike and, although their inducements were usually confined to shouting and jeering, occasionally more violent methods were resorted to.

The spontaneous action of the women could equally be interpreted as a deliberately conceived weapon rather than a reflection of irrationality or confusion. It maximized disruption by being unpredictable and, as a display of united action, could also serve to heighten the self-respect and self-regard of the women and fuel the communal solidarity of the mill and factory.

There was little evidence of women electing a committee or leadership to organize their disputes, although there usually emerged from each strike a number of women who were particularly indefatigable in their efforts to muster support for the action. During a strike at Cox's in 1911, *Glasgow Forward* referred to the zealousness of one of these anonymous organizers:

> The Girl with the 'Green Felt Hat' deserves special praise. She has proved herself a born organiser, leading the strikers in all their frolics during the first week, arranging processions etc., but when want was making itself felt, some serious work had to be done, she proved herself a veritable Trojan, leading the amount collected every week, even going to the International Football Match at Glasgow, only to be refused admittance.[12]

Although there was rarely an identifiable leadership, the manner in which strikes were initiated, spread, and enforced was also coherent and organized, and is testimony to the power of the communal basis of solidarity. The unskilled nature of the work performed by the majority of the jute workers, and the consequent lack of any organizational apparatus which included rules regulating apprenticeships, did not mean that there was little basis for the development of group solidarity. Their shared experience both in and out of the workplace could provide a basis for united action, which was as powerful as that derived from craft autonomy, skill, and pride in one's work.

To understand the form and character of the Dundee women's industrial militancy, it is necessary to take account of much more than their economic experience at the level of the workplace. The organization of the jute industry, its labour process, and the structure of authority relations in the home, in work, and in society generally, all provide part of the explanation.

As has been illustrated, the division of labour and authority in the workplace paralleled conventional patriarchal family relations and this was reinforced by a definition of skilled work which reflected gender divisions and patriarchal authority. However, the absence of a family economy in the jute industry meant that the supervisory role of the small number of men was not sustained or buttressed by family ties which might have confirmed its legitimacy, facilitated the subordination of the women, and guaranteed their quiescence.

Although the spontaneous nature of the strikes could be seen as a rational and instrumental response to the objective conditions of the jute industry, it could also be interpreted as an assertion of independence from the control of both employers and to some extent male-dominated trade unions. The unpredictable nature of the action might have been equally important as a declaration of their autonomy and a reminder to their employers that they could not exercise unfettered control over their workforce. In his evidence to the Labour Commission on the state of the jute industry the Reverend Williamson doubted whether conciliation boards would meet with any success in the trade as:

> It is not easy to know what to do with women. They are governed by impulse . . . all at once, without notice 50 or 100 of them are in a state of rebellion, and it requires someone to come in just to advise them, for as a rule neither master, manager nor any other official can get anything from them.[13]

This defiance could equally be directed at the organized labour movement. The constant complaints of the trade union movement that the women's action was 'hasty' or 'ill-advised' are testimony to the difficulties they encountered when attempting to exercise a restraining influence. At a meeting of the Dundee Trades Council in 1899 which condemned the strike action of the jute workers a motion was passed recording sympathy with the unions 'in the predicament in which they found themselves owing to the rash acts of individuals over whom they had no control'.[14]

It was not only the manner in which strikes were unleashed but the tone of the protest which encapsulated a spirit of resistance and defiance. Strikes were often characterized by behaviour and gestures which challenged patriarchal authority by ridicule and teasing. A favourite ploy of strikers was to visit the Cowgate, the business haunt of the employers and merchants, and indulge in catcalling and heckling. The conscious intention of the strikers was to puncture the dignity of these prominent members of Dundee society by subjecting them to public ridicule and mocking. Invading the territory of the manufacturers and indelibly imprinting their presence on the scene was yet another way of challenging their masters' authority and asserting their independence, so that for a brief period the terms of the relationship were determined by the workers. An account of such an invasion in 1906 is a typical illustration of how this was enacted:

> Strikers invaded the Cowgate . . . 'in a twinkling', a circle, the diameter of which extended from the Queen's Statue to the portals of the shelter was formed, and a couple of score of shrieking, shouting spinners spun round in the gyrations of jingo ring . . . ere long Panmure Street was thronged from end to end by an uproarious crowd of lassies. Number gave them the boldness and they made a rush for the shelter, in which for the most part millowners seeking to escape personal allusion and recognition had taken refuge . . . A hooting band made a rush for the last door, but the police, who acted with commendable discretion intervened and the portals were closed.[15]

It was commonplace for the strikers to carry effigies of particular employers who had aroused their wrath and to dress up in a comic manner for their parades and demonstrations through the streets. The style of dress adopted was also a way of ridiculing patriarchal authority as they often donned men's hats and on several occasions a few of the women wore policemen's helmets.

The hilarity and dancing and singing which invariably accompanied women's strikes sharply distinguished them from men's industrial action, which was altogether a more sober and serious affair. A demonstration of men in 1909 against unemployment displayed a marked reluctance even to march in procession along the street as they felt it might do more harm to their cause than good.[16] The character of women's strikes bore a striking similarity to their leisure activities and commentators often noted how a strike amongst women took on the aspects of a public holiday or carnival, with fun and high spirits the order of the day. They usually roamed the streets in bands or paraded them in processional order singing popular music-hall songs and dancing 'jingo ring'.

The demonstrations were not only carried on during working hours, they frequently spilled over into the evenings with crowds of women converging on the high streets and indulging in what was usually described as 'unruly' behaviour. Parading up and down streets with workmates, who were invariably leisure time companions, and engaging in banter with other groups, was an integral part of 'play', especially for the younger unmarried girls, and could almost be described as a form of street life. It was surely no accident that the behaviour of women on strike should be analogous to their leisure activities for it was the only time they were free from direct control and supervision. Leisure involved self-expression and fun, which the daily grind at work denied them, and, by stamping their strike action with the flavour of their leisure time, they could recapture it as their own time. Although their action had quite definite and specific objectives, it also assumed a symbolic significance. It was a flight from work, a collection expression of defiance, however temporary, and, by imbuing it with a sense of fun, they underscored the fact that they were expropriating this time from the masters and repossessing it themselves.

However, subverting male authority was clearly a central part of women's actions and, by using ridicule, embarrassment, and sexual impropriety, they turned sexual divisions into an effective weapon which left the victims of their *badinage* emasculated and without redress. The converse of the dominance and persuasiveness of male power was the submission and deference of women, who were expected to have respect for this power and to conform to their culturally prescribed gender roles, which were largely determined by men. Therefore, not surprisingly, women's resistance symbolized a rejection of male control and dominance by subjecting them to ridicule and mocking, thus demonstrating disrespect, whilst, by breaching the codes of modesty and flaunting sexual differences, they denied men's power to control their behaviour.

The organized sections' references to the state of their trade and their quest for respectability reflected acceptance of the permanence of existing social arrangements. The informal organization of Dundee women and their culture displayed a subversive disrespect for authority, but it also reflected a fatalistic acceptance of class divisions and inequality as part of the natural order of things. This view is expressed in the Jute Mill Song written by Mary Brooksbank, a Dundee jute worker;

> Oh dear me, the warld's ill divided,
> Them that work the hardest are aye wi' least provided,
> But I maun bide contented, dark days or fine,
> But there's no much pleasure living' offen ten-and-nine.

The weapons of teasing and ridicule may have brought authority to the point of exasperation, but they were highly unlikely to topple the edifice of capitalism. Although the ebullience and gaiety of strikes were important aspects of the pattern of resistance, they were manifestations of an essentially defensive culture where primacy was placed on fun and high spirits as a means of escaping from the drudgery of work. Whatever the inadequacies of the ideology developed by the jute workers for the purpose of mounting a significant challenge to capitalism, it is important to stress that it was oppositional and that resignation or non-committed compliance to the social order did not signify complete submission.

The labour process of the jute industry and the social structures of the locality displayed certain features which may have fuelled working women's militancy;

for example, the pattern of migration into the city contributed to population instability and, coupled with the accompanying disruption of kinship relations, had the effect of dislocating conventional family authority relations. Similarly, conventional family authority relations had no analogue in the workplace, in contrast to Lancashire's workplace authority structures. Dundee's social structure may have been unique, but the widespread evidence throughout Scotland of women's workplace militancy suggests that in this respect it was not an aberration.

CONCLUSION: WOMEN AND THE LABOUR MOVEMENT IN SCOTLAND, 1850–1914

The history of women's employment in Scotland from 1850 until the First World War provides strong confirmation of the view that women's subordinate position in the labour market was linked to prevailing ideologies of gender and domesticity. However, the evidence suggests that women's experience of waged labour was mediated by these ideologies and not determined by them. The analysis of the development of the Glasgow cotton-spinning industry demonstrated that decisions about when and how to employ women were contingent on the interaction of a number of variables and could not be explained by one general theoretical model whether it was based on patriarchal ideology, the exclusionary practices of trade unions, or the assumption of any inherent logic of capital to deskill and cheapen costs. Managerial strategies were influenced by wider market conditions, relations between capital and labour, and the kind of technology employed. However, these categories, which are derived from the labour process, are insufficient and partial in their explanatory value and have to be integrated with consideration of the wider social relations outside the workplace, crucially gender ideologies, in order to provide a comprehensive analysis of the structuring of labour markets.

Clearly women's entry into social production did not release them from male domination or replace gender subordination with exploitation as waged labour, but rather their experience as workers was premised upon their subordination as a gender. Even in a town such as Dundee, where female employment was widespread and many women were the major or sole contributors to the family income, the yoke of patriarchal authority and control hung heavily, defining the nature of their work, earnings, modes of supervision, and codes of behaviour. In Dundee and elsewhere wider social relations penetrated the workplace so that the capitalist labour process was also shaped by the relations between the sexes and not solely by the imperatives of capital accumulation. Therefore, gender relations were constituted in both the workplace and the home. Women's identity as members of a gender was not discarded when they became workers as in practice their entry into production was in part shaped by a domestic ideology which prescribed appropriate roles for women and appropriate relations between the sexes.

The pervasiveness of domestic ideology and the notion of separate sexual spheres, which percolated throughout society, did not mean it was digested in exactly this form by the working classes. It was forged and elaborated by the bourgeoisie, and, whilst providing the touchstone of culturally acceptable gender roles, it was recast by the working classes to make sense of their experience. For the organized minority of the working class who were either in possession of skills or strategically placed in the production process, it was an ideal to be realized. However, the recognition that it could not always be achieved meant that separate spheres were reinterpreted to include work for women, provided it did not encroach on men's province or usurp men's prior rights to work, and was compatible with women's culturally prescribed role. The reformulated version of the separate spheres ideology meant that the critical issue which was contested was the site of female labour rather than its exclusion from the labour market.

Labour historians have drawn attention to the exclusivist practices of Victorian trade-unionism which sought to maintain differentials of skill and earnings with the labour force. They have ignored, however, the ways in which such practices embodied assumptions about gender roles and the familial ideology that women's place was in the home. The notion of the male provider and protector reinforced the claims of skilled, semi-skilled, and unskilled trade-unionists to a prior right to work and their demand for a family wage, which meant that frequently their strategies disadvantaged women workers, even when other sectional policies had been eroded or abandoned. The corollary of the demand for a family wage for men was the conception of women as economic dependants whose earnings did not need to cover their living costs. This contributed to one of the most pressing problems for working women in this period, their appallingly low wages; and yet the response of the trade union movement to a situation which they helped to create was to view women's low pay as a consequence of their inability to organize and as a threat or a problem to be overcome by excluding them from the labour market or at least controlling their entry. Because trade unions related to women as dependants and failed to recognize the ways in which women's gender roles structured their status and experience as waged workers and created many of the problems which they faced in the labour market, they represented in practice the interest of male workers.

Trade-unionists did not always set their face like flint against organizing women, but their support was conditional and contingent. Instances of supportive action by trade-unionists were usually confined to well-defined areas of women's work which did not compete with male labour, and where combination was viewed as an indirect means of moral and social regulation by providing the lever to raise wages and thus dispel the spectre of prostitution. Regulation and control of female labour motivated attempts by male trade-unionists to organize women workers in the same industry or workplace where employers had succeeded in introducing female labour over the heads of male workers. Trade union organization was often advocated as a way of out-manoeuvring employers' attempts to use women to undercut and undermine male labour's wages and organization. Alternatively, trade union controls were advocated when non-unionized women in an industry persistently bypassed established negotiating procedures and took independent initiatives which not only had a disruptive effect on production but undermined the legitimacy of workplace trade union organization and threatened the economic interests of the organized men. In these instances support for organizing women was cynically exploited as a means of channelling collective action along more manageable and containable routes. The experience of women workers in this period illustrates that the problems that women faced in the labour market derived from the wider sexual division of labour in society, and that, if trade unions were to represent their interests adequately, the structures and practices of trade-unionism would have had to recognize and challenge these divisions rather than reflect them. This would have involved developing alternative forms of organization and moving beyond the traditional concerns of trade-unionism in order to encompass issues which tackled gender divisions.

Whilst subordination was the keynote of women's labour market position, it is not the full story. Underlying the somewhat bleak general structures lurks a more complex reality which breaks down the gender stereotype associated with over-reliance on general abstract models to explain women's waged work. Although invariably classed as unskilled labour, women workers often possessed genuine skills from which they derived immense satisfaction but which were socially unrecognized. Although women usually had little formal authority in the workplace, their centrality to production and their possession of valued skills, as in Dundee's jute industry, enabled them to exert informal levers of influence, if not legitimately sanctioned authority. Both spinners and weavers in Dundee were responsible for the on-the-job training of new recruits which placed them in a strategic position they were not slow to exploit, particularly when their labour was in short supply.

Women did not always perceive their experience of work as unalloyed drudgery and tedium or as a period of marking time until they could occupy their rightful and proper place in the home as the helpmeet of a husband. Despite the diffusion and force of Victorian domestic ideology, the experience of waged work could generate an ambivalent or even oppositional response to this ideology among women who might not have consciously challenged it but who none the less articulated positive and enthusiastic attitudes to their work. The confinement of women to well-defined sectors of the economy where they occupied a subordinate position in the labour force in terms of authority, skill, and pay is indisputable, but this did not mean that work was an arid and negative experience which lacked the compensating skills and status of men's work.

Whatever qualifications are applied to the general theory of women's subordination in the labour market, the history of working women in Scotland demonstrates its limitations as an explanation for their workplace behaviour. The copious evidence of women workers' collective action indicates that one cannot ascribe typical characteristics to women workers which are derived from general models of gender. More recent contributions to labour process debates have restored to labour a key role in the formation of the labour process, and illustrate the contested character of managerial authority. Similarly, women's structural and ideological subordination in the workplace and society did not mean complete submission to patriarchal control and authority. By concentrating on formal trade union organizations, assumptions have been made about women based on their absence from these spheres, as if these areas exhausted all collectivist tendencies. Consequently, the received view of non-unionized women is one of either irrationality and impulsiveness or deference and docility. However, it is clear that the history of women workers is one of struggle and opposition and that they frequently displayed a strong commitment to collective action. This is not to suggest that women's forms of resistance were superior to those of the organized trade union movement or that they displayed a higher level of class consciousness, but to reappraise the view that women represented the most backward section of the working class.

The nature of sexual divisions in society mediated women's experience of class and therefore shaped the form of their class consciousness. It would therefore be a mistake to view the form of working women's resistance in this period as outmoded, anachronistic, or irrelevant simply because it did not conform to the practices of nineteenth-century trade-unionism.

The controls and constraints placed upon every aspect of women's lives derived from a male-dominated culture. Therefore, not surprisingly, women's resistance often took the form of subverting male authority and challenging gender divisions. Women's collective struggles in the workplace, even when they were expressions of economic grievances, displayed an awareness of their common experience and identity as women and as workers. Waged labour, by drawing women together as a gender and as workers, created the potential for them to struggle as both workers and as a gender. Although there is little basis for the unqualified optimism of Engels's prediction concerning the liberating consequences of women's entry into social production, intensification and reinforcement of gender subordination was not the only alternative. Women's entry into waged labour generated struggles which both strengthened their capacity for self-organization and contained implicit challenges to prescribed gender roles.

The nature of women's resistance may be dismissed as a temporary release which did not threaten the basic order of society or undermine the gender of authority relations, but the style of confrontation where emboldened women mimicked and ridiculed patriarchal authority did question and challenge existing gender divisions and the dominance of masculinity. Therefore, their resistance contained an additional dimension to the traditional masculine style of confrontation which left the existing social relations untouched.

In arguing that women's identity as members of a gender was not discarded when they became workers, it is not suggested that their experience of work was undifferentiated and that women were a homogeneous group, but that their experience was mediated through their gender subordination. Nor is it suggested that the process was one way and that ideology shaped work experience. Clearly work-related factors had some impact on women's consciousness and responses. What was decisive for women's (and men's) experience of waged labour and their responses to it was the interaction between social relations and processes within the workplace and those outside.

Historical debate about divisions within the British working class has largely centred on the divisions between skilled and unskilled workers and more precisely between a labour aristocracy of workers and the rest. The concept of the labour aristocracy has recently been subjected to vigorous criticism which has seriously questioned its explanatory value and drawn attention to the fact that its central weakness is that it is too simplistic to capture all the distinctions between British workers in the second half of the nineteenth century. The present study provides further evidence of the inadequacy of an explanation of the social formation of the working class which poses a simple dichotomy between workers and fails to recognize either the complexity of divisions or more profound divisions than skilled versus unskilled. In arguing that gender divisions were central to the formation of the workforce, it is not intended to substitute one polarity for another, but to draw attention to the interaction of class and gender and indeed to the interconnectedness of different elements of the social structure such as the family and the workplace. The orthodox Marxist definition of class which concentrates on the realm of production and economic experience at the point of production has proved inadequate for an understanding of the differential experience of men and women in the labour market. This points to the need for a broader consideration of the social formation and an analysis of the interrelationship of production and reproduction if we are to conceptualize the position of women in the world of work.

NOTES

1 Dundee and District Union of Jute and Flax Workers (hereafter DDUJFW), Executive Committee Minutes, 14 Feb. 1914.
2 DDUJFW, Copy Letter Book, 20 Jan. 1912.
3 Annual Reports on Strikes and Lockouts, 1906–14.
4 Ibid.
5 The major proponent of the 'crisis' school, which argues that there was a fusion of industrial, political, and social grievances which threatened the stability of the political and social order, is S. Meacham, in 'The Sense of an Impending Clash: English Working Class Unrest before the First World War', *American Historical Review*, 77 (5) (1972). See Ch. 7 for a discussion of local political activity in this period.
6 DDUJFW, Executive Committee Minutes, 21 Jan. 1912.
7 *Dundee Year Book*, 1912.
8 *Dundee Advertiser*, 23 Dec. 1911.
9 E.J. Hobsbawm, *Primitive Rebels* (Manchester University Press, 1959).
10 *Dundee Advertiser*, 24 Feb. 1906.
11 Interview with Mrs MacDowall.
12 *Glasgow Forward*, 1 Apr. 1911.
13 Royal Commission on Labour, *The Employment of Women*, C. 6894 (London: HMSO, 1893).
14 *Dundee Advertiser*, 8 Sept. 1899.
15 Ibid., 27 Feb. 1906.
16 *Dundee Advertiser*, 17 Aug. 1909.

The Scottish Agricultural Labour Market, 1900– 1939: a case of institutional intervention

Richard Anthony 1993 *Economic History Review* 46, 558–74.

This article examines the nature of institutional intervention in the Scottish agricultural labour market during the early twentieth century, focusing in particular on the rise and fall of collective bargaining, and the differing circumstances under which wage regulation was introduced in 1917 and 1937.[1] It argues that in the case of the labour market, institutional intervention was an important factor both as a cause and an indicator of change, and that the nature of these activities identifies continuing differences between the market for farm labour in Scotland and that elsewhere in Britain.

With a satisfactory balance between the supply and demand for farm workers in Scotland, there was little demand in the trans-World War 1 period for statutory wage controls: Scotland was excluded from the provisions of minimum wage regulations in 1924. Institutions emphasized policies promoting voluntary collective bargaining. However, the depression, with declining product prices and a dramatic cut in alternative employment opportunities both at home and abroad, caused significant readjustments as real wages fell and unemployment rose. This instigated the collapse of earlier negotiating arrangements and forced the state to intervene, imposing minimum wages and unemployment insurance on an industry that a decade earlier had resoundingly rejected them. In assessing the reasons behind the adoption of these policies, a greater understanding emerges not only of agricultural development in a country where, in 1921, farming still employed 194,000 people (nearly 9 per cent of the working population),[2] but also of the role of institutional policy in labour market operations in general.

I

In assessing institutional intervention in the economy we need to understand the general economic background. During the decades prior to the outbreak of war in 1914 much of lowland Scotland can be regarded as a high wage region, a function of rapid industrialisation during the nineteenth century,[3] which, combined with a high level of geographical mobility among Scots, ensured significant population movements. Recent research by Brock indicates the impact on the population growth of the different counties of Scotland, the prime losers not surprisingly being predominantly rural areas.[4] Devine's work on nineteenth-century Scotland has demonstrated how high outmigration from rural areas ensured a relatively tight agricultural labour market.[5] In explaining the social stability of lowland Scotland at a time of agrarian disturbances in the south of England, he concluded that the labour market operated in such a way as to ensure that there was no permanent labour 'surplus' which employers could exploit. Most lowland rural areas were relatively close to the major centres of industrial development, which absorbed the population surplus that occurred as rural population growth continued and agricultural productivity rose.

On the 'push' side of this migration model, the combined long engagement and tied housing system meant that an individual who failed to get a permanent post in agriculture had little chance of doing so for another six months or a year, and without a job had no house. These factors provided significant incentives to migrate, which were further reinforced by the harsh attitude adopted by the Scottish poor law to the able-bodied unemployed.[6] By the late nineteenth century, high rates of external migration had added further opportunities for Scottish population mobility, ensuring a continued flow of labour out of the least productive sectors of the economy. Therefore, those who remained on the land retained a stronger bargaining position in the labour market than their counterparts in the south of England.[7] The patterns of Scottish agricultural output further enhanced this, by demanding a highly skilled labour force, a response to the concentration on specialist livestock production in conjunction with complex cropping rotations with ordinary labourers making up a minority of regular workers.[8] In 1907 a Board of Trade survey of 18,400 Scottish male farm servants found that 61.8 per cent were horsemen and·11.2 per cent 'orramen'; this compared to the English breakdown of 31.5 per cent horsemen and 42.8 per cent ordinary labourers.[9] The result was, as Carter has shown, a fiercely independent labour force that was confident in its ability to negotiate freely for satisfactory wages and conditions.[10] As an assistant commissioner working for the Royal Commission on Labour in 1893 observed of the situation in Mid and East Lothian:

> There is an amazing amount of independence about a Lothian hind. He is a sterling, honest, hard working man, perfectly well able to make his own bargain, and prepared to discharge his duties so long as his engagement lasts. To watch his proceedings at a hiring market, a stranger might be led to think that the men were engaging the masters, and not the masters the men. This, however, does not blind him to the fact that there is a security about a yearly engagement and a comfortable house for at least twelve months. On the expiry of the term, if he is not satisfied, he can easily get another situation.[11]

Given the lack of any disequilibrium in the labour market, the balance of power between employers and workers, and relative economic stability, there was little demand for any form of institutional intervention. The introduction of National Health Insurance in 1911 drew an unusual reaction from Scottish agriculture, when, for example, in the 'Turra Coo' incident of 1913, farmers and workers united to repossess a cow that had been impounded when a farmer had refused to pay his contributions. Fenton, in his study of this incident, described the attitude of the protesters to Lloyd George's imposition:

> It was actively disliked by many in lowland rural areas because neither employer nor employed wanted to pay good money for stamps, for benefits the workers might never see; for the countryside view was that ill health was rarer there than in the towns and at that period unemployment was not a rural problem.[12]

That is not to say that the workers did not have grievances. The Royal Commission on Labour in 1894,[13] while finding no examples of direct industrial action among the regular workforce, recorded numerous complaints concerning wages, hours, and housing conditions. However it was not until 1912 that a successful trade union, the Scottish Farm Servants' Union (S.F.S.U.) was established, and that was largely due to the backing of the Aberdeen Trades Council and the individual abilities of Joe Duncan.[14] In contrast to the English National Agricultural Labourers' Union, the S.F.S.U. was opposed to any state-sponsored intervention in the labour market, in particular a wages board.[15] The union emphasized voluntary collective bargaining as its main strategy, arguing that a wages board was not required and that more was to be gained by voluntary negotiations with the employers for a shorter working week.[16]

Meanwhile, collective action by the farmers, with the formation of the National Farmers' Union of Scotland (N.F.U.S.) in 1913, was more concerned with the weak bargaining position of dairy farmers vis-à-vis the Glasgow milk wholesalers, than with interfering in the labour market.[17]

II

The impact of the First World War on rural society in England and Wales is a well-researched topic.[18] The war clearly encouraged the spread of agricultural trade unionism, although the actual monetary benefits that Scottish workers received from the enhanced status of agriculture were not so dramatic (see figure 1). The real decline in wages appears to conflict with the conclusions of Winter on agricultural workers.[19] However, certain groups in the workforce made greater gains, most notably single men who were tied to a shorter period of contract (six months rather than a year for married men), and for whom the demand was greater.[20]

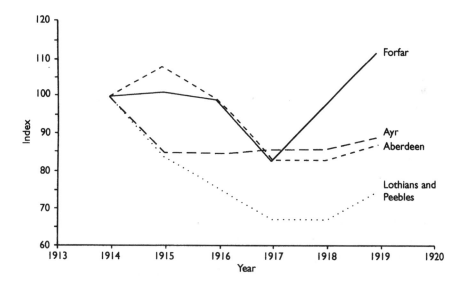

Figure 1: *Index of agricultural wage rates in Scotland, 1914–1919 (at constant prices, 1914 = 100.*
Note: figures for foremen, first cattlemen, and ploughmen.
Source: Scottish Record Office, AF 43/133, Evidence submitted by the Board of Agriculture for Scotland to the Royal Commission on Agriculture, 6 Aug 1919.

Dewey's work on England and Wales has shown that the economy was well able to replace much of the farm labour recruited into the armed forces.[21] The position in Scotland is not altogether clear, but appears to have been different for a number of reasons. First, Scotland was less affected by reduced labour supply. Board of Trade surveys show that between July 1915 and July 1918 the average net loss of permanent male workers in Scotland was 13.7 per cent compared to 25.7 per cent for England and Wales.[22] Second, the greater use of female labour in Scotland before the war meant that Scottish agriculture was disrupted less by the enlistment of men, but that there were fewer farm-based women available to replace those who were lost.[23] Third, the overall increase in tillage was below that in England and Wales, due to the lower proportion of permanent grass being available to be broken up. This resulted in a smaller increase in the demand for labour within Scotland.[24] Finally 'replacement' labour was more widely available in Scotland, partly because the substitution of women for men was more easily accomplished, given their greater prewar role in production, and partly because higher rates of pay in Scottish agriculture increased the opportunity cost of migrating to industrial areas.[25]

Establishing a balance between these factors is not easy. The 1916 War Office Farm Labour Census suggested that there was an approximate 10 per cent surplus of labour on farms in England and Wales, and a 6 per cent surplus in Scotland, less than half of which was located in the lowlands.[26] This implies that Scottish farms were more efficient in their use of labour. However, in terms of the changing balance between the demand and supply of farm labour, Scottish farmers appear to have been more favourably placed than their English counterparts.

III

As in England and Wales, the improved status of agriculture in the Scottish economy and the social upheaval associated with war presented the agricultural trade unions with an opportunity to expand their influence.[27] The S.F.S.U., with a tightened labour market and dramatic shifts in real wages, attempted to intervene in the workings of the market, mainly through collective bargaining at county level with the N.F.U.S. in order to negotiate voluntary wage agreements. These were strictly to provide guidelines to both employers and workers as to the state of the market – both organizations were careful not to usurp their members' independent negotiating rights which had formed the basis of prewar conditions. Negotiations began as early as 1915 in Dunbartonshire and Ayrshire,[28] and soon spread to other lowland areas, in particular around Glasgow and the Lothians. The effectiveness of these agreements in unclear, and was partly related to the strength of organization in the counties; one outside observer concluding that they 'have considerable effect on the individual bargains made between farmers and workers, but they have not been universally adopted in full, even by the members of the Unions themselves'.[29]

In July 1916 the S.F.S.U. proposed to the N.F.U.S. national negotiations on wages,[30] and this produced a draft scheme for permanent local negotiating committees in December 1916. The S.F.S.U. was supported in this by the Board of Agriculture for Scotland (B.O.A.S.), which was keen to reduce the high levels of labour turnover resulting from uncontrolled individual bargaining.[31] However, it soon became clear that the government was considering the formation of district wage committees under the Corn Production Bill, and so the scheme was dropped.[32] The Corn Production Act (C.P.A.) of 1917 provided the first major state intervention into the agricultural labour market with its provisions for the establishment of district wage committees to set minimum wage rates, which was part of a general strategy to increase agricultural production.[33] Some prominence has been given to the impact of the C.P.A. on the agricultural labour market in England and Wales. Pretty, writing on trade unionism among Welsh farm workers, described 1917 as 'the major turning point in the history of the agricultural labourers' with the act awarding them 'the cachet of recognition and status'.[34] In Scotland, the N.F.U.S. as an institution agreed to the C.P.A. as a temporary wartime measure, which also guaranteed wheat and oat prices, but there was widespread opposition to wage control from both farmers and workers, as evidence given to the Agricultural Policy Sub-Committee of the Reconstruction Committee in the winter of 1916/7 shows. For example, on behalf of the S.F.S.U.:

> Mr Duncan said that the Union's fundamental objection to the setting up of wages boards was that the conditions of the farm workers in Scotland were not before the War nor at the present time such as to demand special assistance from the state. The only ground for intervention would be if farm servants were in a specially disadvantageous position. The Union felt that farm servants would obtain better wages by trade union methods than by means of state assistance, and he could not conceive of legislation bringing any improvement in the position of Scottish farm servants without their own organisation.[35]

Such condemnation of the provisions of the C.P.A. proved correct in its predictions for Scotland. The district wage committees concentrated on setting minimum subsistence rates,[36] which were consistently well below the market rates in nearly all lowland areas (except Dumfries and Galloway), and had little impact on the local collective bargaining agreements that the S.F.S.U. and the N.F.U.S. continued to set. In October 1919 the *Scottish Farm Servant* (the journal of the S.F.S.U.) commented that 'the Act, in respect of the minimum wage clauses, has been a farce, a big farce, and nothing but a farce. When one finds the standard rate in a county 15s. above the legal minimum rate, it is time to stop talking and start laughing.'[37] The failure of the C.P.A. in Scotland also comes to light in the evidence given to the 1919 Royal Commission on Agriculture by Sir James Wilson (Chairman of the Scottish Central Agricultural Wages Committee), who was forced to admit that the minimum wages rates were ineffective. In addition to this, there had been no prosecutions under the act, and both the S.F.S.U. and the N.F.U.S. effectively ignored it.[38]

Following the fiasco of the C.P.A., and the success of local wage negotiations, the S.F.S.U. reinforced its collective bargaining policy with a campaign to reduce the length of the working week, in particular the establishment of a Saturday half-holiday as an accepted part of the employment contract. Local and national negotiations with the N.F.U.S. followed the earlier pattern, and again there is little evidence as to the success of this campaign at the farm level, although in June 1919 Duncan (general secretary of the S.F.S.U.) reported to his executive committee that in only two counties (Dumfries and Caithness) was the policy not being actively pursued.[39] In January 1919 the N.F.U.S. consented to a national conference on the issue, and an agreement was signed in the spring, but then collapsed due to a dispute over coverage, though this scheme does appear to have become the basis for the hours worked by ploughmen in some areas.[40] The union's campaign was further boosted by the announcement of the government's intention to include agriculture in the Hours of Employment Bill (aimed at restricting the working week to 48 hours), although the S.F.S.U. supported state-sponsored arbitration rather than statutory limitation.[41] Along with other farmer organizations, the N.F.U.S. opposed this; but by the autumn of 1919 both the B.O.A.S. and the Ministry of Labour had added their support to the inclusion of agriculture.[42] However, the Cabinet, after months of indecision, finally decided to drop agriculture from the bill in June 1920 for reasons of short-term political expediency.[43]

The postwar boom saw a peak of institutional intervention in the agricultural labour market, both effective and ineffective. The S.F.S.U. and N.F.U.S. continued to negotiate throughout much of lowland Scotland over wages and hours at a local level, and this was accompanied by a dramatic rise in the membership of both organizations,[44] while the state reinforced its general policy of official support for agriculture with the 1920 Agriculture Act. The sharp depression of 1921 brought about a rapid U-turn by the government on its proclaimed policy, with the repeal of both the C.P.A. and the Agriculture Act on the grounds of cost.[45] In England and Wales the termination of the minimum wage committees brought howls of protest from the farm worker unions.[46] In Scotland the

S.F.S.U. happily accepted the situation, adding that 'the wages committees in Scotland had never been of any service to the workmen in Scotland'.[47]

The year 1921 also marked the end of the period of prosperity in agriculture associated with the war, and the 1920s in general were not good years for farmers. Employment among regular agricultural workers in Scotland, however, stabilized, indicating a steady demand for permanent labour (figure 2).[48] Meanwhile, the alternative to agricultural employment diminished, but not dramatically. General industrial unemployment undoubtedly increased, but not to the spectacularly high rates of the early 1930s: the Scottish unemployment rate stood at 14.3 per cent in 1923 and 10.6 per cent in 1927, remaining significantly lower than in the north-east of England.[49] Therefore industrial employment opportunities remained open. The other factor in external labour demand, emigration, soon rose to its pre-1914 levels.[50] Agriculture remained an important supplier of emigrants: for example, in the period 1924–6 agriculture accounted for 19 per cent of Scottish adult male emigrants, but only 10.5 per cent of the occupied male population in the 1921 census.[51] The Dominions in particular offered potential opportunities for workers to mount the 'farming ladder'.[52] Even by 1931, when the census gives the first indication of unemployment among farm workers, rates among the skilled elements of the workforce in Scotland – the ploughmen, shepherds, and cattlemen – remained at around 3 per cent.[53]

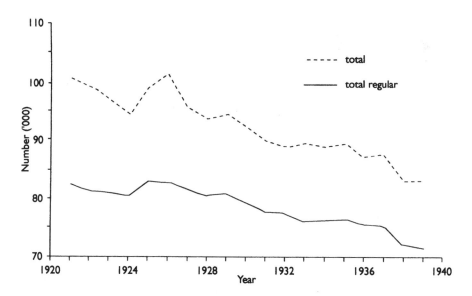

Figure 2: *Numbers of farm workers in Scotland, 1921–1939 (excluding highlands)*
Source: Agricultural statistics, 1921–39.

IV

The continued satisfactory balance between supply and demand in the agricultural labour market meant that the pattern of institutional intervention through the 1920s was relatively unchanged. S.F.S.U. and N.F.U.S. county branches continued to negotiate over 'recommended' levels of wages, though these negotiations became increasingly concentrated within the central belt, whence the S.F.S.U. drew most of its declining support. In common with other trade unions, the S.F.S.U. saw its membership drop from the high of the postwar boom, so that by 1928 it had only about 6,000 members.[54] Agreements were not always forthcoming, but the rationale behind the negotiations remained for both sides the provision of guidelines to farmers and workers unsure of market conditions as the day of a hiring fair approached.[55] The position of the labour market, the independent attitude to bargaining by its members, and the memory of the low minimum rates set under the C.P.A., meant that the S.F.S.U. continued to oppose the introduction of wages boards. In 1924 the union made it clear to the Labour government that it did not expect the extension of its agricultural wage regulation proposals to Scotland, and accordingly the Agricultural Wages (Regulation) Act covered England and Wales only. At the time Duncan wrote:

> as it stands the argument for a legal minimum wage is a confession that the method is a second best, and something in the nature of a desperate remedy to cure a desperate disease. If we are considering a body of workers living at a standard denoted by 25s. a week, there is force in the argument. If the workers cannot escape that condition by their own efforts, some form of crutch must be provided, but a crutch is nothing but an encumbrance to a man with a pair of healthy legs.[56]

Similarly when, in 1923, a Labour M.P. introduced a bill into Parliament providing for a statutory half-day on Saturdays for farm workers in Scotland, the union saw it as a distraction from its primary task of organization and voluntary collective bargaining.[57] This feeling also applied to the extension of unemployment insurance to agriculture, to which both the S.F.S.U. and the N.F.U.S. were opposed. Again the argument was simple; there was little evidence of unemployment among Scottish farm workers, and workers and employers would therefore be paying contributions but seldom claiming benefit.[58] This view was supported by the 1926 Interdepartmental Committee on Unemployment Insurance in agriculture, which recommended the establishment of a scheme in England and Wales, but not in Scotland.[59]

However, the membership of both the employers' and workers' organizations was declining.[60] This was further hastened by the reversal suffered by agriculture in the late 1920s, when the agricultural price index, having stabilized in the years 1923–5, following the depression of 1921–2, started to fall again.[61] In addition, there was a gradual rise in the general Scottish unemployment rate to 12.1 per cent by 1929. These forces on both the demand and supply side fed through into agricultural unemployment, especially for the less skilled whose unemployment rate by 1931 was over 11 per cent. In reaction to this weakening in the position of labour in the market, the S.F.S.U. declared its support for unemployment insurance in October 1929.[62]

It was, however, the depression of the early 1930s which radically changed the state of the Scottish agricultural labour market, precipitating a switch in the policies of both the government and the S.F.S.U. on institutional intervention. Two factors resulted in a reduced demand for agricultural labour: a dramatic fall in product prices[63] and increases in real wages (figures 2 and 3).[64] Meanwhile, general unemployment soared (the Scottish rate peaking in 1932 at 27.7 per cent), and emigration collapsed as the Dominions shut their doors.[65] The traditional escape routes of occupational migration and emigration were now closed to unemployed agricultural workers. The fall in employment was halted only in 1933 following a decline in real wages (figure 3) and a stabilization of product prices; by that date a new level of labour market equilibrium had been established.[66] A very different situation prevailed in England and Wales, where minimum wage rates ensured that real wages did not fall markedly after the early 1930s figure 4).[67]

The N.F.U.S., in a buyers' market, dropped the remaining local collective bargaining agreements. As an S.F.S.U. pamphlet commented, 'It was easier to take advantage of a favourable labour market when there was no collective agreement'.[68] By the winter of 1933/4 the N.F.U.S. refused even to consider meeting local S.F.S.U. officials.[69] In this period of transition and crisis, the S.F.S.U. faced major difficulties. First, its membership plummeted, so that by the end of 1932, when it was forced to seek the financial security of an amalgamation with the T.G.W.U., it had only 1,800 fully paid-up members.[70] Second, although its changed policy on unemployment insurance received some sympathy from the Royal Commission on Unemployment Insurance, the commission's 1932 report only recommended the setting up of a statutory committee to look into the matter, due to the potential complexities in constructing an agricultural unemployment insurance system which included the possibility of a separate scheme for Scotland.[71]

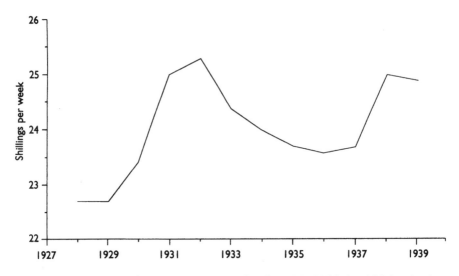

Figure 3: *Agricultural wage rates in Scotland, 1928–1939 (at 1914 prices)*.
Note: using 'weighted average' wage figure for all regular male workers (as calculated by the Department of Agriculture for Scotland).
Source: P.R.O., MAF 38/816, 'Agricultural wage costs, Scotland, 1943–5'.

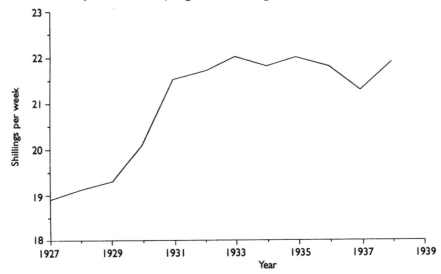

Figure 4: *Agricultural wage rates in England and Wales, 1927–1938 (at 1914 prices)*.
Note: average minimum wage per week for adult male workers.
Source: Department of Employment, *British labour statistics*, tab 8.

At the same time, the S.F.S.U. continued to reject the idea of minimum wages, despite the recent fall in wages, haunted by the failure of the C.P.A. and the concern that minimum rates might reduce wage differentials for the predominantly 'skilled' labour force. The emerging conflict between established policy and the facts of the market was clearly demonstrated in an article written by Duncan in 1933:

> Neither the farmers nor farm workers in Scotland have been in favour of legal minimum wages. They believe that it is possible to work out a satisfactory system of collective bargaining in Scotland which would avoid the necessity of statutory fixing of wages and yet secure the maintenance of reasonable standards. We have had experience of collective bargaining in Scotland, and it has been shown that, when agreements have been made they have been accepted by the great body of farmers and workers, and have been generally observed without the need for legal enforcement.

At the same time he was forced to admit that: 'if the standard of living continues to fall the state will be forced to protect the workers on the grounds of social policy, and that will mean the legal enforcement of minimum rates'.[72]

In line with this statement, and in reaction to the fall in real wage levels, the S.F.S.U. approached the Department of Agriculture for Scotland (D.O.A.S.) and the Secretary of State for Scotland officially in December 1933 with proposals for a national collective bargaining scheme, involving local D.O.A.S. conciliation officers. The department viewed this proposal favourably, but publicly adopted a neutral stance so as to avoid any clash with the N.F.U.S., whose approval of the scheme was then sought. The N.F.U.S. appears to have stalled, and the S.F.S.U. became increasingly irritated by the lack of activity, while the department felt obliged to wait until it had received an official N.F.U.S. view. The issue was further complicated by the intervention of the industrial relations department of the Ministry of Labour in February 1934, opposing any idea of compulsory arbitration by the state and doubting that the scheme would work if voluntary negotiations broke down.[73] This is not surprising, given Rodney Lowe's description of ministry policy at the time as one of 'minimizing state responsibility (and embarrassment) and maximizing industrial freedom (and self-discipline)'[74] and in particular the philosophy of the head of the industrial relations department, Frederick Leggett, whose 'fanatical defence of free collective bargaining led him to resist any move by the state to give an industrial lead unless it had the full backing of both sides of industry'.[75]

Although those inside the D.O.A.S. considered the Ministry of Labour's attitude to be 'childish', this forced the department to proceed more cautiously in its promotion of collective bargaining. Like the S.F.S.U., the D.O.A.S. preferred such a scheme to any form of wage regulation. Matters were made worse when Duncan, in an effort to force some activity, wrote to the Secretary of State in August 1934 saying that his union had no intention of negotiating directly with the N.F.U.S., and that he regarded the proposed scheme as 'a matter for government action'.[76] However, by December 1934 the D.O.A.S., with Ministry of Labour backing, managed to get both sides around the table; and in March 1935, a draft scheme was drawn up. In a concession to the Ministry of Labour and the N.F.U.S., it was decided that a D.O.A.S. conciliator would only be brought in if the formation of a Joint Area Committee failed due to opposition from one side, or if the sides failed to reach an agreement; and even if the conciliator did intervene he had no statutory powers. The central executive of the N.F.U.S. had negotiated this in the belief that it was the way to avoid minimum wages, but their branch membership resoundingly rejected the scheme and the employers were forced to withdraw.[77] Why, given the increasing threat of minimum wage regulation, did the farmers act in such a manner?

It appears that opposition from members in the north-east, incensed at the refusal of the state to extend to oats and barley the deficiency payments scheme in operation for wheat, worked against any form of negotiations involving the government.[78] In addition, the poor financial situation of most farms meant that farmers were not in the mood to tolerate any form of intervention. As a result of these attitudes, the N.F.U.S. was split over whether voluntary wage regulation was a preferred option, and both officials and national representatives appear to have been concerned at the possible repercussions on membership levels, leading the central executive to act in a very cautious manner:

> It was very evident that the Executive really wished to evade all responsibility in the matter and to place the whole onus upon the Department of Agriculture. Their timidity may have been due to the fact that they have no real authority over the branches for the National Union is a comparatively loose federation of district unions. Whatever the reason, it was manifest that the Executive had come to a decision that the only scheme of collective bargaining which they would push would be one in which the Department of Agriculture took the initiative at every stage and which imposed practically no obligations on themselves.[79]

Not surprisingly, a majority of branches abstained from directly voting for or against the scheme when it was put forward, although 'the view of some of the leading people in the Farmers' Union [is] that the remaining 90 [branches] are more or less indifferent and certainly are in favour of a voluntary scheme if the

alternative is statutory regulation'.[80] The result, however, finally provoked the
S.F.S.U. to demand the same protection for its members as had been given to
farm workers south of the border.[81]

V

The years 1935 and 1936 saw two critical reports on the state of the agricultural
labour market in Scotland: the Unemployment Insurance Statutory Committee's
report on the proposed extension of unemployment insurance to agriculture,
and the report of the Committee on Farm Workers in Scotland.[82] The former, in
the light of increased rural unemployment, recommended the extension of
unemployment insurance to agriculture, but on a separate scheme with lower
contributions and benefits, given the lower wage rates in the industry. It believed
there was little difference between agricultural unemployment rates in England
and Scotland, but accepted that those on long engagements in the north of
Britain were less likely to become temporarily unemployed, and therefore
recommended a 25 per cent reduction in contributions for those on annual
and six-monthly contracts. The initial hypothesis was confirmed when unemployment figures for agriculture in 1937 and 1938 showed that unemployment
in Scotland was fairly similar to the overall British figure.[83]

The latter report, a consequence of the failure of negotiations in 1935 and
with a specific remit to look into the possibility of minimum wage regulation for
Scotland, concluded that wages boards, similar to the system under the C.P.A.,
should be set up as soon as possible. This time the minimum wage, established
under the 1937 Agricultural Wages (Regulation) (Scotland) Act, appears to
have had an impact in Scotland. Real wages rose and employment fell, creating
the classic 'minimum wage' effect, a situation in direct contrast to the failure of
the Corn Production Act (see figures 2 and 3).[84] Unlike the 1917–21 period, the
position of labour had now weakened and the S.F.S.U. gave full support to wage
regulation, which produced a regulatory regime entirely different in its impact
from the previous experience.

VI

Thus the introduction of effective state intervention in the Scottish agricultural
labour market was not the result of the rapid advance of agriculture in the
national political economy (as during both world wars), or of some whiggish
progression that had been opposed by employers and demanded by workers for

decades until the government finally saw the 'light'. It was a response to a complete change in the nature of the labour market resulting from the depression, which had led to rising unemployment and falling comparative wages, evoking the requirement for state-sanctioned minimum standards of living. Prior to the 1930s these standards had been provided through the free operation of the market, a fact most notably demonstrated by the ineffectiveness of the C.P.A. in Scotland when state intervention was an unnecessary exercise. Effective institutional intervention prior to the 1930s concentrated on improving the efficiency of market operations, that is, voluntary collective bargaining to produce guidelines on the market rate for wages and hours, and even the refining of market facilities. In the 1920s the S.F.S.U. had a policy of hiring halls to provide a more 'civilised' environment for the hiring fair.[85] Right up until 1929, the S.F.S.U. rejected any suggestion of state intervention in market operations, and as late as 1935 it was still trying to avoid the necessity of a minimum wage. The union firmly believed throughout the 1920s that unemployment insurance would place an unnecessary burden on its members and that minimum wages would result in lower average wages. In such a position the state had little incentive to intervene, and so in Scotland the attitude to rural labour relations and social policy was less interventionist than in England.[86] With the existence of an acceptable equilibrium position in the market prior to the depression, the state had no reason to interfere with the individual bargaining rights of either employers or workers, a situation that both sides were keen to protect. Therefore, institutional intervention was ultimately a function of the demands of the labour market, and the key to evaluating the role of institutions in Scottish agriculture is to understand the economics of market operation.

University of Edinburgh

NOTES

1 A version of this article was given to the Economic & Social History Society of Scotland's conference on 'Rural history' at Dundee in December 1991. The research was funded by an E.S.R.C. studentship. I am most grateful to Bob Morris, Roger Davidson and an anonymous referee for their helpful comments.

2 *Report of the thirteenth decennial census of Scotland*, tabs. A and B. This figure includes all those engaged in agriculture, i.e. farmers, farm managers, workers, and crofters.

3 Hunt, *Regional wage variations in Britain*, pp. 50–3, and *idem*, 'Industrialization and regional inequality'.

4 Brock, 'The importance of emigration'.

5 Devine, 'Introduction: Scottish farm service', p. 6; *idem*, 'Social stability and agrarian change'; *idem*, 'Farm servants and labour in East Lothian'.

6 For the position of the unemployed with regard to the poor law in the early twentieth century see R. C. on Unemployment Insurance, Final report (P.P. 1931–2, XIII), pp. 49–50; and Levitt, 'The Scottish poor law and unemployment'.

7 Devine, 'Scottish farm labour'; the position in the north of England was similar; see Caunce, 'Twentieth-century farm servants', pp. 144 and 160–1.

8 For a useful summary of the structure of Scottish agricultural production see Whitby, 'Some changes in the structure'. Even in predominantly arable areas there was steady demand for regular labour throughout the year; see R. C. on Labour, III, 2 (P.P. 1893–4, XXXVI) p. 45.

9 Report of an enquiry by the Board of Trade into the earnings and hours of labour (P.P. 1910, LXXXIV), p. xxi. 'Orramen' were workers whose employment did not involve the use or care of livestock (including horses).

10 Carter, 'Class culture among farm servants'.

11 R. C. on Labour, III, 3 (P.P. 1893–4, XXXVI), p. 100.

12 Fenton, The Turra Coo, p. 2; for the trade union attitude see Scottish Farm Servant, June 1926, p. 26.

13 R. C. on Labour (P.P. 1893–4, XXXVI).

14 Smith, Joe Duncan, pp. 31–2.

15 For the policy of the National Agricultural Labourers' Union see Howkins, Poor labouring men, chs. 5–6.

16 The S.F.S.U. met farmers in Moray, Perth and Inverness and also met the Scottish Chamber of Agriculture in 1913, but it appears that no definite agreements were obtained: Scottish Farm Servant, Nov. 1926, p. 128. For opposition to a wages board see Scottish Farm Servant, July 1913, p. 2, and Sept. 1913, p. 14.

17 National Farmers' Union of Scotland Archives (National Farmers Union of Scotland, Edinburgh; hereafter N.F.U.S.), National Farmers' Union of Scotland in 1913 (small black book), cuttings from Glasgow Herald, 11 July 1913 and Scottish Farmer, 27 Sept. 1913. For a comparison with the National Farmers' Union (England and Wales), see Cox et al., 'Origins and early development'.

18 Dewey, British agriculture; Horn, Rural life in England.

19 Winter, The Great War, p. 235.

20 Duncan, 'The Scottish agricultural labourer', pp. 206–7. Women also obtained greater wage gains.

21 Dewey, 'Agricultural labour supply', pp. 102–5.

22 Board of Trade, Industrial (War Inquiries) Branch, 'Reports on the state of employment in the United Kingdom in July 1915 . . . October 1916; idem, 'Reports on the state of employment in agriculture in Great Britain at the end of January 1917 . . . July 1918' (unpublished reports, available in British Library of Political and Economic Science). Dewey has shown that these figures are subject to significant sample bias, but their importance is in the comparative rather than the absolute levels and there is no indication that the bias was significantly different between England & Wales and Scotland (see Dewey, British agriculture, app. H). My thanks to Peter Dewey for locating these records for me.

23 Board of Agriculture and Fisheries, *The agricultural output of Great Britain* (P.P. 1912–3, X), p. 18; *Report of the Board of Trade on the increased employment of women* (P.P. 1918, XIV), p. 13.

24 Dewey, *British agriculture*, p. 203.

25 Board of Trade, unpublished reports cited above, n. 22. However the replacement labour lacked the skills required to handle livestock and horses.

26 Scottish Record Office (hereafter S.R.O.), HH 31/28, *Recruiting, appeals tribunals, conscientious objectors, agricultural workers, 1915–24*, Box 3. Dewey has questioned the accuracy of this survey, but it seems likely that any bias does not mitigate against comparative analysis (see Dewey, *British agriculture*, p. 47, n. 29).

27 For England and Wales see Howkins, *Reshaping rural England*, pp. 268–9; Pretty, *The rural revolt that failed*, pp. 64–76; Howell, 'Labour organization', pp. 73–5.

28 *Scottish Farm Servant*, June 1915, p. 7; July 1915, p. 5.

29 Wilson, 'Farm wages in Scotland', p. 404.

30 N.F.U.S., central executive committee minutes, 11 July 1916.

31 S.R.O., AF 43/96, *Agriculture and recruiting; substitution of labour, 1916–8.*

32 N.F.U.S., central executive committee minutes, 26 Jan. 1917.

33 Whetham, *The agrarian history of England and Wales*, pp. 94–7; Dewey, *British agriculture*, pp. 93–5. In an earlier article ('The Agriculture Act, 1920', p. 39) Whetham claimed that Scotland was excluded from the wage committee provisions of the Corn Production Act; this is incorrect.

34 Pretty, *The rural revolt that failed*, p. 90; for England see Howkins, *Poor labouring men*, pp. 122–3, and Groves, *Sharpen the sickle*, pp. 163–70.

35 *Summaries of evidence taken before the Agricultural Policy Sub-committee* (P.P. 1918, v), p. 41.

36 *R. C. on Agriculture: evidence* (P.P. 1919, VIII), Sir James Wilson, p. 114.

37 *Scottish Farm Servant*, Oct. 1919, p. 78.

38 *R. C. on Agriculture: evidence* (P.P. 1919, VIII), Sir James Wilson, pp. 110–9.

39 Scottish Farm Servants' Union records (Mitchell Library, Glasgow; hereafter S.F.S.U.), central executive minutes, 19 June 1919.

40 Wilson, *Report to the Board of Agriculture for Scotland on farm workers*, pp. 33–47.

41 P.R.O. LAB 2/740/12, memo. on the application of the Hours of Employment Bill to agriculture in Scotland by the S.F.S.U., March 1920.

42 S.R.O., AF 43/138, *Hours of Employment Bill (1919), 1919–20*; P.R.O., LAB 2/740/12. *Hours of Employment Bill, 1919: requests for exclusion, 1919–20.*

43 Cooper, *British agricultural policy*, p. 50; Lowe, 'The failure of consensus in Britain'.

44 S.F.S.U. membership: June 1914: 12,000; Nov. 1918: 11,000; May 1920: 38,000 (S.F.S.U., minutes A.G.M. 20 June 1914, central executive minutes, 10 Nov. 1918 and 31 March 1920; membership appears to have fallen during the early part of the war due to the disruption caused by military recruitment). N.F.U.S. membership: 1915: over 2,000; March 1920: 14,000 (N.F.U.S., central executive minutes, 23 Dec. 1916 and 31 March 1920).

45 Whetham, 'The Agriculture Act, 1920'; Cooper, *British agricultural policy*, ch. 3.

46 Pretty, *The rural revolt that failed*, p. 149; Howkins, *Poor labouring men*, ch. 7; Groves *Sharpen the sickle*, pp. 163–70; Howell, 'Labour organization', p. 91.

47 S.F.S.U., A.G.M., 17 June 1921.

48 For possible reasons behind this see Gilchrist, 'Agriculture in the south-west of Scotland', p. 233.

49 Smout, *A century of the Scottish people*, p. 114.

50 Carrier and Jeffery, *External migration*, p. 93.

51 Anon., 'Emigration of Scottish agricultural workers', p. 341.

52 Constantine, *Emigrants and empire*.

53 *Report on the fourteenth decennial census of Scotland*, calculated from tabs. 1 and 6.

54 S.F.S.U., central executive minutes, 1 April 1928.

55 Duncan, 'Scottish farm labour', pp. 501–2; *Scottish Farm Servant*, Oct. 1925, p. 112.

56 Duncan, 'The fixing of farm wages', p. 376.

57 *Scottish Farm Servant*, May 1923, p. 24.

58 Ibid., June 1924, p. 33.

59 *Report of the Unemployment Insurance Statutory Committee . . . on the question of the insurance against unemployment of persons* (P.P. 1934–5, XIV), p. 5.

60 N.F.U.S. membership 1929: 10,240 (S.R.O., AF 43/339, *Agricultural workers' unemployment insurance: conference on extension of and Royal Commission on Unemployment Insurance, 1929–31*); 1931: 8,621 (R. C. on Unemployment Insurance: *evidence* (P.P. 1919, VIII), p. 1071).

61 Whetham, *The agrarian history*, p. 230; Brown, *Agriculture in England*, pp. 80–1.

62 S.F.S.U., central executive minutes, 27 Oct. 1929.

63 Brown, *Agriculture in England*, pp. 107–10.

64 The relationship between rising real wages and declining labour demand has been well established for the depression: see Beenstock and Warburton, 'Wages and unemployment in interwar Britain'; and Dimsdale, Nickell, and Horsewood, 'Real wages and unemployment in Britain'.

65 Carrier and Jeffery, *External migration*, p. 93.

66 Brown, *Agriculture in England*, p. 123. By January 1934 agricultural unemployment was a particular problem in eastern Scotland, with rates up to 15 per cent in the north east: S.R.O. AF 43 349, D.O.A.S. memo, 'Unemployment among agricultural workers in Scotland', March 1934.

67 S.R.O., AF 59/38, D.O.A.S. memo., 'Agricultural wages in Great Britain', Nov. 1934; AF 59 49, Ministry of Agriculture memo, 'Agricultural wage regulation in England and Wales'.

68 T.G.W.U., *1919 then and now, 1946*, pp. 2–3.

69 S.F.S.U., branch circular, Feb. 1934.

70 S.F.S.U., central executive minutes, 3 Dec. 1932.

71 R. C. on Unemployment Insurance: *final report* (P.P. 1931–2, XIII), p. 197.

72 Duncan, 'The economic crisis and the Scottish farm worker', pp. 281–2.

73 S.R.O., AF 43/184, *Agricultural wages: scheme for promoting collective agreements, 1921–34*.

74 Lowe, *Adjusting to democracy*, p. 120.

75 Ibid, p. 70.

76 S.R.O., AF 43/184, *Agricultural wages: scheme for promoting collective agreements, 1921–34.*

77 S.R.O., AF 43/185, *Agricultural wages: scheme for promoting collective agreements, 1921–34.*

78 N.F.U.S., central executive minutes, 30 July 1936.

79 P.R.O., LAB 2/2017/5, *Agriculture-Scotland proposal of the SFSU for a scheme for the promotion of collective agreements in the industry in Scotland, 1934–5*, letter from Galbraith (Chief Conciliation Officer, Glasgow) to Leggett, 13 Feb. 1935.

80 Ibid., 31 July 1935.

81 S.R.O., AF 43/185, *Agricultural wages: scheme for promoting collective agreements, 1934–5.*

82 *Report of the Unemployment Insurance Statutory Committee . . . on the question of the insurance against unemployment of persons* (P.P. 1934–5, XIV); *Report of the Committee on Farm Workers* (P.P. 1935–6, VIII).

83 *Reports of the Unemployment Insurance Statutory Committee . . . , on the financial condition of the Unemployment Fund on the 31st December, 1937* (P.P. 1937–8, XVIII); *on the 31st December, 1938* (P.P. 1938–9, XVIII).

84 Some of this wage rise may have been caused by a general tightening of the labour market, but there is no evidence of a sudden rise in the demand for labour in agriculture. See *Twenty-seventh report of the Department of Agriculture for Scotland* (P.P. 1938–9, IX), pp. 13–5.

85 *Scottish Farm Servant*, Dec. 1925, p. 43.

86 For a comparison with the Ministry of Agriculture see Savage, 'Friend to the worker'.

OFFICIAL PUBLICATIONS

Royal Commission on Labour, *The agricultural labourer* (P.P. 1893–4, xxxvi).

Report of an enquiry by the Board of Trade into the earnings and hours of labour of workpeople of the United Kingdom, V: agriculture in 1907 (P.P. 1910, lxxxiv).

Board of Agriculture and Fisheries, *The agricultural output of Great Britain* (P.P. 1912–3, x).

Report of the Board of Trade on the increased employment of women during the War in the United Kingdom (P.P. 1918, xiv).

Summaries of evidence taken before the Agricultural Policy Sub-Committee of the Reconstruction Committee Appointed in August 1916 (P.P. 1918, v).

Royal Commission on Agriculture: evidence (P.P. 1919, viii).

Board/Department of Agriculture for Scotland, *Agricultural statistics*, annually (Edinburgh, 1922–39).

Wilson, J., *Report to the Board of Agriculture for Scotland on farm workers in Scotland in 1919–20* (Edinburgh, 1921).

Report of the thirteenth decennial census of Scotland, III: occupations and industries (Edinburgh, 1924).

Royal Commission on Unemployment Insurance; final report (P.P. 1931–2, xiii). Minutes of evidence (1931).

Report of the fourteenth decennial census of Scotland, III: occupations and industries (Edinburgh, 1934).

Report of the Unemployment Insurance Statutory Committee, in accordance with section 20 of the Unemployment Insurance Act, 1934, on the question of the insurance against unemployment of persons engaged in employment in agriculture (P.P. 1934–5, xiv).

Report of the Committee on farm workers in Scotland (P.P. 1935–6, viii).

Report of the Unemployment Insurance Statutory Committee in accordance with section 59 of the Unemployment Insurance Act, 1935, and section 8 of the Unemployment Insurance (Agriculture) Act, 1936, on the financial condition of the Unemployment Fund on the 31st December 1937 (P.P. 1937–8, xviii); on the 31st December 1938 (P.P. 1938–9, xviii).

Twenty-seventh report of the Department of Agriculture for Scotland, for the year 1938 (P.P. 1938–9, ix).

Carrier, N.H. and Jeffery, J.R., External migration: a study of the available statistics, 1815–1950 (Studies on medical and population subjects, 6, General Register Office, 1953).

Department of Employment, British labour statistics, historical abstract, 1886–1968 (1971).

SECONDARY SOURCES

Anon., 'Emigration of Scottish agricultural workers', Scot. J. Agric., X (1927), pp. 340–3.

Beenstock M. and Warburton P., 'Wages and unemployment in interwar Britain', Exp. Econ. Hist., 23 (1986), pp. 153–72.

Brock J.M., 'The importance of emigration in Scottish regional population movement, 1861–1911', in T.M. Devine, ed., Scottish emigration and Scottish society (Edinburgh, 1992), pp. 104–34.

Brown J., Agriculture in England: a survey of farming, 1870–1947 (Manchester, 1987).

Carter I., 'Class culture among farm servants in the north-east, 1840–1914', in A. A. Maclaren, ed., Social class in Scotland: past and present (Edinburgh, 1976), pp. 105–27.

Caunce, S., 'Twentieth-century farm servants: the horselads of the East Riding of Yorkshire', Agric. Hist. Rev., 39 (1991), pp. 143–66.

Constantine S., ed., Emigrants and empire: British settlement in the Dominions between the wars (Manchester, 1990).

Cooper A.F., British agricultural policy, 1912–36: a study in Conservative politics (Manchester, 1989).

Cox G., Lowe P. and Winter M., 'The origins and early development of the National Farmers' Union', Agric. Hist. Rev., 39 (1991), pp. 30–47.

Devine T.M., 'Social stability and agrarian change in the eastern lowlands of Scotland, 1810–1840', Soc. Hist., 3 (1978), pp. 331–45.

Devine T.M., 'Farm servants and labour in East Lothian after the Napoleonic wars', Scot. Lab. Hist. Soc. J., 15 (1981), pp. 15–25.

Devine T.M., 'Introduction: Scottish farm service in the agricultural revolution', in idem, ed., Farm servants and labour in lowland Scotland, 1770–1914 (Edinburgh, 1984), pp. 1–8.

Devine T.M., 'Scottish farm labour in the era of agricultural depression, 1875–1900', in *idem*, ed., *Farm servants and labour in lowland Scotland, 1770–1914* (Edinburgh, 1984), pp. 243–55.

Dewey P.E., 'Agricultural labour supply in England and Wales during the First World War', *Econ. Hist. Rev.*, 2nd ser, xxviii (1975), pp. 100–12.

Dewey P.E., *British agriculture in the First World War* (1989).

Dimsdale N.H., Nickell S.J. and Horsewood N., 'Real wages and unemployment in Britain during the 1930s', *Econ. J.*, 99 (1989), pp. 271–92.

Duncan J.F., 'Scottish farm labour', *Scot. J. Agric.*, II (1919), pp. 498–507.

Duncan J.F., The fixing of farm wages', *Scot. J. Agric.*, VII (1924), pp. 374–80.

Duncan J.F., 'The Scottish agricultural labourer', in D.T. Jones, H.M. Conacher, J.F. Duncan and W.R. Scott, *Rural Scotland during the war* (1926), pp. 189–220.

Duncan J.F., 'The economic crisis and the Scottish farm worker', *Scot. J. Agric.*, XVI (1933), pp. 275–82.

Fenton A, *The Turra Coo: a legal episode in the popular culture of north-east Scotland* (Aberdeen, 1989).

Gilchrist J.A., 'Agriculture in the south-west of Scotland: past and present trends', *J. Proc. Agric. Econ. Soc.* III (1935), pp. 227–39.

Groves R., *Sharpen the sickle: the history of the farm workers' union* (1949, repr. 1981).

Horn P., *Rural life in England in the First World War* (Dublin, 1984).

Howell D.W., 'Labour organization among agricultural workers in Wales, 1871–1921', *Welsh Hist. Rev.*, 16 (1992), pp. 63–92.

Howkins A., *Poor labouring men: rural radicalism in Norfolk, 1870–1923* (1985).

Howkins A., *Reshaping rural England: a social history, 1850–1925* (1991).

Hunt E.H., *Regional wage variations in Britain, 1850–1914* (Oxford, 1973).

Hunt E.H., 'Industrialization and regional inequality: wages in Britain, 1760–1914', *J. Econ. Hist.*, XLVI (1986), pp. 935–61.

Levitt I., 'The Scottish poor law and unemployment, 1890–1929', in T.C. Smout, ed., *The search for wealth and stability: essays in economic and social history presented to M.W. Flinn* (1979), pp. 263–82.

Lowe R., 'The failure of consensus in Britain: the National Industrial Conference, 1919–1921', *Hist. J.*, XXI (1978), pp. 649–75.

Pretty D.A., *The rural revolt that failed: farm workers' trade unions in Wales, 1889–1950* (Cardiff, 1989).

Savage G.A., 'Friend to the worker: social policy at the Ministry of Agriculture between the wars', *Albion*, 19 (1987), pp. 193–208.

Smith J.H., *Joe Duncan: the Scottish farm servants and British agriculture* (Edinburgh, 1973).

Smout T.C., *A century of the Scottish people, 1830–1950* (1986).

T.G.W.U.: Scottish farm servants section, *1919 then and now, 1946* (Airdrie, 1946).

Whetham E.H., 'The Agriculture Act, 1920, and its repeal: the "Great Betrayal"', *Agric. Hist. Rev.* 22 1974), pp. 36–49.

Whetham E.H., *The agrarian history of England and Wales, VIII, 1914–39* (Cambridge, 1978).

Whitby H., 'Some changes in the structure of Scottish agriculture since 1870', *J. Proc. Agric. Econ. Soc.*, VIII (1950), pp. 312–36.

Wilson J., 'Farm wages in Scotland in summer 1926', *Scot. J. Agric.*, IX (1926), pp. 401–5.

Winter J.M., *The Great War and the British people* (1986).

The Independent Labour Party in Glasgow, 1888–1906: the struggle for identity

Extracted from James J Smyth 1990 in Richard Morris and Alan McKinlay (eds) *The Independent Labour Party in Scotland*, Manchester (Manchester University Press), 20–29.

The history of the Independent Labour Party (ILP) in Scotland does not begin with the Bradford Conference of 1893 but with the earlier formation – in 1888 – of the Scottish Labour Party (SLP). Originally titled the Scottish (Parliamentary) Labour Party, the SLP was, in the words of Keir Hardie, 'The Pioneer of the ILP'.[1] Whether or not Hardie's description is strictly accurate, it is unquestionably the case that it is with the formation of the SLP that a Labour political presence was established in Scotland and particularly Glasgow which has continued unbroken to the present day. The SLP can be regarded, or even dismissed, as a relatively insignificant body; it had a small membership, enjoyed no electoral success and eventually subsumed itself with the larger (national) ILP.[2] Yet, it is with the birth of the SLP that Labour politics, as we understand them even today, first emerged.

In seeking to explain why Scotland made this original breakthrough the question of organisation is paramount.[3] This did not mean, however, that Scotland became a bastion of strength for this new movement. Prior to 1914 there were only three Labour MPs elected in Scotland and, overall, Labour's electoral performance was 'relatively weaker' than in England.[4] Yet, there were a number of indicators of a potentially more propitious development: there was the formation of the Scottish Workers Representation Committee (SWRC) prior to the formation of the Labour Electoral Committee (LEC); the creation of the Scottish Trade Union Congress (STUC) in 1897; and the formation of the SLP itself. The existence of such bodies has led David Howell to comment upon the apparent conundrum of how, 'Scottish labour could claim to be organisationally in advance of its English counterpart . . . [yet] individual prominence and organisational precocity neither indicated nor produced mass support'.[5]

I

In fact, this precocity can be explained in terms of the weakness of the Labour movement in Scotland – due to the lack of a strong trade union base political questions assumed a greater importance than they did in England. Certainly, Scottish trade unions were not as strong as their southern counterparts. The smashing of the Glasgow Cotton Spinners' Association in 1837–8 was a body-blow to Scottish trade unionism which was further debilitated by the depression of the early 1840s.[6] When unions began to re-build in the 1850s they had to do so mainly from scratch and tended to be 'small and localised'.[7] Even where all-Scottish national unions were formed they were, 'federal in structure, with power and financial control remaining firmly in the hands of local societies' – a pattern that was repeated in the 1880s.[8]

Overall, the level of trade unionism in Scotland was lower than in England; the Webbs calculated the proportionate number of trade unionists in the United Kingdom in 1892 as 3.98 per cent of the total population but which for England and Wales was 4.55 per cent and for Scotland 3.64 per cent only.[9] While Scotland shared in the general growth of trade unionism over the following two decades, its level of union membership remained lower than England and Wales.[10]

Another particular aspect of Scottish trade unionism is that it was largely concentrated in the Glasgow area. For 1892 the Webbs deduced that there were 147,000 trade unionists in Scotland – 'two-thirds of the total, indeed, belonging to Glasgow and the neighbouring industrial centres'.[11] As the Webbs were aware, it was not total numbers which gave the trade union movement its significance but, rather, the concentration of members in particular industries and localities.[12] Nevertheless, the 'greater-Glasgow' mass of trade unionists did not overcome Scottish localism but, if anything, exacerbated it.[13] The weakness and localism of Scottish trade unions meant that trades councils played a much more significant role north of the border than they did in England, and they did embrace political matters as well as union affairs.[14] However, while providing a much-needed focus for unity among trades, trades councils could still not play the dominant role of a strong trade union.

The discrepancy between Scotland and England in this respect is most clearly shown in the case of the mining unions. The suffrage and redistribution reforms of 1884–5 led to a sudden increase in the number of trade union MPs from two to eleven in the General Election of 1885. No union was able to exploit the new situation better than the miners – of the eleven Lib-Labs six were miners representing 'mining' constituencies.[15] The miners did not have to run their candidates in three-cornered contests but used their weight to secure quid pro quo arrangements with the Liberals.[16] There were no such agreements in Scotland where the miners simply did not have sufficient density of numbers in constituencies or the organisational strength to force any recognition from the Liberals.

The build-up of the Scottish mining unions under the leadership of Alexander MacDonald reached a high point in 1874 but thereafter went into a rapid decline and, by 1880, only the Fife and Kinross Miners' Association remained. In 1886 there was a new phase of union growth with 'county' unions established in Ayrshire and for the Forth and Clyde Valley led by Keir Hardie and Chisholm Robertson respectively and, by the end of the year the Scottish Miners' National Federation (SMNF) was formally constituted.[17] The SMNF was by no means a 'national' union however – it had no central authority and real power remained with the localities.[18] Even local organisation remained weak and in its first year the SMNF shrunk from an original twenty-six districts and 23,570 members to fifteen districts and 13,000 members.[19] Within a couple of years the SMNF was defunct. By the late 1880s and early 1890s the mining unions in Scotland were in better shape than they had been in 1880 but, even so, 'only the Fife organisation . . . could be called a really established union'.[20]

It is from this perspective – of the general weakness of Scottish trade unionism and the particular vulnerability of the miners – that Hardie's 'independent' challenge to the Liberals at Mid-Lanark and the subsequent formation of the SLP is best understood. It was the inability of Scottish trade unionists to make local Liberal Associations accept trade union or working-class candidates that forced miners' leaders such as Keir Hardie into a reappraisal of the organisational link with Liberalism.[21] The Mid-Lanark by-election campaign has been extensively chronicled and its details need not concern us too much here.[22] What is of more concern is to set Hardie's election effort and the subsequent formation of the SLP within the context of the contemporary debate on the need for a 'labour party'.

II

There were three main constituent parts to the SLP – the Socialists, the Trade Unionists and the Radicals – all of whom had their own views of what a labour party should be. The trade union element of the SLP, originally at least, was largely confined to the miners of central and west Scotland. The argument in favour of the independent representation of miners and for a labour party, as articulated in the pages of *The Miner*, was clearly based upon the weakness of the mining unions in Scotland and the necessity, therefore, of looking to the state to play an interventionist role in the industry.

This view had to confront the 'independent' attitude of the Lib-Lab MPs of North-East England. In the very first issue of *The Miner*, the Northumberland miner MP, Thomas Burt, wrote about the demand for the eight-hour day, 'it seems to me to appeal to Parliament to fix the hours of adults [ie adult men] is to weaken the motives for union and self-reliance'.[23] Burt was arguing from a position of strength – his union was strong enough to compel the Liberals to recognise its officials as candidates and both the Northumberland and Durham miners already enjoyed a working day of less than eight hours.[24] The Scottish miners (with the partial exception of Fife which was the only area in Scotland to have won the eight-hour day)[25] were unable to accomplish either and Hardie focused his strategy upon the reality of their position. In reply to Burt, Hardie drew a comparison between the plight of 'the Irish and Highland tenant farmers' and that of the Scottish miners:

> The classes named had the opportunity, as the miner has, of putting things right of themselves; but that which looks well in theory is often found to be very difficult in practice. So it is in this case. The miner finds it next to, if not quite impossible to continue an eight-hour day without some outside help, and he therefore looks with confidence to Parliament to respond to his cry by voting for the Bill.[26]

These words were published in the immediate aftermath of a bitter strike in Lanarkshire which had ended in violence and defeat for the miners. Although Hardie had proposed the tactic of a 'holiday' to restrict output rather than strike action, the use of troops against a mining community set him at odds with the local Liberal establishment.[27] From around this time Hardie can be seen to question the validity of working-class support for the Liberal Party. Increasingly his concern lay not only with securing reforms through Parliament but also in some form of direct labour representation. There was no sudden break in Hardie's thinking, however, and his emphasis could switch from the theoretical end of Liberalism and its ultimate replacement, to the practicality of establishing a labour political presence – a task which might still be integrally related to the Liberal Party.[28]

Hardie was constantly looking for a broader perspective than the merely local or the 'simple' trade union approach.[29] At one stage he came close to arguing that the unions would have to be transformed into political bodies: 'We want a new party – a Labour party pure and simple and the Trade Unions have the power to create this.'[30] However, speaking at the SMNF annual meeting in

August 1897 he presented a more modest proposal when he said that: 'The Labour Party will be a distinct organisation from the Trade Unions.'[31] Hardie was consistent in regarding the unions as an essential component but the structure of this intended labour party remained unclear. His decision to contest Mid-Lanark in opposition to the Liberal effectively forced the issue and his campaign made concrete the need for a definite organisation. Hardie was aware of the lack of organisation during the campaign[32] and a month later, on 19 May, the first meeting of the SLP was held in Glasgow.[33] In fact, even before this meeting Hardie claimed that his supporters in Mid-Lanark were busy establishing branches of the SLP.[34]

The formal inauguration of the new party took place at a conference on 25 August, again held in Glasgow,[35] and, increasingly, the centre of gravity of the SLP shifted from the Lanarkshire coalfield into Glasgow. The motivation for Hardie's candidature at Mid-Lanark may have come from the miners and the locality but the significance of his challenge to the Liberals went beyond both. Furthermore, if there was to be a distinct organisation rather than just a series of individual deals with the Liberals[36] it was clear that the mining unions could not sustain this on their own. Hardie's campaign had received widespread comment and support and this was reflected in the inaugural conference.

Hardie's backers could by typified largely as radicals or left-wing Liberals. They included the Crofters' MP, Dr Clark and the Irish Nationalist leader in Glasgow, John Ferguson, who were elected Honorary Vice-Presidents of the new party.[37] This was no accident. The radical wing of the Liberal Party tended to see the cause of labour representation as their own and Hardie's position appeared that of a radical. In the month before the election Hardie explained his strategy thus: 'Better to split the party now, if there is to be a split, than at a general election, and if the labour party only make their power felt now, then terms will not be wanting when the general election comes.'[38]

This, in fact was the key to the radical involvement. Among Hardie's supporters was the London-based, land-restorationist journal, *The Democrat*, edited by the ex-MP William Saunders.[39] *The Democrat* regarded Hardie as: "the Radical candidate', who was being snubbed by an unrepresentative 'clique', ie the Mid-Lanark Liberal Association'.[40] This identification of labour representation with the radicals' own interest also meant, ultimately, labour's identification with the Liberal Party. Saunders argues: 'If the labour classes are to form a reliable wing of the Liberal Party their just and equitable claims must no longer be either tampered with or evaded.'[41] However, taking an 'independent' line at a by-election was one thing, the pressure for 'unity' against the Tories at a general election was a completely different matter. In 1892 the editor of *The Democrat* had moved firmly back into the Liberal camp. The SLP was running candidates against Liberals and was forced to expel John Ferguson and Dr Clark for speaking in support of Liberal candidates in seats the SLP was contesting.[42] The basic problem confronting the radicals was what to do when the Liberal Party refused to countenance Labour representation. For some, like James Shaw Maxwell the solution was to move completely towards an 'independent' line and socialism.[43] For most, however, the only course of action was to remain within the Liberal Party where, in Hardie's words he (ie the radical) 'has to grin and bear the situation as best he may'.[44] There was also a fundamental difference between the ambitions of the radicals who saw Labour as being a 'reliable wing of the Liberal Party' and the socialist-inclined views of men like Hardie who could, at least theoretically, consider a future beyond the Liberal Party. During the Mid-Lanark campaign Hardie wrote:

> But don't let us be mistaken: sending a 'working man' representative to Parliament is only a beginning, but it is a beginning . . . We must get rid of this talk of working men having a right to a 'share' in the representation. Why working men and women (using that term to embrace all workers) must have *all* the representation.[45]

Sentiments like this had an obvious appeal for socialists as did the SLP's founding programme which, as well as 'constitutional' demands such as adult suffrage, abolition of plural voting, triennial parliaments, payment of election expenses and salaries for MPs, also included social demands for an eight-hour day, nationalisation of the land and minerals, state acquisition of railways, waterways and tramways, and a cumulative income tax.[46] The formation of the SLP occurred at a time when socialists in Scotland were re-considering their existing strategies and the issue of electoral activity.

The socialist movement was in the process of establishing itself in Scotland when it split at the end of 1884, leaving the Social Democratic Federation (SDF) under the leadership of HM Hyndman and the breakaway Socialist League (SL) led by William Morris.[47] In Scotland the SL emerged the stronger with Edinburgh (which styled itself the Scottish Land and Labour League (SL&LL) going over to the SL more or less unanimously and in Glasgow the branch divided in two.[48] Although Edinburgh had been the most active city initially, Glasgow eventually made progress in its propaganda activity and the SL appears to have held an edge over the SDF. As well as establishing itself within Glasgow, the SL sought to take the socialist message into the surrounding districts.

One of the areas where they were relatively successful was Hamilton where William Small established a branch of the SL&LL in late 1884.[49] Thanks to

Small, who was a miner's agent and became Secretary of the Lanarkshire Miners' County Federation when it was formed in 1893[50] a high level of activity was maintained amongst the miners with regular speakers from Glasgow. On one such occasion Bruce Glasier, the major activist of the Glasgow SL, addressed a meeting of between two and three thousand miners.[51] During the bitter strike of February 1887 these links were intensified. The SL opened their branch rooms as a temporary strike headquarters and organised a mass demonstration which drew twenty thousand to Glasgow Green.[52]

Activity like this, however, posed uncomfortable problems for the socialists since it begged the question of what to do next. The whole strategy of the SL in particular could be summed up as education for revolution. Its position was stated unequivocally in the founding document: 'our view is that such a body [ie a socialist party] has no function but to educate the people in the principles of Socialism'.[53] Although this emphasis was partly due to the desire to clearly disassociate the SL from the perceived opportunism of Hyndman, it did, nonetheless, reflect a genuine belief that partial reforms (the 'dreaded palliatives') could not help the working class but only serve to further reinforce its subordination.[54] However, increasingly, the Glasgow socialists found themselves in the position of getting involved in campaigns which led to the formulation of precisely such demands. As well as their solidarity with the miners, the socialists also took a leading role in the unemployed agitation during the 1880s.

In May 1886 the Glasgow SL organised a mass meeting of the unemployed on the Green to protest at the stopping of outdoor relief and which demanded that the City Council provide work. This demand was not met but, as a direct result of the agitation, the Council decided to keep the soup kitchens open for another week.[55] This partial success cut across the strategy of the SL which had an official policy of 'non-intervention' in the unemployed agitation.[56] The following year, 1887, the Glasgow membership divided over this precise issue. On the one hand there were those who supported the policy of the national executive while, on the other, were those who believed that it was possible to secure a significant amount of relief for the unemployed through the common good fund of the City Council and, more than this, to demand that the Council provide work directly.[57] This section also argued that it would be to the advantage of the SL if it provided leadership – as it had done in the Lanarkshire miners' strike.[58]

At the same time the SL nationally was split over the question of electoral activity. Those who supported parliamentary action were defeated and eventually expelled in 1888.[59] However, there was a crucial debate on the issue at the 1887 Conference which was conducted over a resolution submitted by Hamilton, William Small's branch. This included the demand for the, 'overthrow of the capitalist system' but also called for socialists to be involved in trade unions and co-operative societies, to campaign in local and national elections and, crucially, 'organising the people into a Socialistic labour party'.[60]

Although both the SL and the SDF were national organisations, local branches had a tendency to follow their own lines of development. The differences between the national leaderships were not that clearly drawn in Scotland and, by the end of 1888, there appeared to be a rough consensus among Scottish socialists on the need for a more efficient organisation. This was fuelled partly by a dissatisfaction with London and resulted in the formation of the Scottish Socialist Federation (SSF).[61] A Conference was organised by the Edinburgh SDF at which most of the socialist forces in Scotland were present and which resolved to form, 'a Delegate Committee to thoroughly organise the propaganda in Scotland'.[62] This Committee was to be based in Edinburgh for the first year and John Leslie was appointed as Secretary.[63] According to Lowe the SSF represented a conscious break from London[64] but, whatever the ambitions behind it, the SSF did not emerge as a separate party. It remained an Edinburgh organisation with the SL and SDF branches linking up and, with the rapid decline of the SL nationally after 1888, it operated, ultimately as the Edinburgh branch of the SDF.

Given this state of flux and debate over tactics, strategy and organisation, it is hardly surprising that socialists began to gravitate towards the SLP. In 1893 Andreas Scheu approached Bruce Glasier about the possibility of a delegate from Glasgow attending the International Congress at Zurich. Glasier informed Scheu that, with the disintegration of the SL there were only the SDF and the Fabians left as socialist organisations and, keen as they would be to send a delegate, it was unlikely they could afford to do so. However, Glasier did suggest that Scheu approach the Labour Party which he was sure would be sympathetic, since many of its members had previously been in the SL.[65] In fact it was Glasgow Trades Council which decided to send a delegate to Zurich and their choice was John Warrington, President of the Council, active in the SLP and who had been an early member of the SL.[66] Around this time the *Labour Leader* commented on the disintegration of the SL that: 'One section of its members drifted more and more towards political action, and identified themselves with the Labour Party programme'.[67]

At the same time the SDF also made an input to the SLP, though its members did not have to leave their own organisation but could maintain membership of both. The SDF contribution was recognised by George Carson who wrote that, 'many of its best members are also active and zealous members of the Labour Party'.[68] In Edinburgh it was the SSF which originally established the SLP in 1892.[69] This action represents a considerable change of opinion amongst the Edinburgh socialists who had not considered the SLP 'worthy of their support' four years earlier.[70] In accepting the need to contest elections and agitate over specific issues the SSF was following the national lead of the SDF which had consistently argued this line. As Hyndman put the 'electoral' case to William Morris: 'we cannot separate ourselves from our epoch in this respect, any more than we can in the matter of dealing with capital and capitalist . . . You cannot keep an organisation healthy and vigorous without having some immediate work and some immediate aim'.[71] In Scotland the existence of the SLP allowed the SDF to pursue this line in a particular way and its involvement was encouraged by the peculiar structure of the SLP.

NOTES

1 *Socialist Review*, April 1914.

2 James Kellas, 'The Mid-Lanark By-Election (1888) and the Scottish Labour Party (1888–1894)', *Parliamentary Affairs*, XVIII, 1965, pp 318–29.

3 If Scotland took the lead other areas were not far behind. See Jack Reynolds and Keith Laybourn, 'The Emergence of the Independent Labour Party in Bradford', *International Review of Social History*, XX, 1975, pp 313–46.

4 Ian Hutchison, *A Political History of Scotland 1832–1924: Parties, Elections and Issues* (John Donald, Edinburgh, 1986), p 257.

5 David Howell, *British Workers and the Independent Labour Party 1888–1906* (Manchester University Press, Manchester, 1983), pp 133–44.

6 WH Fraser, 'Trades Councils in the Labour Movement in Nineteenth Century Scotland', in Ian McDougall (ed), *Essays in Scottish Labour History* (John Donald, Edinburgh, 1978), p 1.

7 *Ibid.*

8 *Ibid.* The Webbs, writing in 1894, identified 1879 as 'distinctly a low-water mark of the Trade Union Movement', which in Scotland had ruinous consequences due to the failure of the City of Glasgow Bank – 'a blow from which Trade Unionism in Scotland has even yet not recovered; Sidney and Beatrice Webb, *The History of Trade Unionism* (Longmans, London, 1911), p 334.

9 Webbs, *ibid*, pp 490–91.

10 Roy H Campbell, *Scotland Since 1707: The Rise of an Industrial Society* (John Donald, Edinburgh, 1985), p 237.

11 Webbs, *op cit*, p 412.

12 *Ibid*, p 411.

13 Fraser, *op cit*, pp 1–2.

14 *Ibid.*

15 GDH Cole, *British Working Class Politics: 1832–1941* (Methuen, London, 1941), pp 98–9.

16 Roy Gregory, *The Miners in British Politics 1906–14* (Clarendon Press, Oxford, 1968), p 16.

17 R Page Arnot, *A History of the Scottish Miners* (Allen & Unwin, London, 1955) p 66–70.
18 *The Miner*, January 1887.
19 Arnot, *op cit* p 68.
20 *Ibid*, p 70.
21 'Assessment of Hardie's relationship with Liberalism must distinguish between organisational and ideological aspects.' Howell, *op cit* p 144.
22 Kellas, *op cit*; KO Morgan, *Keir Hardie: Radical and Socialist* (Weidenfeld, London, 1975), pp 25–33, Fred Reid, *Keir Hardie: The Making of a Socialist* (Croom Helm, London, 1978), pp 110–115.
23 *The Miner*, January 1887.
24 E H Hunt, *British Labour History 1815–1914* (Weidenfeld & Nicolson, London, 1985), pp 253–4.
25 Arnot, *op cit*, p 51. The Fife coalfield was only on the brink of expansion, however.
26 *The Miner*, March 1887.
27 See Fred Reid, 'Keir Hardie's conversion to Socialism', in Asa Briggs and John Saville (eds), *Essays in Labour History 1886–1923* (Macmillan, London, 1971).
28 On the end of the Liberal Party see Hardie in *The Miner*, July 1887, and Chisholm Robertson in same, August 1887; see also May 1887 on the end of the capitalist, 'His day is now nearly past.'
29 See Arnot, *op cit*, p 67.
30 *The Miner*, April 1887.
31 *Ibid*, August 1887.
32 See Howell, *op cit*, p 147.
33 *The Miner*, June 1888.
34 *Ibid*, May 1888.
35 *Ibid*, September 1888.
36 See Howell, *op cit*, p 146.
37 David Lowe, *Souvenirs of Scottish Labour* (Holmes, Glasgow, 1919), p 4.
38 *The Miner*, March 1888.
39 *Ibid*, January 1888.
40 *The Democrat*, May 1888.
41 *Ibid*, August 1888.
42 Kellas, *op cit*, p 327; Low *op cit* pp 112–13.
43 Shaw Maxwell had been a 'land radical' in the early 1880s. He became the first chairman of the SLP in 1888 and the first secretary of the ILP in 1893. Lowe, *op cit*, pp 4, 117.
44 *Labour Leader*, 5 January 1894.
45 *The Miner*, April 1888.
46 Lowe, *op cit*, pp 3–4.
47 The best treatment of socialism in the 1880s remains EP Thompson, *William Morris: From Romantic to Revolutionary* (Merlin, London, 1977).
48 *Ibid*, pp 350–57. This is also dealt with in James Smyth, 'Labour and Socialism in Glasgow 1880–1914: The Electoral Challenge Prior to Democracy' (unpublished PhD thesis, University of Edinburgh, 1987), ch 1.

49 Reid (1978), *op cit*, pp 80–2.

50 Arnot, *op cit*, pp 91–2.

51 *Commonweal*, October 1885.

52 Thompson, *op cit* p 437.

53 *To Socialists*, 1885.

54 Thompson, *op cit*, pp 337–42.

55 *Commonweal*, 22 May 1888.

56 Socialist League, *Report 1888*.

57 J Bruce Glasier (Glasgow) to Socialist League (London), 24 October 1887, Socialist League Collection, International Institute of Social History, Amsterdam.

58 *Ibid*.

59 Thompson, *op cit*, pp 446–56.

60 *Our Corner*, June 1887.

61 Lowe, *op cit*, p 128.

62 *Justice*, 8 December 1888.

63 *Ibid*.

64 Lowe, *op cit*, p 132.

65 J Bruce Glasier to Andreas Scheu, 25 May 1893, Socialist League Collection.

66 Lowe, *op cit*, p 122.

67 *Labour Leader*, June 1893.

68 *Ibid*, March 1893.

69 Paolo Vestri, 'The Rise of Reformism', *Radical Scotland*, April-May 1984.

70 *Ibid*.

71 *Justice*, 31 March 1888.

The Battle of George Square

Extracted from W Gallagher 1936 *Revolt on the Clyde*, London
(Lawrence and Wishart), 232–36.

. . . In the meantime the main body was closing in on the police across the
square and forcing them right back into the Building.

Inside, we had been taken from the quadrangle into one of the corridors
where we were able to sit down. We didn't know what was happening or how
the fight was going, except that, in the early stages, workers were brought in
hurt and bleeding to receive first aid or hospital treatment. Then after a bit, the
workers ceased coming and policemen were carried in instead. We knew then
that things were not going all the one way.

The police who were with us knew it too and they didn't look so good. Bailie
Whitehead came along while we were sitting there and said 'How are you
feeling?' 'Fine!' I replied. 'Could I get you a glass of whisky?' he asked me. 'No,
thank you, Jimmy,' I answered. 'You know I never touch it.' 'I know, I know,'
he said, 'but it wouldn't do you any harm just now.' After a word or two more
he went off, then the policeman who had tried to smash my face with his baton
said, 'You should have taken it, Willie, and gi'ed it to me.' I looked at him. He
was white and nervous. 'By Christ,' I said, 'I believe you could do with it.' 'I
could,' was his frank reply.

But now the battle was coming near the chamber itself. We were removed
from the corridor to a room upstairs, where we were shut in with several
policemen. These policemen were glad to be out of it and were anxious to be on
friendly terms with us. Anyone who wanted could get in to see us. The first
visitors were Wheatley and Rosslyn Mitchell. Some remarks were made about
our personal condition and then Wheatley informed us that we didn't have to
worry about anything, that Mr. Mitchell would take charge of our affairs.

'Not mine,' I said. 'I've had some. I'll look after my own affairs and if I go to
quod I'll know what I'm going for.' That was the finish for me and Mr. Mitchell.

A few minutes later 'Jock' McBain came in to see us with his head bandaged.
He informed us that the police had been driven right up against and into the
chambers. They wanted the crowd to march to Glasgow Green for a great
protest demonstration there. But they wouldn't leave without word from us.

'Would we go out and speak from the balcony?' This we eventually did, and the strikers formed up and marched off to Glasgow Green.

Had we been capable of planning beforehand, or had there been an experienced revolutionary leadership of these great and heroic masses, instead of a march to Glasgow Green there would have been a march to Maryhill Barracks. For while troops, mostly young raw recruits, with tanks, machineguns and barbed wire were being brought forward for the encirclement of Glasgow, the soldiers of Maryhill were confined to barracks and the barrack gates were kept tightly closed. If we had gone there we could easily have persuaded the soldiers to come out and Glasgow would have been in our hands.

That night Shinwell was arrested and during the following days Harry Hopkins, George Ebury of the B.S.P., young Brennan and several others were brought in. We were all taken to Duke Street Prison.

On the Saturday morning the troops marched with all the paraphernalia of war and took possession of the city.

The *Herald* for February 8 commenting on these developments said:

> The panic of the civic and national authorities can only be explained thus.
> They actually believed a Spartacus coup was planned to start in Glasgow,
> and they were prepared to suppress it at all costs.

This is correct. A rising was expected. A rising should have taken place. The workers were ready and able to effect it; *the leadership had never thought of it.*

All the London newspapers sent up special correspondents to write up the 'revolt'. They came in to find the military in control and the leaders of the 'revolt' safe behind the bars. One of these special correspondents was Siegfried Sassoon, the young poet who, while showing exceptional bravery as a soldier, distinguished himself by his fierce hatred of and opposition to the war.

What an experience! There he was just a youngster, with all the desire of creative genius surging up within him – in the midst of the 'abomination of desolation', mud and slime – and blood – all churned up into an awful 'Devil's Broth'. Destruction all around, destruction and death. Mad, searing, shrieking death, while at home the mothers, wives and sisters were poisoned by a continuous stream of unholy lies about the glory of a 'holy' war.

From out of his scarred and wounded soul came the cry:

> O German mother dreaming by the fire,
> While you are knitting socks to send your son,
> His face is trodden deeper in the mud.

As I read that I had a vision of the mothers of all nations searching the shell-torn battlefronts for their children and as they gathered up the broken, tortured bodies, they cursed in their bitter agony the criminal gang that had sent their young to such a death.

With intense hatred of the social system responsible for the past black years, he came to Glasgow ready to welcome a change whatever course it took.

While in Duke Street Prison where we were committed to await trial, bail having been refused, I received a short note from Sassoon, dated February 7, which read:

> Dear Gallacher,
> I was very sorry to have been unable to see you yesterday. I should have enjoyed a talk with you – even through a grating! Best of luck.
> > Yours sincerely,
> > Siegfried Sassoon.

He, like a good many others, was sadly disappointed at the turn of events. So many were not only expecting, but hoping, that a rising would take place in Glasgow.

A week later the strike was called off and the Clyde settled down to its normal life once more. Two weeks after that a Judge in Chambers granted bail of £300 for the principal leaders with lesser amounts for the others. When we came out of Duke Street Prison we found Glasgow still showing the 'scars of war'. All around the centre of the city, shop fronts were boarded up. Despite its short duration the fight had been a costly one.

From Independent Collier to Militant Miner: Tradition and change in the trade union consciousness of the Scottish miners, 1874– 1929

Extracted from Alan Campbell 1989 *Scottish Labour History Society Journal* 24, 8–23.

INTRODUCTION

This article attempts to survey the changes which occurred in the trade union consciousness of the Scottish miners during the decades between the 1870s and the 1920s.[1] Our period of study is marked at one extreme by the collapse of the miners' unions after the failure of strikes to resist huge wage cuts in 1874; it is bounded some fifty or so years later by the election of a Communist Party leadership among the Scottish miners. In 1927 William Allan, a prominent young communist, was elected secretary of both the Lanarkshire Miners' County Union (LMCU) and the federal National Union of Scottish Mine Workers (NUSMW) while his Fife comrade John Bird secured the presidency of the national union against Robert Smillie, the veteran socialist; these communist gains were further reflected in the results of the executive elections of the Fife and Lanark County Unions. In a complex series of manoeuvres, the non-communist leaders of the Scottish miners succeeded in preventing the newly elected communists from taking up national office. In an atmosphere of bitter acrimony and organisational chaos, a communist-led breakaway union, the United Mineworkers of Scotland (UMS) was established in 1929.

Previous historians have paid considerable attention to particular facets of this process of change between 1874 and 1929. For example, Fred Reid has analysed Keir Hardie's conversion from the values of Liberalism and the 'independent collier' to socialism.[2] Historians of the Communist Party and its industrial arm, the Minority Movement have paid some attention to the formation of the UMS within the context of national and international communism, and there are unpublished accounts of industrial relations in the Scots coal industry after 1926.[3]

However, it is important to bear in mind that by the mid-1920s, a cadre of communist activists with a significant popular base was already established in the largest county unions of Lanarkshire and Fife. Any analysis which takes this as its unproblematic starting point is necessarily incomplete. What is lacking from these existing accounts is an attempt to go beyond either a geographically or chronologically restricted institutionalism and locate the emergence of a communist politics among the Scots miners within a longer, overarching analysis of changes in the industry, the composition of the workforce, and in the trade union cultures of the coalfield.[4] Only by adopting such a perspective can we hope to explain the Communist victories in 1927 or understand the virulence and deeply-rooted nature of the disputes within the miners' unions which was their consequence.

A TYPOLOGY OF TRADE UNION CULTURES IN THE SCOTS COALFIELDS

In attempting to outline the main features of such an analysis, this article examines the consciousness of trade union activists among the Scottish miners by reference to three ideal-typical orientations to union activity: the 'independent collier', the 'bureaucratic reformist' and the 'militant miner'. The components of these ideal types are summarised schematically in Figure 1.

The writer and others have analysed the miners' unions in Scotland for the earlier years of the nineteenth century by reference to the work culture of the 'independent collier'.[5] This culture informed the policies of successive Scots controls on the supply of labour and collective restriction of coal output to maintain prices and therefore wages. Although these policies displayed a considerable tenacity into the twentieth century, their failure to prevent wage reductions in the collapsing coal market of 1874 and the subsequent rout of the miners' unions have been described as the 'crisis of the independent collier'.[6] (That year also marked the zenith of the career of Alexander Macdonald, the secretary of successive Scots miners' unions and the embodiment of the strategies associated with the independent collier, when he was elected to parliament as one of the first two 'Lib-Lab' MPs.)[7]

As we outline below, the failure of the policies of the independent collier led to 'bureaucratic reformism', with its goal of state regulation of the industry, coming to dominate the consciousness of Scottish miners' leaders from the 1880s onwards. The years immediately preceding the First World War marked the emergence of our third ideal type.[8] Although the government's acceptance of the principle of a minimum wage after the first national miners' strike in 1912 and the imposition of state control of the mines during the war can be seen as significant fulfilments of the aspirations of bureaucratic reformism, they also created strong oppositional currents within the miners' unions. The creation of a revolutionary-led reform committee movement during the war was to provide the nucleus of the Minority Movement in the mid-1920s. The experience of the war, it will be argued, was a crucial moment in the transformation of the consciousness of a section of the Scots miners.

These ideal types represent at best a skeletal summary of the components of the miners' consciousness, and we readily acknowledge their crudity. Bureaucratic reformism, for example, encompassed not only the anti-war Robert Smillie, (sometimes described by labour historians as exemplifying the 'militant reformism' of the immediate post-war years), but also David Gilmour, the conservatively respectable pro-war secretary of the LMCU and James Brown, the Ayrshire miners' leader who reflected many of the cultural values of the traditional Scots colliers.[9] Nevertheless, all shared an ideological commitment to political reformism – both Brown and Smillie were Labour MPs – coupled with a bureaucratic trade union practice. Despite their bluntness as analytical tools, it is intended that these categories will assist in conceptualising the ideological clashes and cultural crosscurrents which developed within the Scots coalfields.

We should also emphasise that the relationship between ideology and the labour process indicated in Figure 1 was not a simple nor a reductionist one. Indeed, the impact of mechanisation in the years prior to the First World War initially evoked a reaffirmation of 'exclusive' policies associated with the independent collier. Therefore although our ideal types display a chronological sequence in their emergence, it is not suggested that they were historically discrete and all three orientations can be discerned as coexisting or competing within the miners' unions during the early decades of the twentieth century. It is suggested, however, that struggles for control of the labour process and the contours of industrial concentration conditioned the plausibility of the differing industrial and political strategies advocated by our ideal types. We begin, therefore, by describing the context of the Scots mining industry.

THE SCOTTISH COAL INDUSTRY

We are mainly concerned here with Lanarkshire and Fife, the largest and second largest coal producing areas in Scotland at this time, employing approximately 55,000 and 23,000 workers respectively in 1919. Space does not permit any detailed account of the economic history of these coalfields but it is relevant to draw attention to a number of structural features which are significant for our later analysis. Firstly, the pattern of colliery ownership varied considerably in its degree of concentration. In Lanarkshire, a few very large companies were surrounded by many small companies owning only one or two mines. The later development of the eastern coalfields led to a more concentrated industrial structure so that by the mid-1920s, Fife and Clackmannanshire were dominated by four large companies.[10]

We should also note that individual collieries in Lanarkshire remained small by the standards of other British coalfields. By 1927, the average number employed per mine in Lanarkshire was only 193, compared with 364 in Fife; the British average was 362.[11] The averages conceal a wide range however. In 1919 some five and a half thousand miners worked in the four pits employing more than 1,000 workers in the Blantyre and Bothwell districts of Lanarkshire.

The generally small scale of the mines in the large Lanarkshire coalfield was reflected in mining technique. The division of labour was relatively undeveloped and the Scots collier remained more of an all-round, underground tradesman in the early years of the twentieth century than his counterparts in other British coalfields. Such features helped perpetuate the traditional underground autonomy of the independent collier. However such autonomous job control was increasingly contested by employers, particularly in the larger collieries, following the introduction of coal cutting machinery after 1900. By 1919, almost a third of Scottish output was cut mechanically. The more complex production cycle necessitated closer supervision and greater division of labour. A further consequence was the deskilling of the hewers at the coalface since the skilled work of 'holing' or undercutting was now done by machinery.[12]

THE EMERGENCE OF BUREAUCRATIC REFORMISM

Trade union organisation had been characterised for much of the 19th century by a succession of short-lived federations of local unions established on the cyclical upswing of the coal market. These sought to maintain wage levels through restriction of output and control of entry to the trade, but were then destroyed during strikes to resist wage reductions when the market declined. However the repetition of defeat finally prompted union activists to contemplate alternative, or at least additional, strategies to the traditional attempts to regulate the markets for coal and labour.

The 1880s saw a revival of attempts to organise anew the Scottish miners' unions in which socialists such as Keir Hardie and Robert Smillie played a prominent part. By 1913, 80% of Scots miners were union members.[13] What were the policies of these new unions? In response to the weakness of the Scots miners' organisations and the failure of the policies of the independent collier, socialist miners adopted a strategy of legislative reform based on independent labour representation. Their programme included a state-enforced restriction of output through a legal eight hour day, state insurance for miners (to be financed out of nationalised mineral royalties), nationalisation of the mines, and state arbitration of wage disputes in the coal industry.[14]

While such a socialist political programme clearly represented a break with the older Lib-Lab tradition, we should note that in their everyday practices the Scottish miners' unions only slowly abandoned the policies derived from the independent collier. Thus in 1906 the Scottish miners' conference voted not only for nationalisation of the mines, but also to campaign for a two or three year apprenticeship.[15] The persistence of traditional union orientations, and in particular the defence of skill, was most clearly seen in the reactions to mechanisation. For example, in response to fears over the employment of boys at low wages in machine sections, a resolution was passed at the 1910 Scottish Miners' Federations (SMF) conference 'with a view to protect the trade' which sought to revive the traditional system whereby boys entering the mines were permitted to put out only a proportion of a man's output. Not only was the resolution carried unanimously, discussion of it re-emphasised a further theme from the consciousness of the independent collier when one delegate declared that 'if the trade were a trade . . . a full apprenticeship should be served, of say, four years at face before a workman was entitled to claim full wages'.[16] The following year, the conference agreed to impose a heavy entrance fee on all unskilled workers entering the mines.[17]

The greater productivity of machinery also threatened wages and jobs. In 1914, the SMF Executive sought to resist a proposed reduction in the statutory minimum wage, by restricting output to a four days week. Smillie stated that 'if the owners could not regulate prices owing to the insane competition, they would have to attempt it themselves, with a view to protecting the 7/- minimum . . . it would stiffen prices and kill mad competition'.[18] This was more the authentic voice of the independent collier than of reformist socialism, as the editor of the *Colliery Guardian* recognised when he described it as nothing 'but the recrudescence . . . of the ca' canny policy'.[19]

The reasons for the Scots miners' continued adherence to their traditional union policies can be sought both in the unchanged nature of the labour process until 1900 and in the uneven introduction of mechanisation thereafter. A further factor was the failure of bureaucratic *reformism* as an electoral strategy. Despite the repeated efforts of Scots miners' leaders in parliamentary elections, starting with Keir Hardie's pioneering attempt at Mid-Lanark in 1888, by 1914 only one – William Adamson – had been elected an MP. The goal of nationalisation of the mines seemed a distant dream. But in the face of mechanisation and growing monopolisation, the policies of the independent collier were likely to be even more ineffectual in the 20th century than they had proved in the 19th. However, an alternative conception of trade unionism, which took account of both these processes, began to emerge in opposition to the *bureaucratic* reformism of the existing miners' leadership.

THE GROWTH OF THE REFORM COMMITTEES

The unions which had been built up since the 1880s were distinguished from their predecessors by their permanence and their county-wide coverage. As a consequence they were the first among the Scots miners to move away from the 'primitive democracy' of the local district unions and employ a permanent staff of full-time officials. The nurturing of stable bargaining relationships with employers and the need for careful stewardship of the finances of the recently established unions by this new bureaucracy led to conflicts with sections of the membership.

The first expression of anti-bureaucratic sentiments is found in 1912. It took place against a background of syndicalist agitation in the British coalfields and dissatisfaction with the outcome of the first national miners' strike which had sought a national minimum wage but had succeeded in securing only district minima. A demonstration in Hamilton, which had been organised by a 'Miners' Indignation and Reform Committee', was addressed by a number of speakers including WF Hay of South Wales, one of the authors of 'The Miners' Next Step'. The meeting called for a reconstruction of the Lanarkshire County Union 'in order that the miners of the county might have more say in their own affairs' and demanded re-election of all agents and their exclusion from executive positions.[20] The demonstration was brought to an abrupt end by a sudden thunderstorm, and nothing more was heard of this committee. But the motivation behind it re-emerged in 1917.

In August of that year about a hundred miners met in Hamilton to form the Lanarkshire miners' reform committee. The aims of the committee included: a repudiation of nationalisation and the demand for direct control of the mines by the miners; 'the methods of the union to be based on the principle of class

struggle'; the annual election of agents and officials, who would attend the
executive in a purely consultative capacity; the establishment of pit committees
to handle local disputes; the organisation of all men and women working in the
coal industry within one union; and that the union purchase a building 'for the
purpose of educating trade unionists in Social Science'.[21]

At least twenty four branches of the Lanarkshire Union affiliated to the
committee (out of a total of 126) and it was claimed that active minorities
existed in the majority of branches.[22] By October 1917 a Fife miners' reform
committee had been formed, and similar committees were established in Stirling
and the Lothians.[23] One former member recalled the Fife committee as being 'a
fairly loose organisation' of activists which met monthly to co-ordinate support
for militant policies among the branches.[24] In Lanarkshire, the reform committee played a more leading role in campaigns against rising food prices and
conscription.

In August 1917 the cost of living index stood at 80% above the figure at the
outbreak of war, whereas Scottish miners' wages had been advanced only 43%.
In June of that year, a Lanarkshire Miners' Union delegate from Blantyre who
was a prominent member of the reform committee, had won the delegates'
support for a one day strike against food profiteering.[25] In August, some 50,000
Lanarkshire miners struck work and attended meetings which condemned the
high cost of provisions. The following year, the reform committee organised
unofficial strikes in the Blantyre district demanding 'a more equitable distribution of the food supplies'.[26]

At the Blantyre and Coalburn mass meetings in August, several thousand
miners had also passed resolutions threatening strike action against the further
extension of conscription.[27] Although almost 36,000 Scottish miners – 26.8%
of the industry's workforce – had rallied to the colours by August 1915, as the
war continued, opposition to it increased, particularly after the Government
withdrew the exemption from conscription from younger miners in the summer
of 1917. In 1918, 23 of the Lanarkshire unions' branches voted for a 'down
tools' policy if any more miners were conscripted.[28] 1918 also saw a miners'
official lose office as a consequence of the reform movement's agitation when
David Gilmour, the pro-war Lanarkshire Union secretary was dismissed on the
recommendation of a ballot vote of the membership for taking up a Government post on the Labour Advisory Board. In addition to the vote removing
Gilmour from office, there was a majority of 4,400 out of a total vote of 26,000
against the union assisting further in recruitment.[29]

In attempting to explain the emergence of the reform movement we can point
to a number of causes which reverberated through the Scots coalfields at this
time. In the workplace, we have already alluded to the problems associated with

mechanisation, conscription and the cost of living. In the mining communities there was increasing dissatisfaction on the housing question. Housing and sanitation provision in the Scottish mining areas, particularly Lanarkshire, had been appalling before the outbreak of war; with the subsequent expansion of population associated with the munitions industry in the Clyde valley, overcrowding became intolerable.

A vital factor in focusing these grievances and imbuing them with a political content was the agitational intervention of revolutionary socialists such as John Maclean and his 'first lieutenant' James MacDougall. As is well known, Maclean had conducted lectures on Marxism in Glasgow and throughout Scotland for a number of years prior to the outbreak of war and was the leading campaigner for the Scottish Labour College which was established in 1916. Although considerable debate has taken place concerning his influence on the shop stewards movement in Glasgow, his significance (and that of Mac-Dougall) for the miners' reform movement has only recently been emphasised.[30] Both had established Marxist education classes in the Lanarkshire and Fife coalfields before the war, and they had also established links with the unofficial reform movement in South Wales: MacDougall recalled being 'indoctrinated by one of its founders' who toured Fife during the Cambrian Combine dispute in 1910; at the invitation of the Cambrian strikers, Maclean conducted a week's campaign in the Rhondda the following year.[31] Maclean's commitment to industrial unionism was a continuous feature of his political life (although one often neglected by his biographers). Unlike the South Wales syndicalists, however, he combined demands for industrial unionist reforms with Marxist political action.[32] A further source of industrial unionist strategy was the presence in Lanarkshire of miners who had been members of the United Mine Workers in the USA and Canada.[33] One of Maclean's 'principal assistants' was George Pettigrew, a former UMW official in British Columbia who had played a prominent role in the Vancouver Island miners' strike of 1912–14.[34]

MacDougall had been jailed in 1916 for anti-war activity and had suffered a nervous breakdown during his imprisonment. Upon his release in 1917, Maclean secured him a job working as a pithead labourer at a mine in Blantyre.[35] As his health improved, he threw himself back into political activity and was the leading figure in the Lanarkshire reform committee. It was probable, concluded Scottish Command's military intelligence summary after the Lanarkshire miners voted against assisting recruitment in 1918, 'that many of these miners have been influenced by James MacDougall who has recently been very active in that part of the country'.[36] By the winter of 1917, MacDougall was teaching six classes each week in Lanarkshire while Maclean was tutor for four in Fife; the following year, 1,500 students were enrolled in

Scottish Labour College classes in the counties of Lanark, Renfrew, Dumbarton and Fife.[37] In January 1919, Maclean announced himself to be the 'appointed spokesman of the unofficial miners' movement' and added that he was as proud of this position as he was of being the Glasgow consul of the Bolshevik government.[38] Later that year military intelligence sources lamented that:

> for some considerable time now the working class interest in sociological, economic and historical subjects has been entirely directed by the extremists and 'unofficial' party[39]

The reform committee movement, under the guidance of such teachers and their students, drew upon Marxism to make sense of the changes taking place within their industry and their unions. For example, George Russell, the treasurer of the Lanarkshire committee, had been a member of Maclean's Glasgow economics class, and James Ferguson, a member of the committee was the tutor of a class in industrial history at Blantyre.[40] The manifesto of the Lanarkshire reform committee, of which 50,000 were circulated, drew attention to changes in technology and the growing monopolisation within the Scottish coal industry; it argued that while the formation of the Lanarkshire Miners' Union had been a progressive step in the 1890s, 'there is no such thing as finality in working class organisation' and that 'nothing can cope with the highly trustified condition of the British mining industry' but an amalgamation of all existing unions into one industrial union.[41]

The height of the reform committee's activities took place in the early months of 1919. At the end of January, against the background of a shipbuilding and engineering workers' strike on Clydeside for a 40 hour week and the Miners' Federation demanding that the government introduce a 30 hour week and full nationalisation, a widespread unofficial strike by Fife miners broke out over the surface workers' hours.[42] The Fife reform committee broadened it into a demand for the Miners' Federation claim.

This was sufficient for the Lanarkshire committee to initiate a wave of unofficial strikes in support of the MFGB's demands. Mass pickets brought out a number of pits which did not respond to the committee's call. As MacDougall later recalled, 'it could scarcely have been called peaceful picketing'.[43] On the night of 31st January, for example, in scenes reminiscent of Zola's *Germinal*, columns of pickets had marched from Tollcross and Blantyre to Craighead and Hamilton Palace collieries where they broke into the lamp cabins and smashed the lamps, before dispersing before police baton charges.[44] On the evening of the 29th several thousand miners had demonstrated outside the Lanarkshire union offices to demand the strike be made official. A 'score of young men' forced their way into the offices and took control, allegedly compelling the officials into handing over the keys at gunpoint, and informing them that henceforth they were going to 'run the show'. Reform committee leaders addressed the crowd from the building's balcony and the demonstrators sang 'The Red Flag'. Under this duress, the union leaders agreed to make the strike official. However, they condemned it and the committee and demanded a return to work as soon as they could safely do so from the security of an office in Edinburgh. A ballot of the Fife miners supported a return to work by the narrow majority of 724 out of a total vote of over 13,000 and after a week the strike movement in Fife and Lanarkshire collapsed.[45]

The Scottish militants had been under no illusion that they could achieve anything in isolation from the rest of the British coalfields: 'The general strike cannot last very long' wrote MacDougall in the *Call* of the 6th February. 'That is its very nature. Either the strike will rapidly extend over the whole of Britain or it must be terminated'. But their organisational links with other coalfields and with the Clyde engineers were too embryonic to achieve such co-ordinated action. Although MacDougall had visited South Wales at the end of 1918, and AJ Cook had completed a propaganda tour of Lanarkshire in January 1919 – no preparation had been made to spread the strikes there, perhaps because of their spontaneous origin.[46] Similarly, when unofficial strikes broke out in South Wales at the end of March over the 'vagueness' of the Government's assurances on the Miners' Federations' claims, there was no echo of them in Scotland.[47]

Moreover, the base of support for the reform committees was very unevenly distributed within Scotland. It is significant that the reform committee's strong-holds in Lanarkshire were in the large, highly mechanised pits around Hamilton, Burnbank and Blantyre, and in the recently exploited coal seams of Douglas and Coalburn. Significant too that Marxist education classes had been conducted at Burnbank since 1908 and Coalburn since 1912. Similarly, the Fife Committee was strong at Bowhill, the largest pit in the coalfield, where Maclean had taught a class since 1910 and for which 100 miners enrolled in 1918.[48] But as we have seen, the technical and economic development of the Scots coal industry was extremely uneven. In the smaller coalmines of the Larkhall district, for example, class relations continued to display the collaborative tendencies within the culture of the independent collier. Thus in September 1917, when the manager of Dykehead colliery was promoted to company assistant manager, his workforce presented him with a gold watch and well-filled wallet and sang 'Auld lang syne'.[49]

As well as these structural divisions, we should note also the differential impact of the war upon the Scots miners' militancy. We have described the opposition to conscription led by the reform movement and this clearly had a generational dimension. The Manpower Bill and the call for a further 50,000 miners for the army in January 1918, aroused, in the words of a Scottish military intelligence summary, 'an element of opposition among the younger men affected'. Protest meetings in Dunfermline and Shettleston were attended by 700 and 1,000 young miners respectively; in Hamilton 3,000 young miners demonstrated outside the union offices 'where the socialists harangued the crowd'.[50]

In contrast was the involvement of the miners' union officials in the machinery of conscription – for example, the four colliery recruiting courts in Scotland which enforced the conscription regulations each contained two union officials and two employers' representatives. Union committees of 'middle-aged or elderly miners' at each colliery superintended the ballots to select recruits.[51]

We must also bear in mind that the reform committee militants were active in a particularly youthful workforce. The effect of the expansion of the coal industry up to 1919 upon the demography of its labour force meant that in 1911 and 1921 over a third of the Scottish miners were under 25 years old, and in the latter year almost 60% were under the age of 35.[52] A crucial formative influence upon this new generation was the experience of the War, whether it was spent in the pits or in the trenches.

FROM REFORM COMMITTEES TO THE UNITED MINEWORKERS OF SCOTLAND

As a result of the debacle of the 1919 strikes and the government's shrewd payment of the Sankey award later that year, the reform movement among the Scots miners went into some decline. It also underwent several changes of nomenclature and organisation. Maclean and MacDougall were prominent in the establishment of a short-lived 'One Union Movement' in 1919.[53] In 1921 the various unofficial 'rebel' groups within the Scots miners' unions merged into the mining section of the National Workers' Committee Movement, which was committed to supporting the newly formed Communist Party, and which became its industrial arm, the Minority Movement, in 1924.[54] However, following the crushing defeat of the miners' unions in the three month lockout of 1921, the situation in the Scots coalfields was scarcely conducive to union militancy as unemployment rose and wages plummeted.

Despite the general weakness of trade union organisation and divisions within the unofficial movement (a breakaway Reform Union was established in Fife against the advice of the Communist Party) Marxist education classes were maintained and expanded.[55] In 1920–21, nine full-time students attended the Scottish Labour College under the tuition of Maclean and others; seven were miners, including William Allan and John Bird.[56] In the coalfields, evening classes continued under SLC auspices. In 1923, there were seventeen such courses in the Lanarkshire coalfield, including one in Blantyre taught by William Allan; in Fife in 1925 there were 10.[57]

The effects of such propaganda and the continuing inability of the existing union leadership to defend wages or maintain union organisation were reflected in the Lanarkshire union elections in 1925. William Allan, by then a leading Communist and Minority Movement activist, secured a significant share – 42.4% – of the votes in a straight contest with William S Small for the post of General Secretary. It is noteworthy that Allan received most support in areas where the Reform Committee had previously been strong. Of the seventeen branches where he received 60% or more of the votes, sixteen were within a circle six miles in diameter based on the Hamilton, Blantyre, Bothwell and Motherwell districts; the 17th was Douglas.[58]

FIGURE 1   IDEAL TYPES OF ORIENTATION TO TRADE UNIONISM IN THE COALFIELDS

Ideal Type	'Independent Collier'	'Bureaucratic Reformist'	'Militant Miner'
Historical Period	18th Century...1930s	1880s..	
Union Recruitment	Exclusive	Open	Open including Miners' 'Womenfolks'
Union Organisation	Federations of local and district unions	Federations of County Unions	One Industrial Miners' Union
Industrial Relations Methods	Unilateral regulation of recruitment and output (and hence wages) by hewers	Collective bargaining within context of State regulation of hours and minimum wage	Militant waging of all disputes as expression of class struggle
Politico-industrial Goal	Co-operative production	Nationalisation of the mines	Socialist Revolution involving socialisation of the mines
Political affiliation	Liberal	Independent Labour	Communist
Typified by	Alexander Macdonald (1821–1881) General Secretary Scottish Coal and Ironstone Miners' Assoc 1855–1881 Elected liberal MP for Stafford 1874	Robert Smillie (1857–1940) President NUSMW 1894–1912, 1922–1928 President MEGB 1912–1921	Willie Allan (1900–1970) President M OD General Secretary NUSMW 1927 General Secretary UMS 1929–31
'Corresponding' Stage of Labour	Hand mining	Hand and Machine mining	Machine mining
Process and Mine Ownership Structure	Small Mining Enterprises Local Markets	Larger Mining companies National Market	Monopoly Combines International Markets

NOTES

1 This article is a revised and shortened version of a paper first delivered at the British Sociological Association 1988 Annual Conference. I am grateful to Rob Duncan and Bill Knox for their helpful comments on it.

2 F Reid, 'Keir Hardie's Conversion to Socialism', in A Briggs and J Saville (eds) *Essays in Labour History*, vol 2 (1971) and *Keir Hardie: The Making of a Socialist* (1978).

3 LJ MacFarlane, *The British Communist Party: its origin and development until 1929* (1966), pp 265–274; R Martin, *Communism and the British Trade Unions, 1924–1933* (Oxford, 1969), pp 127–9; N Branson, *History of the Communist Party of Great Britain 1927–1941* (1985), pp 41–2; P Long, 'The Economic and Social History of the Scottish Coal Industry, 1925–39', unpublished PhD thesis, University of Strathclyde, 1978, ch 12; M Sime, 'The United Mineworkers of Scotland' and 'The United Mineworkers of Scotland – an appraisal of its origins'. I am grateful to Martin Sime for allowing me to photocopy these unpublished papers.

4 The only study which attempts such an approach is Stuart McIntyre's excellent analysis of Lumphinnans in Fife, but it is deliberately confined to this atypical 'Little Moscow'. See S McIntyre, *Little Moscow: communism and working-class militancy in inter-war Britain* (1980).

5 For the 'independent collier' see: A Campbell and F Reid, 'The Independent Collier in Scotland' in R Harrison (ed) *Independent Collier: the coal miner as archetypal proletarian reconsidered* (Hassocks, 1978); AB Campbell, *The Lanarkshire Miners: a social history of their trade unions, 1775–1874* (Edinburgh, 1979), especially ch 2.

6 F Reid, 'Alexander MacDonald and the Crisis of the Independent Collier, 1872–74' in Harrison, op cit.

7 GM Wilson, *Alexander MacDonald, Leader of the Miners* (Aberdeen, 1982).

8 The suggestion of this 'new tradition' was originally made by Stuart McIntyre, op cit p 169.

9 For biographical details of Gilmour, see the *Hamilton Advertiser*, 25th August 1917; for details of James Brown see entry in W Knox, *Scottish Labour Leaders 1918–39: A Biographical Dictionary* (Edinburgh, 1984) and A Gammie, *From Pit to Palace: The life of the Right Honourable James Brown MP, Lord High Commissioner to the General Assembly of the Church of Scotland* (1931); the latter book is probably the only biography of a trade union leader which has more index entries under 'King, His Majesty the' (11) than to the union (4)!

10 Long thesis, op cit, p 88.

11 Ibid, pp 483–4.

12 For a fuller discussion of mechanisation in Lanarkshire, see A Campbell, 'Colliery Mechanisation in Lanarkshire', *Bulletin of the Society for the Study of Labour History*, no 49, Autumn 1984, and 'The Independent Collier and Mechanisation in the Lanarkshire Coalfield, 1900–1914' in G Schmidt (ed), *Bergbau im Grosbritannien und in Ruhrgebiet* (Bochum, 1985); for Fife, see McIntyre, op cit p 153.

13 R Church, *The History of the British Coal Industry, vol 3*, p 693.

14 Reid, (1971), op cit p 42.

15 *Glasgow Herald*, 29th December 1906.

16 *Proceedings of the Seventeenth Annual Conference*, Scottish Miners' Federation, 28th-31st December 1910, National Library of Scotland (hereafter NLS).

17 *Glasgow Herald*, 18th August 1911.

18 *Colliery Guardian*, 17th July 1914.

19 Ibid, 31st July 1914.

20 *Hamilton Advertiser*, 3rd August 1912. Another speaker was 'J Dougherty, Northumberland' who was a sympathiser with the South Wales movement, see David Egan, 'The Unofficial Reform Committee and the Miners' Next Step', *Llafur*, vol 2, no 3, Summer 1978, p 77.

21 *Plebs*, October 1917.

22 *Call*, 11th April 1918, JD MacDougall, 'The Scottish Coalminer', *Nineteenth Century*, December 1927, pp 768–9.

23 *Plebs*, October 1917, JD MacDougall, ibid.

24 I MacDougall, *Militant Miners*, (Edinburgh, 1981), pp 18–19.

25 *IMCU Minutes of Council Meetings*, 30th June, 12th August 1917, NLS Deposit 227/35.

26 *Bellshill Speaker*, 11th October 1918.

27 *Call*, 9th and 23rd August 1917.

28 WR Scott and J Cunnison, *The Industries of the Clyde Valley during the War* (Oxford, 1924), p 29; *Bellshill Speaker*, 24th August 1917; *Hamilton Advertiser*, 6th April 1918.

29 *Call*, 15th August 1918; *Hamilton Advertiser*, 23rd August, 2nd March 1918.

30 W Kendall, *The Revolutionary Movement in Britain 1900–1921* (1969); J Hinton, *The First Shop Stewards' Movement* (1973); I MacLean, *The Legend of Red Clydeside* (Edinburgh, 1983); N Milton, John MacLean (1973) makes a number of references to MacLean's agitation among the miners, but it is only recently that David Howell has indicated the significance of this for an evaluation of MacLean's political strategy. See D Howell, *A Lost Left: three studies in socialism and nationalism* (Manchester, 1986).

31 MacDougall recalls the man as 'Jack Hay', JD MacDougall, op cit p 767. He may have mistakenly meant W E Hay or Jack Hughes, a leading member of the Cambrian Combine Committee; see Egan, op cit pp 78–79. For MacLean's visit to Wales, see Recollections (c 1936) 'written down from the dictation of JD MacDougall' *John MacLean Papers*, NLS Acc 4251, Box 2, File 9, and *Justice*, 29th July 1911.

32 Milton distinguishes MacDougall's support for industrial unionism from MacLean's views (Milton, op cit p 144) but for MacLean's advocacy of industrial unionism see for example *Justice*, 15th April 1911 and 'John MacLean's Electioneer', 7th November 1922, *John MacLean Papers*, NLS Acc 4251, Box 2, File 7; cf Howell, op cit p 162.

33 JD MacDougall, op cit, p 767.

34 Recollections (c 1936) 'written down from the dictation of JD MacDougall', *John MacLean Papers*, NLS Acc 4251, Box 2, File 9. I am grateful to Bill Burrill of Simon Fraser University for providing me with information on Pettigrew.

35 See entry on MacDougall in Knox, op cit.

36 GHW *Intelligence Summaries, Scottish Command*, 19th-25th February, 1918, Public Record Office (hereafter PRO), AIR 1, 560, 16/15/59.

37 Milton, op cit, pp 43, 68; *Plebs*, December 1917; *Call*, 21st March 1918.

38 *Motherwell Times*, 31st January 1919.

39 GHQ *Military Intelligence Summaries, Scottish Command*, 18th-24th May 1919, PRO, AIR 1, 554, 16/15/43.

40 Milton, op cit, 142; *Call*, 4th October 1917; *Glasgow Herald*, 3rd February 1919.

41 'Manifesto of the Lanarkshire Miners' Reform Committee', NLS; *Plebs*, October 1917.

42 For the Fife dispute, *Dunfermline Press*, 25th January, 1919. For the 40 Hour Strike, see Hinton, op cit, MacLean, op cit. MacLean's comments on the insignificance of the 40 Hour Strike are facilitated by him almost totally ignoring the simultaneous events in the coalfields.

43 JD MacDougall, op cit p 772.

44 *Hamilton Advertiser*, 3rd May 1919.

45 Glasgow *Herald*, 27th January-5th February, 1919; *The Times*, 31st January 1919; *Hamilton Advertiser*, 1st and 8th February, 1919; *Colliery Guardian*, 7th February 1919; *Dunfermline Press*, 25th January 1919.

46 *Call*, 23rd and 30th January 1919.

47 M Woodhouse, 'Rank and file movements among the miners of South Wales, 1910–1926', unpublished D Phil Thesis, University of Oxford, 1969, pp 163 et seq.

48 Milton, op cit, pp 43, 68, 71; Recollections (c 1936?) 'written down from the dictation of JD MacDougall; *John MacLean Papers*, NLS, Acc 4251, Box 2, File 9; *Call*, 11th October 1918.

49 *Hamilton Advertiser*, 15th September 1917.

50 *Bellshill Speaker*, 8th February 1918; GHQ *Intelligence Summaries, Scottish Command*, 5th-11th February 1918, PRO, AIR 1, 560.16/15/59.

51 *Third General Report of the Departmental Committee appointed to Inquire into the conditions prevailing in the coalmining industry during the War*, PP 1916 VI, 480; *Bellshill Speaker*, 19th April 1918.

52 Calculated from the *Census of Scotland*, 1911 and 1921.

53 *Worker*, 24th May 1919; *Motherwell Times*, 31st January 1919.

54 *Stirling Journal and Advertiser*, 28th April 1921; R Martin, op cit, p 33.

55 For the Fife Reform Union see Martin, op cit, p 32, McIntyre, op cit, p 155 and I MacDougall, op cit, pp 64–67.

56 I MacDougall, op cit, pp 33–38.

57 *Worker*, 22nd September 1923; *Miner*, 17th January 1925.

58 IMCU *Minutes of Council Meetings*, 1925, NLS Deposit 227/41.

In Search of the 'Lad of Parts': the Mythical History of Scottish Education

Extracted from R Anderson 1985 *History Workshop Journal* 19, 82–104.

I

Other countries may have shown a finer flower of scholarship, but in none has the attitude towards education been so democratic, so thoroughly imbued with the belief that learning is for the whole people, so socialised as to afford the spectacle of the sons of the laird, the minister, and the ploughman, seated on the same bench, taught the same lessons, and disciplined with the same strip of leather.

In no other country has there been in the past the same free path for ability, in whatever rank produced, not only through the schools, but into all the learned professions . . .

Today in our country it is almost true to say that there is no boy or girl of good natural ability, however poor or straitened in circumstances, however remote or isolated the home, who cannot break a way into the mysteries of the highest learning that the Universities supply.

By what steps has such a system of national education developed? Through what onrushes and eddies and backwaters has its stream run? What haltings and advances and retrogressions have marked its onward progress? In what manner has the Scottish educational ideal persisted and grown and expanded with the passage of the centuries? Finally, what defects are still to be removed, what work is still to be done?[1]

This extract from the introduction to a popular history of Scottish education published in 1912 encapsulates a view of its 'democratic' character which has been characteristic of Scottish attitudes from the early 19th century until the present day. Much more than in England, a certain view of the educational past has underlain current controversies, a view which may be called 'mythical' not because it was necessarily untrue, but because it idealized and simplified the facts and had an inspirational or creative function which took on a life of its own. Scots have generally been proud of their education system, tracing its origins back to the days of John Knox, and linking it with more general 'democratic' virtues claimed for Scottish society, such as absence of class feeling and respect for merit and ability rather than social status. According to the historians of the Scottish Church, the First Book of Discipline of 1560, which embodied the educational views of the Reformers,

> both reflected and created the essentially democratic quality of Scottish life, the inherent equality and disregard of wealth and title, and the respect for intellectual achievement, which have distinguished the country from her southern neighbour.[2]

As a small country living in the shadow of a larger neighbour, Scotland has prized its educational system as part of the cluster of institutions and values by which its separate national identity has been maintained, and when the democratic tradition has been invoked, it has often been against the persistent threat of assimilation and 'anglicization'. It has been characteristic to see the democratic virtues as in decline, part of a golden age of Scottish education located in the just-vanished past. Today this type of nostalgia frequently takes a conservative cast, as any reader of the correspondence columns in the Scottish press will know: there was a time – perhaps in the writer's youth, perhaps when he started his teaching career – when Scottish education was the 'envy of the world', and when 'standards', whether of discipline or of academic achievement, were maintained with old-fashioned robustness. In the 19th century, this way of thinking often took a more radical form, and tradition was appealed to in order to resist southern innovations which threatened to make education narrower in scope or more constrained by class distinctions. For the link between 'mythical' thinking and resistance to anglicization means that the content of the myth has changed over the years, reflecting the ways in which the two systems have actually differed at particular times. For a long period, for example, Scotland had a tradition of public provision and state intervention while laissez-faire ideas prevailed in England, and many disputes and complaints arose from the neglect of this Scottish tradition in 'British' legislation. But once English opinion caught up with Scottish in this respect, this aspect of Scottish distinctiveness ceased to be an issue and was forgotten.[3] . . .

[The article then looks at some origins of the myth in the early nineteenth century, and continues]

Collective memory of the Scottish educational past chose to lay the emphasis on the lad of parts, the individual who escaped from his working-class origins through the classics and a university education. But that past also contained some very different traditions, of a communitarian rather than an individualist kind. Why were these forgotten? Partly, no doubt, because the old popular culture was especially linked with groups, notably the handloom weavers, who were the victims of mechanization.[4] Artisan communities declined, and there was no direct link between them and the new working class being formed by the factories; when in due course this industrial working class forged its own vigorous culture, it was not particularly marked by intellectualism. But the lad of parts ideal also prevailed because it suited the kind of stratified educational system thought appropriate for an industrial society, one in which a basic elementary education for the masses co-existed with a small secondary sector for the middle class; allowing a small number of talented children to cross the barrier satisfied the demand for merit to be rewarded, and was not incompatible with retaining a rather mediocre education for those who were not selected. Moreover, it was well suited to the new emphasis in the 19th century on formal educational institutions, carefully regulated, standardized, and age-graded. In the new era of examinations, individual mobility through education depended on special training; behind every lad of parts stood the 'dominie', the teacher who encouraged him and shared in his triumphs. The cult of the lad of parts therefore ministered to the growing self-esteem and professional mystique of the schoolteachers, who came to control the keys of knowledge. For if modern civilization has tended to increase social mobility through education, it has also closed off non-educational channels of mobility by imposing ever greater needs for formal qualifications, and handed power over individual destinies to the authorities who create educational systems and the professionals who staff them.

III

In the middle decades of the 19th century, it is difficult to find much reference to the wider democratic purposes of education in the abundant polemical literature, which concentrated on the practical problems of schooling in the cities or on religious and political controversy. The Disruption of the Church of Scotland in 1843 (creating the rival Free Church) shattered the hope of a revived godly commonwealth, and the clergy, the main purveyors of educational ideology in Scotland, turned their energies to internecine warfare. Only in the 1860s, with the controversies over the Revised Code of 1862 and the various bills which preceded the Scottish Education Act of 1872, did the parish school, whose distinctive character now seemed threatened by the inappropriate application of English policies, again become a focus of sentiment.[5]

In this period, however, there was an important expansion in the literary treatment of Scottish education, especially in the magazines which flourished to serve the middlebrow reader. The parish schools and their 'dominies' often figured in these magazine articles, whose authors could draw on a tradition of the dominie as a village character – socially uncouth but intellectually zealous, naive and unworldly, comic in his classical pedantry yet devoted to his pupils' interests – which went back to Dominie Sampson in Scott's *Guy Mannering*. But even more popular were articles on 'Scottish student life', which appeared in large numbers between the 1850s and the 1870s, using the same themes in a repetitive and derivative way.[6]

For English readers, whose image of a university was formed by Oxford and Cambridge, the Scottish universities had some striking and picturesque features. Apart from St Andrews, they were situated in large towns, and their students lived at home or in lodgings; the authorities did not attempt to control the students' social lives, and teaching took the form of impersonal professorial lectures. Some students were as young as 14, others were in their twenties and thirties, and because university education was cheap they came from wider and lower social strata than the aristocratic undergraduates of England. As an article on Glasgow put it, with some exaggeration:

> A university education in Scotland comes far down in the social scale; and while at the universities of England the great majority of the young men are the sons of gentlemen, in Scotland the vast preponderance consists of sons of farmers, tradesmen, and working men; and of poor lads, without relations or friends, struggling on amid unheard-of difficulties and privations . . . there is really a deep pathos in the story of toil, privation, and resolution, which is the story of many a Glasgow student's college days.[7]

Glasgow probably had more poor students than elsewhere, and the contrast between the old college with its red-gowned students and its grimy and insalubrious surroundings (until the university moved to a new suburban site in 1870) appealed to the literary imagination. But all these accounts emphasized the 'peer and peasant' theme of social diversity combined with intellectual democracy:

Their doors are open to the richest as well as the poorest in the land; and on their benches will be found, side by side, the son of the laird and the son of the cottar, with no social distinction, no badge of rank, but each appreciated by his class and professors according as he displays ability or scholarship.[8]

Most articles too gave a stereotyped picture of the life of the poor students, emphasizing their straitened lives, their lack of social contacts outside the lecture-room, the jobs which they took in the summer to pay for each year's session, and their habit of overworking in their chilly garret lodgings, leading all too often to broken constitutions and an early death. Perhaps their diet also had something to do with this:

> A bag of meal, in which some eggs have been carefully packed, and another of potatoes, with a small kit of salt herrings, form their staple articles of food, on which they will be contented to live during the whole winter, provided they can drink in the words of knowledge that fall from their professors' lips.[9]

Oatmeal had a special place in the legend. At Edinburgh University, a holiday in mid-February was (according to an article of 1894) 'still called by its ancient name of "Meal Monday". It was then that in days of yore the poor student went home for the second supply of meal, ham, and potatoes, on which, like Carlyle, he might board himself through his half-year of plain living and hard work'. In fact, as D. B. Horn has shown, this holiday was a recent innovation, and both the name 'Meal Monday' and its supposed purpose were Victorian inventions.[10]

The wide social and geographical recruitment of the universities was thought to bring special advantages to Scottish life. One result was that the universities

> are the national educational heart of the country. They receive large annual accessions of fresh blood from every corner of the land; and they return it throbbing with new life, to invigorate even the remotest regions, and to quicken the entire intellectual soil. The intellectual circulation is complete. The Universities are in touch with the entire community . . . Those who study there reflect the academic light on those who don't; and all, in some measure, breathe the academic atmosphere.[11]

Daniel Fearon, an English school inspector who reported on Scottish education in the 1860s, claimed similarly that:

> The intensely national and popular character of the Scotch Universities causes their influence to be felt in every part of that wild and rugged

country. In every corner of the kingdom; in the Islands as well as the Highlands; among the shepherds of the Grampians and the fishermen of Argyleshire, as well as among the weavers of Paisley, and the colliers of Ayr and Dumfries, the influence of one or other of the universities is keenly felt, not merely through the connection of their own parochial schoolmasters and the governors of their churches with the universities, but because the cheapness and the elementary character of university instruction renders it accessible to a very large proportion of the population.[12]

There was an element of romanticism in this idea of the universities influencing even those who did not go to them. In practical terms, it was used to justify maintaining graduate teachers and classical instruction even in small rural schools, but it also looks back to the earlier theory of 'kindly' ties linking the classes vertically, and forward to a new mystique of ruralism which, as we shall see, was to appear in the early 20th century.

Another popular argument was that the competitive atmosphere of the universities, and the self-sacrifice demanded of the poorer students, formed a school of character which accounted for the enterprise and worldly success of the Scots, and their role as a nation of empire-builders. At the opening of the new Glasgow University in 1870, John Caird, professor of Divinity, proclaimed that:

The University of Glasgow is . . . an institution . . . which has struck its roots deep into the soil of our national life, and with the other and kindred educational institutions has rendered Scotland, long one of the poorest of European nations in material wealth, one of the foremost in intelligence and civilisation, an institution which has contributed to the formation of that type of character, that sobriety of mind, reasonableness, steadiness, sagacity, sturdy independence, self-reliance, not unrelieved by quiet humour or ungraced by the love of poetry and song – that peculiar combination of qualities, intellectual and moral, which renders the typical Scotchman remarkable all over the world.[13]

These were purple passages, no doubt, but they are no less significant for that, for it is in the clichés of the public platform or the after-dinner speech that the myth of educational democracy (along with other stereotypes of Scottish national character) has particularly flourished.

IV

The university life of Aberdeen received special literary attention. The university
was more closely linked than others in Scotland with its surrounding region, the
north-east, where the parish school system worked with particular vigour. There
were more graduate schoolmasters in the north-east and more classical teaching
in rural schools, whose ambitions were directed towards the large number of
university bursaries at Aberdeen. These were awarded by open competition, and
the annual bursary competition, in which the prestige of schoolmasters and local
communities was at stake as well as the fate of the candidates, became a part of
local folklore. According to one of the many accounts,

> these endowments are open to free universal competition, and are in this
> shape one of the most interesting and remarkable specimens of the ancient
> literary republics, in which each man fought with his brains, and held what
> his brains could achieve for him. Annually, at the competition for bursaries
> in Aberdeen, there assembles a varied group of intellectual gladiators – long
> red-haired Highlanders, who feel trousers and shoes an infringement of the
> liberty of the subject – square-built Lowland farmers – flaxen-haired
> Orcadians, and pale citizens' sons, vibrating between scholarship and the
> tailor's board or the shoemaker's last. Grim and silent they sit for a day,
> rendering into Latin an English essay, and drop away one by one, depositing
> with the judges the evidence of success or failure as the case may be.[14]

According to one Aberdeen professor, the local boys had an advantage in this
contest, for

> the people along the east coast are a different race, with Scandinavian blood
> and larger heads, industrious, careful, and pushing, in marked contrast to
> the naturally lazy, superstitious, Gaelic-speaking race of the north-west
> coast.[15]

Since he was professor of Anatomy, he was presumably an expert on the
question: anthropologically-based theories of racialism, combined with the
application of Darwinism in the social field, gave a new 'scientific' justification
in this period to competitive individualism and the emergence of the fittest from
the struggle between brains.

In 1874 there appeared a novel on Aberdeen student life, *Life at a Northern
University*, by Neil Maclean, the author of one of the magazine articles cited

above. This was not the first fictional treatment of the subject. John Gibson Lockhart's *Peter's Letters to his Kinsfolk* (1819) had already featured Edinburgh students who 'live in a garret upon porridge or herrings',[16] and there were university episodes in Lockhart's *History of Matthew Wald* (1824) and in the Aberdeenshire novels of George Macdonald, such as *Alec Forbes of Howglen* (1865) and *Robert Falconer* (1868). But Maclean's was the only novel devoted entirely to the theme. It was based on his career at King's College in the 1850s, but it also owed something to English university novels like *The Adventures of Mr Verdant Green* (1853–7). Although the hero is prepared for the university by a classic village dominie, he and his friends come from comfortable backgrounds and speak a slangy 'varsity' English. The novel underlines the social distance between them and the poorer students, who remain more purely Scottish. One of these is taken up by the hero and persuaded to leave his garret; but too late, for his health has already been undermined by overwork, and he dies at the end of the book after taking the first prizes in his final examinations. 'Bury me within sight of the old college tower' is his last wish.[17] This theme of early death was a popular one, appearing for example in 'Shon Campbell', a poem about a Highland student written in 1894 which became a favourite Aberdeen student song.[18] In an age when tuberculosis stalked the cities there were some real life examples – like the brother of the Biblical scholar William Robertson Smith, who died in 1866 a few weeks after graduating at Aberdeen with the highest honours – but perhaps they were not as numerous as the Victorian taste for deathbed scenes makes them appear.[19]

Another Aberdeen graduate, William Robertson Nicoll, was the literary entrepreneur who created the 'kailyard' school of literature in the 1890s, and it was his special discovery, 'Ian Maclaren' (the Rev. John Watson, a Presbyterian minister in Liverpool), who popularized the phrase 'lad of parts'.[20] In his collection of stories about the fictional Lowland village of Drumtochty, *Beside the Bonnie Brier Bush* (1894), the 'lad o' pairts', George Howe, is prepared by the village dominie for the university, where he graduates with a triumphant 'double first'. But he is worn out by his endeavours, returns to the village mortally ill, and dies.

> It was a low-roofed room, with a box bed and some pieces of humble furniture, fit only for a labouring man. But the choice treasures of Greece and Rome lay on the table, and on a shelf beside the bed College prizes and medals, while everywhere were the roses he loved. His peasant mother stood beside the body of her scholar son, whose hopes and thoughts she had shared, and through the window came the bleating of distant sheep. It was the idyll of Scottish University life.

The two college friends who came to his funeral were a Harrow-educated aristocrat and a crofter's son from Barra, symbolizing the scholastic unity of pre-industrial Scotland.[21] Apparently Watson based his story on a friend of his own schooldays at Stirling High School, and it is characteristic that he transposed it from this urban secondary school to a mythical rural setting.[22]

Dominies and ministers – lads of parts who had survived to achieve their goal – were prominent in other classics of the kailyard school like James Barrie's *Auld Licht Idylls* (1892) and S. R. Crockett's *The Stickit Minister* (1893): the stickit (failed) minister in Crockett's story had given up his theological studies when TB was diagnosed so that his brother could be sent to the university instead to study medicine, and had returned to the family farm to die. Even George Douglas Brown's *The House with the Green Shutters* of 1901, which turned the kailyard novel on its head by depicting small-town life as an unrelieved saga of greed and brutality, had an inverted lad of parts in the shape of John Gourlay, the central character's son. Instead of being coached by the local dominie, he commutes by train to the nearest High School (as was indeed normal by this time); he gets to Edinburgh University, but fails to make his mark, takes to drink, returns in disgrace, and kills his father in a violent quarrel before himself committing suicide.

Beside the Bonnie Brier Bush was not an original or a distinguished piece of work,[23] but it was an immense best-seller, in America as well as Britain, and made its author famous. It also put the term 'lad of parts' into circulation. This may have been in colloquial use, but I have not found it in discussions of education before 1894; in later years it was often vaguely supposed to go back to John Knox, but this is not the case, and the frequent use of the Scots version 'lad o' pairts' appears to derive from Watson's folksiness, not from any sixteenth or seventeenth-century origin.[24] The phrase 'pregnant parts' can indeed be found earlier; the scientist Lyon Playfair, for example, claimed in 1870 that in the past 'Every presbytery had the pious duty imposed upon it of sending up lads 'of pregnant parts' to the nearest university at the cost of the Church.[25] But I have not found an earlier example of this, and its real origin was perhaps Matthew Arnold's well-known poem *The Scholar-Gypsy* (1853):

> The story of the Oxford scholar poor,
> Of pregnant parts and quick inventive brain . . .

[The remainder of the article discusses later development of the myth, and its relationship to policy in the twentieth century.]

NOTES

1 W. J. Gibson, *Education in Scotland. A Sketch of the Past and the Present*, London 1912, pp. ix-xi.

2 Andrew L. Drummond and James Bulloch, *The Scottish Church 1688–1843. The Age of the Moderates*, Edinburgh 1973, p. 187.

3 R. D. Anderson, 'Education and the State in Nineteenth-Century Scotland', *Economic History Review*, 2nd series, vol. 36 no 4, 1983, pp. 518–34. Other recent discussions of the Scottish tradition and its 'mythical' aspects are J. Gray, A. F. McPherson and D. Raffe, *Reconstructions of Secondary Education. Theory, Myth and Practice since the War*, London 1983, pp. 36–46; Andrew McPherson, 'An Angle on the Geist: Persistence and Change in the Scottish Educational Tradition', in Humes and Paterson, *Scottish Culture and Scottish Education*, pp. 216–43.

4 Smout, *History of the Scottish People*, pp. 395–6; Norman Murray, *The Scottish Hand Loom Weavers 1790–1850: A Social History*, Edinburgh 1978, pp. 161–4.

5 The Revised Code introduced the principle of 'payment by results' for the 'three Rs', which ignored the more advanced teaching often given in Scotland, and assumed that elementary schools were exclusively for the labouring poor. The Act of 1872 abolished parish schools as a distinct category, and created elected school boards to administer all public schools.

6 On the parish schools, examples are [Andrew Halliday], 'My Scotch School', *Cornhill Magazine*, vol. 4, 1861, pp. 220–8; 'A Bundle of Scotch Notes', *All the Year Round*, vol. 14, 1865–6, pp. 349–55; 'Reminiscences of a Scottish Parish School', *Leisure Hour*, vol. 16, 1867, pp. 357–9. On student life, apart from those cited below: 'University Systems – English and Scotch', *British Quarterly Review*, vol. 65, 1877, pp. 305–38; [A. I. Shand], 'North-Country Students', *Cornhill Magazine*, vol. 37, 1878, pp. 452–67; 'Scottish University Students', *All the Year Round*, new series, vol. 24, 1879–80, pp. 80–2.

7 [A. K. H. Boyd], 'College Life at Glasgow', *Fraser's Magazine*, vol. 53, 1856, pp. 509–10.

8 [Neil Maclean], 'University Life in the North of Scotland', *Chambers's Journal*, 4th series, vol. 9, 1872, p. 279. On 'peasant and peer', see also [E. S. Dallas], 'Student Life in Scotland', *Cornhill Magazine*, vol. 1, 1860, pp. 374–5.

9 *Chambers's Journal*, 4th series, vol. 9, 1872, p. 279.

10 'Scottish Student Life', *Chambers's Journal*, 5th series, vol. 11, 1894, p. 596; D. B. Horn, 'Meal Monday', *University of Edinburgh Journal*, vol. 23, no. 1, 1967–8, pp. 63–5.

11 *Educational News*, vol. 18, 1893, pp. 118–9. Similar picture in [A. C. Sellar], 'School and University System in Scotland', *Fraser's Magazine*, vol. 78, 1868, pp. 342–4.

12 *Schools Inquiry Commission. Vol VI. General Reports of Assistant Commissioners*, PP 1867–8 vol. XVIII, part 5, p. 32.

13 *Introductory Addresses Delivered at the Opening of the University of Glasgow, Session 1870–71*, Edinburgh 1870, p. 15.

14 [J. H. Burton], 'Student Life in Scotland', *Blackwood's Magazine*, vol. 77, 1854, pp. 144–5. This closely resembles an early example of the genre, 'The Two Great Northern Universities', *Tait's Edinburgh Magazine*, vol. 3, 1833, pp. 184–7.

15 *Report of the Royal Commission on the Universities of Scotland, Evidence – Part II*, PP

1878 vol. XXXIV, p.16. This theory about 'broad-headed' Aberdonians was still going strong fifty years later: James Ritchie, 'The Genius of the Aberdonian', *Aberdeen University Review*, vol. 15 no. 45, 1928, pp. 204–5.

16 John G. Lockhart, *Peter's Letters to his Kinsfolk*, 3rd edn., Edinburgh 1819, p. 196.

17 Neil N. Maclean, *Life at a Northern University*, 4th edn., Aberdeen 1917, p. 327.

18 *The Scottish Students' Song Book*, 6th edn., London 1897, pp. 11–13. This *Song Book*, which first appeared in 1891, was a product of the new student 'corporate life' of the late 19th century which was making the traditional literary picture obsolete.

19 John S. Black and George Chrystal, *The Life of William Robertson Smith*, London 1912, p. 62.

20 On the kailyard school, see J. H. Millar, *A Literary History of Scotland*, London 1903, pp. 657–9; George Blake, *Barrie and the Kailyard School*, London 1951; Tom Nairn, 'Old Nationalism and New Nationalism', in Gordon Brown (ed.), *The Red Paper on Scotland*, Edinburgh 1975, pp. 36–7.

21 Ian Maclaren, *Beside the Bonnie Brier Bush*, 4th edn., London 1895, pp. 44–5.

22 J. Lascelles Graham (ed.), *'Old Boys' and Their Stories of the High School of Stirling*, Stirling 1900, pp. 145–6.

23 Elements of the story, including the deathbed scene, are in 'The Poor Scholar', in *Lights and Shadows of Scottish Life* (1822) by 'Christopher North' (John Wilson). On Wilson and the Tory *Blackwood's Magazine* circle as precursors of the kailyard, see David Craig, *Scottish Literature and the Scottish People 1680–1830*, London 1961, p. 223.

24 The *Scottish National Dictionary*, under 'Pairt', gives Watson's novel as the first reference for the phrase.

25 *Transactions of the National Association for the Promotion of Social Science, Newcastle-upon-Tyne Meeting, 1870*, London 1871, p. 58.

An Angle on the Geist: Persistence and Change in the Scottish Educational Tradition[1]

Extracted from A McPherson 1983 *in* W Humes and H Paterson (eds) *Scottish Culture and Scottish Education, 1800–1980*, Edinburgh (John Donald), 216–43.

INTRODUCTION

The ebb and flow of nationalist fortunes in the past fifteen years has been accompanied by renewed public and academic interest in the nature of Scottish identity and its place in the political process. A variety of commentators has tried to resolve the central and enduring Scottish paradox, symbolised by the political Union and most recently restated in the inconclusive devolution referendum of 1979: how could a national sentiment of such continuity and consequence persistently prove so inconsequential? Was the very idea of a Scottish identity merely a misplaced metaphor, a deluded personification of altogether more complex events? Or was there indeed such an identity, but one so labile, divided or insecure as to be incapable of sustained and coherent political expression? Or was the resolution of the paradox to be found, not in the pathology of Scottish social personality, but in the pathology of a governance that was unresponsive to stable and distinctive features of Scottish civil society? Had Scotland been sold out? Were the rules of the political game manipulated against it? Alternatively, was the government and administration of the United Kingdom altogether *too* responsive to Scottish national sentiment, periodically purchasing Scottish political quiescence through acts of administrative devolution whose long-term effect could only be to extend centralised political control and ultimately to absorb Scottish institutions into alien metropolitan forms?

The mood of the current reappraisal is self-critical, iconoclastic and demythologising. Harvie's twentieth-century Scotland, for example, is a country of 'no gods and precious few heroes'[2], and Nairn describes Scotland as 'the land where ideal has never, even for an instant, coincided with fact'. In its popular culture he finds 'the pathetic symbols of an inarticulate people unable to forge valid correlates of their different experience . . .' and he talks of 'the universality of (Scotland's) false consciousness and the multiplicity of its forms': 'Scotland's myths of identity are articulated sufficiently to suit everyone . . . [M]inisters of the Kirk, lawyers, lairds, tycoons and educationalists all have their own contrasting angles on the Geist'.[3]

This essay is mainly concerned with one central aspect of the educationist's 'angle', with the nature of Scottish community, its social differentiation and solidarity, and the relationship of its school system to these. In exploring the symbolic and material basis of this world I want, in particular, to suggest how élite educationists' and others' experience of Scottish education, broadly in the first half of this century, was selectively structured so as to confirm for them the validity of an inherited, traditional and egalitarian, view of Scottish culture and institutions. I shall also suggest – there will be little space for elaboration – some consequences of this for educational advice and policy-making in the 1950s and 1960s. My discussion is offered partly in an attempt to relate the substance of Scottish education to social and political process, and partly as a corrective to analyses that dismiss tradition and myth solely as 'false facts' and that fail to cope with the resultant problem of how one explains the persistence of traditional beliefs which facts appear to contradict. The demythologiser is as likely to dehistoricise, to discount the significance of the interplay over time of changing forms and ideas, as is the prisoner of myth who interprets present institutions as the unchanged expression of a timeless ideal. And therein lies a danger in the summary description of tradition, and my reason for not offering one here. Either one describes the forms – for example, the parochial school, the omnibus school, the five-subject Highers curriculum, the open-doors university, and the general degree – and risks assembling merely a catalogue of 'pathetic symbols', of 'invalid correlates of experience', some of which have demonstrably changed, in form or significance, in recent history; or else one tries to describe that experience more directly in terms, say, of the essential egalitarianism of the Scots. One then, however, risks a somewhat mystical metaphysic of the type that recently attracted the reaction: 'It is as if Scots are judged to be egalitarian by dint of racial characteristics, of deep social values which apply at the level of the individual in an undifferentiated manner. Man (or at least Scotsman) is judged to be primordially equal . . .'[4]

The authors of this gentle lampoon observe that '(n)o myth is more prevalent and persistent than that asserting Scotland is a 'more equal' society than England (or Britain) and that Scots are somehow 'more egalitarian' than others in these islands'. They trace the myth to various sources, among them seventeenth and eighteenth-century Presbyterianism, the late eighteenth-century romantic discovery of the 'sturdy clan communalism' of Scottish Gaelic culture, and the late nineteenth-century flowering of Scottish Kailyard literature, which 'celebrated egalitarianism at its most clannish and communal'. 'The myth', they conclude, 'describes putative conditions in the typical pre-capitalist and pre-industrial community, rural or urban. Social identity is one of community, not of class . . . The locus of egalitarianism is the parish, religious and secular, whether in the country village or the small town.'

But did literature imitate life? Did life imitate literature? My exploration of these questions will reinforce the view that the locus of social identity has indeed been that of the village and small town and not that of the city; and especially not that, I would add, of the Clydeside conurbation with Glasgow at its centre. Yet, in 1951, this conurbation accounted for one-third of the Scottish population; over half the population lived in the four cities and the large burghs, and over 80 per cent was urbanised. In 1901 this last proportion had already been about three-quarters.[5] I shall point also to a close and puzzling parallel between the persisting locus of social identity and the locus of influence in the formation of Scottish educational policy and advice, a parallel that is all the more intriguing in the light of Hanham's characterisation of Scottish nationalism as a 'small man, small town' movement.[6] However, I must warn that my essay is intended to extend, and not be a substitute for, the account of the changing Scottish tradition that my colleagues and I have offered elsewhere; it is essentially programmatic in that I have preferred here to strike the balance between suggestiveness and conclusiveness in favour of the former; further evidence and elaboration is required on a number of points; and I do not deal directly with epistemological problems concerning the explanation of actions and beliefs and the representation of beliefs as true or false.[7]

ASPECTS OF THE FORM AND CONTENT OF THE SCOTTISH TRADITION

Since Durkheim sociologists have often wanted to reserve the term 'myth' not for beliefs that could simply be dismissed as false but for folk stories that had two simultaneous functions: to celebrate identity and values and to describe and explain the world in which these are experienced or sought. Logically, myths may be expressive *and* true, or expressive *and* false; though the explanations that they offer and the 'facts' that may confirm or refute them are never closed to dispute.

Public statements about Scottish education often have the logically dual character of myth. For example the nineteenth-century Scottish concern to maintain a socially accessible national education system was often made explicit in the form of a story about the burgh and parochial school since Knox.[8] This story was simultaneously celebratory, descriptive and explanatory. The descriptions contained a measure (sometimes large, sometimes changing) of truth. By the mid-nineteenth century, for example, the parochial school could not sustain a weight of empirical interpretation commensurate with its symbolic importance to contemporaries. [9]

Examples of the continuity of public statements about equality and tradition in Scotland between the 1860s and 1960s have been given elsewhere[10] and one alone must suffice here. McClelland wrote in 1935 that the 'key' to the Scottish education system was that 'the Scottish people value education and that the central and unbroken strand in our long educational tradition is the recognition of the right of the clever child, from whatever social class he may come, to the highest and best education the country has to offer'.[11] Here the present is explained as the realisation of an inheritance that is made potent for the future through the public consent it commands. McClelland's later, and highly influential, work on selection for secondary education derived from this view.[12] Thus the secondary account may mesh with the primary action. Can one pull the stories away without some of the facts sticking? . . .

There are . . . several reasons why the egalitarian claim should have appeared valid to the educationists who made and influenced policy for the post-war period. First, teachers who became involved in advice and policy-making at a national level after the second war had received their education during a period when, relative to England, the Scottish myth had real substance. Second, there is evidence from as late as the 1960s and 1970s that the bipartite areas of the Scottish secondary system had a higher level of class inequality of educational attainment than the rest of the system where the omnibus schools, mainly serving the small towns and other non-city areas, were common. This 'may in large part have been a result of the much older tradition of the omnibus school' whose long history in certain areas 'might be both a consequence and a cause of a more egalitarian class structure, which in turn influenced the educational attainment of children'.[13] The omnibus school was, of course, only a part of the Scottish tradition, but it had been a larger part before the second world war, and especially before Circular 44 of 1921 denied it to the cities . . .

Then, third, there are considerations relating to the way in which educational selection structured the experiences and perceptions of this generation of educationists, both as pupils and later as secondary school teachers. 'Academic' secondary education was, of course, selective, but generously so.[14] The individualist ethic could explain away the relatively high 'wastage' of able working-class pupils through 'early' leaving.[15] Among those who lasted the five-year course for Highers, social class differences in attainment were smaller than in the general school population. Indeed, by the early 1960s, within the population attempting Highers, mean social class differences in Highers attainment were very small indeed (they would of course have been larger if all pupils in the age-group who did not take Highers were 'scored zero').[16] At this time class differences in Highers attainment within the Highers population were non-existent in the omnibus sector,[17] and non-existent also in the six-year schools for areas of scattered population wherein local communities were served by 'truncated' secondary schools.[18] Until the 1960s the Scottish universities maintained an 'open doors' policy for virtually all applicants with minimum Highers qualifications, or better.[19] A relatively high proportion of graduate entrants to school teaching had working-class origins,[20] and anecdotal evidence indicates that such teachers were well represented among those who rose from teaching to the Inspectorate in the 1950s: 'I remember once entertaining a group of Russian educationists . . . with a group of inspectors . . . [O]f the eight I think seven were of working-class origin, which impressed the Russians so much that [they thought] we had chosen them deliberately, but we frankly hadn't. This kind of thing happens more frequently in Scotland than anywhere I know, that's one of the features of Scottish education that pleases me.'

LITERATURE, POLITICS AND EDUCATION

The Senior Chief Inspector (HMSCI) who said this was one of sixteen influential educationists, politicians and administrators of the post-war period whom Charles Raab and I interviewed at length between 1976 and 1980.[21] In section 4 I shall look further at these interviews. But first I want to use some biographical and literary evidence to suggest how the first half of the twentieth century made a version of the nineteenth-century tradition available to Scotland after 1945 . . .

[After discussing this early twentieth-century evidence, McPherson continues:]

. . . such sentiments seem to have been pervasive. We found, for example, that the majority of the eleven Scottish-educated educationists whom we interviewed spontaneously identified their own origins with the lad o' pairts and that, with differences of emphasis, virtually all described the post-war Scottish system as socially open. One ex-HMSCI told us that many in the influential Association of Directors of Education shared this view, as did his colleagues in the SED. Both former Secretaries to the Department confirmed this last judgement, one of them saying 'it was something in our blood'. And, in a radio interview in 1973, Bruce

Millan, Parliamentary Under-Secretary of State with responsibilities for Scottish education at the time of comprehensive reorganisation, commented, 'I think there is a stronger democratic tradition in Scottish education . . . perhaps we tend to over-emphasise it now and believe that equality of opportunity has gone further in Scotland than it has in England . . . it's perhaps not quite as true nowadays but I still think there is a stronger democratic tradition'.[22]

THE SYMBOLISM OF THE KIRRIEMUIR CAREER

I shall now suggest one other way in which the reception of the egalitarian myth into the world of post-war policy-making may have occurred. Sir James Robertson, a 'classic' and also the author of the 1947 SACE report, *Secondary Education*, subsequently became vice-chairman of the SACE of 1957–1961 and chairman of the Scottish Council for the Training of Teachers. In 1962 he was interviewed on television by Esmond Wright:

Let's look at your own career – It started in Kilmarnock?

(JJR) In Kilmarnock, a co-educational school, then moved to Glasgow, a little while in Hutcheson's Grammar School; and then . . . a sixth year in the High School of Glasgow.

Until you retired three years ago you were Rector of Aberdeen Grammar School . . . Before that you were Rector of the Royal High in Edinburgh; before that you were Rector of Falkirk High School for nine years; before that you were Rector of Fort William Senior Secondary. Why so many moves?

(JJR) Well . . . when I trained after the First World War, I started in Glasgow; and Dr. William Boyd – wise counsellor as well as a great teacher – said to us 'Now get out of Glasgow. Glasgow is so big, the schools are so big, that of necessity promotion will come very late, be very slow – get out of Glasgow.' I got out of Glasgow, I quickly got promotion as a principal teacher, I tried that out in two schools and then I applied for a smaller school, in the Highlands . . . Fort William was a typical small town school, the one which is repeated almost endlessly in the pattern of Scottish life. It had a wide range of ability, it had quite a wide social and economic range, and a school like that was a very good apprenticeship. The same in a measure was true of Falkirk High School, though it was more highly selective. In Aberdeen Grammar School the selection, intellectually, was not too rigorous. There was a certain selection socially – it was a fee-paying school – but we had great variety of types and many levels of ability . . .

This movement is still somewhat unusual, surely, in the experience of Glasgow?

(JJR) It's bound to be. You see, there are no small schools . . .[23]

William Dewar, another 'classic', also served on the SACE of 1957–61 and on other public bodies (section 5). In 1976 he gave us the interview from which the following extracts are taken:

(WD) I myself had been a bursar at Morrison's [Morrison's Academy, Crieff] . . . many a 'lad o' pairts' wanted to go into teaching . . . the tremendous advantage that I had over most teachers in Scotland [was that] I served in four different areas and I knew my own country town of Crieff as well . . . I was unemployed for about two months when I came out in 1929 . . . A post appeared in Aberdeen . . . The Grammar School was fee-paying . . . but there were bursaries . . . After three and a half years there I went as Senior Classics Master to Dumfries Academy, which was quite a contrast; from a city and large port to a relatively small town of about 36,000 inhabitants with one senior-secondary school [in] a sprawling county, but with several well formed, almost independent communities, Annan, Langholm, Lockerbie, Beattock, Moffat . . . Each of these towns had its own identity. In each there was a three-year secondary school, comprehensive in the sense that, in Moffat, for example, all the children from the country schools round about Moffat . . . came to that school. Nobody was sent to Dumfries in the very first year; but at the end of year III those who were judged fit . . . were transferred . . . There was no question of class distinction, none whatever, although Dumfries Academy had its own primary department, and this was still a common thing in Scotland. We hear, incidentally, if I may go off slightly at a tangent, far too little about this practice in Scotland, of having the whole of the child's education in one school, and it is not confined to the grant-aided schools. You get it . . . in Kirriemuir, if you want a present example. There's any number up and down Scotland . . .

Largely rural schools?

(WD) Provincial, I prefer to use the expression 'provincial'.

What's the distinction?

(WD) I think of 'rural' as embracing a very large number of very small schools . . . whereas for me 'provincial schools' are larger without being large absolutely, and they serve a wider area . . .

Provinces with respect to Glasgow and Edinburgh?

(WD) These are urban areas, big urban areas. Suppose you go out into Angus. Now that's a province . . .

Dewar later remarked, 'I have always been keenly aware of the situation of the fellows and the women who are away out on the periphery of Scotland in the provinces . . . (see section 5). After Dumfries he moved to Greenock Academy and thence to George Heriot's School, Edinburgh. He emphasised how, at all his schools, poor boys had had bursaries.[24]

Several points may be made from these extracts. Robertson and Dewar between them named eleven six-year secondary schools where they had been pupils or heads. At the time of their association with them, all were either burgh schools (mostly fee-paying) or city schools (all fee-paying); in 1968 seven of the eleven were still fee-paying. All of the eleven but Fort William, a 'good apprentice-ship', had either been among the 52 burgh and parish schools classed as 'secondary' by Grant in 1876 (I shall call these 52 'Grant 1876' schools),[25] or else were city foundations of the seventeenth century or earlier (though Heriot's Hospital only became a boys' day school for fee-paying pupils in 1886). There is no mention of an education authority (EA) secondary school in a city that was non-fee-paying by 1946 (there were 24 such schools in 1921.). Robertson saw the school at Fort William as 'typical', and 'repeated almost endlessly in the pattern of Scottish life'. When Dewar searched for examples, he turned to Angus and to Kirriemuir. The 'provinces' were prominent in his mental map of the country.

There is here, I suggest, a symbolic axis that parallels the axis of careers that were traced through the historical heartland of the pre-industrial education system. One might say that this symbolic world is bounded by Angus, standing for the East and North and with Kirriemuir at its heart, by Dumfries in the South and, in the West by a Glasgow academy, perhaps the Academy. In this world, I suggest, the secular career is also a moral career. We might call it the Kirriemuir career after J. M. Barrie, educated in Angus at Kirriemuir and Forfar High School, at Dumfries Academy and at Glasgow Academy (not entirely fortui-tously since he attended the two Academies whilst lodging with his teacher brother who went to a classics post at Glasgow Academy and thence to

Dumfries and promotion to the Inspectorate).[26] On the basis of the empirical evidence summarised in section 2, I contend that the Kirriemuir career took one through schools and communities in which social intercourse and educational attainment were less deeply differentiated by social class relationships than they were in the cities. The education authority schools of the city had no place on this career path ('Get out of Glasgow') and no place, either, on the symbolic map. For the ambitious lad o'pairts the career frontier lay, not in the West, but in the East, North or South; not in the city and the future but in the parish and the past.

This, then, may be one reason for the relatively uncritical reception that was given to the egalitarian myth after 1945; namely that it was not subject to the challenge of the city, or of Glasgow, or of the West in the day-to-day experience of the secondary teachers who came to influence advice and policy.

[McPherson goes on to discuss post-war policy in detail, including the part played by several of the officials whom he and Raab interviewed.]

NOTES

1 I am grateful to R. Bell, P. Burnhill, P. Cuttance, D. Raffe and P. Weston for comments on an earlier draft; to the Moray Fund of Edinburgh University for financial help with the interview-study of policy-making; to the participants in that study, named and unnamed; to C. Raab, the co-director of that study, for his numerous suggestions and comments; to T. Bone for permission to use his doctoral thesis; to J. Hughes for research assistance; to the staff of the National Library of Scotland; to N. Phillipson and O. Dudley Edwards for advice; to M. MacDougall and C. Holliday for their patient and skilled word-processing; and to A. Arnot. Responsibility for any remaining errors is mine. The pun in the title is pre-emptive.

2 C. Harvie, *No Gods and Precious Few Heroes* (London, 1981).

3 T. Nairn, 'The Three Dreams of Scottish Nationalism', in *Memoirs of a Modern Scotland*, ed. K. Miller (London, 1970), pp. 34–54. See also H. J. Hanham, *Scottish Nationalism* (London, 1969), 'With the myths of Scottish culture this book is largely concerned' (p. 25) and, more recently, articles by C. Harvie, T. Gallagher, J. Hunter and others in *The Bulletin of Scottish Politics*, 2, Spring 1981.

4 D. McCrone, F. Bechhofer and S. Kendrick, 'Egalitarianism and Social Inequality in Scotland', Paper given at the Annual Conference of the British Sociological Association, University College of Wales, Aberystwyth, 6–9 April 1981. They contend that '[s]trictly speaking egalitarianism and social inequality are not directly comparable. Egalitarianism refers essentially to a set of social values, a social ethos, a celebration of sacred beliefs; social inequality is a characterisation of the social structure referring specifically to the distribution of resources and opportunities'.

5 D. J. Robertson, 'Population and Movement', in *The Scottish Economy*, ed. A. K. Cairncross (Cambridge, 1954), pp. 9–20. 'Urbanised' in this context pertains to communities of over 1,000 persons.

6 Hanham, *op cit.*, p. 175; my phrase.

7 See A. F. McPherson, 'The Generally-Educated Scot: an Old Ideal in a Changing University Structure', in A. McPherson, D. Swift and B. Bernstein, *Eighteen-plus: The Final Selection* E282 Units 15–17 (Open University, Bletchley, 1972) pp. 5–52; A. F. McPherson, 'Selections and Survivals: a Sociology of the Ancient Scottish Universities', in *Knowledge, Education and Cultural Change: Papers in the Sociology of Education*, ed R. Brown (London, 1973), pp. 163–201; A. F. McPherson and G. R. Neave, *The Scottish Sixth: A Sociological Evaluation of Sixth Year Studies and the Changing Relationship Between School and University in Scotland* (Slough, 1976), especially chapters 6 and 7; and J. Gray, A. F. McPherson and D. Raffe, *Reconstructions of Secondary Education: Theory, Myth and Practice Since the War* (London, 1982 *in press*). Chapters 16 and 17 in particular discuss epistemological problems in the explanation of myths and other beliefs and take a somewhat different view from that offered in McCrone, Bechhofer and Kendrick, *op cit.*, and n. 4 above.

8 See McPherson 1973, *op cit.*, p. 190, nn. 24 and 25.

9 *Ibid.*, p. 171 and p. 192, n. 39.

10 Gray, McPherson and Raffe, *op cit.*, chapter 3.

11 W. McClelland, 'Distinctive Features of Scottish Education', *The New Era in Home and School*, 16, 17, pp. 172–174, C. Raab drew this to my attention.

12 W. McClelland, *Selection for Secondary Education* (London, 1942), and Gray, McPherson and Raffe, *op cit.*, Part 2.

13 Gray, McPherson and Raffe, *op cit.*, chapter 14. Re-analysis of extant data-sets from the 1947 Scottish Mental Survey (*ibid.*, chapter 2) and the Scottish Mobility Study . . . could throw further light on this conclusion.

14 McPherson 1973, *op cit.*, pp. 164–170, 173.

15 *Ibid.* and Gray, McPherson and Raffe, *op cit.*, chapter 16.

16 *Ibid.*, chapters 12 and 14.

17 *Ibid.*

18 Unpublished calculations by the author from the Scottish Education Data Archive (for which see Gray, McPherson and Raffe, *op cit.*, chapter 2).

19 McPherson 1973, *op cit.*, n. 9.

20 A. F. McPherson and G. Atherton, 'Graduate Teachers in Scotland – A Sociological Analysis of Recruitment to Teaching Amongst Recent Graduates of the Four Ancient Scottish Universities', *Scottish Educational Studies*, 2, 1, pp. 35–55, National, Scottish evidence is not systematically available for the first half of the century, but see A. Kelly, 'Family Background, Subject Specialisation and Occupational Recruitment of Scottish University Students: Some Patterns and Trends', *Higher Education*, 5, Table 3, for supporting evidence from the 1930s and 1950s.

21 The fullest published account of this research to date is to be found in C. Raab, 'The Changing Machinery of Scottish Educational Policy-Making', *Scottish Educational Re-*

view, 12, 2, 1980, pp. 88–98. The sixteen include two former Secretaries to the SED, a former Minister, and a number of 'educationists', among them two former HMSCIs and three former Directors of Education. Raab and I plan to publish a further account of this research at a later date.

22 B. Millan, transcript of interview, Open University Education Programme FW004.

23 Sir J. Robertson, transcript of interview with Professor Esmond Wright, 4 April 1962.

24 Transcript of interview of W. McL. Dewar with A. F. McPherson and C. D. Raab, 22 June 1976, with amendments 13 May 1977. All interviewees received an interview transcript to edit and amend with a view to agreeing with the researchers on a version for public use.

25 J. Grant, *History of Burgh and Parish Schools in Scotland* (London and Glasgow, 1876), pp. 507–510. Unless the context says otherwise, the term 'fee-paying' refers to the status of the school in 1968; see J. Highet, *A School of One's Choice* (London and Glasgow, 1969).

26 D. Mackail, *The Story of J. M. B.* (London, 1941), pp. 1–51.

Celtic and Rangers, or Rangers and Celtic

Extracted from Simon Kuper 1995 *Football Against the Enemy*, London (Phoenix), 205–19.

Celtic were playing Rangers in Glasgow, and I travelled there by way of Northern Ireland.

I spent months preparing for the game. On a train in France, I met a rare Protestant Celtic fan, who assured me that the ancient Glaswegian custom of asking passers-by their religion had fallen into disuse. He said: 'Nowadays they don't ask, 'Prod or Catholic?', or 'Billy or Dan?', they just ask, 'Which team do you support?' I always say, 'Partick Thistle', and they laugh and go away.' But if I were to go about in team colours, said this man, 'They'll just back-stab you without even talking to you.' I decided not to go about in team colours.

I also prepared by reading Celtic and Rangers fanzines. I read them in Moscow, in Cameroon, in the bath of the house I stayed in in Cape Town. From the bathtub you looked out onto Table Mountain. You also looked out onto the patio, from where your housemates looked back at you, so it was not the most soothing place to read fanzines. Reading them tended to remind me of the Yugoslav war anyway. The following is taken from *Follow, Follow*, a Rangers fanzine. Bear in mind that Rangers are Protestant, that Celtic are Catholic, that a 'Prod' is a Protestant, and a 'Tim' a Celtic fan, or simply any Roman Catholic.

> *Only one of Hitler's main henchmen was a Prod, the foreign minister von Ribbentrop . . . The three most distinguished non-Jewish anti-Nazi resisters, Raoul Wallenberg, Dietrich Bonnhoffer and Pastor Niemoller were all Prods. And let's not forget that Hitler was a Tim!*

Follow, Follow has a circulation of 10,000, and is quite a force in Glasgow.

Possibly Rangers and Celtic fans are the only people who live in the real world. Certainly they live in a world rather different from ours, and ours only matters to them when it connects with their rivalry. And it never matters all that much, for even as World War II raged several of their derbies ended in riots. An Old Firm game in 1975 inspired two attempted murders, two cleaver attacks, one axe attack, nine stabbings and 35 common assaults. On the other hand, the clubs also inspire great love. Rangers no longer allow the ashes of dead fans to be scattered on the Ibrox pitch, because, in the words of John Greig, former Rangers player and manager, 'we were doing so many that we were ending up with big bald patches – even in the middle of summer.' Scarcely a Glaswegian novel fails to touch on the Old Firm game, and it is in the main thanks to Rangers and Celtic fans that Scots watch more football matches than do any other Europeans except Albanians. This suggests that there is less to do in Albania than in Scotland.

I say that Celtic are Catholic and Rangers are Protestant. This has to be qualified. Celtic have always fielded Protestants, and players like Bertie Peacock were even rumoured to be Orangemen – members of the extreme Protestant Orange Order. It was different at Rangers.

The punk group Pope Paul and the Romans (also known as The Bollock Brothers) once sang 'Why don't Rangers Sign a Catholic?', and sometimes Rangers directors would reply honestly. 'It is part of our tradition', said Matt Taylor in Canada in 1967. 'We were founded in 1873 as a Presbyterian Boys' Club. To change now would lose us considerable support.' The *Bush*, a Presbyterian Church newspaper, raised the issue in 1978 and saw its circulation fall from 13,000 to 8,000. The paper soon folded. Today, the table-tennis and snooker tables at Ibrox are still painted blue, but in 1989 the club signed the Roman Catholic striker Maurice Johnston.

Not the View, a Celtic fanzine, scooped with the news that 'Rangers are to break with a 100–year tradition and in a shock move sign a good looking player.' In fact, Johnston was not the first Catholic to play for Rangers: rather, he was the first Catholic the club had knowingly signed since World War 1 (even if his stepfather was a Protestant and a Rangers fan). To Rangers fans, Mo Johnston was the worst Catholic of them all. He had head-butted Stuart Munro of Rangers in the 1986 Skol Cup final, and while being sent off had made the sign of the cross 'at' the Rangers fans. Just before joining Rangers he had seemed on the point of signing for Celtic. When he chose otherwise, the Shankill, Belfast branch of the Rangers Supporters Club folded in protest. Meanwhile, Celtic fans nick-named him *La petite merde*, in honour of his spell in France. *Scotland on Sunday* called Johnston 'the Salman Rushdie of Scottish football', for offending two sets of fundamentalists at once, and the player took Rushdie-like measures. Fearing Glasgow, he took a house in Edinburgh. It was petrol-bombed by Celtic fans. He hired a 24–hour bodyguard. Celtic fans attacked his father.

During his time at Rangers, *Follow, Follow* writers debated whether he was trying his best for the team. He was certainly trying his best to please. It was soon reported that he had sung The Sash, a Protestant song, at a supporters' dance, and also that years before he had spat on a Celtic crest. The Govan R.S.C. voted him Player of the Year after his first season, but a year after that he was gone. He never transformed Rangers into a Catholic club. 'Rangers could sign Pope John Paul himself and I don't think it would make any difference', as William English told me.

English is a young Royal Mail worker and Ibrox regular who finds some of his fellow fans hard to explain. When I placed an advertisement in *Follow, Follow* he phoned me, eager to talk, and we met in a Glasgow café. He told me: 'There were guys who, when Mo scored, didn't count that goal, so if the result was 1–0 they'd count it as a 0–0 draw. I've seen guys almost get into fights at matches for encouraging Mo Johnston. The strange thing is that once the booing stopped, Mo got *worse*.' Johnston is an eccentric.

Now Mark Hateley, the Rangers centre-forward, is rumoured to be a Catholic. English said: 'When Hateley plays, you get guys shouting, 'Come on the Queen's Ten!' They won't say 'Queen's Eleven' because they don't count Hateley.' Before, there had been doubts about Trevor Francis (said to have sent his children to a Catholic school) and Mark Falco (a Protestant with a habit of crossing himself), while even Terry Butcher ('Celtic, you hate 'em so much') finally had to deny publicly that he was Catholic.

Hateley was accepted most of the time, said English. 'But if he misses a couple of chances, they go: 'He's a Fenian, isn't he?'' I asked, 'So he can't have three bad matches in a row?', and English said, 'I wouldn't recommend it.' I asked how anyone *knew* that Hateley was a Catholic. 'They say Hateley's *wife* is a Catholic. I don't know how *anyone* knows that.' Did English think Hateley was a Catholic? 'It's a terrible thing to say, but he doesn't *look* like it.' What? 'Well, Catholics, I'd say, are more likely to have jet-black hair, with no tan at all, or else tight orange hair.' He pointed at a group at the other end of the café: 'For instance, I don't think those four guys are Catholics.'

'I paid for my season-ticket one week', Danny Houston recounted to me mournfully, 'and they signed Mo Johnston the next.' Houston, an honorary Deputy Grand Master of the Orange Lodge in Glasgow and Scotland, boycotted Rangers during the Johnston era. I visited him at his house. He was dressed in a tracksuit.

The Orange Order is an Irish Protestant society founded in 1795, and is strongest in Scotland and Ulster. Every summer the Order holds Orange Marches, which often end in brawls with Catholics. 'We're working-class people who are Loyal and Royal', as Houston defined it. 'Orangemen support all sorts of teams. You get Airdrie supporters, Falkirk supporters . . .' But few of them are Parkhead regulars, and most just support Rangers. One man who walked up to an Orange March while dressed in a Celtic shirt was arrested for breach of the peace.

Houston insisted he had no objection to Rangers signing a foreign Catholic, but 'Roman Catholicism in the West of Scotland is synonymous with Irish Republicanism.' That was his catchphrase. Real Sociedad, he said, signed only Basques, and in the German league before the war there had been a Jewish team called Maccabi, which the Nazis had banned. 'So why should anyone act like the Nazis? Why does Scotland have this hang-up about Rangers being a Protestant team? There's not a *Scottish* Protestant in the current Celtic team. Does anyone ever say that?'

Graeme Souness, the Rangers manager who signed Johnston, was making a point to fans like Houston. Before capturing Johnston, Souness had done his best to buy the Welsh Catholic Ian Rush from Juventus (the living person Rush would most like to meet is the Pope), and had bid for the Catholics Ray Houghton and John Sheridan. Yet the change in policy was also down to David Murray, the Rangers chairman.

Matt Taylor in 1967 was afraid of losing fans, but Murray in 1989 was more interested in luring sponsors. 'Football is no longer a pie-and-Bovril game', he liked to say. Fans (or some of them) want Rangers to be a Protestant club, but sponsors do not. Murray has gone for sponsors, and they have responded.

Max Weber, the German sociologist, famously observed that where Protestants and Catholics live together, the Protestants tend to be richer. There used to be a wealth divide of this kind in Glasgow, but today Rangers fans like to insist that they are just as poor as Celtic fans. That is the accepted wisdom – and yet Rangers F.C. are rich and Celtic F.C are poor, and Bluenoses at Old Firm games chant, 'You Haven't Got Any Money'. The Kelly and White families run Celtic far more laxly than Murray does Rangers, yet it would be wrong to give Murray all the credit. He could never have done at Celtic what he did at Rangers: for most businessmen in Glasgow are Protestants, who would not buy executive boxes or pay £75 for a five-course meal at Parkhead.

Colin Glass is a prominent Glasgow insurance agent and a Rangers fan. He grew up in Dundee, but moved to Glasgow at the age of 18 to be near his team. Now he owns a house in Florida, and says that but for Rangers he would have moved there. 'I didn't become a Rangers fan because of religion. I did it because I liked the colours, the red, white and blue', he assured me.

'And Rangers get the image in the press of being the religious bigots! You know these stories about thousands of Rangers fans returning their season-tickets when Johnston signed? Well, I happen to know the Rangers director in charge of season-tickets. Do you know how many tickets were returned? One!' Yes, but other fans burned their season-tickets in front of Ibrox. 'A media stunt.'

I said that Celtic fans were quite as convinced that the press was biased against them. 'But they have got a *general* paranoia that there is discrimination against Catholics.' Then he said: 'There is discrimination against Catholics, but not so much in the media. There is discrimination in jobs, by a lot of businesses in Western Scotland. So when, say, a referee's decision goes against them for perfectly legitimate reasons, they get paranoid. A Catholic friend of mine told me that he walked out of chapel recently when the priest started on about how everyone was against Catholics, right down to football referees.'

When it comes to job discrimination, Glass, given his position, is a strong witness. I asked for his evidence. 'If you take a look and see the number of Masonic handshakes at places like the Chamber of Commerce. The police too. I remember once, at a police retirement do, the Chief Inspector talking about Catholics. He said, 'I promoted two of them, and you know, one of them turned out not bad!' This man had no idea what he was saying!'

Glass told me that three of his four assistant-managers were Celtic fans. But: 'If someone called Patrick O'Leary applied, I wouldn't put him in a job approaching normal executive businessmen, because when he phones up and gives his name, they'll say 'No'.' Catholics should dissemble more, he said. 'They call their kids Bridget Teresa or names like that. My view is, why do they give their children that handicap when neither they nor I have the power to change people's prejudices?' Could he tell a Catholic from a Protestant? 'Catholics speak slightly differently. The police here will ask, What *exactly* did the suspect say?' Take 'stair': we say 'steer', they say 'stayer'.

'But it works on both sides: the Labour council of Glasgow is totally dominated by Catholics. There was a firm called Lafferty's Construction, now bust. Every single tender from the district council that Frank Lafferty went for, he was *just* under the next bird. He used to sit in the directors' box at Celtic Park.'

'The worst club match in the world, without a doubt', said Jim Craig, a well-coiffed, grey-haired Glaswegian dentist about the Old Firm game. What was it like to play in? 'I loved it! I'm of the warrior class, and a warrior is trained to fight. Sometimes I went through the whole game without ever doing anything constructive, and got praised at the end.'

Craig used to be Celtic's right-back, and he once scored an own goal against Rangers. '23 years ago – people still tell me about it – and it wasn't even a very good one', he lamented. 'I tried to glance it beside the post. It hit the inside of the post and went in. A few years ago Terry Butcher scored an absolute smasher in the game for Celtic: the ball came across and he threw himself at it and it *screamed* into the corner. I wrote to him, 'I scored a mediocre own goal in the Old Firm match back in 1970 and I'm still reminded of it. You'll be remembered for all time for that one!'

'The tribal supporters don't want the game to change. It's a great day for them, to go out there and hate the opposition. If you played behind closed doors, they'd stand outside at either end and shout. It's hard for me because I'm not a passionate person. It's hard for the players, because very often your whole season is judged on how you do in the Old Firm games.' We shook our heads and deplored the fans. Then Craig said: 'Don't forget, though: you'll get a summer holiday, I'll get a summer holiday, but they won't get a summer holiday.' In Ulster in the 1970s, he had met a man whose father was dying of cancer. 'The son asked me to come round and see the guy, who was a Celtic fan, and I did, I brought along some pennants and badges, and then I went back to Scotland and, I must admit, clean forgot about it. That November I got a letter from the son. His Dad had lived much longer than anyone had expected him to, and all he talked about for the last six months of his life was that a Celtic player had been to see to him. Not 'Jim Craig', but a Celtic player. It's hard for players: you're fighting with the manager, you're injured, you're carrying an injury, you're coming back from injury, and it's very much a job. You forget that that other side of football is a tremendous thing.'

The most famous Celts in history are Jock Stein's 'Lisbon Lions'. In 1967 they became the first British team to win the European Cup, beating Helenio Herrera's Inter Milan 2–1 in the final in Lisbon. Craig is a Lisbon Lion, and I asked what he remembered of the game. 'I'm still always asked about it, and I still don't think it was a penalty. I was determined he wasn't going to turn past me, and I thought, 'If I bump into him the referee isn't going to give a penalty, not at this stage of the game.' How wrong I was.' But later he set up Tommy Gemmell's equalizer, and then Chalmers scored the winner. The post-match banquet was the one at which the Celtic coaches abused Herrera. 'We had Scotsmen falling out of cupboards for weeks afterwards', said a British diplomat in Lisbon. Three years later, Craig was on the bench when Celtic lost their second European Cup final to Feyenoord. What had gone wrong? He thought it might have had to do with the biorhythms of the two teams.

Few footballers go on to become dentists, I said. 'Nowadays there are a lot of Catholic lawyers, doctors and so on. You didn't have that 40 years ago. These people were fighting a system. That's why when Jock came and the team suddenly picked up, it was wonderful for these people.'

I told him about my book. He shook his head. 'It's hard for someone from beyond Glasgow to understand the place. This is a strange city. I'll give you an example. The other night, I was walking down the street, past this building that's just been bought by the Ministry of Defence, and I saw a light on inside, so I climbed up on the ledge to see what was in there. This guy comes past, looks at me, and says: 'You're a nosy bastard!' Then he says: 'What's up there anyway?''

The Old Firm divides Scots all over the world, from the USA to South Africa, but the region it affects most is Ulster. The Province, after all, is like an Old Firm game got out of hand, and when the Old Firm meet it grows tenser than usual. A week before Celtic *vs*. Rangers at Parkhead, I went to Ulster.

I started from Dublin, capital of the Republic. 'I'm Irish aren't I', one Dubliner wrote to me, explaining why he supported Celtic. 'From a very early age in Ireland your father embeds the words Glasgow Celtic into your system. You will be very grateful for this introduction to the world's finest club, and it will probably be the only time in your childhood that you will obey your father's orders most willingly.'

From Dublin I took the bus up to Derry, in Ulster. Recently, a Derry family scattered a relative's ashes over the running track at the Rangers ground only to watch groundsmen sweep up the ex-fan seconds later. From Derry I took another bus to the small town of Limavady. On its deserted main street, David Brewster has a solicitor's office. I asked him whether I could leave my rucksack at the reception desk. 'Better take it with you', he said. Politicians in Ulster are careful people.

Brewster, who was wearing a blue pullover, is tipped as future MP. He is an Ulster Unionist, and so, naturally, is a Rangers fan. He was the first of many lucid Old Firm fans I met. 'This', he said, indicating a scar around his eye, 'is, as a matter of fact, a souvenir of Glasgow. But in Glasgow, 99% of the time you can be as bigoted as you want and the worst you'll get is punched. All the stuff that you've bottled up for months in Ulster, you can let go there in 90 minutes. Things get very intense over there, but you won't get shot.' In Ulster itself, he said, Old Firm fans kept quiet. Celtic and Rangers shirts were read as simple sectarian symbols. 'Pat Rice, a Roman Catholic, was killed in about 1971. He was educationally subnormal, and he used to walk around in his neighbourhood, one of the toughest areas of Belfast, wearing a Rangers scarf. He had been warned – he got on people's nerves – and in the end he got murdered. So the Old Firm is not that tribal.'

In other words, there was no street rivalry between Celtic and Rangers fans in Ulster? No teasing, no fist-fights? 'In Belfast, Catholics and Protestants who do work together avoid religious topics. The phrase is 'Whatever you say, say nothing.' If you ever ask the folk here anything, by way of an opinion poll for example, they'll be very guarded about expressing an opinion. Yet they know the religious affiliation, or the *perceived* religious affiliation, of virtually every club in England and Scotland.' I went straight back to Derry, and caught a bus to Belfast, arriving there late on the Thursday evening.

Belfast used to have its own Old Firm games. Belfast Celtic, a clone of Glasgow Celtic, were founded in 1891, and their matches against Protestant clubs were always hairy affairs. There was gunfire at games against Linfield in the 1930s and 1940s, and finally, after fans invaded the pitch and broke a player's leg in 1949, Belfast Celtic folded.

Later, the tiny Belfast club Cliftonville began to attract Catholics, simply because their ground, Solitude, lies near a Catholic area. Matches between Cliftonville and Protestant teams can produce quite spectacular violence. Graham Walker, a Rangers fan and a Queen's University lecturer in politics, has even seen Protestant fans throw a grenade: 'It went off at the back of the Spion Kop, where the Cliftonville fans were. The back of the Spion Kop is where the Falls Road is, so the fans started cheering and singing, 'We've Got Another One' – they thought the bomb was one of theirs.' But Cliftonville is a very small club. Belfast Catholics look to Glasgow for most of their football.

I stayed at Queen's University, which has a Celtic Supporters' Club and a Rangers one. All the committee members of the Queen's R.S.C. that year were also members of the Unionist Party. On the Friday morning I found Lee Reynolds, the R.S.C. Chairman, waking up under a Union Jack in his room. 'You probably can't go into a Protestant house in Ulster where there isn't a Rangers scarf, or a mug, or something', he told me. I mentioned that I also wanted to speak to the chairman of the Celtic Supporters' Club. 'Oh yes, D.J. We'll go and find him.' We met Thomas 'D.J.' McCormick, draped in Celtic scarf, outside the Student Union, and Lee introduced us. The two were overly polite to one another, like diplomats of warring states at a UN meeting. D.J. told me he would take me to the match the next day. He decided that instead of sitting in the press box I would stand on the terrace with the Celtic fans . . .

D.J. and I took the train to his parents' house in Larne, the port for the Stranraer ferry, and the next day, rather early on a very cold morning, we walked to the boat. I was staying on in Glasgow after the match, but D.J. was making a 22–hour round trip that would cost him at least £70. Ulster Old Firm fans are almost quantifiably the most loyal supporters in Britain. The Glasgow academic Raymond Boyle surveyed Belfast fans of Celtic and found that:

– less than 50% of them had full-time work.

– 80% made all 16 organized trips to Parkhead each season.

– 49% spent more than £500 a year on Celtic. Some told Boyle he should have allowed a category for over £1000.

– 80% of those who filled in the political section of the questionnaire voted Sinn Fein. However, 40% of the sample left the section blank.

Ours was an all-Celtic boat – Rangers and Celtic fans travel best separately – and on it was a rubber-faced man the others called 'Reeva'. He was probably the one person in the world who could jump on a table in front of a ferryload of Celtic fans and shout, 'Can You Hear the Rangers Sing?', without getting a response. Reeva was the Larne village idiot, and he gave me a barrage that he insisted I quote verbatim in my book. He never made the match that day: he was arrested in Glasgow before kick-off for talking to a policeman's horse. 'In Northern Ireland you belong to one side or the other', Paul Hamill, head of the Larne C.S.C., told me. 'Either you are, or else you aren't. If I miss the boat tonight, I'll be given a bed, be given money. It's happened before. Celtic is a big family: it's essentially an Irish club, an Irish club playing in a foreign league.' Many Rangers fans agree, and think that Celtic players never try their best for Scotland because they feel Irish. 'He'd rather be wearing a green shirt than a blue one', is the terrace phrase.

Our coach finally reached the East End of Glasgow and D.J. gave me a Celtic scarf, for safety's sake. When we passed Rangers fans we looked away, and so did they.

It was still cold, I was still sleepy, and I found it hard to feel partisan. No one else did: Parkhead was full, *Follow, Follow* had called for a Flag Day, and the Rangers end looked like a crowd at a Royal Wedding. Their Union Jacks are considered so provocative in Glasgow that the police regularly confiscate them, which, as *Follow, Follow* points out, is peculiar: 'After all, it is the national flag.' . . .

Other countries have no history. German fans can hardly reminisce about great matches of the 1930s, not with the old photos showing swastikas and Hitler salutes. In Russia, many clubs changed their names after the Bolshevik revolution, and Stalin once even disbanded CSKA Moscow – by accident, but that is another story. Some countries just have no time for tradition. Ajax, the club with the most glorious past in Holland, are to move to a new stadium outside Amsterdam later in the 1990s, and none of their fans seems to mind. The British bent for the past extends even beyond football. Take our Parliament: when the

Conservative Party broke its election promise and levied VAT on fuel in 1993, Michael Heseltine pointed out that Harold Wilson had once raised VAT after vowing not to. What happened 30 years ago seemed relevant still, because like Celtic, the Labour Party is a unit with a history. When Labour play the Tories, their histories play each other too. Margaret Thatcher liked to invoke Winston Churchill; the Tories never tire of discussing 1979; and on the Labour side, Tony Benn and Peter Shore complain that Labour is drifting away from its traditions. When John Motson tells us that 'these two sides last met in the Cup in 1954, Rovers winning 1–0 thanks to a 31st minute own goal', he is making a very British point.

British fans enjoy fan culture, and most of all they enjoy hating their rivals. Celtic and Rangers fans need each other. Perhaps their rivalry is still based on real religious divides in Glasgow, but I question whether these divides alone are strong enough to make the Old Firm such a phenomenon. After all, more than 40% of Catholics who marry now marry Protestants. And if Celtic and Rangers really do stand for two poles in the city, then this is not reflected in Glaswegian politics: Celtic and Rangers fans alike vote Labour. Yet perhaps that is because the political divide in Glasgow – Labour, Conservatives and Scottish Nationalists – is a Westminster divide.

Had Labour won the 1992 elections, it would have created a Scottish assembly. Soon, truly Scottish parties would probably have replaced the Labour and Tory Parties. How to know what kind of new parties these would have been? By using the Old Firm rivalry as a guide to feeling, in the West of Scotland at least. By this guide, it would appear that in an independent Scotland, a left-wing, republican, Catholic party would oppose a centre-left, Unionist, Protestant party.

Unless, that is, the Old Firm rivalry has outlived religious hatred. I suggest that that is the case, and that the Old Firm has survived as a phenomenon because the fans enjoy it so much. They are not about to give up their ancient traditions just because they no longer believe in God.

That day's *Celtic View* (known to fans as *Pravda*) had an Old Firm quiz that started with an easy one: 'True or False – it took Rangers nearly five years to beat Celtic for the first time?'

Our end sang for the IRA hunger-striker,

Bobby Sands MP
Bobby Sands MP
Will you swear to bear allegiance to the flag of Ireland?
Will you wear the black beret?

Will you serve the IRA?
If you can,
You're a man,
BOBBY SANDS!

and, 'Get the Brits, get the Brits, get the Brits out NOW!', and, even more simply, in praise of the IRA, 'Ooh aah up the Ra, say ooh aah up the Ra!' That very afternoon, an IRA bomb killed two children in Warrington.

The Rangers fans were singing,

The cry was no surrender,
Surrender and you'll die, die, die
With heart in hand . . .
We'll guard old Derry's walls

and 'Nooooo Pope of Rome!'

As for me, I was just freezing. Being a neutral among fanatics is tiring. Had I really left Ulster that morning? Was this really part of the country I lived in?

The Ninety Minutes' Hate kicked off, and the man leaning into my ear became the ten millionth person in history to shout 'Fuck off, you Orange bastards!' during an Old Firm game. Celtic scored, and a few dozen people hurled themselves down the stands at my back while Rangers nearly equalized. As the Celtic board later noted, Rangers kicked off while Celtic players were still celebrating, and Stuart McCall's shot came just 12 seconds after Celtic's goal hit the net: the referee's an Orange bastard. Then Celtic scored again.

The match was poor – Old Firm games tend to be. As the Glaswegian joke goes, 'And in the middle of it all, a football match breaks outs!' Tradition is that Celtic have a more refined style than Rangers, but all I could see was two teams running around much too fast. Half the players are fans in jerseys, and they play in a frenzy of rage. Peter Grant of Celtic is known to Rangers fans as 'Rasputin', 'The Mad Monk', or 'The Mad Priest', and according to Gary Lineker, Terry Butcher used to sing Rangers songs in the England changing-room.

The match ended at last, Celtic winning 2–1, though since Hateley had scored the Rangers goal many would consider it 2–0. I returned my scarf to D.J., turned left into the London Road, and realized my mistake. No one else was coming my way, and Rangers fans were walking down the road towards me: on Old Firm days, the fans of the two clubs use separate routes. The first few fans to pass gave me uncharitable glances, and then one man carrying a banner threw me a fake head-butt (a 'Glaswegian kiss') as he went by. I say it was fake, but I only knew that when his nose stopped moving an inch from mine. I pretended not to notice and walked on . . .

The Body in the Kit Bag: History and the Scottish Novel

Cairns Craig 1979 *Cencrastus* 1, 18–22.

Moseby, one of the principal characters in Alan Sharp's *A Green Tree in Gedde*, waiting for his friend Harry Gibbon, encounters an old man in a pub, a Tiresias of the modern Scottish wasteland, whose conversation revolves around the First World War: 'Things weren't the same after the war . . . If you'd seen that you couldn't be the same again'. His monologue concludes with the story *of a young man who had been to the war and had gone melancholy and had suffocated himself in his old army kit bag . . . 'He got up on the dresser and got in the kit bag and he had a rope through the holes in the kit bag and then just rolled off and pulled the neck tight and he just suffocated, couldn't get air, and that's how they found him, hanging up from the pulley . . .' Moseby could see it, the kit bag and the little kitchen, swinging slightly, and finding him in the canvas shroud.* (1970, p 70)[1]

Two antithetic meanings flow from this image. For the old man it symbolises a historical experience so horrific, so overwhelming that it cannot be escaped even in the safety of one's own home: the enclosed, domestic pre-war world, an idyllic world evoked by an earlier part of his conversation – 'Before the war they were real summers, before your time . . . They really were summers' – has been violated by contact with an external history that is brutally destructive. To Moseby, however, the image has a resonance of a completely different kind: it is the claustrophobic kitchen the melancholy Tommy has tried to escape from, it is the experience of history, however brutal, he seeks. After knowledge, no matter how horrific, of that other realm the enclosed domestic world is unacceptable, and wrapping himself in his kit bag he asserts significance that has been offered and then withdrawn by history – 'Pack up your troubles . . .'. Turning slowly in his inverted womb the young man insists that what the Scottish wasteland needs and finds impossible is rebirth through the coupling of the domestic and the historic.

The image acts as chorus to an underlying pattern in many twentieth century

Scottish novels which oppose a static community, by-passed by the mainstream of history, to a world beyond whose essential meanings are defined by history. The opposition is not only of thematic interest, it is the key to central problems of narrative technique within the tradition of the Scottish novel. The point is made clear in Sharp's novel by Harry Gibbon:

> *Paris is quite a place, to look at as well as the people. I suppose it's because so much has happened here and you know it has even if you don't know what it is. In Greenock, you know nothing ever happened nor ever will happen, in the historical sense I mean, so you look at it differently or you don't look at it at all.* (232)

The static world of Scotland is unknowable because nothing in it, nothing historical, forces one to look at it, to understand it. Like Greenock in Sharp's world it has a graveyard at its core – 'the dead centre' (27) – a graveyard which is the denial of change rather than the repository of it as it is, for instance, in Orwell's presentation of the graveyard in *Coming Up for Air*. English grave-yards are the story of a community and its continuity in history; Scottish graveyards are the denial that there is any history – all is reduced to a smooth equality. That deadness at the heart of Sharp's conception of the town is a deadness to the power of narrative: a society apparently static offers no purchase to narrative art, no pattern upon which the particular lives of a novelist's characters can be modelled. In his famous study *Philosophy and the Historical Understanding* W. B. Gallie argued that all history was founded upon the processes of narrative: history is the construction of story out of the amorphous, fragmented, hypothetical totality of what has happened to occur. Narrative, however, is essentially teleological: 'it is chiefly in terms of the conclusion – eagerly awaited as we read forward and accepted at the story's end – that we feel and appreciate the unity of a story' (London, 1964, p 29); and the ultimate teleology of the historical story is the present: 'to be studied as history, a set of past human actions must be felt by members of some human group to belong to its past, and to be intelligible and worth understanding from the point of view of its present interests.' (52) The writing of history and the writing of novels developed side by side: each is the attempt to understand the present by the construction of a narrative which leads to, which explains or justifies its given nature. The individuals of the novelist's work become universal by mimicking in their personal relations patterns which can be projected on to or derived from the society at large; the individuals of the historian's narrative are subsumed into the generalities of a total pattern. History and the novel look through opposite ends of the telescope of narrative, one seeing through individuals general pattern, the other seeing under general pattern individuals. That either can exist, however, we need a sense of change, of development to which we ourselves are attached – we need to feel, whether it is true or not, that history is not just the account of the events of the past but the process which accounts for the events of the past; in other words, that we are not just relating ourselves to past events but relating past events which shape our present.

As Gallie points out there are various different kinds of history, some of which claim to be non-narrative, but these are all parasitic on a central strand of narrative. Without such a narrative there can be no awareness of a process of which the present is the outcome and it is precisely such a vacuum, I want to suggest, which characterises Scottish life in the nineteenth century. Without that central narrative strand it is extremely difficult to construct a novel, because novels take their shape primarily, if not exclusively, from their establishment of a relationship between the pattern of history and the pattern of a set of individual lives. Other narratives can give such pattern – but the novel, by its 'solidity of specification', by its concentration on a world of objects with social meanings, is primarily tied to the narrative of history. In this sense all novels are historical novels.

What Scottish novelists have had to do again and again in recent times is to link their novel to some moment of historical dynamism which intrudes upon the historyless Scottish community: Scotland can only be known through narrative in these moments when narrative possibilities are forced upon a society that has lost all sense of its own narrative. The incident in Sharp's *A Green Tree in the Gedde* from which I began is only a minor instance of the predominance in the Scottish novel of two related and crucial event of intrusive history – the First World War and the Clearances. The war haunts the Scottish imagination. The two great novels of the inter-war years – Grassic Gibbon's *Sunset Song* and Neil Gunn's *Highland River* – set the pattern, but it is one repeated in William McIlvanney's *Docherty* and, on a lesser level, in Davie Toulmin's *Blown Seed*. The haunting is literal in Mackay Brown's *Greenvoe*, in which one of the central characters, Mrs McKee (and key to the novel), is visited by a ghostly tribunal investigating her actions in 1916 while her fiancé was at the Front; the haunting is metaphorical in Muriel Spark's *The Prime of Miss Jean Brodie* as two of that eminent schoolmistress's pupils bring her fiancé, killed in the war, back to life to stalk her subsequent fantasies about him. In Gordon Williams's *From Scenes Like These* the still centre of the fragmentary plot is another Tiresias whose name, Archie Stewart, advertises his belief that all Scottish history from 1745 is a falsification of the country's true being: he lives, symbolically, on a worked-out mine to assert the failure of the industrial unconsciousness within which the country is trapped. For the Highland novel the Clearances play the same role. If the first war is a sudden end to the industrial Scotland which had boomed through the nineteenth century and which crashed into the depression, the Clearances are seen again and again in Highland novels as the intrusion of modern capitalism upon a historyless society. The best known are Gunn's *Silver Darlings* and *Butcher's Broom*, the latter leading up to, the former following upon, the event itself, but the same pattern is evident in Fionn MacColla's *And the Cock Crew* and Crichton Smith's *Consider the Lilies*. What is significant is not the historical accuracy or otherwise of these novels: on both sides of the Highland line Scottish novelists have insisted in their best works that the potentiality of narrative itself can only be harnessed to those moments when an external dynamic intrudes itself destructively upon a culture which has divorced itself from history. Lowland Scotland, of course, is inescapably part of the post-industrial world of technological progress, but it is a progress which has become, in the eyes of the novelists, sclerosed, ossified, set in a fixed pattern that seems to have evaded the transforming power of the history upon which it was founded. The creation of an industrial society has been effected only at the cost of complete exhaustion, so that there seems no more historical dynamic left in Lowland society than in that pre-industrial society of the Highlands before the Clearances.

Since Lukacs, of course, we are all aware that Scotland was the seedbed of the historical novel, the form which was the dominant mode of the novelistic imagination throughout the nineteenth century. Scott's *Waverley* wakens Europe to the explicit forming of the pattern of fictional lives in parallel with or in counterpoint to the pattern of history; through Scott Europe realises the medium of historical fiction at precisely the moment when Hegel's philosophy alerts it to the fact that history is its medium. But there is a strange ambivalence in Scott's view of history, a view developed out of Enlightenment thinking in the eighteenth century and creating the sense of vacuum which is characteristic of the modern Scottish novel. In the 'Postscript' to *Waverley* Scott sums up the sixty years between the action he has recounted and his own time:

> There is no European nation which, within the course of half a century, or little more, has undergone so complete a change as this kingdom of Scotland. The effects of the insurrection of 1745 . . . commenced this innovation. The gradual influx of wealth and extension of commerce, have since united to render the present people of Scotland a class of beings as different from their grandfathers as the existing English are from those of Queen Elizabeth's time . . . But the change, though steadily and rapidly progressive, has, nevertheless, been gradual, and like those who drift down the stream of a deep and smooth river, we are not aware of the progress we have made,

until we fix our eye on the now distant point from which we have drifted.
(*Waverley*, ed A Hook, p 492)

The double sense here, of incredibly rapid change, achieving in sixty years what England had taken two hundred to achieve, and, at the same time, of no consciousness of change, is striking. The image of the amnesiac drift of progress offers vividly Scott's underlying sense that the entry into the modern world is an entry into a storyless environment. Narration and history are divorced for Scott: contemporary history is a silent drift, unparticularised by name or deed; narrative can only connect with a disconnected past. If history is narration then the present is post-history; it inhabits a new realm in which there is progress without narrative. At the very moment, therefore, at which history becomes in Europe a living force, the reality in which people live, act and die, Scott divorces the Scottish present from history.

Scott's transference of narrative to the historical past, dehistoricising the present, is a direct outcome of the Scottish Enlightenment's theories on history and society. As Annand Chitnis points out (*The Scottish Enlightenment* (1977) p 117) the Scottish philosophical historians contributed largely to the evolution of that Whig view which regards the real nature of history as the diffusion of political liberty through the social effects of commerce. They did so, however, by projecting on to the actualities of English history a theoretical model of man's development which was obviously lacking from their own barbaric, fragmented past. The sudden emergence of Scotland into an advanced, civilised society is an act of incorporation into a history which comes much closer to their underlying philosophic model of how a society ought to develop, so that Scottish history becomes a source of local narratives no longer teleologically attached to the present. In terms of Gallie's theory this is hardly history at all, but in the Scottish context it remains history by casting the present into a post-historical limbo.

Scott's greatness lies in the fact that it is precisely this tension between the historical past and the dehistoricised present that his novels explore: the famous passive hero is the representative of the post-historical world who is suddenly pitched into the alien world of narrative. Thus Waverley ends looking at a painting of himself and his Jacobite companion Fergus MacIvor 'in highland dress; the scene a wild and mountainous rocky pass' (489); his life in history has been turned into art and he turns away from art – 'Men must, however, eat, in spite both of sentiment and virtue', as Scott snidely puts it – to the world of progress and stability. As an Englishman he has learned that his Jacobite sympathies are a romantic perversion of the true course of history, a reversion to narrative which has been ended by the non-narrative history of Hanoverian harmony. What the Enlightenment and Scott between them achieved, in the very decades when they were providing Europe with a historical conception of how societies evolve, was the reduction of Scottish history to a set of stories which could not form a connected evolution but could only be used in juxtaposition with and as a justification of the progressive and progressively non-narratable present. The insistence was ideological: the assertion of a separate Scottish historical impetus would have upset the new harmonious totality upon which North Britonism was founded, and though there may have been justification for such a view it was destroying the foundations in Scotland upon which the European novel was to be built in the nineteenth century. After Scott – or rather, perhaps, after Hogg's *Confessions of a Justified Sinner* – the tension between the historical and the post-historical, between the Scottish past and the British present, was dissolved, and the land of romance lay in wait for successive waves of colonisation while the real Scotland lay unlooked at.

There is a history of Scottish society in the nineteenth century, of course, in the sense that there are events and records, but there was not until recently, hardly is still, a Scottish history in the sense of a narrative 'of past human actions . . . felt by members of some human group to belong to its past, and to be intelligible and worth understanding from the point of view of its interests.' (Gallie, 52). When Marx wrote in a famous passage that there is 'no country in Europe that does not possess, in some remote corner, at least one remnant people, left over from an earlier population, forced back and subjugated by the nation which later became the repository of historical development' (*Political Writings* I, Penguin (1973), p 221), he cited the Gaels in Scotland, but the paradox of nineteenth century Scottish culture lay deeper than Marx could see: it was that the repository of historical development, the industrial world of Lowland Scotland, had, at a conscious intellectual level, annulled its own sense of its development as historical. History was always elsewhere: Europe, the Empire, England: and that sense of a dehistoricised present, turned sour since Scott's time, was enshrined for our own time in Edwin Muir's poetry and criticism:

> *Here a dull drove of faces harsh and vexed,*
> *We watch our cities burning in their pit,*
> *To salve our souls grinding dull lucre out,*
> *We, fanatics of the frustrate and the half,*
> *Who once set Purgatory Hill in doubt.*
> *('Scotland 1941')*

Scotland in the present is a purgatorial eternity, beyond history, beyond transformation.

In England Scott was mentor to two generations of English novelists who used his awareness of historical disjunction to understand the relation of agricultural to industrial England, but in Scotland, lacking any sense of historical dynamic, Scott's achievement was not followed through and by the time the novelists of the 'sixties and 'seventies of the nineteenth century turned to direct depiction of contemporary society Scotland had become invisible. Carlyle's work projected a history upon England which could become the model of Dickens's narrative strategies; George MacDonald inherited only the tunnel vision in which Scottish society was left when the likes of Carlyle put on English spectacles. Waverley, lapsing back into romantic history and by luck managing to grow into post-history, is grandfather to the Peter Pan who cannot get out of the world of romance into the adult post-narrative world of (English) adults. Barrie's work reveals superbly the problems of narrative in late nineteenth century Scottish fiction: his stories have a location, but his Thrums is a town in stasis which can offer no general narrative movement to which the lives of individual characters can be related. Their lives, like the narratives, become discrete, fragmented, significant only through personal relations that cannot have general meanings except as a focus for the reader's patronising pity for their insignificance. For Barrie narrative is of its essence an escape from a storyless environment, and it is part of Barrie's honesty as an artist, in the midst of all his dishonesties, that he turns increasingly in his later years, in *Peter Pan* and, finally, in *Farewell, Miss Julie Logan*, to an examination of the incompatibility of the world of narrative with the world of history. As part of nineteenth century Scottish culture, however, he could not see the world of history sufficiently clearly to make the tension truly effective except, perhaps, in that last story. This is why, I think, Barrie so insistently places his narrator, in *Auld Licht Idylls* as in *Julie Logan*, in houses cut off by snowstorms: The suspended animation of the environment mirrors the historical white-out, in which his characters exist. By-passed by history, the weavers of Thrums gain their significance not from their centrality to the social condition of Scotland in the 1880s, but because they act as an image of a Scottish society in which felt history, history people are aware of living through, has disappeared and even the silent drift of progress is no longer discernible because there is no longer any visible or distinguishable point from which the speed of the current can be measured.

If a recent book of recollections of childhood by contemporary Scottish writers had been called *JM Barrie's Bairns* instead of *Jock Tamson's Bairns* (ed Trevor Royle, 1970) it might not have been far wrong, for nearly all of the contributors describe a Scotland whose essential condition is still recognisably Thrums: a world trapped, suspended, storyless. Alan Bold quotes one of his own poems, 'I have imprisoned myself in four small rooms/and decayed there'; Alan

Spence recalls that Vera Lynn had promised 'joy ever after/Tomorrow/When the world is new', but that his 'new world was a room and kitchen with a narrow lobby in between' – all it needs is the body in the kit bag; Martin MacDonald writes of the effects of Suez in 1956: 'as that week progressed the violence in Old Quad swelled and overflowed into the street, to be contained by the police, and for an illusory moment students in Edinburgh almost believed they might be as effective as their continental contemporaries in Europe. The feeling died, of course . . .' The intrusion of narrative, the potentiality of a parallel with significant history, 'dies of course'. And yet it is precisely those kinds of intrusions that Scottish novelists have had to depend on to create their narrative impetus; without such narrative moments Scottish society allows them no point of entry at which the particular and the general can be linked together, no perspective within which they can look at their historyless past.

What these contemporary writers are describing in autobiographical terms had already been given fictive form by Grassic Gibbon and Neil Gunn between the wars. In *Sunset Song* the village of Kinraddie has 'some twenty or thirty holdings in all, the crofters dour folk of the old Pict stock, they had no history' (*Scots Quair* (1950), 17); in *Highland River* the hero has 'a fugitive smile, secretive as those dark Picts who left, as their record of thousands of year of habitation of that land, his own slim dark-eyed body' (1974, 86), and he belonged to a people who were 'sounds in the empty spaces of history' (62). In *Butcher's Broom* Gunn describes a self-contained Highland community and pleads, 'surely the forces that had so shut them in could do without them and forget them' (1977, 21), and though the economic basis is different Gunn's plea could be offered too for the community McIlvanney describes in *Docherty*: 'Like a messenger who has come so far he forgets exactly what his message is, word of the war limped stammering into High Street' and the people 'found themselves searching the recent past for significant events, like the torn pieces of a picture they had carelessly thrown out.' (1975, 132) Similarly the community in Mackay Brown's *Greenvoe* is an echo chamber for distant history that leaves the lives of its people untouched till the arrival of a military establishment clears them from the island altogether: Timmy Folster, for instance, the village idiot, picks up on the beach a bottle with a letter inside: 'This bottle with contents was dropped into the North Atlantic Ocean of 12 April 1912 from the S.S. *Titanic* on her maiden voyage . . .' (1976,134) As the iceberg to the Titanic, so the War or the clearances to that smoothly drifting Scottish society.

The focus in the Scottish novel on such narrative moments is an index of how patternless the rest of Scottish experience has been, and without such significant general patterns too many Scottish novelists have to give up the Scottish scene altogether (Muriel Spark, Giles Gordon, Gordon Williams, even Robin Jenkins), or run dry (Alan Sharp most sadly, Archie Hind seemingly), or look, like Catherine Gavin, to other histories for their material. What we are left with is the storyful non-historical fictions about Wallace or Bruce or Charles Edward or Mary – 'sounds in the empty spaces of history'. For those who try to tackle the Scottish reality two distinct paths have emerged by which they attempt to get round the narrative vacuum. The first, regularly used by Lowland writers, is to construct a plot in which the historical dynamic of intrusive history can be harnessed to revolutionise Scottish society. The most recent example is *Docherty*, in which the eldest son, returned wounded from the war, becomes a communist: having experienced history he tries to introduce its motive force into his own community by adopting a creed which will offer the Scottish proletariat a non-national historical significance. What seems unsatisfactory here is that we know that such a desire for political transformation was ineffective: the location of the narrative around the point of real historical intrusion defeats the effort to assert that any dynamic can flow from it, because in fact it did not. But McIlvanney's structuring of his narrative on this basis testifies to the power of the fictional tactic that Grassic Gibbon had developed in *A Scots Quair*. There Chris Guthrie's son, Ewan, product of a marriage between Highland and Lowland and so of the harmony upon which so many Scott novels close, is cut off from any such harmony by the death of his father in the war. His growing up is the internalisation of the message of history, even although history has been destructive for his family, and he too becomes a communist in order to control, to be history:

> And for a while his words and the image they painted abided with Ewan when Trease himself had gone shambling away across Windmill Place, turning, stout, shabby, to wave ta-ta. A hell of a thing to be History! – not a student, a historian, a tinkling reformer, but LIVING HISTORY ONESELF, being it, making it . . . (459)

Gibbon's rhetoric has often been criticised for its naiveté and simplicity in passages like this, but the tone is carefully judged, studiedly distanced. History is inhumane, is hell – 'a hell of a thing' – but at least by accepting the destructiveness of history one maintains the only possibility there is for transforming an inhumane environment – history itself.

The pattern of immersion in history as cure for the wounds of history is one strand of *A Scots Quair*, but that pattern is balanced by, perhaps superseded by, another, focusing on Chris Guthrie herself. It is a pattern which has dominated much of the best writing by Scottish novelists and it is part of the greatness of the *Quair* that it is able to incorporate both the Lowland drive for harnessing history and the Highland drive to deny it. For Chris Guthrie the intrusion of history is a revelation not of the deprived condition of a historyless community but of the fragile and illusory nature of its escape from history. The historyless condition which has been broken by the War must be recreated in a new spiritual form, an individual form which will be free from all possibility of fracture by history. The historyless lacuna in which Scottish society has existed before the introduction of narrative becomes a model for a higher perspective in which the character realises an ultimate set of values that precede all history – an eternal, non-linear pattern that denies the need for history altogether. At the end of *A Scots Quair* Chris Guthrie, like Kenn in Gunn's *Highland River*, accepts an ultimate isolation from the human community and so escapes the temporality that community necessarily suffers, a temporality that invites the intrusion of history. Each is identified at the end of the novel with the eternal principles of a landscape that is untouched by human changes, its granite permanence implacably opposed to human transformations.

Such an ultimate dehistoricising of truth, making the historyless condition of Scotland the model of a higher ideal, is itself, of course, a denial of narrative. The most successful Scottish novels of our century accept narrative from history only to deny history and narrative as ultimate revelations of human truth. Again and again Scottish novels conclude with the recognition that the pattern of an individual life is not a unique and particular fact of history, but the re-enactment of some archetypal pattern of myth or ritual. Once that recognition is made there is no further need for particular and individual narrative. In Gunn's novels the individual escapes the intrusive effects of history by realising that he is not moulded by its forces but by the primordial underlying patterns of his culture's myths and legends. Similarly in *Greenvoe* Mackay Brown's displaced islanders return to their island and by their secret ritual defeat the forces of history. In these novels it is not the silent drift of post-history, but the archetypal cycle of pre-history that is their escape from the historical. Given such beliefs narrative itself is difficult if not impossible to sustain: the novel, by its commitment to narration, can never be the medium of ultimate truths: it can only be the prelude to the realisation of truths which will make the form itself irrelevant.

This double pattern, the Lowland desire for re-entry into history, the Highland desire for re-entry into mythic pre-history, is enacted beautifully in Muriel Spark's *Prime of Miss Jean Brodie*. Jean Brodie herself is a woman desperately desiring an entry into the history which has deprived her of her lover: her fascism is an attempt to introduce from without what she sees as significant narrative in contemporary history. Opposed to her is Sandy Stranger (truth is stranger than . . .) who becomes a nun in denial of history. Between the two drifts Mary McGregor, Spark's equivalent of Sharp's melancholy soldier, Mary dies in a hotel fire during the war, a death that has no significance in the narrative of history:

> *Back and forth along the corridors ran Mary Macgregor, through the thickening smoke. She ran one way: then, turning, the other way: and at either end the blast furnace of the fire met her. She heard no screams, she gave no scream, for the smoke was choking her. She ran into somebody on her third turn, stumbled and died.* (1965,15)

Like the Scottish novel Mary runs between the fire of history and the fire of myth, from narrative to ritual, being destroyed by both. To enter history will be to leave Scotland behind, as Muriel Spark herself has done, as Ewan Tavendale does in *Grey Granite*; to enter myth will be to destroy the narrative potentialities of the novel by replacing them with a primordial, non-temporal set of relationships. The Scottish novelist sits in the kitchen and wonders if there is any life in the kit bag, or climbs into the kit bag to escape the confines of the kitchen.

NOTES

1 All references are to the most easily available editions of the novels.

Beyond the Caledonian Antisyzygy: Contemporary Scottish poetry in between cultures

Ursula Kimpel 1995 in H-W Ludwig and L Fietz (eds) *Poetry in the British Isles: Non-Metropolitan Perspectives*, Cardiff (University of Wales Press), 135–56.

I

Recent literary and cultural theory has come to perceive multi-culturality or cross-culturality as the inevitable condition of modern societies world-wide – the result of colonial and imperial expansion and of labour migration – and, what is more, as the inevitable condition of creativity. Thus, in their important study of *Theory and Practice in Post-colonial Literatures* (1989), Bill Ashcroft, Gareth Griffiths and Helen Tiffin write:

> Both literary theorists and cultural historians are beginning to recognize cross-culturality as the potential termination point of an apparently endless human history of conquest and annihilation justified by the myth of group 'purity', and as the basis on which the post-colonial world can be creatively stabilized.[1]

According to Ashcroft, Griffiths and Tiffin,

> impetus towards decentering and pluralism has always been present in the history of European thought and has reached its latest development in post-structuralism. But the situation of marginalized societies and cultures enabled them to come to this position much earlier and more directly.[2]

But in any case, such a position had to be hard won against a dominant discourse which privileged homogeneity rather than heterogeneity as the basis of cultural identity. 'The problem is that we have been taught to see culture in terms of unity and completeness', the Scottish critic Cairns Craig writes in the official programme of a Commonwealth Writers Conference which took place in Edinburgh in July 1986. Speaking not only for Scottish literature, but also for the experience of the writers from all over the English-speaking world assembled at the conference, Craig spells out the condition of what he calls 'Being Between':

> Most of us inhabit a fractured culture, a bi-culturalism of language, nation, tradition or class, whose effects we expect to be destructive because we assume that the self-division of our language and our culture cannot help but be reflected as a fissure in the organisation of our poetry. We do not live, however, within a language or a tradition, but between languages and traditions. It is those poets who have lived 'in between' who have made the most powerful contributions to the literatures of English in the twentieth century.

Craig goes on to maintain that in 'Scotland the dialectic between Scots and English and between Gaelic and English has generated an immense amount of linguistic experiment which may act as a kind of map for the possibilities of such biculturalism'.[3] But the history of Scottish literature in this century also provides a kind of map of the powerful obstacles inherent in the process of coming to terms with the experience of cultural heterogeneity when confronted with the strong pressure of inherited homogenizing ideologies.

A tension between the experience of cultural heterogeneity on the one hand and a strong pressure for cultural homogeneity on the other hand may be said to be the main driving force behind the development of Scottish literature throughout the twentieth century. From this tension the process of cultural self-determination which was started by the Scottish Literary Renaissance at the beginning of this century derived its momentum. It was perpetuated by a key term of the Scottish Renaissance: G Gregory Smith's self-consciously apologetic conception of the 'Caledonian antisyzygy' (or combination of opposites) as formulated in his history of Scottish literature of 1919.[4]

In modern Scotland a number of factors make for a patchwork of the most heterogeneous cultural fields, such as Scotland's history between independence and the United Kingdom of Great Britain; its three language communities – the Gaelic, the Scots, and the English – often overlapping, more often mutually indifferent or even hostile; and its long history of being involved in different waves of pre-industrial and industrial migrations. Yet the model of a homogeneous national culture inherited from the nineteenth-century United Kingdom has exerted a very strong pressure throughout the present century. As a result, for the greater part of the century the dominant discourse in which Scottish writers have located themselves tends to view the multiplicity of Scotland's cultural inheritance as an embarrassment and a major predicament for creative work. And ever since the Scottish Literary Renaissance, considerable effort has been spent on an attempt to construct a homogenous unity out of the disparate elements of Scottish culture.

Most notably the challenge was taken up by two major Scottish poets in this century, Edwin Muir and Hugh MacDiarmid. Their work in the late thirties, in particular – criticism and poetry – was wholly dominated by a colossal effort of 'Seeing Scotland Whole', as MacDiarmid put it in his autobiography *Lucky Poet*.[5] They both took their cue from Gregory Smith's conception of the 'Caledonian antisyzygy'. Between them, Muir and MacDiarmid succeeded in inflating this problematic conception to such proportions that for decades to come it almost paralyzed any debate on what modern Scottish culture might be. Contemporary Scottish culture has been persistently haunted by the spectre of the 'antisyzygy'. Its favourite hunting ground seems to be sweeping statements on the state of Scottish culture of the more maudlin kind. But as a close second comes 'serious' criticism. Indeed, many critics, poets among them, have gone out of their way to provide an ample, and seemingly inexhaustible, supply of blood for the ghosts.[6] Yet contemporary Scottish poetry and criticism have also provided spaces beyond the 'antisyzygy' in which a new attitude towards the heterogeneous experience of Scotland could be developed.

2

The 'Caledonian antisyzygy' is the problematic offspring of a discourse commonly known as 'Eng. Lit.'. The discourse of 'Eng. Lit.', as developed in the late nineteenth century, is based on a conception of English nation literature as expressing the spirit of English national life, its history mirroring the growth of the national mind. It was largely developed by writers from the peripheries of Britain, mainly Scottish and Irish intellectuals (drawing on continental, mainly German models), as part of a strategy by which they wrote themselves into English culture.[7]

In this century, the discourse of 'Eng. Lit.' turned out to be much more tenacious than the United Kingdom itself. Originally developed as a strategy supporting integration into the United Kingdom by writers from the peripheries themselves, it proved to be hard to get rid of when, at the beginning of the century, Scottish and Irish writers began to reassert their own cultural traditions. Their acts of reassertion typically took the form of an attempt to establish an *Irish* or *Scottish* national identity independent of the English. Yet this is precisely the point where trouble started for Scottish writers: in their attempts to construct a national literature of their own, these writers, often trained within the discourse of 'Eng. Lit.', inevitably came up against the standards set by English literature. Compared with the 'Great tradition' of English literature, Scottish literature to their embarrassment looked a very patchy affair. Nowhere is this clearer than in a history of Scottish literature written at the beginning of the century by a Scottish lecturer in English at Edinburgh University: G. Gregory Smith's *Scottish Literature: Character and Influence* (1919). It was a passage of this book which provided the Scottish Literary Renaissance with its famous phrase, the 'Caledonian antisyzygy'. In reflecting on the course of Scottish literature, Gregory Smith here notes 'two considerations of contrary bearing':

> One is of encouragement; that the literature is a literature of a small country, that it runs a shorter course than others, and that there is no linguistic divorce between its earlier and its later stages, as in southern English. In this shortness and cohesion the most favourable conditions seem to be offered for the making of a general estimate. But, on the other hand, we find at closer scanning that this cohesion, at least in formal expression and in choice of material, is only apparent, that the literature is remarkably varied, and that it becomes, under the stress of foreign influence and native division and reaction, almost a zigzag of contradictions. The antithesis need not, however, disconcert us. Perhaps in the very combination of opposites – what either of the two Sir Thomases, of Norwich and Cromarty, might have been willing to call ' the Caledonian antisyzygy' – we have the reflection of the contrasts which the Scot shows at every turn, in his political and ecclesiastical history, in his polemical restlessness, in his adaptability, which is another way of saying that he has made allowance for new conditions, in his practical judgement, which is the admission that two sides of the matter have been considered. If therefore Scottish history and life are, as an old northern writer said of something else, 'varied with a clean contrair spirit,' we need not be surprised to find that in his literature the Scot presents two aspects which appear contradictory. Oxymoron has ever been the bravest figure, and we must not forget that disorderly order is order after all. We can be indifferent to the disciples of De Quincey who will suspect us of making 'ambitious paradoxes' and 'false distinctions'. We may dwell on these incongruities, the better to explain their remarkable synthesis in Scottish literature; as we may, in a later chapter, on the breaks and thwarts, the better to show the continuity of a literary tradition.[8]

Gregory Smith here is at pains to prove that Scottish literature is a true expression of the Scottish mind. The idea of an organic national literary tradition, as exemplified in the discourse of 'Eng. Lit.', is clearly present in the background as the standard of comparison and it provides the framework in which the passage is enclosed. Thus the passage begins and ends by naming the most important aspects of the standard: 'cohesion' and 'continuity'. This framework at the same time reveals what Gregory Smith perceives as the chief characteristic of Scottish literature, namely its *lack* of coherence and continuity, and it contains the discontinuity it has revealed in a semblance of coherence and continuity. Working from within the interpretative framework of 'Eng. Lit.', Gregory Smith clearly perceives Scottish literature as deficient (hence his all too frequent assurances to the effect that nobody needs to be worried by the worrying state of affairs he describes). He therefore adapts the framework in such a way that it fits Scottish literature.

Of crucial importance here is the paradoxical term around which the whole passage is set. 'Antisyzygy' means a combination of opposites. With the help of this term, Gregory Smith performs a conjuring trick of admirable, if doubtful, ingenuity: he locates the phenomenon which he is describing in a tradition which embraces both English and Scottish literature. The trick works by tentatively ascribing the freakishly quasi-humanist term to two seventeenth-century authors, both well-known for their idiosyncratic style and masters of 'ambitious paradoxes', one from Scotland: Sir Thomas Urquhart of Cromarty, author of *The Jewel* and translator of Rabelais, and one from England: Sir Thomas Browne of Norwich, author of *Religio Medici, Pseudodoxia Epidemica, Hydriotaphia* and *The Garden of Cyrus*. These two 'Sir Thomases' might well have coined a phrase like 'Caledonian antisyzygy' and, more importantly, like seventeenth-century literature in general,[9] they both took great delight in any 'zigzag of contradictions'. By naming them as possible authors of his term, then, Gregory Smith indicates a tradition comprising both Scotland and England, in which the embarrassing lack of coherence and continuity displayed by Scottish literature might look more normal than otherwise. Despite the ingenious conjuring trick, however, the idea of the 'Caledonian antisyzygy' clearly bears the traces of its origin in some deeply troubled thinking about Scottish literature, the trouble arising mainly from Gregory Smith's desperate need to make sense of Scottish literature in terms of the discourse of 'Eng. Lit.' within which he was working. In the final analysis the 'Caledonian antisyzygy' is an expression of a sense of inferiority induced by the uneasy existence of Scottish literature in between conflicting cultural fields.

3

In 1936 the poet Edwin Muir published a famous book of criticisms *Scott and Scotland. The Predicament of the Scottish Writer*,[10] in which he spells out the implications of the 'Caledonian antisyzygy' as formulated by Gregory Smith and takes it to its logical extreme. The argument offered in *Scott and Scotland* could be summarized as follows: if one accepts the notion that a homogeneous culture reflected in a homogeneous body of literature is the highest aim to be achieved, then no amount of clever reasoning and no 'ambitious paradoxes' can explain away the fact that a fragmented cultural inheritance must be ultimately harmful. The only solution, then, would be to join the one cultural tradition available which does seem to fulfil the norm.

For Muir, as for Gregory Smith, this meant English culture. Throughout his book, English culture as the standard of comparison applied stands for completeness, Scottish culture for fragmentation. The whole book is pervaded by a juxtaposition of images of completeness and fragmentation: England possesses an organic society, a homogeneous language, a rich and continuous literary tradition; Scotland's society is fragmented, it does not possess a homogeneous language, its literary history is nothing but a series of disconnected figures. Through this set of juxtapositions Muir re-enacts a fable of loss. In the particular story of *Scott and Scotland* this loss is identified as 'the lack of a whole mind' (p 9) brought about by a 'far-reaching dissociation' (p 72). This dissociation had set in as a result of the loss of Scots as an autonomous language and the concomitant introduction of English into Scotland. Both were brought about by a complex interaction of historical and religious events (the Reformation had introduced the English Bible; the Unions of Crowns and Parliaments in 1603 and 1707 meant that Scots was replaced by English as the official language of all Scotland). According to Muir, this meant 'that Scotsmen feel in one language and think in another; that their emotions turn to the Scottish tongue with all its associations of local sentiment, and their minds to a standard English which for them is almost bare of associations other than of the classroom' (p 8). It also meant the loss of a common language, capable of expressing the full range of modern experience on all levels of discourse and in all literary genres and it finally led to a fragmentation of Scottish culture as a whole. Muir maintains that 'Scotland will remain a mere collection of districts' unless Scottish literature finds an 'adequate language' in which to recreate a sense of a full national life (p 112). This, according to Muir, could only be achieved by an 'act of faith' (p 113) similar to that performed by Yeats in Irish literature, an act of faith by which Scottish writers would take full advantage of English as the only language capable of full expression still available to them (Scots being disqualified by its fragmentation into numerous local dialects and its impoverished literary tradition, and Gaelic by its minority status). This would still involve a loss, be only a partial solution to the 'Predicament of the Scottish writer', since English could never be invested with those 'associations of local sentiment' which belong to the vernacular. Writing in English, then, in Muir's view could only be an approximation to the ideal of wholeness, but certainly the closest approximation possible. Indeed, it is only in the dreamlike vision of his poetry, written in the classical blank verse of Shakespeare, Milton, and Wordsworth (the great tradition of English poetry which Muir chose to join), that Muir can finally perceive fragmented Scotland as 'a difficult country, and our home' ('The Difficult Land'),[11] in which the violence and waste of its history is bound into a mythical pattern, the scene fixed in the timelessness of myth, the speaker's voice gathered into the collective 'we' of a national community.

4

Whereas Muir, facing what he perceived as Scotland's fragmentation, opted for the English language and the English tradition in literature as a cultural field in which to root his poetry, MacDiarmid, at about the same time, firmly opted for the indigenous Gaelic tradition. By the 1930s, MacDiarmid, partly in a furious reaction against Muir, had come to see the Gaelic as the only genuinely Scottish tradition. Given his own background in Lowland Scots culture and given that Gaelic culture is only a minority culture in modern Scotland (and a much beleaguered one at that), this decision was fraught with obvious difficulties. It was a decision, in fact, which may seem even more problematic than Muir's decision for the English tradition. But, interestingly, MacDiarmid's understanding of the Gaelic tradition offered him a way of dealing positively with Scotland's fragmentation, a way which may be described as love of the land itself in all its diversity. In Gaelic nature poetry he found a praise of place and the minutest detail of nature which delights in diversity rather than homogeneity. This attitude to place gave MacDiarmid not only a precedent for his own tendency to value equally each and every patch of Scottish soil, irrespective of the different histories and traditions encoded in them. It also gave new resonance to his favourite notion of the 'Caledonian antisyzygy' which he increasingly came to associate with the value system of Gaelic nature poetry:

In the wonderful diversity and innumerable
Sharp transitions of the Scottish scene,
The source of our Scottish antisyzygy,
I . . . See now the reconciliation of all opposites.[12]

('Direadh I')

Thus the notion of the 'Caledonian antisyzygy' undergoes an important transformation in the work of the later MacDiarmid (cf. particularly the travel-book *The Islands of Scotland* and the 'Direadh' sequence of poems with its three bird's-eye views of Scotland[13]). It is no longer rooted in a supposed common English/Scottish tradition, going back to the seventeenth century, as it was in Gregory Smith's text, but in the utterly un-English, much older, indigenous Gaelic tradition. And whereas Muir, faced with Scotland's linguistic diversity, mournfully opted for English as the lesser evil, MacDiarmid energetically embraced the vision of a future 'world language'[14] which would thrive precisely on a diversity of languages such as Scotland had inherited. Although this 'world language' would not be identical with any of Scotland's three languages, its roots would be in Gaelic, not in English.

This shift of perspective made it possible for MacDiarmid, firstly, to prove that contemporary Scottish culture could be explained in terms of an indigenous tradition, in other words, that against all appearances contemporary Scottish culture was based on a continuous tradition and, secondly, to attach positive value to Scotland's fragmentation, which had proved so troublesome to Gregory Smith and Muir. In fact, 'fragmentation' increasingly comes to be replaced by 'diversity', a term with much more positive connotations, in MacDiarmid's writing of the thirties, prose and poetry. MacDiarmid thus prepared the way for a view of Scottish culture which no longer needed to be apologetic about its fragmentation. Indeed, the 'Caledonian antisyzygy' in his hands came close to meaning a diversity *no longer in need of* the reconciliation of opposites indicated in the term 'antisyzygy'. Nevertheless, in the final analysis both Muir *and* MacDiarmid still share Gregory Smith's basic assumption that a country's culture is valid only in so far as it can be shown that it is based on a common national identity. Hence their attempts to link Scottish culture to a single line of tradition, the English in Muir's case, the Gaelic in MacDiarmid's case. Yet the enormous 'act of faith' involved in *both* attempts indicates that the idea of a common national identity has finally arrived at breaking point. This is true for both Muir and MacDiarmid, regardless of the fact that their respective 'acts of faith' take very different forms. It is difficult, indeed, to imagine how Scots from all backgrounds could rally round either Muir's vision of 'The Difficult Land' or MacDiarmid's Gaelic 'Vision of a World language'.

5

With Muir and MacDiarmid the project of 'Seeing Scotland Whole' arrived at a point where it could hardly be continued. A witty epitaph to the whole project may be found in Edwin Morgan's concrete poem 'A Chaffinch Map of Scotland' (1965)[15] which teasingly takes up Muir's and MacDiarmid's triple concern with the diversity of Scotland, a focus on the country as a whole, and a language to express its true tradition. The 'Chaffinch Map of Scotland' consists of an accurate inventory of the local variations of the bird-names as they occur in Scotland, typographically arranged on the page in such a way that it resembles the outlines of the map of Scotland. Read aloud, this map of Scotland is onomatopoeically transformed into a chorus of birdsong (rhythmically patterned by different line lengths, the line breaks and gaps in the lines shaping the contours of Scotland on the page) which takes the sound shape of the word 'chaffinch' through a series of variations: 'chaffinch / chaffinchaffinch / . . . / chaffie chye chaffiechaffie / . . . / shillyshelly / . . . / shilfyshelfyshelly / shellyfaw / shielyshellyfaw / . . . / shilfy-shelfyshelfy chaffiechaffie / . . . / shilfy / shilfyshelfy', and then laconically breaks off with the *one* term in the whole list – located in the southernmost corner of Scotland – which is *not* phonetically related to 'chaffinch': 'brichtie'. This 'Chaffinch Map of Scotland (a pun on 'half-inch map', of course) wittily and playfully satirizes any attempt at charting 'Scotland Whole'.[16] It totally lacks the searching seriousness of either Muir's or MacDiarmid's visions (Scotland a birdsong: 'syzygy, 'syzygy, 'syzygy . . .). At the same time it demonstrates at a very 'concrete' level how effectively the linguistic variety of Scotland may be used for poetic purposes, thus at one sweep brushing aside both Muir's argument for English as the only possible language for Scottish literature and MacDiarmid's heady metaphysical construction of a Gaelic 'world language'.

Indeed, many contemporary Scottish poets after Muir and MacDiarmid seem to be tired of the subject of Scotland altogether. Iain Crichton Smith has spoken of his feeling that 'there is nothing real in Scotland that you can actually operate on to make real poetry', that there is 'just talking about what has gone on in the past' and he compares the case of Scotland with the very different case of contemporary Ireland where the pressure of everyday violence *does* create a powerful commitment to the question of Ireland: 'I think the Irish poets are very lucky, in a sense, because they have to deal with real things.'[17] Norman MacCaig, asked about his Scottish loyalties, gave a scornfully polemical answer which betrays his extreme exasperation with a nationalism locked into mournful contemplation of Scotland's past and his refusal to deal with any generalizations about national character as against a concern with the individual:

I don't like the Scots, and I don't like their history. Liars, murderers, traitors, not only in the Highlands, the Borders as well. I think the Scots are awful . . . I think everybody's awful, except when you meet a particular instance, and some of them are so wonderful and marvellous . . . and don't tell me they came from their filthy history.[18]

Whereas Crichton Smith in a way regrets the absence of a cause which might generate commitment to the idea of Scotland, MacCaig utterly refuses to join any such cause, even if it would present itself. The jibe against the Scots' 'filthy history' is a refusal to consider at all seriously Muir's contention that Scotland's history must be a 'predicament of the Scottish writer'. MacCaig's insistence on the individual instance would allow neither generalizations about the collective identity of '*the* Scottish writer' nor about the meaning of Scottish history as a whole.

6

In contemporary Scottish poetry there is still a powerful commitment to the experience of Scotland. But the attempt to imagine a common national identity seems to have been abandoned for good. Instead, poets tend to express their sense of Scotland through an exploration of the landscapes, the history, the traditions, the languages of those Scottish regions and places which more immediately belong to their own personal background. In the attitude to place in contemporary Scottish poetry we thus observe a phenomenon which – adapting Tom Nairn's famous phrase of 'The Break-Up of Britain'[19] – we may call 'The Break-Up of Scotland': a shift from a predominantly national to a predominantly regional concern. This is certainly a shift towards places more clearly recognizable and closer to the actual experience of Scotland than Muir's and MacDiarmid's Scotlands of the mind. But the regional places of contemporary Scottish poetry are by no means less resistant to attempts to imagine them in a single vision, encoded securely in a single unbroken line of tradition or a single perspective. They tend to be precarious inter-spaces between landscape, history, and the traditions and languages involved in Scottish culture. Three examples from the work of Sorley MacLean, Norman MacCaig, and Edwin Morgan may serve to illustrate the point.

Sorley MacLean's 'Hallaig' (1954)[20] is perhaps the most famous poem of place in contemporary Scottish poetry and has become a touchstone for any concern with the difficult regional places of Scotland. It is a meditation on the changes worked by time on the place where the poet's family lived for centuries

('Time, the deer, is in the wood of Hallaig'), written in Gaelic and translated into English by the poet himself. Hallaig is seen as a place of desolation where the old vegetation has taken over from the people driven away in the clearances; yet in the speaker's vision the desolation seems alive with the people who once lived there:

Na fir 'nan laighe air an lianaig
aig ceann gach taighe a bh' ann,
na h-igheanan 'nan coille bheithe
direach an druim, crom an ceann.

The men lying on the green
at the end of every house that was,
the girls a wood of birches,
straight their backs, bent their heads.

The place of Hallaig in this poem is an inter-space, encoded in the *difference* between past and present and in the *difference* between two languages. In fact, the poem itself has ceased to be monolingual: MacLean's English translation from his Gaelic is not only an expendable concession to the multilingual publishing situation in Scotland, but an essential part of the poem, reflecting the fact that the speaker's perspective on Hallaig no longer allows for a space in which Gaelic would *not* have to compete/coexist with English. The inter-space from which Hallaig emerges is frozen in time by the speaker's loving vision:

and when the sun goes down behind Dun Cana
a vehement bullet will come from the gun of Love;

and will strike the deer that goes dizzily
. . .
his eye will freeze in the wood,
his blood will not be traced while I live.

Yet the speaker sees himself as a poacher illegally hunting time, his prey, at nightfall. Thus his vision is an extremely precarious one which has to be guarded in secrecy as long as he lives.

Norman MacCaig's poem 'A Man in Assynt' (1967)[21] is also concerned with a difficult place in Gaelic Scotland. But its speaker – in not belonging to the Gaelic language community himself – is yet further exiled from the place than MacLean's poacher in the country of his ancestors. The landscape of Assynt,

scene of the notorious Sutherland Clearances which left it as desolate as
MacLean's Hallaig, is seen with the eye of a visitor from Edinburgh who loves
it but does not belong to it:

> Up there, the scraping light
> whittles the cloud edges till, like thin bone,
> they're bright with their own opaque selves. Down here,
> a skinny rosebush is an eccentric jug
> of air. They make me,
> somewhere between them,
> a visiting eye,
> an unrequited passion,
> watching the tide glittering backward and making
> its huge withdrawal from beaches
> and kilted rocks. And the mind
> behind the eye, within the passion,
> remembers with certainty that the tide will return
> and thinks, with hope, that that other ebb,
> the sad withdrawal of people, may, too,
> reverse itself and flood
> the bays and the sheltered glens
> with new generations replenishing the land
> with its richest of riches and coming, at last,
> into their own again.

The Assynt of MacCaig's poem is neither just primordial landscape, nor just a
place defined by its history of loss. At the beginning of the paragraph quoted
here it seems completely governed by the mind of the observer which gives it a
structure between 'Up there' and 'Down here' and encodes it in striking conceits
('a skinny rosebush is an eccentric jug/of air'). Yet the observing mind,
oscillating between memory and hope, is itself governed by the cyclical rhythms
of nature, ebb tide and flood tide. The place of Assynt thus is at the intersection
between the landscape, its history, and the mind of the outside observer.

Even more than Assynt, the urban wasteland of Edwin Morgan's 'Glasgow
Green' (1968)[22] resists the attempt to be defined by a single voice. Glasgow Green
in this poem is encoded between different voices, harshly set against each other.
The scene is set by a strictly conventional, somewhat melodramatic, poetic
evocation of mood: 'Clammy midnight, moonless mist . . . Meth-men mutter
on benches,/pawed by river fog . . .'. Into this scene, the immediacy of direct
speech intrudes violently, a Glasgow dialect voice enacting a homosexual rape:

'What d'ye mean see me again?
D'ye think I came here jist for that?
I'm no finished with you yet,
I can get the boys t'ye, they're no that faur away.
You wouldny like that eh? Look there's no two ways aboot it.
Christ but I'm gaun to have you Mac
if it takes all night, turn over you bastard
turn over, I'll -'

And here a different voice interrupts with a sharp 'Cut the scene'. This voice
insists on the brutal reality of the scene, not to be defused and made acceptable
by any conventions of horror fiction: 'the sweat/is real, the wrestling under a
bush/is real, the dirty starless river/is the real Clyde'. Yet this voice also notes an
aspect of the place very different from the violent nocturnal incident, coming to
another break in the poem with the first naming of the place:

> . . . washing blows
>   where the women watch
> by day,
>   and children run,
>   on Glasgow Green.

By the time the place is named for the first time, then, the poem has moved
through a number of different voices and aspects all belonging to the place, thus
constituting it as a multidimensional reality. At this point, another voice breaks
in, the passionately insistent voice of popular pulpit oratory, searching for a
meaning between the violence and the peacefulness, culminating in a prophetic
appeal to reinvent the place:

> Water the wilderness, walk there, reclaim it!
> Reclaim, regain, renew! Fill the barns and the vats!
>
> Longing,
>   longing
>   shall find its wine.

Yet this vision of renewal is denied its fulfilment in the poem. In the last
paragraph an altogether more sceptical voice takes over from the passionately
prophetical voice and encodes the place in a metaphor defining it as a place in
which the universal principle of desire acts itself out perpetually:

Let the women sit in the Green
and rock their prams as the sheets
blow and whip in the sunlight.
But the beds of married love
are islands in a sea of desire.
Its waves break here, in this park,
splashing the flesh as it trembles
like driftwood through the dark.

The place of Glasgow Green thus remains suspended in a space of never-fulfilled desire between the violence and the peacefulness, between acceptance and the hope for renewal. None of the voices in this poem is ultimately allowed to gain control over the others.

These three examples all testify to a continuing process of reinventing Scotland. They all take Muir's and MacDiarmid's investigations one important step further: having abandoned the attempt to construct a common national identity out of a diversity of elements in favour of a commitment to places which have a more immediately personal significance for them, MacLean, MacCaig, and Morgan discover the experience of heterogeneity *within* the very place they have singled out for closer inspection. The important point, however, is that they do not attempt to reconcile this heterogeneity in one single vision but let their places exist, precariously and changeably, in the spaces between conflicting influences. Thus they do justice to the experience of Scotland in all its diversity – and they do so without recourse to a concept like the 'Caledonian antisyzygy'.

7

Yet critical concepts, once established, tend to acquire a life of their own which lasts long after their usefulness has been exhausted. Contemporary criticism, at any rate, was rather slower in discarding the 'Caledonian antisyzygy' than poetry. Thus the discourse of the 'Caledonian antisyzygy' and the 'Predicament of the Scottish Writer' resurfaced with a vengeance when, in 1979, the referendum on the 'Scotland and Wales Act' failed to produce enough support for even a modest degree of Scottish independence. Initially writers, in an attempt to make sense of their cultural situation, responded to this failure by reviving the debate Muir and MacDiarmid between them had already thoroughly exhausted. Muir's *Scott and Scotland* was reissued in 1982. The publisher's blurb announced it as still 'one of the most important and provocative criticisms of Scottish literature to be written in this century' and made it the subject of a conference which was to discuss the implications of Muir's analysis for contemporary writers. This proved to be the 'Cultural Non Event of the Year', as Joy Hendry noted at the time.[23] Any number of mournful clichés about 'the Scottish Writer' were freely bandied about, the claims of Gaelic and Scots to the true inheritance of Scotland were discussed with more or less conviction, and where Muir's book was confronted at all it was indiscriminately dismissed without even the attempt to place it in a broader perspective. The question of what the 'Predicament' of Scottish writers might be and how it could be overcome was lost beyond recovery in this debate.

In fact, apparently unnoticed by the prophets of doom, the question itself was becoming obsolete. Against all expectations, the 1979 debacle proved to be far from detrimental to Scottish culture. On the contrary, the 1980s saw an upsurge of creativity which amounted to something like a new Scottish Renaissance. Among the signs of the times was the appearance of an important new magazine, started by young writers and intellectuals directly in the wake of 1979. *Cencrastus*, which in its subtitle self-confidently links Scottish to 'International Literature, Arts and Affairs', offered a forum for a lively and fiercely intellectual debate on Scottish culture – certainly not a cosy hunting ground for the ghosts. At about the same time Tessa Ransford and Tom Hubbard began building up quite literally a 'room of their own' for Scottish poets, the Scottish Poetry Library in Edinburgh, which made it possible for the first time for a wider public to become acquainted with a wide range of poetry published in all three of Scotland's languages. Thus it became possible to acquire a knowledge of Scottish poetry which was no longer dependent on what the institutions of 'Eng. Lit.' might or might not provide.

This process was continued in the eighties with the appearance of several new histories of Scottish literature, notably Roderick Watson's *The Literature of Scotland*, which paved the way by giving 'a straightforward account of the lives, times and major works of Scotland's writers',[24] and the four-volume *History of Scottish Literature* edited by Cairns Craig,[25] which charts the terrain more closely through individual essays by a wide range of specialists focusing on particular aspects of Scotland's literary inheritance. Watson still paid cautious tribute to 'the presence of such factors as the 'Caledonian antisyzygy' . . . without proposing these as necessary, or exclusive proofs of Scottishness'.[26] In the volumes edited by Craig, any such considerations are notably absent. And it was Craig who formulated, in his introduction to the volume on the twentieth-century, the critical dogma which seems to be beginning to supplant that of the 'Predicament of the Scottish Writer':

> In defiance of critical theories that assert otherwise, the apparent lack of a
> coherent tradition, the lack of a coherent national culture, far from impeding
> development have been major stimuli to creativity. Scottish writers have been
> inspired by the condition of being between cultures rather than within a
> culture . . .[27]

This statement appears somewhat too purposefully optimistic when applied
retrospectively to the whole story of Scottish literature in this century. Muir
and MacDiarmid clearly aspired to 'the condition of being . . . *within* a
culture'. If this has certainly not prevented them from writing very fine poetry,
it has not exactly helped them either. And by no stretch of the imagination
could it be said that the discourse of the 'Caledonian antisyzygy' which they
bequeathed to contemporary Scottish culture did anything at all towards
creating a lively intellectual climate which might prove a positive stimulus to
creativity. On the contrary, this discourse proved positively stifling, as
becomes painfully obvious when reading the documents of the 1982 debate
on the 'Predicament of the Scottish Writer'. And even in 1992 Douglas Dunn
still senses a 'skeleton' rattling in the 'Caledonian cupboard'.[28] But Craig's
statement does indeed summarize the new spirit of the Scottish cultural
renaissance of the eighties. This renaissance took its intellectual stimulus
certainly not from the outworn discourse of the 'Caledonian antisyzygy'
but rather from the new international discourse of the multicultural society
which became prevalent throughout the eighties and provided a fresh perspective on Scottish culture, too. With regard to the most recent Scottish
poetry Douglas Dunn notes: 'If anything explains the unclenched nationalism,
or refusal of any kind of nationalism on a poem's surface, it is the eclectic
reading and wider range of influences to which younger writers have exposed
themselves'.[29] The national perspective on Scottish culture was beginning to
give way to a comparative perspective. This new comparative perspective was
evident in the programme for the Edinburgh Commonwealth Writers conference in July 1986. It was perhaps best summarized by Seamus Heaney,
speaking at the 'International Conference on the Literature of Region and
Nation' which took place one month later, in August 1986, at the University
of Aberdeen. 'I have a sense that nowadays the writers on the outskirts know
more about one another than ever before and have begun to take cognisance
of each other in ways that are fortifying and illuminating',[30] Heaney said, and
he concluded his 'regional forecast' by maintaining that

> poets in these various regional, post-colonial or off-center situations have
> long ago been freed to throw away the cracked looking-glass of the servant

and to scan the world instead through the cunningly arranged and easily manoeuverable periscope of their submerged sensibility.[31]

As Craig points out, the 'fragmentation and division which made Scotland seem abnormal to an earlier part of the twentieth century came to be the norm for much of the world's population'[32] – as it is, indeed, for the disintegrating English society of our days. Which means, of course, that the standards of 'Eng. Lit.' have become obsolete even in England. Consequently, there is no longer any reason why Scottish writers should apologize for not conforming to these standards.

8

Diversity in itself is hardly a meaningful concept. In order to be experienced as meaningful, the 'situation between cultures rather than within a culture' requires the continuing effort of defining places in between from which speaking and writing becomes possible. Such places will have to be scrupulously exact as to the details of landscape, history, and language; but above all, inevitably, changeable and eminently precarious. In fact, places such as Edwin Morgan's 'On the Needle's Point: 'Of course it is not a point at all./ We live here, and we should know.'[33] The place on the needle's point may eventually even turn out to be something like a precarious paradise:

> But I like it on the point, good
> is the dark cavern, good the craggy walks,
> good the vertiginous bare brightness,
> good the music, good the dance
> when sometimes we join wings and drift
> in interlinking circles, how many thousands
> I could never tell, silent ourselves,
> almost melting into light.[14]

At any rate, 'On the Needle's Point' is probably as good a place as any from which to develop a poetics of the truly multicultural society.

NOTES

1 Bill Ashcroft, Gareth Griffiths, Helen Tiffin, *The Empire Writes Back. Theory and Practice in Post-colonial Literatures* (London, 1989), 36.

2 Ibid, 12.

3 Cairns Craig, 'Being Between', official programme of the Commonwealth Writers Conference, Edinburgh, 17–21 July 1986, 7. Craig's argument here is based on several previous publications, in particular his important essay, 'Peripheries' in *Cencrastus*, 9 (1982), 3–9.

4 G. Gregory Smith, *Scottish Literature, Character and Influence* (London, 1919).

5 'Seeing Scotland Whole' is the title of a chapter in MacDiarmid's *Lucky Poet* (1943) (reprinted London, 1972).

6 Witness, most recently, Robin Bell's relentlessly facetious introduction to his otherwise useful anthology of contemporary Scottish poetry, *The Best of Scottish Poetry. An Anthology of Contemporary Scottish Verse* (Edinburgh, 1989).

7 Important contributions were made, for example, by the Scottish writer Thomas Carlyle and the Irish critic Edward Dowden. This is not sufficiently realized in recent English accounts of 'The rise of English' (Eagleton) which tend to over-emphasize the role played by Matthew Arnold, Cf. Terry Eagleton, 'The rise of English', in his *Literary Theory* (Oxford, 1983), 17–53; Chris Baldick, *The Social Mission of English Criticism, 1848–1932* (Oxford, 1987).

8 *Scottish Literature: Character and Influence*, op. cit., 3–5.

9 For complex reasons, seventeenth-century English literature proved to be a useful point of contact with 'mainstream' English literature for poets from the 'peripheries' throughout this century, Cf. T.S. Eliot's 'Metaphysicals' essay of 1921 and, more recently, Seamus Heaney's praise of George Herbert in *The Redress of Poetry. An Inaugural Lecture Delivered Before the University of Oxford on 24 October 1989* (Oxford, 1990).

10 Rpt Edinburgh, 1982. Subsequently, page numbers in brackets refer to this reprint.

11 Edwin Muir, *Collected Poems* (London, 1984,), 238.

12 Muir's and MacDiarmid's contributions to the discourse of the 'Caledonian antisyzygy' are discussed in more detail in a previous version of this essay: Ursula Kimpel, 'Modern Scottish Poetry. Beyond the "Caledonian antisyzygy"', in Lothar Fietz, Paul Hoffmann, Hans-Werner Ludwig (eds.), *Regionalität Nationalität und Internationalität in der zeitgenössischen Lyrik* (Tübingen, 1992), 284–302.

13 *The Complete Poems of Hugh MacDiarmid*, ed. Michael Grieve and W.R. Aitken (Hardmondsworth, 1985), vol. II, 1170.

14 Extracts from *The Islands of Scotland* (1939) are reprinted in Alan Bold (ed.), *The Thistle Rises, An Anthology of Poetry and Prose by Hugh MacDiarmid* (London, 1984); the 'Dìreadh' sequence, written as part of MacDiarmid's 'Mature Art' project submitted to Faber and Faber in 1938, although it was not published independently before 1974, is reprinted in *The Complete Poems of Hugh MacDiarmid*, vol. II, 1163–93.

15 'A Vision of World Language' was to be the title of a long poem which MacDiarmid began writing in 1939. The only part of this project which was ever completed is 'In Memoriam James Joyce; (*Complete Poems*, vol. II, 737–889). This poem develops the idea of and itself acts out the movement towards a 'world language'.

16 'A Chaffinch Map of Scotland' was one of Morgan's contributions to Emmett Williams's famous *Anthology of Concrete Poetry* (New York, 1967).

17 Christopher Carrell (ed.), *Seven Poets* (Glasgow, Third Eye Centre, 1981), 47. The seven poets presented in this attractive publication (with portraits by the Scottish painter Alexander Moffat, photographs by Jessie Ann Matthews, interviews, selections of their poetry, biographical and bibliographical material) are Hugh MacDiarmid, Norman MacCaig, Iain Crichton Smith, George Mackay Brown, Robert Garioch, Sorley MacLean and Edwin Morgan.

18 Ibid., 38.

19 Tom Nairn, *The Break-Up of Britain* (2nd edn. London, 1981).

20 Reprinted in Sorley MacLean, *Spring Tide and Neap Tide, Selected Poems 1932–72/ Reothairt is Contraigh, Taghadh de Dhàin 1932–72* (Edinburgh, 1981), 142–5.

21 'A Man in Assynt' was commissioned by the BBC and broadcast in 1967. It was printed in MacCaig's collection *A Man in My Position* (1969) and reprinted in his *Collected Poems* (London, 1985), 214–20.

22 'Glasgow Green' appeared in Morgan's collection *The Second Life* (1968) and was reprinted in his *Selected Poems* (Manchester, 1985), 30–3.

23 In her editorial to the special issue of *Chapman* devoted to the question 'The State of Scotland – A Predicament for the Scottish Writer?' *Chapman*, 35–26 (1983), 1.

24 Roderick Watson, *The Literature of Scotland* (London, 1984), Macmillan History of Literature series), 4.

25 *The History of Scottish Literature*, general ed. Cairns Craig, 4 vols., (Aberdeen, 1987–8). Watson and Craig provide the best general introduction to Scottish literature. The individual essays in Craig's *Aberdeen History of Scottish Literature* also provide suggestions for further reading.

26 Roderick Watson *The Literature of Scotland*, op. cit. 4.

27 Cairns Craig (ed.) *The History of Scottish Literature*, vol. IV, (Aberdeen, 1987), 3.

28 In his introduction to the *Faber Book of Twentieth-Century Scottish Poetry* (London, 1992), xlv.

29 Ibid.

30 Seamus Heaney, 'The Regional Forecast', in R.P. Draper (ed.), *The Literature of Region and Nation* (London, 1989), 22.

31 Ibid, 23.

32 *The History of Scottish Literature*, vol. IV, op. cit., 7.

33 Edwin Morgan, *Selected Poems*, op. cit., 105–6.

34 Ibid., 106.

ANTHOLOGIES OF MODERN SCOTTISH POETRY:

Bell, Robin (ed.), *the Best of Scottish Poetry. An Anthology of Contemporary Scottish Verse* (Edinburgh, 1989).

Dunn, Douglas (ed.), *The Faber Book of Twentieth-Century Scottish Poetry*, (London, 1992) (with an introductory essay by Douglas Dunn: 'Language and Liberty', xvii-xlv).

Kerrigan, Catherine (ed.), *An Anthology of Scottish Women Poets* (Edinburgh, 1991).

King, Charles (ed.), *Twelve Modern Scottish poets*, (London, 1971).

King, Charles and Smith, Iain Crichton (eds.), *Twelve More Modern Scottish poets* (London, 1986).

MacAulay, Donald (ed.), *Nua-Bhardachd Gailidhlig/ Modern Scottish Gaelic Poems* (1976) (rpt. Edinburgh, 1980).

FOR A COMPARATIVE PERSPECTIVE ON MODERN SCOTTISH POETRY SEE ALSO:

France, Peter and Glen, Duncan (eds.), *European Poetry in Scotland. An Anthology of Translations* (Edinburgh, 1990).

Hulse, Michael; Kennedy, David and Morley, David (eds.), *The New Poetry* (Newcastle upon Tyne, 1993).